PRAISE FOR

Criminal Woman,

the Prostitute, and the Normal Woman

by Cesare Lombroso and Guglielmo Ferrero

translated and with a new introduction by

Nicole Hahn Rafter and Mary Gibson

"[Lombroso's] still-relevant works haunt contemporary ideas of criminality and jurisprudence. Current debates over the biology of mind versus the role of environment ably show that we haven't resolved the nature-nurture fray Lombroso entered—nor do we actually know much more about what makes a criminal than he did. Although maybe we doubt it has *quite* so much to do with the mandible."—ALEXIS SOLOSKI, *Village Voice*

"*Criminal Woman, the Prostitute, and the Normal Woman* is a major publishing landmark in criminology. Nicole Hahn Rafter and Mary Gibson have achieved a remarkable feat in translating this pivotal work and presenting it for scholars to study in a well-edited text. It gives new insights into positivism and the history of the subject. It will be required reading for anyone interested in developments in the field. It may even lead to new evaluations of Lombroso's contribution, not least by feminist scholars."—FRANCES HEIDENSOHN, coauthor of *Gender and Policing: Comparative Perspectives*

"Cesare Lombroso created the field of criminology, but there has been a lack of available textbooks making his arguments accessible to today's students of history, law, and sociology. This volume fills that void. Offering work previously not translated along with a scholarly introduction and new visual evidence, it reveals Lombroso's argument without distorting the peculiar and genuinely contradictory character of his reasoning."—PETER BECKER, coeditor of *Criminals and Their Scientists: The History of Criminology in International Perspective*

Criminal Man

Cesare Lombroso

Criminal Man

TRANSLATED AND WITH A NEW INTRODUCTION

by Mary Gibson and Nicole Hahn Rafter

with translation assistance from Mark Seymour

DUKE UNIVERSITY PRESS

Durham and London

2006

2nd printing, 2007

© 2006 Mary Gibson and

Nicole Hahn Rafter

All rights reserved.

Printed in the United States of

America on acid-free paper

Designed by

C. H. Westmoreland

Typeset in Carter & Cohn

Galliard with Univers display

by Tseng Information

Systems, Inc.

Library of Congress

Cataloging-in-Publication

Data appear on the last printed

page of this book.

Mary Gibson dedicates her
share in this book to Jim Cohen for
his love, friendship, and humor.

Nicole Rafter dedicates her
share in this book to her dear friend
Frances Heidensohn, who has helped
so greatly with this project and
many others.

Contents

List of Tables

Note: Lombroso did not usually title his tables, especially when they were short. We have added brief titles for clarity and ease of reference.

List of Illustrations

Acknowledgments

This volume completes our project of providing new English translations of Cesare Lombroso's classic companion works, *Criminal Man* and *Criminal Woman*. When looking back over the many years devoted to this project, we will undoubtedly remember our 2004 research trip to the Lombroso Museum of Criminal Anthropology at the University of Turin as its high point. We are indebted to Delia Frigessi for her generous hospitality in arranging our visit to the museum and to Renzo Villa for providing a fascinating historical tour of Lombroso's Turin. Our many hours of conversation with these two authorities on the history of Italian criminology provided invaluable insights for our project. Professor Paolo Tappero and Dr. Elena Gay of the Lombroso Museum graciously guided us through the exhibit and answered our numerous questions; we thank the museum for permission to photograph objects from Lombroso's collection for this book. Mary Gibson would also like to thank Professor Mario Portigliatti Barbos, emeritus professor at the University of Turin and the last person to hold Lombroso's chair in criminal anthropology, for welcoming her to the museum during an earlier visit in 1997 and providing her with photocopies of several original Italian editions of *Criminal Man*.

From the beginning of this project, we have enjoyed the support and counsel of Peter Becker of the Johannes Kepler University in Linz, Piers Beirne of the University of Southern Maine, and Frances M. Heidensohn of Goldsmiths College, University of London, and the London School of Economics. Other colleagues who provided assistance and encouragement are Bernard Cohen, Simon Cole, Neil Davie, Ellen Dwyer, Jeffrey Feldman, Sarah Hahn, Steven Hughes, Dario Melossi, Graeme Newman, and Amy Srebnick. We fondly acknowledge the help of Raphael Allen, the editor at Duke University Press who originally championed our project and guided us through the preparation of *Criminal Woman*. We had the unusual good fortune to work with an equally fine editor, Courtney Berger, for *Criminal Man*. Courtney combines two invaluable qualities as an editor: efficiency and levelheadedness in offering practical guidance, and a deeply intellectual understanding of the historical significance of Lombroso and his writings. We thank her for her commitment to our project.

A grant from the National Library of Medicine, part of the National Institutes of Health, supported our research trip to Turin and the preparation of this manuscript. Jacob Marini, director of Sponsored Programs at John Jay College, offered invaluable assistance in obtaining this funding. We want to thank Mark Seymour of the University of Otago for his willingness to wrestle with Lombroso's long-winded and often baffling prose in order to produce a first draft of our translation. Tamar Pitch again graciously served as our Italian consultant on the text; Corinna Riva of St. John's College, Oxford, provided additional help.

The reproduction of Lombroso's original illustrations would have been impossible without the expertise and generous assistance of the photographer Robert Roher and members of the John Jay Library including professors Ellen Belcher, Nancy Egan, Bonnie Nelson, and Larry Sullivan. Others who contributed to this project include Raul Cabrera, Brian Fox, Noah Simmons, and Ellen Zitani.

As a visiting research fellow of St. John's College, Oxford University, Nicole Rafter enjoyed excellent conditions for working on this project during the winter and spring of 2004. We would like to thank Robert Hahn and Jim Cohen for their emotional support, thoughtful advice, and willingness to share their lives with Cesare Lombroso over the many years of this project.

Criminal Man

Editors' Introduction

This book offers English-language readers the first critical, scholarly translation of *Criminal Man* (*L'uomo delinquente*), the classic work by the Italian physician and psychiatrist Cesare Lombroso (1835–1909). It provides a companion volume to our previous translation of Lombroso's other major work, *Criminal Woman, the Prostitute, and the Normal Woman*.[1] *Criminal Man*, first published in 1876 as one slim volume, went through five editions during Lombroso's lifetime, each one greatly expanded in both length and number of topics addressed.[2] The final edition, published in 1896–97, appeared in four volumes, the last of which, entitled *Atlas* (*Atlante*), consists almost entirely of tables, maps, drawings, and photographs. This new translation offers lengthy excerpts from all five editions, so that readers can follow the development of Lombroso's thought over his professional lifetime. Unlike earlier English translations, which are fragmentary and almost a century old, this volume reveals for the first time the complexity of Lombroso's ideas.[3]

Lombroso is best known for his theory of the born criminal (*delinquente nato*), a dangerous individual marked by what he called "anomalies"—physical and psychological abnormalities. For Lombroso, these anomalies resembled the traits of primitive peoples, animals, and even plants, "proving" that the most dangerous criminals were atavistic throwbacks on the evolutionary scale. Because anomalies can be examined, counted, and classified, Lombroso promised to turn the study of criminality into an empirical science. He called his new field of research "criminal anthropology," reflecting his desire to reorient legal thinking from philosophical debate about the nature of crime to an analysis of the characteristics of the criminal.

We began this project with a disdain for what we understood as the simplemindedness of Lombroso's theory of atavism and with a fear that his biological determinism was prejudicial to women, blacks, and other social groups that he deemed inferior. Many of his conclusions seemed silly, and his project a particularly frightful example of bad science. But our views have changed, based on our careful reading of his criminological oeuvre, our investigation of his place in Italian history, and our research on the evolution of criminology in other countries. Lombroso now appears to have been a curious, engaged, and energetic polymath with a tremendous appetite for literature, art, and folklore, as well as for natural science, medicine, psychiatry, and law. That he was careless and often wrong about the conclusions that he drew from the disparate data provided by these fields does not detract from the significance of his enterprise.

Although deservedly known for its biological determinism, Lombroso's criminological theory also embraces sociological causes of crime. As a young liberal supporter of Italian unification and later a member of the Italian Socialist Party, Lombroso sympathized with the working classes and advocated a series of sometimes radical reforms to lessen poverty and prevent lawbreaking.[4] He proposed humanitarian alternatives to incarceration for so-called occasional criminals, or those individuals driven to crime by bad environment, and he became an ardent champion of special medical institutions for the criminally insane. This new edition of *Criminal Man* captures the complexity of Lombroso's multicausal theory of crime and documents his wide range of proposals for turning that theory into practical policy.

The most famous Italian thinker of his era, Lombroso emerged as the leader of an international movement called the positivist or scientific school of criminology. He led the revolt against the classical school of penology, which traced its roots back to the eighteenth-century Enlightenment and Cesare Beccaria's famous tract, *On Crimes and Punishments* (1764).[5] In opposition to Beccaria's emphasis on the free will of criminals and his dictum that punishment be proportional to the crime, Lombroso urges that the severity of punishment match the dangerousness of the criminal, whose lawbreaking is not the result of free choice but determined by biological, psychological, and social factors. Although this so-called medical model of crime—according to which criminality, like disease, required clinical examination and individualized treatment—was not completely new, Lombroso was the first to envision criminology as a new academic discipline independent of law and public hygiene. *Criminal Man* was translated into French (1887), German (1887–90), Russian (1889), and Spanish (1899), and Lombroso's theory of the born criminal became the center of debate at the first International Congress of Criminal Anthropology.[6]

Both at home and abroad, Lombroso was known for his lively curiosity, innovative thinking, and dedication to translating ideas into practical reforms. A prodigious researcher and writer, he produced over thirty books and one thousand articles during his lifetime.[7] Respected as a leading intellectual in Italy, he was invited to write for newspapers and popular magazines on the major issues of the day, even those unrelated to crime. He inspired several generations of disciples and students, many of whom implemented his theories as members of parliament, judges, prison directors, or police administrators.[8] His journal, the *Archives of Criminal Anthropology*, listed 68 collaborators on its masthead in the founding issue of 1880, a number that grew to 106 within ten years. Both lists included many foreign names, a pattern repeated in his lengthy footnotes to *Criminal Man*, where he thanks numerous colleagues for use of their data and cites additional studies supporting his conclusions. These footnotes show the international breadth of Lombroso's reading; fluent in a number of languages, he was able to follow developments across Europe and North America.

Despite the almost iconic status of *Criminal Man* as the founding text of criminology, no complete English translation exists of any of the five editions. Only two books in English can claim any relationship to Lombroso's classic, and both offer a fragmentary and distorted view of his larger project. In 1911, Lombroso's daughter, Gina Lombroso-Ferrero, issued a short compendium of his writings entitled *Criminal Man* that has mistakenly been taken as a translation of the original work.[9] Although Lombroso-Ferrero, herself a doctor and a secretary to her father, offers an accurate summary of Lombroso's notion of the born criminal, she radically oversimplifies a theory that is complex and even contradictory in the original editions of *Criminal Man*. In her 1911 volume, we hear her words rather than those of her father, and readers are left with the impression that his theory was static rather than constantly in flux. The latter problem also mars the volume entitled *Crime: Its Causes and Remedies*, also published in 1911, which translates the third volume of the fifth edition of *Criminal Man*.[10] Over half of *Crime* is comprised of a synthesis that, like Lombroso-Ferrero's volume, flattens out the nuances and erases the chronological development of Lombroso's thought. It leaves out all material from the first two volumes of edition 5, including important topics that had preoccupied Lombroso as early as the first edition of 1876. Our new translation, by providing excerpts of all five editions in their chronological order, fills the need for an English edition of *Criminal Man* that traces the history of Lombroso's notion of the born criminal and of criminal anthropology in general.

Goals of the New Edition

This new edition of *Criminal Man*—like the already published companion volume *Criminal Woman*—has a twofold purpose: to provide, for the first time, an adequate English translation of a classic work by Lombroso and to lay foundations for an emerging new generation of Lombroso scholarship.

Until the publication of our recent edition of *Criminal Woman, the Prostitute, and the Normal Woman* (2004), few of Lombroso's original texts were available in English, and existing translations were incomplete and out of print. *La donna delinquente* (*Criminal Woman*) was the only criminological work by Lombroso to appear in English during his lifetime and therefore became the conduit for his thought to the Anglo-American world.[11] Issued in 1895 under the title *The Female Offender*, the first translation omitted major sections on so-called normal women, female sexuality, and prostitution. The two versions of *Criminal Man* mentioned above that appeared after Lombroso's death constitute incomplete summaries of the final form of his theory. Presenting his ideas in a congealed and artificial form, these earlier versions are of limited use for scholars attempting to trace the origins of criminology. They have misled generations of students to adopt a simplistic and stereotypical view of Lombroso, the man named in many of their textbooks as "the father of modern criminology."[12]

A recent upsurge in research on Lombroso makes the appearance of this new edition of *Criminal Man* especially timely. Even scholars who read Italian have great difficulty locating all five editions of the original text, especially the rare first edition. This holds true not only in English-speaking nations but also in Italy, where even the Lombroso Museum in Turin possesses only three of the five editions. Despite the early translation of *Criminal Man* into French, German, Russian, and Spanish, only one or two editions are available in each of these languages. Thus this new edition provides the only resource in any language with selections from all five editions of *Criminal Man*.[13]

In part because of the misleading nature of existing translations,

Lombroso has long been ridiculed as a simplistic biological determin-ist with reactionary ideas. English-language readers have had little un-derstanding of the Italian context of Lombroso's criminological theory or the political goals of his proposals for reform of police, courts, and punishment. Furthermore, the contribution of biologically determin-istic thinking to the rise of the international eugenics movement made hereditarian theories of crime an anathema to most scholars after World War II. After Nazi death camps exterminated Jews on the basis of their "race," scholars became unwilling to recognize distinctions among pro-genitors of biological theories of racial difference. They overlooked the fact that Lombroso himself was Jewish and that his ideas, while prop-erly labeled as racist, were not analogous to those of Nazi—or even Ital-ian fascist—anti-Semitic ideologues.

Recent scholarship has begun to reevaluate the place of Lombroso in a variety of contexts, including the histories of criminology, science, race, and sexuality. These new works demonstrate that many of Lom-broso's views were standard for his time and rooted in humanitarian impulses. In a pioneering work entitled *Il deviante e i suoi segni: Lombroso e la nascita dell'antropologia criminale* (*Deviancy and Its Signs: Lombroso and the Birth of Criminal Anthropology*), the Italian historian Renzo Villa places Lombroso's quest to identify signs of deviance on the criminal body and in the criminal mind within the context of nineteenth-century penal science and medicine.[14] Mary Gibson argues in *Born to Crime: Cesare Lombroso and the Origins of Biological Criminology* that the com-plexity of Lombroso's theory inspired both liberal and conservative policy shifts within the Italian criminal justice system.[15] In *Cesare Lom-broso*, Delia Frigessi offers a detailed account of the close relationship between Lombroso's intellectual biography and broader developments in science and psychiatry.[16] David Horn demonstrates in *The Crimi-nal Body: Lombroso and the Anatomy of Deviance* how new instruments of measurement encouraged Lombroso and other nineteenth-century criminologists to see moral truths inscribed on the physical body.[17] The new scholarship agrees that Lombroso's theory shared many assump-tions, methods, and conclusions with a wider scientific and legal com-munity. Instead of dismissing criminal anthropology as a naive or aber-rant science, scholars are beginning to locate it in the broader context of the production of scientific knowledge in the late nineteenth century.

New studies of nineteenth-century criminology in Europe and the Americas are also documenting Lombroso's international stature. Due to a dearth of research on the origins of criminology, Lombroso's influence outside of Italy has until recently either remained unrecognized or been deemed insignificant compared to national legal traditions. The well-known denunciation of the concept of the born criminal by French criminologists at the International Congress of Criminal Anthropology in 1889 has encouraged scholars to underestimate Lombroso's international impact. The historians Laurent Mucchielli and Marc Renneville, however, have recently argued that French opposition to Lombroso was based more on nationalist sentiment than substantive disagreement.[18] Despite naming themselves the school of social milieu, French criminologists agreed that biology and heredity play important roles in the etiology of crime; moreover, their theory of degeneration differed from atavism principally in its emphasis on adverse social conditions that might initiate the biological decline of a family. Richard Wetzell has made a similar argument for Germany, where criminologists who rejected Lombroso's definition of the born criminal nevertheless accepted the medical model for identifying and treating lawbreakers.[19] According to a new book by Neil Davie, Lombroso's criminal anthropology had significant influence even in England, whose criminological tradition has previously been described as too embedded in the practical activities of prison doctors to incorporate continental theory.[20]

Nations outside of Europe also adopted Lombrosian ideas and methods, often in an attempt to set criminology on a modern, scientific footing. In her book *Creating Born Criminals*, Nicole Hahn Rafter has shown how biological theories of crime shaped new policies and institutions for individuals considered criminal, insane, or feebleminded in the United States.[21] A number of American criminologists became conduits for Lombroso's thought, thus compensating for the paucity of English translations of his work. Historians of Latin America are beginning to document the deep impact of criminal anthropology on legal and penal reformers in that region.[22] Latin American jurists and criminologists gained access to Lombroso's ideas both from Spanish translations of his books and from lecture tours in 1908 and 1910 by Enrico Ferri, another prominent member of the Italian positivist school. That Lombroso's influence reached even to Asia is documented in the forthcoming collection of essays entitled *Criminals and Their Scientists*.[23]

Lombroso is becoming a touch point for a variety of fields outside of the history of criminology and medicine including women's studies, race studies, and the history of sexuality. The status of Lombroso as an early sexologist has been obscured by the deletion of explicit references to sexual organs and behavior by English translators, which we have now restored to the text. He also deserves recognition as a collector of art by and about criminals. The Lombroso Museum in Turin has preserved Lombroso's original collection of drawings and photos of criminals, as well as paintings, sculpture, and furniture made by criminals. This volume includes over forty examples of this art, taken from his original books and from photographs shot in the museum itself. Included as well are examples of another body of work collected by Lombroso—criminal writing. As an early student of prison culture, Lombroso analyzed poems, graffiti, and the shape of inmates' script for clues to their moral character. Lombroso's mixture of contempt and admiration for the creativity of the criminal becomes evident, too, in his extensive analysis of tattoos, an artistic form combining drawing and writing.

Lombroso's Explanation of Criminality

In *Criminal Man*, Lombroso's major claim is to have turned the study of crime into a science that draws its conclusions from empirical data and clinical case studies. Such an approach was consistent with his medical training at the universities of Pavia, Padua, and Vienna. His dissertation on cretinism, a mental disorder widespread in impoverished areas of Italy, showed his early interest in psychiatry and his humanitarian impulse to address social issues. As a young military doctor during the wars of Italian unification, Lombroso quickly developed his signature approach of measuring and observing the bodies of his patients, in this case soldiers. He later applied this method, supplemented with psychological interviews, to mental patients and, finally, criminals. Holding posts in both mental asylums and prisons, Lombroso examined thousands of individuals during his lifetime, carrying out his own famous prescription to study the criminal rather than the crime.

Lombroso's intellectual trajectory was not unusual for the late nineteenth century, when the prestige of science, and particularly biology, was in its ascendancy. Lombroso drew on the popularity of Charles Darwin's theory of evolution to convince readers of *Criminal Man* of the scientific validity of his theory of criminal atavism. For liberal and secular thinkers like Lombroso, science offered a counterweight to religion and a tool for progress toward a more liberal society. Seeking to incorporate empirical methods into their disciplines, scholars in the nascent social sciences and even traditional humanities joined natural scientists in creating the dominant intellectual movement of the late nineteenth century—positivism. It is not surprising, then, that Lombroso and his followers proudly labeled themselves the positivist school of criminology and criticized the heirs of Beccaria for abstract philosophizing when they could have been collecting data through actual contact with offenders.

Despite his claim to be a lonely pioneer in the application of science to penology, Lombroso drew on earlier movements that had initiated research on the physical and psychological traits of criminals. The first of these was early-nineteenth-century phrenology, which located intellectual and emotional faculties in specific areas of the brain. While rejecting the phrenologists' map of the skull, Lombroso adopted their assumption that exterior corporal features mirror interior moral states.[24] He fully accepted a second concept developed by early-nineteenth-century psychiatrists, moral insanity, as a diagnosis of individuals who performed depraved acts while remaining rational and logical.[25] Mentioned briefly in the first edition of *Criminal Man*, moral insanity becomes a key component of Lombroso's theory of born criminality in the third edition. Throughout the editions of *Criminal Man* Lombroso also cites the findings of Adolphe Quetelet and A.-M. Guerry, who in the 1820s and 1830s initiated the study of moral statistics, or the quantification of patterns of human behavior like crime.[26] Finding that aggregate national crime rates remained steady over time, they argued that crime was rooted not in individual choice but in larger and more constant social and biological factors. This insight informed Lombroso's frequent declaration that crime was "natural," rather than a product of free choice, and that it would always remain a part of the human experience.

For modern readers, Lombroso's methodology appears unscientific and even laughable. While his books are filled with statistical tables, these tables are often sloppy and unsophisticated in their lack of standardization. Control groups appear as early as the first edition of *Criminal Man*, but they are not employed systematically. Even more questionable is Lombroso's mixture of quantitative data with qualitative evidence such as proverbs, historical anecdotes, and examples drawn from painting and literature. Rather than distinguishing among more or less objective types of data, Lombroso treats all evidence as equal and reenforcing. For him, proof results not from following a rigorous and clearly defined methodology, but from the accumulation of examples, no matter how disparate. Despite these failings, however, Lombroso's approach did not fall outside the mainstream of social science research of his day. Statistical procedures were rudimentary and reliable data scarce in new fields like criminology. Many of Lombroso's flawed assumptions were shared by his colleagues in the fields of medicine and anthropology, including the belief that physical traits constituted visible signs of interior psychological and moral states. In short, its methodological flaws notwithstanding, Lombroso's criminal anthropology formed part of a general intellectual trend in all the new social sciences of the late nineteenth century to medicalize human behavior.

Classification of Criminals

By the time of Lombroso's death, criminal anthropology had become world famous for its elaborate classification of criminals. This penchant for classification, however, remains absent from the first edition of *Criminal Man*, where Lombroso lumps all lawbreakers together in a single, undifferentiated group, which he compares to the insane and, sporadically, to control groups of "healthy" men (usually soldiers). In fact, the phrase *born criminal* was coined four years later by Ferri and did not appear in the first edition of *Criminal Man*.[27] Yet in the earliest formulation of his theory, Lombroso already focused on atavistic criminals, describing those physical and psychological features that quickly became associated with criminal anthropology. One reads in the first edition that criminals, compared to "healthy" individuals, have smaller and more deformed skulls, greater height and weight, and lighter beards. They are more likely to have crooked noses, sloping foreheads, large ears, protruding jaws, and dark skin, eyes, and hair. They also tend to be physically weak and insensitive to pain. This last trait, according to Lombroso, constitutes the exterior sign of inward moral obtuseness that explains why criminals rarely exhibit remorse for their crimes. Unable to control their passions, they indulge in drinking and gambling. In edition 1, Lombroso also includes chapters on tattoos among prisoners, as well as on their jargon, poetry, and art. From Lombroso's eclectic point of view, the scientist must be alert to any and all clues to atavism, even when those clues are more social than biological in nature. The criminal is a diseased person, and the criminologist has to be creative in locating and reading the symptoms.

In the second edition of *Criminal Man*, Lombroso begins to build a rudimentary system of classification by establishing a new category, that of the so-called criminal of passion. Criminals of passion are unlike other criminals in many ways: they tend to have good reputations before committing their crime; they repent immediately; and their motives are "generous and often sublime."[28] These might include anger against an adulterous spouse or commitment to a banned political ideal. Both jealous husbands and political rebels may lose control of their emotions momentarily, but in neither case do they typically exhibit the physical or moral anomalies of common murderers.

In the third edition of *Criminal Man*, Lombroso adopts Ferri's label of the born criminal, a tag that quickly gained international recognition. It also drew instant criticism, as opponents ridiculed the inability of Italian criminal anthropologists to identify a single anomaly that disfigured all born criminals. In response, Lombroso proposed that any individual exhibiting a cluster of five or more anomalies be classified as "the full criminal type," although he also maintained that even an isolated anomaly marked an offender as constitutionally flawed and therefore potentially dangerous.[29] Pronouncing 40 percent of all offenders as born criminals in the third edition of *Criminal Man*, Lombroso reduces his estimate to 35 percent in the fifth edition.[30] *Crime: Its Causes and Remedies* names an even lower figure of 33 percent.[31] That Lombroso decreased his estimate of the extent of born criminality even after the publication of the final edition of *Criminal Man*, bowing to pressure from critics, is confirmed by Gina Lombroso-Ferrero's English summary, which repeats the lower figure of 33 percent.[32]

Edition 3 of *Criminal Man* not only introduces the term *born criminal* but also reconfigures the relationship between criminality and insanity. In the first two editions, Lombroso seeks to differentiate criminality, an inborn condition present at birth, from insanity, a disease usually developed later in life. In edition 3, however, he concedes that crime and mental illness merge in the morally insane, individuals who appear normal in intelligence but are unable to distinguish between good and evil. When tested for physical sensitivity, they exhibit, according to Lombroso, a dullness of touch compatible with their moral vacuity. To support his thesis of "the complete similarity between the morally insane and the born criminal," he identifies studies that had found moral insanity widespread among the prison population.

In this same edition, Lombroso also declares that the concept of atavism is inadequate to explain the presence of multiple anomalies in all born criminals, particularly in the morally insane. But rather than abandoning his beloved notion of atavism, Lombroso simply adds disease to atavism as a possible cause of arrested development or the degeneration of biological and mental functions. Although Lombroso criticizes other criminologists for relying too heavily on degeneration theory, he finds it useful for explaining how social factors—such as alcoholism, venereal disease, or malnutrition—might initiate biological and psychological regression in individuals and their progeny. Lombroso's adoption of degeneration theory, originally a French concept, might seem to signify a defeat for criminal anthropology; but instead it broadened its scope and applicability. Lombroso could now count any malformation, even if attributable to disease rather than atavism, as one of the cluster of anomalies that identify the born criminal.

In the fourth edition of *Criminal Man*, Lombroso adds epilepsy to atavism and moral insanity as causes of born criminality. While subscribing to the notion (common in his time) that epileptics might commit crimes during convulsions, he goes even further by identifying "hidden epilepsy" (*epilessia larvata*) as a catalyst for lawbreaking in individuals free of physical symptoms. Thus by 1889, epilepsy becomes for Lombroso a universal substructure of all criminal behavior, encompassing both moral insanity and atavism. He explains the differences among the three categories as primarily those of scale: "The most serious cases of moral insanity overlap with those of congenital criminality, while epileptic criminals who experience fits of violence resemble the morally insane. Overall, the three phenomena are similar." However, as this quotation indicates, Lombroso never precisely articulates the relationship among atavism, moral insanity, and epilepsy in his born-criminal theory.

Lombroso returns to the insane criminal in edition 4, identifying three additional subcategories: the alcoholic criminal, the hysterical criminal, and the mattoid. Alcoholic criminals are usually free of physical anomalies, but excessive drinking causes them to develop the same psychological traits as born criminals: impulsiveness, cruelty, lack of remorse, and laziness. Often inheriting a weak constitution from alcoholic parents, offenders of this type are predisposed to violent acts like murder, rape, and homicide. The category of the hysterical criminal also proves elastic, since its members may display few signs of mental illness and be free of convulsions; but their character is marked by "an egotism and a self-preoccupation which leads to a desire for scandal and public attention." Most hysterics are female, whereas members of the third category of insane criminals, mattoids, are invariably male. The term *mattoid* was coined by Lombroso for self-fashioned prophets and revolutionaries who rise from the lower classes to spout utopian ideas. Lombroso points to mattoids' voluminous writings as a sign of their madness, for these tomes combine concepts that are "well-expressed and even sublime" with others that are "mediocre, ignoble, and paradoxical."

Finally, the fourth edition of *Criminal Man* introduces a major new category—the occasional criminal. In Lombroso's schema, the occasional criminal encompasses four subgroups: pseudocriminals, marked by few if any anomalies; criminaloids, who exhibit enough anomalies to be predisposed to crime; habitual criminals, recidivists who begin their careers as pseudocriminals but reach the depravity of born criminals through repetitive lawbreaking; and latent criminals, who channel their malicious instincts into alternative channels. In all cases, occasional criminals break the law because environmental pressures or temptations overcome their natural goodness. Ultimately, however, Lombroso never became comfortable with the category of the occasional criminal, complaining in edition 4 that it "does not offer a homogeneous type in the same way as born criminals and criminals of passion. Rather, the category is composed of disparate groups."

In the final edition of *Criminal Man*, Lombroso recognizes a spectrum of deviant types beyond the born criminal.[33] This proliferation of categories across the five volumes of *Criminal Man* increases the weight of sociological factors in Lombroso's explanation of the causes of crime. However, because of the notoriety of the concept of the born criminal, Lombroso has rarely been credited with recognizing environmental factors as significant to the etiology of deviance. Yet as early as in the first edition of *Criminal Man* he argues that "there is no crime which is not rooted in multiple causes," and by the final edition, he has enumerated these social factors in great detail.[34] Despite his increasing emphasis on the social causes of crime, in the final analysis Lombroso is able to continue denying free will by conceptualizing environmental and biological forces as equally determinate.

Practical Applications

Over the five editions of *Criminal Man*, Lombroso continually enlarged his sections on public policy. After unification in 1861, as Italians debated the shape of a new criminal justice system, Lombroso was eager to offer increasingly specialized recommendations for reform of the police, courts, and prisons. In ever-expanding sections on the prevention and punishment of crime, Lombroso showed how these recommendations flowed logically from the principles of his general criminological theory. He also drew on his vast knowledge of legal reforms in other nations, many of which he urged on the Italian government.

Although his practical advice became increasingly specialized over the years, Lombroso's basic philosophy of punishment never changed. In opposition to the Enlightenment principles of Beccaria, he counseled that punishment be tailored to individual criminals rather than to their crimes. He explicitly rejected the principle of moral responsibility, arguing that criminals acted out of compulsion from either their innate physical and psychological degeneracy or from the social environment. Yet even if criminals did not freely choose to break the law, society still had the right to punish them in its own defense. This principle of social defense is not entirely distinct from Beccaria's belief that the major purpose of punishment is to prevent those guilty of crime from further threatening society. Lombroso directly breaks with Beccaria, however, over the mode of determining appropriate punishments. For Lombroso, it is illogical to construct a proportional scale of crimes and punishments since both born and occasional criminals steal and even murder. Therefore, the law should allow wide discretion to judges to assess the degree of dangerousness posed by each defendant as a basis for issuing the appropriate sentence.

In place of the classical scale of crimes and punishments, Lombroso argued for a correlation between types of criminals and punishments. He counseled that occasional crime could be prevented, and the five editions of *Criminal Man* recommended a growing list of political, social, and economic reforms designed to eliminate the causes of crime. These preventive measures, which he called "penal substitutes" (*sostitutivi penali*), included technical measures like street lighting and alarm systems to discourage robberies and theft; new laws like the introduction of divorce to eliminate domestic violence and spousal murder;

and major social reforms like land redistribution to mitigate the dire poverty of the southern peasantry. Lombroso showed surprising ambivalence, however, toward the spread of public education and of "civilization," that is, urbanization and industrialization. Worried that primary education would help criminals perfect their craft, he opposed schools in prisons, though he grudgingly admitted that the spread of literacy among the general population would decrease crime in the long run. Uncertainty also marked Lombroso's discussion of civilization: while he recognized that modernization had reduced levels of violence and fostered moral, intellectual, and political progress, industrialization had encouraged alcoholism among the working classes, and urbanization the formation of criminal gangs. In addition, civilization had led to fraud and other new types of property offenses that were replacing more atavistic crimes against persons.

Because civilization would never eliminate crime, Lombroso turned his attention to prisons, even while seeking alternatives to incarceration for occasional criminals and criminals of passion. While the classical school had championed prisons as a humane and efficient alternative to corporal punishment, positivists believed that incarceration corrupts reformable criminals by mixing them with congenital deviants. When unavoidable, prisons should be modeled on the so-called Pennsylvania or cellular system, where inmates lived and worked in separate cells to prevent communication and moral contamination. Preferable to prison were fines or, if the defendant was poor, community service. For nondangerous criminals, Lombroso advised judges to recommend house arrest, police surveillance, or simply judicial reprimands. He was also enthusiastic about suspended sentences and parole, two modern alternatives to incarceration pioneered in France and the United States that he crusaded to have introduced into the Italian criminal code.

For dangerous criminals, Lombroso recommended a series of specialized institutions. Born criminals and habitual criminals merited perpetual incarceration in the name of social defense and should be sent to special "prisons for incorrigibles." Insane criminals should also be separated from society for life, but in special criminal insane asylums (*manicomi criminali*), where they would receive psychiatric treatment. A strong advocate of criminal insane asylums as a humane alternative to incarceration, Lombroso also envisioned the establishment of specialized mental institutions for groups like alcoholic or epileptic criminals.

Despite his rejection of the death penalty in the first edition of *Crim-*

inal Man, Lombroso gradually came to advocate it in the case of born criminals convicted of a series of bloody crimes and for members of organized gangs who threatened state security. In so doing, he defied a public consensus in Italy that had abolished capital punishment in the Zanardelli Criminal Code of 1889. To his adversaries he replied in the fifth edition of *Criminal Man* that "to claim that the death sentence contradicts the laws of nature is to feign ignorance of the fact that progress in the animal world, and therefore the human world, is based on a struggle for existence that involves hideous massacres." Society need have no pity for born criminals, who were "programmed to do harm" and are "atavistic reproductions of not only savage men but also the most ferocious carnivores and rodents." Capital punishment, in this social Darwinist view, would simply accelerate natural selection, ridding society of the unfit.

Contexts for *Criminal Man*: Sex, Race, Age, and Class

Over the five editions of *Criminal Man*, Lombroso pays increasing attention to groups that were beginning to elicit anxiety in late-nineteenth-century Europe and America: women; southern Italians, Africans, and other "inferior races"; youth; and the lower classes, symbolized by rural bandits and urban revolutionaries. The emergence of these groups as objects of study by social scientists and of discipline by the state coincided with radical economic and political changes that accompanied industrialization, urbanization, and democratization. The pages of *Criminal Man* often engage in larger debates outside of criminal justice over issues like women's rights in marriage, the alleged backwardness of southern Italians, proper schooling for children, and the political demands of the new industrial working class. Lombroso's discussions of sex, race, age, and class cut across and complicate his formal typology of criminals based on dangerousness.

Lombroso's treatment of the variables of sex, race, class, and age exposes two contradictory tendencies in *Criminal Man*: on the one hand, Lombroso incorporates popular prejudices of his day into his science, while, on the other hand, he takes independent and unpopular stands on certain controversial issues. Although Lombroso always defended his unexpected pronouncements on public policy—such as his support for divorce or opposition to colonialism—as logical outcomes of his criminal anthropological theory, they were also shaped by his personal biography. As the father of two well-educated daughters who were themselves public figures, Lombroso was familiar with, and perhaps influenced by, debates in the early Italian feminist movement. His Jewishness probably strengthened his positive attitude toward race mixing, a stance at odds with that of many other late-nineteenth-century "scientific" racists. As both a physician and a liberal (later a socialist), Lombroso supported progressive political change that would alleviate the poverty of both peasants and urban workers. These personal perspectives helped to temper the harsh teachings of Lombrosian theory: that women, nonwhites, the poor, and children are physically, psychologically, and morally inferior to white men.

Sex. Unlike other criminologists of his day, Lombroso recognized the importance of gender to the understanding of the etiology of crime. As early as in the first edition of *Criminal Man* he included a short section on criminal women. Most of his data on female crime in the early editions came from the famous study of Alexandre Parent-Duchatelet on the prostitutes of Paris.[35] Despite the paucity of evidence, Lombroso enunciated his most fundamental insight into female criminality in the first edition of *Criminal Man*, that prostitution represents the typical form of female crime.

This idea helped Lombroso solve a theoretical contradiction that emerged as he collected statistics and found that crime rates of women were invariably lower than those of men. This rarity of female lawbreaking seemed inconsistent with Lombroso's assumption of female inferiority. He solved this contradiction by arguing that the fundamental characteristic of atavistic women was their exaggerated sexual drive, which leads them more often into prostitution than to traditional male crimes like murder and theft. Thus Lombroso redefined prostitution—legal in Italy and most of nineteenth-century Europe—as a crime typical of women in what he referred to as savage societies.

In 1893, Lombroso expanded his analysis of female offending into a separate book, *Criminal Woman, the Prostitute, and the Normal Woman*. Lombroso should be recognized as one of the few criminologists before the advent of feminist criminology in the 1970s to collect extensive data on female crime and take gender seriously as a category of analysis. His resulting theory, however, represented a setback for nineteenth-century champions of women's rights since it asserted the inferiority of both normal and criminal women, holding that both types had smaller skulls, lighter brains, shorter bodies, less muscle, and weaker sensitivity than their male counterparts. So-called normal women, according to Lombroso, were like children and would always remain emotionally and morally stunted compared with normal men.[36] Only their maternal instinct saved normal women from criminality, for it counterbalanced their innate psychological traits of vanity, mendacity, and cruelty.

His bleak pronouncements on female inferiority notwithstanding, Lombroso expressed sympathy for most female offenders. Weak and impressionable, most women, he believed, committed illegal or immoral acts because of unfavorable social circumstances or pressure from husbands or lovers. For Lombroso, these occasional female criminals and prostitutes did not pose a great danger to society and deserved but mild punishment. He advocated the legalization of divorce—a radical position in late-nineteenth-century Italy—to allow women to escape abusive or criminal husbands without resorting to domestic homicide. In another challenge to conventional attitudes of his day, Lombroso prescribed light punishment for women convicted of infanticide and abortion because their criminal behavior resulted not from inborn atavistic tendencies but from the social stigma associated with unwed motherhood. Thus he deemed only a minority of female offenders to be born criminals; but for those women who *were* "true monsters," Lombroso demanded permanent incarceration.[37]

Race. Race is integrally woven into Lombroso's theory of atavism, which equates white men with civilization and black, brown, and yellow men with "primitive" or "savage" societies. In his earlier work *L'uomo bianco e l'uomo di colore* (*The White Man and the Man of Color*), Lombroso had already concluded that "we must say that there are two general races: the White and the Colored."[38] The first two editions of *Criminal Man* haphazardly compared the traits of criminals with those of "savages," Lombroso's representatives of earlier stages of evolution. In edition 3, Lombroso makes his Darwinist underpinning more explicit by adding a long preliminary section on criminal behavior among plants, animals, and primitive peoples. He argues that violence and sexual licentiousness, which came naturally to organisms in early evolutionary stages, gradually gave way to modern notions of justice and monogamy. Lombroso's contention that non-European peoples were inferior to white men was a commonplace in the society of his day, but his systematic equations of born criminals and savages injected racism into the new field of criminology.

When Lombroso discussed the relation of race to current issues of his day, he seemed less concerned with inhabitants of non-Western lands than with those of the Italian south. Like other northern Italians, Lombroso was perplexed by the so-called Southern Question, the debate about the supposed backwardness of southern Italy, including the islands of Sicily and Sardinia. Home to brigandage and criminal organizations like the Mafia and Camorra, the south seemed violent and lawless to northern observers. Lombroso offered a complex answer to the Southern Question, one that included a social critique of southern elites for monopolizing landownership and a political condemnation of the national government for failing to alleviate southern poverty, disease, and illiteracy. Despite his recognition of these environmental barriers to prosperity in the south, Lombroso nevertheless emphasized the importance of race for explaining high rates of violent crime. Having been conquered over the centuries by a number of foreign peoples—including North African Arabs—the south was inhabited by a racially mixed people, who, in Lombroso's view, shared a propensity for murder with their nonwhite ancestors.

Lombroso offered a more subtle analysis of the behavior of Jews, another group included in his chapter on race. His own Jewish ancestry partially accounts for his refusal to characterize Jewish behavior in simple biological rather than more complex sociological terms. Aware of the frightening rise during the last decades of the nineteenth century of racial anti-Semitism in northern Europe, Lombroso argued that Jewish patterns of behavior derived from the historical legacy of persecution rather than from innate racial characteristics. He contended that Jews have high arrest rates for property crimes like fraud and receiving stolen goods because legislation in most European nations traditionally forbade them to follow any professions besides peddling or commerce. As proof that atavism is not intrinsic to the Jewish character, Lombroso cites the rapid movement of Jews into important positions in politics, the army, and academia once they gained the same civil rights as their Christian compatriots.

Lombroso advocated harsh punishment for members of those races he considered atavistic. True, Lombroso admitted that some supposedly primitive peoples were more honest than others and that poverty turned many normal southern Italians into occasional criminals. But for the most part, Lombroso considered race a biological determinant of atavistic behavior and, in the case of crime, of violence and cruelty as well. For example, in edition 2 of *Criminal Man*, he describes the Gypsies as "a thoroughly criminal race, with all its passions and vices," whose atavistic tendencies even include cannibalism. Criminals of the colored races, therefore, deserved harsh punishment including, at least in the case of mafiosi and other members of Italian criminal organizations, the death penalty.

Age. The variable of age is central to Lombroso's criminal anthropology in two ways. First, he characterizes all children as criminal because they display atavistic psychological traits such as vanity, cruelty, laziness, fickleness, and dishonesty. For Lombroso, such behavior could be explained by the nineteenth-century scientific maxim, attributed to Ernst Haeckel, that "ontology reproduces phylogeny," meaning that the life of each individual recapitulates the evolution of the species; thus the embryo is equivalent to the animal stage of evolution and childhood to that of primitive man. At puberty, according to Lombroso, most children lose their criminal characteristics and mature into normal adulthood, much as savages evolved into civilized men. But despite this generally optimistic prospect, for Lombroso childhood constitutes a continual reminder that man's atavistic past is encoded deeply in each individual's biology and psychology.

Second, precocious or early delinquency in children serves as a warning of the power of bad heredity. Lombroso filled *Criminal Man* with case studies of young born criminals whose parents were atavistic, morally insane, or epileptic, or who passed on debilitating diseases like alcoholism, syphilis, or tuberculosis. Evincing the biological and psychological anomalies of born criminals from a young age, these children never matured into normal adults. Such was the fate of many descendants of the drunkard Max Juke, an American family that fascinated Lombroso and included 77 criminals and 128 prostitutes over the course of seven generations.

Lombroso called for prevention rather than punishment of childhood crime since the law of recapitulation assured that most children were only passing through a temporary phase of occasional criminality. They would mature into healthy adulthood if guided by loving but morally strict parents. For orphans, Lombroso recommended foster homes or humane reformatories, although he generally believed that

institutions of incarceration spread rather than eradicated vice. Internment, however, proved the appropriate response to born juvenile delinquents, who constituted a danger to society even before committing
crimes. Once trained to detect biological and physical anomalies, police, teachers, and even parents could collaborate with criminal anthropologists in identifying atavistic youth and separating them from their
normal peers.

Class. A humanitarian current ran through Lombroso's criminology
from its inception. Assigned to the southern Italian province of Calabria as a young army physician, Lombroso was shocked by the peasants'
extreme poverty that led to malnutrition, disease, and sometimes madness. When he returned to the north, he extended this sympathy for the
poor to the urban working classes. In *Criminal Man*, he indicts both
the southern aristocracy for monopolizing landownership and northern industrialists for exploiting factory workers. Lombroso's close contact with the poor as a doctor and researcher helps explain his embrace
of socialism at the end of his life.

However, in *Criminal Man*, Lombroso sharply criticized rebels and
revolutionaries who called for violent social change. Many of his early
subjects of study were brigands, a group accused of political rebellion by the new Italian state. Historical research has refuted this accu-
sation: most acts of brigandage—like robbing the rich or killing soldiers and state officials—were inspired not by leftist political ideology
but by a desperate determination to preserve regional autonomy. Like
many southerners, brigands viewed the new government in Rome as
an imperialist power whose officials, mostly from the north, were bent
on controlling the wealth and citizenry of the south. As a patriot and
firm believer in Italian unification, Lombroso echoed national policy
by equating brigandage with treason. Claiming that brigands exhibited
anomalies typical of savages, Lombroso denounced the atavistic quality
of their violent crimes.

Lombroso offered a more nuanced analysis of urban revolutionaries
who, unlike brigands, were often educated members of the nineteenth-
century middle class. His own political experience, first as a liberal
supporter of Italian unification and later as a socialist, made him ap-
preciative of the role of courageous leaders in overthrowing absolutist
monarchy and promoting a new era of popular sovereignty. In *Criminal Man*, Lombroso assigned most political criminals to the category

of criminals of passion because he believed their violence to be rooted in idealism rather than atavism. Blessed with pleasing physiognomies unscarred by anomalies, most political criminals seemed to pose little social danger. But Lombroso's admiration did not extend to mattoids, whom he considered truly unbalanced and even insane in their political crusades.

Criminality and Representation

While Lombroso's reputation rests on his scientific work, he had a humanistic side as well, one that was fascinated by criminals' arts and crafts, their handwriting, tattoos, and graffiti, their jargon, songs, sculpture, poetry, and folklore. Lombroso went to great lengths to collect, preserve, and interpret the creative work of offenders; he seems to have been the first person to value such material and collect it systematically. Closely related were his efforts to represent his own criminological theory visually—in charts, drawings, graphs, maps, photographs, and the museum of criminal anthropology that he founded in Turin. In addition, Lombroso produced images of criminal life and culture through the narratives of his texts, one of them a grand master narrative (the story of evolution itself, in which born criminals form an instructive, if gloomy, chapter), others short anecdotes (his myriad brief tales of individual crimes and criminals). Criminal anthropology's success owed a great deal to Lombroso's ability to embody his theory visually and embed it narratively.[39]

Art. To each successive edition of *Criminal Man* Lombroso brought not only previously unpublished images but also new *types* of images (handwriting samples in the second edition, for example, and before-and-after photographs of reformed criminals in the fifth) and innovative *methods* of representation (heredity charts in the second edition, bar graphs in the third, crime maps in the fourth).[40] The first edition of *Criminal Man* (1876) begins simply enough, with four illustrations: two of criminals' faces, one of tattoos, and one of prisoner art.[41] The second edition (1878) includes the same four illustrations and adds ten new ones. The third edition (1884) has twenty-five illustrations, and the fourth edition (1889), a two-volume work, has sixty-five. The fifth and final edition (1896–97) dedicates its entire final volume, the *Atlas*, to visual evidence for criminal anthropology. Considered by Lombroso to be "the most important" part of *Criminal Man*, the *Atlas* has 121 illustrations.[42]

Over the two decades spanned by these five editions, Lombroso rarely discarded an image from his inventory, instead heaping new layers onto his snowballing collection. Other turn-of-the-century texts on crime and forensics, too, carried abundant illustrations, but nothing in criminological history rivals the visual richness of the third, fourth, and fifth editions of *Criminal Man*. As his daughter Gina remarked (teasingly, one hopes), Lombroso was a "born collector."[43]

Lombroso's delight in images of criminality spilled over into some of his other books as well. *Criminal Woman* includes eight full-page illustrations and eighteen others set into the text.[44] Crime-related images also appear in *Palimsesti del carcere* (*Prison Palimpsests*), Lombroso's 1888 collection of prisoner prose, pictographs (annotated drawings), tattoos, and wall writings.[45] Another example can be found in Lombroso's lavishly illustrated *L'uomo bianco e l'uomo di colore*, which, although it mainly depicts exotic Africans, Australians, and "Orientals," also includes several images related to criminology: skulls purporting to demonstrate the superiority of the European cranium; a naked Bushman woman with an anomalous rump; and the skull of the brigand Villella, the body part that, Lombroso claimed, first inspired his realization that criminals are evolutionarily backward and marked by anomalies. Supplementing *Criminal Man*, these books visually pursue aspects of its argument.

Although Lombroso clearly enjoyed images of prisoner arts, crafts, and body parts for their own sake, he felt that he had to justify his interest in scientific terms. Thus of pictographs he observes, "The tendency of criminals to express their thoughts . . . through drawings is a curious fact of atavism."[46] Of a female skull Lombroso writes that it belongs to "a prostitute from Naples. Sloping forehead, prognathism. Negroid type of face. Strong jaws."[47] The staged photograph of men reenacting their crime (reproduced in this volume as figure 9) demonstrates criminals' "incredible vanity."[48] Ironically, such comments undercut Lombroso's empiricism by implying a need for creative interpretation. The pictograph on a prisoner's water jug (figure 22) does not simply show a man sitting in a cupboard; it is also the prisoner's confession of guilt for killing his neighbor and shoving his body in the cupboard. Similarly, tattooed flowers (figure 47) mean more than they seem to, for this motif, Lombroso reports, is found most commonly on pederasts.[49] On a more abstract level, the images signify atavism, vanity, and kinship with savages. Lombroso's displays, then, link science and art, operating simultaneously on the visual and narrative levels, drenching objects with symbolic meanings. Because the displays require explanation, they also, in a sense, call criminology and criminologists into being.[50]

Creativity played yet another role in the production of Lombroso's illustrations. While there is no evidence that Lombroso deliberately misled viewers, in some cases his preconceptions about how criminals should look influenced his preparation of images for publication. This process can be seen most clearly in a portrait of a *Romagnolo trococefalo*, or abnormally round-headed man from the Romagna, that appeared in the very first edition of *Criminal Man* (figure 18). It took us some time to realize that this was the same fellow depicted as the *Romagnolo trococefalo stupratore* (abnormally round-headed rapist from Romagna) of the second and subsequent editions (figure 19). Between the first and second editions, the portrait underwent considerable uglification. The man's head became bald, aside from a wispy outer ring of hair. His ears extended outward to resemble jug handles. He acquired a stubble on his chin and upper lip, deeper wrinkles, and shiftier eyes; overall he aged by at least twenty years. The original image depicts not the monstrous rapist of the later editions but an innocuous-looking man.

Similarly, while doing research in Lombroso's museum, the historian Giorgio Colombo discovered earlier (and far less horrific) versions of some of Lombroso's other brutish characters. "The passage from photo to drawing and from drawing to engraving," Colombo points out, "is a gradual process of deformation—and the formation of a monster. . . . The procedure pushes the recalcitrant image to correspond to the archetype of a wicked man, who naturally is always ugly."[51] Mario Portigliatti Barbos, a successor to Lombroso's chair at the University of Turin, has also remarked on the slippage from likeness to stereotype involved in the production of some of his predecessor's illustrations. "There is an unconscious element of caricature [even] in the pages of the *Album of Delinquents n. 1 and 2* [Lombroso's source material], which dates back to 1871 and includes various drawings, probably from the hand of Frigerio,"[52] a physician who contributed images to Lombroso's collection.[53] Thus even Frigerio's original images, from which Lom-

broso later derived his caricatures, were shaped by theoretical presuppo-
sitions. The boundary between science and art was fluid from the start.

Narrative. In *Criminal Man*, Lombroso employed narrative in two
ways to supplement his quantitative data. First, Lombroso examined
written artifacts and the language of inmates to deepen his understanding of the criminal mind. Second, he himself employed narrative and
literary evidence to supplement his measurements and statistics in creating his portrait of the born criminal. To the modern reader, passages
of *Criminal Man* that cite Dostoyevsky or Italian proverbs as support
for criminological claims seem inappropriate. Yet Lombroso's leaven-
ing of statistics with stories made his theory accessible to an audience
that went beyond the academic and medical communities.

As early as in the first edition of *Criminal Man* Lombroso included
chapters on criminals' literature and jargon. He seemed to delight in
the poetry of prison inmates, which he deemed "a surprise from such
pens." Favorably comparing one prison poet to the Renaissance writer
Petrarch, he concluded that criminals were attracted to poetry because
it lent itself to the expression of strong emotions. Lombroso found
the jargon of criminals equally fascinating and more obviously a sign
of their atavistic nature. Surprisingly uniform across Italy, criminal jargon, he reported, mixed archaic and childish vocabularies. Lombroso
concluded in edition 1 of *Criminal Man* that criminals "speak like savages because they are savages, living amidst the very flower of European
civilization."

In the second edition of *Criminal Man*, Lombroso added a chapter
on what he would later call graphology, or the identification of criminal
character through handwriting analysis. Admitting that "the idea that
a man's handwriting can provide clues to his psychological state may
seem useless and even bizarre," he nevertheless claimed to have discovered significant differences between the script of murderers and thieves.
In the fourth edition, he expanded his graphological experiments by
using hypnosis on a supposedly normal young man who, when told he
was a criminal, began to write in rough, uncivilized script.

In *Palimsesti del carcere*, Lombroso collected over thirty additional
pages of prisoners' writing, including graffiti from cell walls, designs
on inmates' water jugs, comments scribbled in the margins of prison
library books, embroidery on prison uniforms, and tattoos. In his introduction, Lombroso explained that this vast collection of prison artifacts

contradicted the general view that the prison is "a mute and paralyzed organism, deprived of a mouth or hands."[54] Instead, these artifacts constituted "a real collection of autobiographies" that reveal "significant signs of the true fiber and psychology of that new and very unhappy race," born criminals.[55] Comparing himself to a paleographer or translator of ancient texts, Lombroso modestly described *Palimsesti* as a collection of data meant only for the eyes of scientists. Yet his tantalizing hints that prison writing was obscene seem designed to attract a wider audience—readers who, like Lombroso himself, would be fascinated by the criminal underworld.

In *Criminal Man*, Lombroso himself used narrative to buttress his scientific arguments. His psychiatric interviews with prisoners elicited individual and family stories that seemed to prove the tenets of criminal anthropology. Lombroso shaped his case studies of famous criminals like Salvatore Misdea and the brigand Giuseppe Musolino into gripping tales of atavistic monstrosity and bad heredity. At times, Lombroso inserted himself, or other criminal anthropologists, into the drama of court cases, picturing scientists as saviors who alone could determine criminal insanity.

At another level of narrative, Lombroso used historical anecdotes, literary passages, and proverbs as scientific evidence. He did not hesitate to cite, for example, the jug ears of the Roman emperor Nero in edition 1 of *Criminal Man* as proof that this anomaly typified born criminals. Similarly, the figure of Raskolnikof in *Crime and Punishment* confirmed for Lombroso in the fourth edition the existence of atavistic traits in many occasional criminals. Perhaps most surprising to the modern reader is Lombroso's readiness, in the fifth edition, for example, to resort to proverbs as confirmation of his findings that criminals exhibited certain physiognomical abnormalities such as sparse beards, beady eyes, and, in women, virile voices. However unscientific this resort to popular opinion might seem, Lombroso's ideas spread quickly because they were built on what one narrative theorist has called "preconstructs" or prevailing stereotypes.[56] Rather than detracting from the impact of *Criminal Man*, its many narrative devices multiplied its appeal and accessibility to audiences outside of the academic and legal communities.

At a more general level, *Criminal Man* as a whole offers a master narrative of the evolution of law and crime from the plant and animal world to savage society and finally to civilized Europe. This grand story knits together the multiple and fragmented types of evidence offered by Lombroso, including statistics, interviews, historical examples, and proverbs. While Lombroso's narrative differed little from the standard social Darwinism of his day that described the triumph of white civilization over a barbarous past, it added a unique dimension to this story by arguing that the roots of modern law lay in the crime and violence typical of past societies, rather than in religion or lofty philosophical principles.[57] In the final edition of *Criminal Man*, Lombroso added a surprising twist to his master narrative, one that had hitherto painted a vast panorama of criminals and their multiple threats to society. In the end, he suggests that crime is useful and has constituted the motor force of history.

The Lombroso Museum

To house his ever-expanding collection of both visual and written artifacts, in 1884 Lombroso informally opened a museum at the University of Turin.[58] It offered exhibits on a wide range of degenerates—epileptics, freaks, lunatics, prostitutes, and street children, as well as lawbreakers. An incredible array of bizarre displays, many of them contributed by Lombroso's admirers in other parts of Italy and foreign countries, jammed the six rooms of the museum, floor to ceiling: wax death masks and pickled brains; obsessive drawings by the criminally insane; bits of tattooed skin; weapons, manacles, and leg irons; overscale models of carnivorous plants; a mummy; more than three hundred skulls—Abyssinian, Chinese, Indian, and Patagonian, as well as Italian; a huge model of the Eastern State Penitentiary in Philadelphia, illustrating its system of solitary confinement; a lithograph of a Prussian cannibal; remains stolen from ancient Sardinian tombs; bodies of murdered infants; prisoners' water jugs incised with sexual fantasies; and, after Lombroso's death in 1909, not only his entire office but also his own face, dozing through eternity in a jar of preservative.[59] However, as Portigliatti Barbos warns, one should not leap to the ahistorical conclusion that the collection is merely "incomprehensible *bric-a-brac*," for, in fact, it "offers premises, techniques, methods, values, and results," albeit while leaving the determination of meanings to "the subjective fantasy of the visitor."[60]

The opening of the Lombroso museum, like the publication of the

Atlas, marked a triumph of positivism, with its emphasis on empirical research and scientific induction. More specifically, the museum's establishment marked the triumph of criminal anthropology, with its assumption that knowledge somehow inheres in crime-related objects. According to the museum's unspoken premise, criminologists and police officials could derive lessons in crime prevention from the study of these artifacts. For turn-of-the-century visitors to this museum and to its imitators in other European cities, the historian Susanne Regener explains, "an aura of knowledge surrounded the collection of artifacts of deviants, establishing as it were a metaphysics of evil: the object's essence could be grasped merely by gazing at it. The items on view . . . were therefore . . . important because knowledge would manifest itself in them."[61] Lombroso made the same epistemological point in the introduction to his *Palimsesti*, where he claimed that he did not want to influence readers' interpretations—conclusions "which, in my view, must emerge spontaneously and speak by themselves to the eyes of the impartial reader."[62] That he in fact went on to tell readers exactly how to interpret every item in the book merely underscores his faith in artifacts' hidden but extractable meanings.

Other than to store Lombroso's collection, what were the goals of the strange museum? To a great extent, its objectives were identical to those of the illustrations in *Criminal Man*: to preserve, educate, persuade, and celebrate. The pedagogical goal predominated, officially at least: Lombroso hoped that the museum would promote scientific policing, educate future criminologists, and persuade both the general public and specialists of the virtues of criminal anthropology. Less clearly articulated was the goal that Regener calls "trophyization"—demonstrating and celebrating the victory of science over crime and, in Lombroso's case, the triumph of criminal anthropology over rival doctrines.[63] In addition, the museum had a political dimension. Founded not long after Italy became an independent nation, it manifested the hope that science would lead to the control of degeneracy and the creation of a healthy, progressive state. "The function of the museum," Regener observes, "was, in this context, to express symbolically the borders, stigmata, and visionary plans of the contemporary project of 'making Italy.'"[64] Expanding on this theme, another of the museum's historians, Colombo, explains that "for a society that was turning to research for its own identity, for protection against the specter of the past and for guarantees of progress," positivism "offered the exciting prospect of capturing reality through the medium of science—. . . measurable facts and deductions from exact laws, . . . as valid for man as for nature and, especially, for society."[65] Thus the museum signified hope that Italy's future would be guided by the very best that contemporary science had to offer.[66]

Lombroso's museum and book illustrations continue to serve one of their original purposes: to provide a unique record of nineteenth-century prisoners and their subcultures. From the pages of *Criminal Man* and other works derived from the museum, one learns of inmates' hopes and fears; their attitudes toward their offenses and, sometimes, toward their impending executions; secrets of their life in organized crime networks such as the Camorra; their views of police, jailors, religion, and sex; their beliefs about the potential of the tattooed body; their sense of humor. A century before so-called outsider art became fashionable, Lombroso preserved prisoners' autobiographical drawings of crime scenes, criminal careers, firing squads, and suicides. ("I am a disgrace[;] my destiny is to die strangled in prison," reads the inscription under a sketch of a prisoner dangling from a rope tied to his cell window grating [figure 21].) In a period famed for sexual prudishness, Lombroso published tattoos of decorated penises and priapic fantasies, helping to establish the field of sexology. From outlaws valued by no one else he collected playing cards, engravings on dried gourds, and sculptures fashioned from breadcrumbs. He preserved photographs in which violent men staged scenes of impending or remembered violence (figure 9). The images of *Criminal Man* offer valuable perspectives on not only criminals' culture but also on their emotional lives—"precious signs," Lombroso called them, "of the moral and psychological condition of this unfortunate class, who live beside us without our really knowing their true characters."[67]

Lombroso's Influence

Since his death in 1909, Lombroso has remained central to criminological debates, even though his ideas have not always been understood and have often been lambasted by critics. Controversial from its inception, the notion of the born criminal has both fascinated and repelled succeeding generations of criminologists. With the publication of the first edition of *Criminal Man*, Lombroso's image of the atavistic offender—

with his small skull, low forehead, protruding jaw, and jutting ears—fired the imagination of not only jurists and doctors but also writers, journalists, and artists throughout Europe. Criminal anthropology became central to the construction of the new discipline of criminology by offering a seemingly more modern and scientific explanation for crime than did traditional legal philosophy based on free will. In 1885, after the appearance of three editions of *Criminal Man*, Lombroso hosted the first International Congress of Criminal Anthropology in Rome, where his theory of the born criminal went practically uncontested. The international repute of Lombroso and his followers brought them fame within Italy, where positivist criminology was dubbed the Italian School.

By the second International Congress of Criminal Anthropology in Paris in 1889, however, Lombroso had come under attack, particularly from the French delegation. That Lombroso was acutely aware of the many criticisms of his theory is clear from the prefaces to each edition of *Criminal Man*, which constitute increasingly lengthy and defensive responses to his adversaries. The French proposed an alternative theory of social milieu that emphasized the role of social factors in initiating physical and psychological processes of degeneration. In following years, German proponents of the so-called modern school of criminal law rejected the importance of physical anomalies in favor of psychological signs of pathology in the diagnosis of criminality. Neither the French nor the Germans denied the hereditary nature of crime, but their specific rejection of born criminal theory with its emphasis on atavism injured Lombroso's prestige.

The publication in 1913 of *The English Convict* by Charles Goring dealt a further blow to the reputation of Italian criminal anthropology.[68] Using more sophisticated statistical techniques than had Lombroso, Goring claimed to have destroyed the theory of the born criminal by proving that physical anomalies were no more widespread in criminals than in the general population. Despite celebration among Lombroso's enemies, who thought that the born criminal had been laid to rest, Gina Lombroso-Ferrero perceptively realized that "Goring is more Lombrosian than Lombroso" because his conclusion—that offenders are mentally deficient and inherit their tendency to crime—echoed her father's ideas.[69] While Lombroso-Ferrero certainly exaggerated the similarities between Lombroso and Goring, she was correct in noting that the strain of biological and psychological determinism within European criminology owed an enormous debt to her father. This emphasis on heredity as the mechanism most responsible for perpetuating vice, crime, and disease only grew stronger when the eugenics movement peaked in the interwar period.

Not surprisingly, allegiance to Lombroso remained strongest in Italy as several new generations of criminologists continued to apply and update his theory. Two main trends characterized developments within the positivist camp after Lombroso's death. First, his followers increasingly emphasized psychological traits rather than physical anomalies as the defining feature of inborn criminality. Second, others retained an emphasis on physical anomalies but downplayed cranial and skeletal malformations in favor of studies of hormones and body types. Lombroso's intellectual heirs moved into positions of power within parliament and the criminal justice system, assuring the popularity of positivist criminology throughout the fascist period. After a visit to Italy in 1936, the American sociologist Elio Monachesi noted in amazement "the intense loyalty to and reverence for Lombroso displayed by the students of crime in Italy."[70]

For the most part, criminologists in the United States rejected biological determinism in the 1920s and 1930s, adopting sociological explanations of crime. The Chicago school of criminology, with its emphasis on the formative influences of family and neighborhood, came to dominate academic theories of crime. Biological perspectives did not disappear, however, particularly when the offenders were women. While few American criminologists followed Lombroso's lead in devoting serious attention to female crime, those who did echoed his conclusions. In *Five Hundred Delinquent Women*, the prominent Harvard criminologists Sheldon and Eleanor Glueck viewed extramarital sexuality among women as a sign of biological inferiority and bad heredity, part of a syndrome that included feeblemindedness or weak intelligence.[71] In addition, in 1939, the American eugenicist and anthropologist Earnest Hooton published two books that attempted to update Lombroso's criminal anthropology.[72]

Today, criminologists are again considering the possibility that crime may be rooted (at least partially and occasionally) in biological factors. In the United States, where for most of the twentieth century sociological theories dominated explanations of male offending, this shift represents a major change. The change is less radical in Italy, where criminology for decades formed part of the professional territory of medical schools, and where in any case Lombroso's influence remained stronger.[73] The change is also less marked in terms of explanations of female crime, which until the 1970s continued to be shaped by the biological (and specifically Lombrosian) tradition.[74] But although biological theories never entirely died out in some countries or in female criminology, for the most part they were eclipsed—until their recent resurgence.

Of course, the current revival of biological explanations does not mark a simple return to Lombroso's positions. There are at least three fundamental differences between biological theories of crime today and in the past. One lies in the fact that whereas criminal anthropologists often spoke in terms of a nature-nurture dichotomy, theorists today speak of gene-environment interactions, holding that heredity seldom works independent of a context. A second major difference concerns determinism: whereas Lombroso claimed that born criminals are biologically bound to commit crime, criminologists today are likely to speak in terms of probabilities, risk factors, and antisocial predispositions. (To be fair, however, one must recognize that Lombroso's strict determinism applied only to born criminals; for other offender types he recognized a probabilistic interplay of social and biological factors.) A third outstanding difference lies in the type of causational factors studied by biological theorists in the past and today: whereas Lombroso focused on atavism, degeneration, epilepsy, and moral insanity, theorists today study such factors as the evolution of antisocial personality traits, behavioral genetics, hormonal imbalances, and neurocognitive deficits.

Despite these crucial differences, however, there also exist a number of significant parallels between the ideas of criminal anthropologists and present-day biocriminologists. Most striking is the way members of both groups have distinguished between a small inner circle of very serious, habitual offenders and an outer ring of more numerous run-of-the-mill offenders. Lombroso spoke of born criminals, differentiating them from less serious occasional criminals, accidental criminals, criminals by passion, and so on; these basic differentiations resurface in current distinctions between life-course persistent and adolescence-limited offenders.[75] The recent work does not derive from Lombroso's teachings, but in this respect it does reach similar conclusions.

Second, Lombroso foreshadowed one of the major currents in biocriminology today, that of evolutionary psychology. Profoundly influ-

enced by Darwinism, Lombroso perceived a multitude of evolutionary effects on criminal behavior, most obviously in his theory of the
criminal as an atavism or throwback to an earlier evolutionary stage,
but also in his attribution of innate criminality to poorly evolved organisms such as savages, children, animals, and even plants. Today's
evolutionary psychologists argue that our social behaviors, including
perhaps male sexual aggressiveness and women's overall lower rates of
crime, can be explained as by-products of adaptation and sexual selection over long periods of time.[76] But their work, like Lombroso's, uses
Darwinian concepts as a starting point.

A third parallel between past and present biological explanations of
crime lies in Lombroso's anticipation of yet another major current in
today's theories, that of behavioral genetics. While Lombroso did not
think in terms of genes, which were identified just at the time of his
death, he did believe that heritable tendencies, transmitted through the
generations, influenced criminal behavior. This is not far from what
current genetic theories of crime hold when they speak of genetic predispositions or propensities to behaviors such as impulsiveness or sensa-
tion-seeking that may lead to crime, especially if the individual is born
into an environment that does not instill self-restraint. On a fundamental level, criminal anthropology's emphasis on heredity anticipated current genetic explanations of rule-breaking behavior.

Few American criminologists today, no matter how devoted to biological theories, trace their roots to Lombroso; nor does the current resurgence in biological theories mark a return to criminal anthropology.
The resurgence does, however, echo many of Lombroso's key ideas. In
major ways, *Criminal Man* proves to have been a forerunner of current
theories about biology and crime.

A Guide to This Translation

This volume is intended to make available to English-language readers
key excerpts from all five editions of Lombroso's *Criminal Man*. We
have included Lombroso's original footnotes, tables, and illustrations
to show how Lombroso used different types of data to support his
theory of criminal anthropology. In addition, we provide this general
introduction, forewords to each edition, footnotes, a glossary, a bib-

liography, and appendices with information about Lombroso and his historical context.

Our intention is neither to endorse nor to attack Lombroso's theory, but rather to make his works available to criminologists and historians. A careful reading of *Criminal Man* challenges the pat analyses of Lombroso's thought available in most criminological textbooks and collections of criminological readings.[77] While Lombroso's name is well-known to criminologists and historians, the evolution and complexity of his ideas, and even the contradictions within them, are obscured in the standard textbook summary that focuses exclusively on the born criminal. The relationship of Lombroso's ideas to his biography and Italian history has been ignored by scholars who do not read Italian. But this situation is now changing, and as new books on Lombroso appear in English, scholars will be able to judge them in light of Lombroso's original text.

Translation Philosophy. This translation of *Criminal Man* abridges the original five editions, but it does not distort their content; it reveals the direction of Lombroso's thought as it grew increasingly complex over twenty years. We include all the major topics addressed by Lombroso in this English edition, which is divided into sections corresponding to the five original Italian editions. The first section of the book includes every chapter of the first edition of *Criminal Man* aside from those on criminal morality, the etiology of crime, and crime prevention. These three chapters are postponed until our section on the second edition, where Lombroso analyzes these topics in fuller detail. Our second section also includes chapters on suicide, criminals of passion, and criminal handwriting. Entirely new topics (crime in animals and savages, crime among children, and moral insanity) are contained in the next section pertaining to the third edition, while the epileptic, insane, and occasional criminal appear in section four on the fourth edition. Because the fifth edition was mainly a compendium of the previous editions, the final section of this translation returns to previous topics but shows how Lombroso expanded and changed them. For example, we show how the databases of the chapters on criminal craniums and criminal physiognomy expanded over time, and how the fifth edition's chapters on the etiology, prevention, and punishment of crime introduce new subtopics.

We were able to retain the substance and shape of the original Italian texts because Lombroso never eliminated, and rarely revised, chapters. As he identified new causes of crime and categories of offenders, he simply added new chapters to the previous ones. Thus many chapters remained intact through the five editions. This pattern emerges clearly in our appendix 1, where we present a comparative summary of the contents of all five original editions. When important new subsections were added (like those on photographs or handwriting), we include these materials as separate chapters. In a few instances, we break up very long chapters from the original edition (for example, material on the etiology of crime) into several parts for consistency and readability.

Within chapters, we eliminate many of the countless examples that Lombroso presents in support of every facet of his theory. Lombroso believed that an accumulation of examples—whether statistical, clinical, historical, or folkloric—increased the strength of his argument. These examples are so repetitious and lengthy that it is impractical to include them in a streamlined edition intended to keep the attention of the reader. We have, however, included representative examples of every kind of data used by Lombroso to make his mode of argumentation clear. Although our abridgment has resulted in a text that is more manageable and direct than the original, we have also retained many passages in which Lombroso's analysis appears contradictory, pointing out inconsistencies in our footnotes.

Lombroso wrote in formal, scholarly Italian, using medical and scientific terms that are today obsolete. To twenty-first-century Italians, Lombroso's language seems old-fashioned, difficult, and at times even incomprehensible. Its datedness results in part from the passage of time and in part from Lombroso's own sloppy style and hasty writing.[78] To educated contemporaries, Lombroso's language would have seemed appropriately learned, and among nonscientists, his obscure terminology might have increased his credibility; but because one of our goals was to make Lombroso's work accessible, we translated obscure words into more familiar terms. We also tried to relax his prose style, making it slightly more colloquial. We attempted to make his prose comprehensible to modern readers while preserving some of its formality.

Reading Criminal Man.   Each edition of *Criminal Man* was introduced by a preface, four of which we have excerpted at length (the preface to the fifth edition simply repeats material from earlier editions). Lombroso used these prefaces to set out his general theory, identify the topics he had added since the previous edition, and defend himself against opponents. In translating these prefaces, we have tried to preserve the tone of Lombroso's dialogue with his critics, which combined mock humility with combativeness and sometimes sarcasm.

Tables appear frequently in the original texts, usually in an unorganized and practically unreadable form. Unless otherwise noted, we include all the tables from each excerpt, but to make them more understandable, we sometimes rearranged the rows and columns, and we added editors' notes to identify statistical discrepancies within the tables and between the tables and the text. In addition, since illustrations were central to Lombroso's project, this volume reproduces over forty images, most drawn from the various editions of *Criminal Man*, but some made by us during work in the Lombroso museum; we also accompany many of these with editors' notes. Appendix 2 catalogues and compares the illustrations in all five editions.

The text has two sets of footnotes: the first is Lombroso's, the second constitutes our editorial annotations. We include all the notes appearing in the parts of *Criminal Man* that we translate; they appear as footnotes at the bottom of the page. Lombroso's citations indicate his familiarity with a vast range of international scholarship and show that researchers all over Europe were working on similar topics. We have not attempted to translate Lombroso's citations or correct errors in them, partly because most of the works to which they refer were never translated, partly because leaving them the way he wrote them gives readers a clear sense of his documentational decisions and procedures. (Similarly, we simply reproduce without translation the citations that Lombroso inserts directly into the text.) However, in the few cases in which Lombroso uses footnotes to make substantive comments, we do translate his notes.

The second editorial set of notes follows the translated text; in these entries we provide biographical data, historical information, explanations of terms, and glosses on difficult passages in the text. Readers should also consult the glossary at the end of the volume for definitions of terms common to nineteenth-century criminal anthropology.

A final word must be said about our use of terms that may seem offensive to readers. In order to reproduce the flavor and intent of Lombroso's language, we have retained his original terms, including *savages* and *primitives* for nonwhite peoples; *normal* for noncriminal individuals; *madmen* for the mentally ill; and *pederasts* for homosexual men. While these terms prove inappropriate for current academic analysis, they were nevertheless typical of nineteenth-century scientific discourse and provide invaluable insight into Lombroso's worldview.

EDITION ONE

1876

Editors' Foreword

In the first edition of *Criminal Man* (1876), Lombroso sets forth many of the fundamental tenets of his theory; but these ideas, while elaborated and expanded in the subsequent four editions, remain sketchy in this short initial volume of just 255 pages. First, Lombroso calls for a new type of research that focuses on the criminal rather than the crime. He promises that his new criminal anthropology—the scientific study of the physical and psychological traits of criminal man—will identify the causes of crime that have eluded traditional legal experts. Second, Lombroso criticizes the philosophical doctrine of free will that attributes to human beings moral responsibility for their actions. Pointing to rising rates of recidivism, he denies that criminals' behavior is a product of free choice and argues that it is instead determined by forces outside of their control. Third, he proposes atavism, or regression to an earlier stage of evolution, as the most important of these forces. Signs of atavism, which Lombroso calls anomalies in later editions, mark the body and mind of the criminal and provide empirical data for criminological research. As atavistic throwbacks on the evolutionary scale, criminals constitute a group that differs from law-abiding citizens and instead resembles "savages" from less civilized societies.

Where the first edition of *Criminal Man* most differs from subsequent editions is in the absence of any classificatory system of criminals. Not yet employing the phrase *born criminal*, coined later by Enrico Ferri, Lombroso refers to all lawbreakers simply as "criminals" or "real criminals." His main concern is not to distinguish among categories of offenders but to measure the difference between, first, criminals and "honest" individuals, and, second, criminals and the insane. Such comparisons lead him to conclude that the three groups are distinct: while criminals may share some anomalies with the insane, the insane are not atavistic but acquire mental diseases later in life. In this edition, Lombroso's only extended treatment of a specific subgroup of criminals occurs in his discussion of organized crime. Although he does not hold that members of organized crime differ physically or psychologically from other criminals, he does offer valuable descriptions of the structure and rituals of the nineteenth-century Italian Camorra and Mafia.

To identify the physical and psychological anomalies of criminals, Lombroso lays out the methodology that he would pursue through the five editions. He begins with an analysis of the circumferences and abnormalities of sixty-six criminal skulls, including that of the thief and brigand Giuseppe Villella. Lombroso later claimed that his theory of atavism had been sparked by the discovery of a median occipital fossetta, or indentation at the base of Villella's skull, an anomaly which reminded Lombroso of a cranial formation typical of primitive peoples and animals. Lombroso supplements his measurements of skulls from cadavers with data on the anthropometry and physiognomy of 832 living subjects, including their height, weight, and strength. He paints an indelible portrait of the criminal face with its hawklike nose, receding forehead, and jug ears. To emphasize the scientific nature of his research, Lombroso presents a series of statistical tables enumerating the physical abnormalities of criminals, sometimes comparing them with control groups of healthy individuals and the insane.

Lombroso presents a no less striking psychological profile of the criminal, an individual hobbled by moral abnormalities mirroring those of the body. Emblematic of Lombroso's conviction of the close connection between the body and the mind are his tests of sensitivity, which equate dullness of touch in criminals to their moral blindness. Vain, vindictive, and bloodthirsty, criminals shun work and delight in orgy. Education alone cannot instill honesty, he argues, for it often provides new tools for criminal activity. To delineate criminal psychology, Lombroso draws more on sensational anecdotes and historical examples than statistical data. Equally unscientific are the lessons that he draws from criminals' tattoos, jargon, and poetry. Yet these idiosyncratic chapters on criminal art make *Criminal Man* one of the first ethnographies of nineteenth-century prison culture.

Through the accumulation of such disparate types of data, Lombroso hopes to convince the reader of the superiority of his empirical positivist method. This first edition of *Criminal Man* contains the seeds of two ideas that will grow to occupy a more central place in later editions: that the etiology of crime is multicausal and that the sexual nature of women's crime differentiates it from that of men. In addition, later editions will complicate his tripartite comparison among real criminals, honest individuals, and the insane. He ends the first edition with an invocation to the theory of social defense as a rationale for punishment, anticipating criticism that his denial of moral responsibility to criminals will unleash social chaos. The social defense rationale for punishing criminals became a hallmark of Lombroso's applied criminology and informed the detailed policy recommendations of subsequent editions.

Author's Preface

Those who follow criminal trials and study the results by visiting prisons or examining statistics are disheartened by the endless debate over punishment. On the one hand judges almost always ignore the criminal and emphasize the crime, thinking of the latter as a mere anecdote, an incident in the life of the offender, one unlikely to be repeated. On the other hand, there are those who, knowing the rarity of repentance and frequency of recidivism (which reaches 30, 55, and even 80 percent), attempt to show the costliness of crime and to expose the weaknesses of a justice system that provides, ultimately, no more than an illusory shield against recidivism. Those who have had direct contact with offenders, such as members of their families or prison wardens, know that they are different from other people, with weak or diseased minds that can rarely be healed. Psychiatrists in many cases find it impossible to neatly distinguish between madness and crime. And yet legislators, believing exceptions to free will to be rare, ignore the advice of psychiatrists and prison officials. They do not understand that most criminals really do lack free will.[1] In past years, having decided that reform is the greatest goal of their terrestrial mission, legislators established legal criteria that failed to recognize any gradations whatsoever among healthy, diseased, and guilty minds.

It seems to me important to reconcile these opposing views and to determine whether the criminal man belongs in the same category as the healthy man or the insane individual or in an entirely separate category.[2] To do this and decide whether there is a force in nature that causes crime, we must abandon the sublime realms of philosophy and even the sensational facts of the crime itself and proceed instead to the direct physical and psychological study of the criminal, comparing the results with information on the healthy and the insane.

The outcome of such inquiries is presented in this work.

1

Criminal Craniums (Sixty-six Skulls)

I thought it best to begin this study of criminal man with an anatomical table to facilitate a thorough examination of criminal craniums, amounting to a total of sixty-six skulls. Of these

- 16 were provided by Calori, from his superb Anatomical Museum in Bologna;
- 8 were provided by Mantegazza, from the Anthropological Museum of Florence;
- 5 were provided by Zoja, from the Anatomical Museum of Pavia;
- 6 came from the Anthropological Museum of the Academy of Medicine at Turin;
- 18 came from Dr. Roggero's valuable private collection at the town prison of Alessandria;
- 12 were collected by me and form part of my Anthropological-Psychiatric Museum;
- 1 was donated by my esteemed friend, Dr. Golgi.

As shown in table 1, measurement of cranial circumference found very few criminal skulls that were particularly large (one of 580 mm [millimeters], two of 560 mm, one of 550 mm, two of 540 mm) or even normal in size (eight of 530 mm, thirteen of 520 mm),[3] but a high incidence of craniums that were microcefalic or abnormally small: thirty-nine out of sixty-five. More precisely, there were nineteen at 510 mm, twelve at 500 mm, and eight at 490 mm.[4]

The cranial sutures or joins in the bones of the skull were normal in only seventeen cases. In five cases, they were still open at the age of seventy-five or eighty. This was true of men like Villella, Pietrotto, and Soldati, who were famous for committing crimes into old age and repeatedly eluding capture. A few of the skulls with open sutures had a large cranial capacity, but others had a small one accompanied by many monkeylike anomalies. The cranial sutures were completely closed in

Table 1: Cranial Circumference of Criminal Skulls

PROVINCE	NAME	AGE	CRIME	CIRCUMFERENCE (mm)
Piedmont	Magone	35	Murder	500
	Medichino Guercio	—	"	520
	Violini	—	"	525
	Rocca	—	"	505
	X. Y. (Turin)	—	"	535
	R. of Alessandria	24	Forgery	490
	T. of Cuneo	36	Theft	545
	B. of Turin	24	Murder	495
	C. of Cuneo	47	Theft	510
Lombardy	Macchi	38	Theft	495
	Belguardi	40	Murder and theft	510
	Favecchio	35	Theft	510
	X. Y. (Pavia)	60	Procuring	490
	X. Y. (Pavia)	50	"	525
	Nicoletti	49	"	520
	X. Y. (Pavia)	37	Prostitution	510
	X. Y. (Pavia)	60	Theft	532
	Palazzoli	40	"	510
	Rainoldi	37	Fraud	530
	Cochelli	78	Purse-snatching	550
	X. Y. (Pavia)	40	Forgery	580
	Lavecchia	53	Theft	502
	Boggia	—	Murder	530
	Rossi of Voghera	38	Patricide	490
Genoa	X. Y. (Roggero collection)	36	"	510
	X. Y. (Roggero collection)	42	Murder	515
Venice	**Soldati of Treviso**	70	"	560
	X. Y. (Bologna)	39	"	508
	X. Y. (Bologna)	38	"	510
	X.Y. (Florence)	41	"	536
Tuscany	X. Y. (Roggero Collection)	—	"	510
	X. Y. of Perugia	42	"	510
	Rossi	35	Murder and arson	526
	Birro	35	Murder	560
	Pietrotto of Pietrasanta	70	Theft	515
Emilia	X.Y. (Florence)	31	Murder	510
	" "	—	"	490
	X.Y (Bologna)	35	"	520
	"	—	"	500
	"	—	"	522
	"	—	"	505
	"	—	"	510
	"	—	"	510

Table 1: continued

PROVINCE	NAME	AGE	CRIME	CIRCUMFERENCE (mm)
	"	—	"	510
	"	—	"	530
	"	—	"	510
	"	—	"	504
	"	—	"	520
	"	—	"	510
	"	—	"	520
	"	—	"	—
Roma	Cipolla of Vallecorsa	71	Murder	500
Naples	Margiullo of Basilicata	19	Brigandage	500
	Gatti of Calabria	—	Arson and theft	490
	Villella of Calabria	70	"	520
	Malt... of Basilicata	37	Brigandage	500
	X. Y. of Terra di Lavoro	20	"	520
	X. Y. of Calabria	25	Receiving stolen goods	500
	X. Y. of Abruzzi	20	Murder	520
	X. Y. of Naples	55	"	500
	X. Y. of Calabria	34	Theft	530
Sicily	Arnioni	25	Desertion	500
	X. Y. (Roggero Collection)	51	Murder	490
	X. Y. (Roggero Collection)	30	"	510
	Carpintari	27	Murder	530
Sardinia	X. Y. (Roggero Collection)	—	Theft	510

Editors' note: Lombroso is not consistent when identifying his unknown skulls, which he labels "X.Y." Sometimes he locates them by home region and at others, by the museum or collection in which he found them. We have bolded the names of the three famous criminals mentioned in the text. The provinces have been rearranged to go from northern to southern Italy. This table is excerpted from a much larger one listing seventeen additional cranial measurements.

thirty-eight cases—so thoroughly in seven of these that they had become invisible.[5]

In another study of fifty-six criminal craniums, I found that thirteen had one of the most serious of all anomalies, a median occipital fossetta or indentation at the base of the skull. A brigand from Calabria, Villella, had a median occipital fossetta[a] of extraordinary dimensions, 34 mm long, 23 mm wide, and 11 mm deep.[6] He also exhibited atrophy of the

[a] You can find a drawing of Villella's median occipital fossetta in the *Arch.*, 1872, pg. 63; and in Virchow's *Arch. f. path. Anatomie* 1871, LII, tav X *Uber ein Hinterauptsgrube*. [We reproduce the substance of Lombroso's footnotes, even when we know they include inaccuracies, in order to show his approach to documentation.—Eds.]

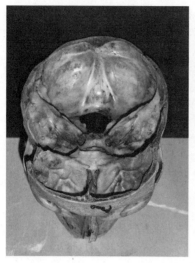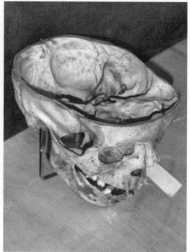

1 and 2 Two Skulls: Villella and a Normal Man
Editors' note: The skull on the left, that of the brigand and thief Villella, has a median occipital fossetta, or an abnormal indentation at its base, in contrast to the bony crest at the base of the "normal" skull on the right. Lombroso interpreted the median occipital fossetta as a sign of atavism.
Source: Photo courtesy of the Museo Lombroso (Turin).

lateral occipital openings, absence of the occipital crest, and two boney parallel projections that gave the occipital opening a trapezoidal shape that ended in a small triangular protrusion near the occipital aperture. From these features, comparative anatomy and human embryology can induce that we are dealing with a fairly small cerebellum. Such a brain suggests not the sublimity of the primate, but the lower level of the rodent or lemur, or the brain of a human fetus of three or four months.

If we compare criminals with the insane, we find the former exhibit a similar or perhaps greater number of cranial abnormalities. This is not surprising, given that most of the insane are not born so, but become mad, while criminals are born with evil inclinations. At the moment I will not go into all the reasons for these cranial abnormalities in criminals, but I cannot avoid pointing out how closely they correspond to characteristics observed in normal skulls of the colored and inferior races.

Criminals have the following rates of abnormality: 61 percent exhibit fusion of the cranial bones; 92 percent, prognathism or an ape-

 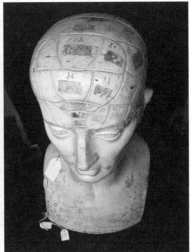

3 and 4 Lombroso's Phrenological Head
Editors' note: Lombroso included this head in his personal collection, showing the importance of phrenology as a source of criminal anthropology. The numbers on the head refer to human attributes like sympathy and aggression, which phrenologists located on specific areas of the skull.
Source: Photo courtesy of the Museo Lombroso (Turin).

like forward thrust of the lower face; 63 percent, overdevelopment of the sinuses; 27 percent, cranial thickness; 9 percent, an open medio-frontal suture; 20 percent, a large jawbone; 25 percent, a receding forehead; 74 percent, wide or overdeveloped cheekbones; 45 percent, overly large wisdom teeth; 59 percent, small cranial capacity, among which 10 percent show true microcephaly; and 14 percent, too many wormian bones. These features recall the black American and Mongol races and, above all, prehistoric man much more than the white races.

These abnormalities are almost always found in large clusters in individual criminals like Villella. Is it possible that individuals with such an enormous variety of cranial anomalies can have the same level of intelligence and sense of responsibility as men with perfectly normal skulls? Note, moreover, that the cranial variations discussed here represent only the most obvious lesions of the brain, that is, alterations of volume and form.

2

Anthropometry and
Physiognomy of 832 Criminals

To many, my attempt to conclude anything at all about the cranial dimensions of the criminal man from a few measurements of cadavers will seem futile and rash. Fortunately, however, I have been able to compare these measurements with those taken from 832 live specimens of criminals, thanks to the help of colleagues who are prison directors and prison physicians.

In terms of height, criminals reproduce their regional types. In Italy, they are very tall in the Veneto (1.69 meters), fairly tall in Umbria and Lombardy (1.66 m), less tall in Emilia, Calabria, and Piedmont (1.63 m), slightly shorter in Naples, Sicily, and the Marches (1.62 m), and shortest of all in Sardinia (1.59 m).[7] Compared with healthy men in the army, criminals appear to be taller than the average Italian, especially in the Veneto, Umbria, Lombardy, Sicily, and Calabria. In the Marches, Naples, and Piedmont, criminals are the same height as healthy men.

These findings, however, are skewed by the preponderance of robbers and murderers in my sample, and thus they conflict with the conclusions of Thomson and Wilson.[8] Robbers and murderers are taller than rapists, forgers, and especially thieves.[b] As for weight, we can compare the findings on 1,331 soldiers, studied by me and Dr. Franchini, with the average for criminals from each region. In the Veneto, healthy men weighed an average of 68 kilograms, while criminals weighed 62.5 kg.[9] But in most other regions, most notably Naples, Sicily, and Piedmont, criminals' average weight exceeded that of healthy men.

There are many erroneous ideas in circulation about the physiognomy, or facial expressions, of criminals. Novelists turn them into frightening-looking men with beards that go right up to their eyes,

---

[b] Thomson found an average weight of 151 pounds among 423 Scottish criminals, 106 pounds among 147 Irish criminals, and 149 pounds among 55 English criminals. The average height was 5 feet 6.9 inches for the Scottish criminals, 5 feet 6.2 inches for the English, and 5 feet 6.6 inches for the Irish.

penetrating ferocious gazes, and hawklike noses. More serious observers, such as Casper, err on the other extreme, finding no differences between criminals and normal men.[10] Both are wrong. It is certainly true that there are criminals with notably large cranial capacity and beautifully formed skulls, just as there are those with perfectly regular physiognomy, particularly among adroit swindlers and gang leaders. Lavater and Polli wrote about a murderer whose face resembled one of the angels painted by Guido (*Saggio di Fisiognomia*, 1837).[11] But criminals whose handsome features make a strong impression can be misleading precisely because they contradict our expectations. They are usually individuals of uncommon intelligence, a trait associated with gracefulness of form.

When, on the other hand, one ignores those rare individuals who form the oligarchy of the criminal world to study the entire spectrum of these wretches, as I have done in various prisons, one has to conclude that while offenders may not look fierce, there is nearly always something strange about their appearance. It can even be said that each type of crime is committed by men with particular physiognomic characteristics, such as lack of a beard or an abundance of hair; this may explain why the overall appearance is neither delicate nor pleasant.

In general, thieves are notable for their expressive faces and manual dexterity, small wandering eyes that are often oblique in form, thick and close eyebrows, distorted or squashed noses, thin beards and hair, and sloping foreheads. Like rapists, they often have jug ears. Rapists, however, nearly always have sparkling eyes, delicate features, and swollen lips and eyelids. Most of them are frail; some are hunchbacked. Pederasts are often distinguished by a feminine elegance of the hair and feminine clothing, which they insist on wearing even under their prison uniforms.

Habitual murderers have a cold, glassy stare and eyes that are sometimes bloodshot and filmy; the nose is often hawklike and always large; the jaw is strong, the cheekbones broad; and their hair is dark, abundant, and crisply textured. Their beards are scanty, their canine teeth very developed, and their lips thin. Often their faces contract, exposing the teeth. Among nearly all arsonists, I have observed a softness of skin, an almost childlike appearance, and an abundance of thick straight hair that is almost feminine. One extremely curious example from Pesaro, known as "the woman," was truly feminine in appearance and behavior.

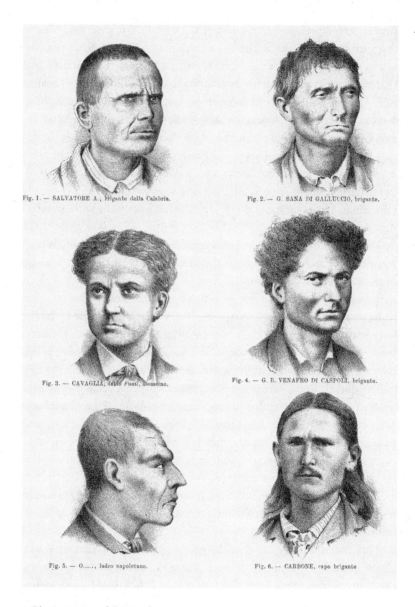

Fig. 1. — SALVATORE A., brigante della Calabria.

Fig. 2. — G. SANA DI GALLUCCIO, brigante.

Fig. 3. — CAVAGLIA, detto *Fusil*, assassino.

Fig. 4. — G. B. VENAFRO DI CASPOLI, brigante.

Fig. 5. — O....., ladro napoletano.

Fig. 6. — CARBONE, capo brigante

5 Physiognomy of Criminals

Editors' note: Lombroso identifies these criminals as brigands (nos. 1, 2, 4, and 6), a Neapolitan thief (no. 5), and Cavaglià (no. 3), the assassin who painted his story on his water jug (see figures 21 and 22).

Source: Lombroso, *L'uomo delinquente*, edition 4.

6 Homosexual Arsonist Nicknamed "The Woman" *Editors' note*: Lombroso characterized male homosexuals, like this arsonist, as feminine in hairstyle and dress. *Source*: Lombroso, *L'uomo delinquente*, edition 4.

Nearly all criminals have jug ears, thick hair, thin beards, pronounced sinuses, protruding chins, and broad cheekbones. Dumollard, a rapist and murderer, had a deformed upper lip and very thick black hair.[12] The rapist Mingrat had a low forehead, jug ears, and an enormous square jaw. Archaeologists have established that the cruelest of the Caesars — Commodius, Nero, and Tiberius — had jug ears and swollen temples.

But anthropology needs numbers, not isolated, generic descriptions, especially for use in forensic medicine. Thus I will provide statistics on 390 criminals from the regions of Emilia, the Marches, and southern Italy. Table 2 compares the hair color of these 390 criminals with that of 868 Italian soldiers from the same regions and 90 insane from Pavia. These figures show that hair color of criminals replicates typical regional characteristics, but only up to a certain point.

Jug ears are found on 28 percent of criminals, but the proportion varies by region: 47 percent of Sicilian criminals have jug ears, as do 33 percent from Piedmont, 11 percent from Naples, 33 percent from the Romagna, 9 percent from Sardinia, and 36 percent from Lombardy. Nine percent of all criminals have very long ears, although that proportion rises to 10 percent in Lombardy and the Romagna and 18 percent in Sicily and Piedmont.

It is difficult to determine the muscular force of criminals even with the best dynamometers because the subjects are completely out of condition after long periods of detention and inertia.[13] The problem is often compounded by the malignant spirit that characterizes prisoners'

Table 2: Hair Color of Soldiers and Criminals

	BROWN (percent)		BLACK (percent)		BLOND (percent)		RED (percent)	
REGION	sol.	crim.	sol.	crim.	sol.	crim.	sol.	crim.
Sicily	51	41	25	54	17	0	0	3
Calabria	39	50	20	33	15	0	0	0
Naples	50	50	28	40	22	5	0.3	0
Central Italy	56	66	20	33	21	5	1	5
Piedmont	47	35	13	35	34	29	0	0
Lombardy	38	33	16	33	32	33	0	0
Insane from Pavia	83	–	12	–	4	–	0	–

Editors' note: The last category, the insane from Pavia, is not consistent with Lombroso's regional categories, but seems to be an attempt to compare the insane with soldiers (normal men) and criminals.

whole existence. They pretend to be weaker than they really are and do not put much effort into pushing the dynamometer. In this regard, it is noteworthy that, as I was able to verify in the penitentiary of Ancona, prisoners are more energetic when they work continuously than in institutions that permit them to be idle. Rapists, brigands, and arsonists are the strongest and thieves and forgers the weakest, based on measurements of traction. Murderers and pickpockets differ in strength only by a slight fraction.

Criminal Women

At this point little can be said about female criminals because I have been allowed to examine only twenty-one of them and did so with much less ease than in the case of men. But this does not pose a complete obstacle because, first, I do not have enough information on normal women to make a comparison with criminal women; and, second, Parent-Duchatelet offers us numerous and reliable statistics on prostitutes, a class of women almost identical to criminal women in moral terms.[14] In addition, the esteemed Dr. Soresina has provided me with measurements on fifty-four prostitutes who were patients in the Milan lock hospital for venereal disease.[15]

The average cranial capacity of the twenty-one female criminals in

Table 3: Cranial Circumference of Insane Women, Prostitutes, and Criminal Women

CRANIAL CIRCUMFERENCE (cm.)	INSANE WOMEN (86)		PROSTITUTES (54)		CRIMINAL WOMEN (21)	
	total	percent	total	percent	total	percent
48	2	0.01	8	4.3		—
49	16	1.04	9	4.8	1	0.2
50	23	1.09	8	4.8	2	0.2
51	20	1.07	15	8.1	4	0.8
52	20	1.07		—	7	1.4
53	3	0.02	3	1.6	6	1.2
54	1	0.05	1	0.5	1	0.2
55			2	1.0		—
56			2	1.0		—

Editors' note: The number of insane women in the second column adds to 85 rather than 86; the total number of prostitutes adds to 48 rather than 54. The percentage columns have no relationship to the other data in the table, illustrating Lombroso's statistical ineptitude or general carelessness with detail.

my sample was 1,442 cc, slightly less than that of twenty insane women without dementia (1,468 cc), and above that of nineteen idiots with dementia (1,393 cc).

Table 3 presents these differences more clearly. Female criminals, and especially prostitutes, have oversized heads, but these are found only in a fraction of insane women. The rate of microcephaly, or a cranial circumference of forty-eight centimeters, among prostitutes is four times greater among the insane, who in turn have a rate double that of criminal women.

The only conclusion about the physiognomy of criminal women that I can draw from my sample is that female criminals tend to be masculine. (Among prostitutes even the voice often seems virile.) The only exception was a poisoner. Two out of twenty-one criminal women closely resembled the insane with their protruding and asymmetrical ears. Where criminal women differ most markedly from the insane is in the rich luxuriance of their hair. Not a single woman in my sample was bald, and only one showed precociously graying hair. Thomson, too, has noted rich manes of hair among female criminals.

Summing up in a few words that which scientific exigencies oblige me to express with arid numbers,[16] I conclude:

—The criminal is taller than the normal individual and even more so than the insane, with a broader chest, darker hair and (with the exception of Venetians) greater weight.

—In head volume, the criminal presents a series of submicro-cephalic craniums, double the number for normal men, but fewer than in the case of the insane.

—Criminals, especially forgers, also exceed the insane in large-volume heads. But the average head size of criminals never reaches the size of healthy men.

—The cephalic index, or shape of the criminal skull, varies with ethnicity but tends to be brachycephalic, or short-headed, particularly among robbers.[17] Criminal skulls present frequent asymmetry, although less often than among the insane.

—Compared to the insane, criminals have more traumatic lesions of the head and oblique eyes. But they less frequently display degeneration of the temple arteries, abnormalities of the ear, thin beards, tics, virility of appearance (if they are female), dilated pupils, and, still less often, graying hair and baldness.

—Criminals and the insane show equal rates of prognathism, unequally sized pupils, distorted noses, and receding foreheads.

—Measured on the dynamometer, criminals reveal greater weakness than normal men, though they are not as weak as the insane.

—More often than in the healthy population, criminals have brown or dark eyes and thick black hair. Such hair is most frequently found among robbers.

—Hunchbacks are extremely rare among murderers but are more common among rapists, forgers, and arsonists.

—Arsonists, and even more so thieves, tend to have gray irises; members of both groups are always shorter, lighter, weaker, and smaller in cranial capacity than pickpockets, who are in turn shorter, lighter, and weaker than murderers.

Among criminal women, one thing that can be said with certainty is that, like their male counterparts, they are taller than the insane. Yet they are shorter, and, perhaps with the exception of prostitutes, lighter than healthy women. All three female groups are identical in their average cranial circumference. Prostitutes show both a greater than average number of large heads and more microcephaly. In prostitutes, extremely small heads are four times more common than among the mad, and the rates among the mad are twice as high as those of the criminal. Prostitutes have dark, thick hair, and in Lombardy, but not in France, they frequently have dark irises. Female criminals are weaker than the insane and more often masculine looking.

Prognathism, thick and crisp hair, thin beards, dark skin, pointed skulls, oblique eyes, small craniums, overdeveloped jaws, receding foreheads, large ears, similarity between the sexes, muscular weakness— all these characteristics confirm the findings from autopsies to demonstrate that European criminals bear a strong racial resemblance to Australian aborigines and Mongols.

3

Tattoos

One of the most singular characteristics of primitive men and those who still live in a state of nature is the frequency with which they undergo tattooing. This operation, which has both its surgical and aesthetic aspects, derives its name from an Oceanic language. In Italy, the practice is known as *marca* [mark], *nzito*, *segno* [sign], and *devozione* [devotion]. It occurs only among the lower classes—peasants, sailors, workers, shepherds, soldiers, and even more frequently among criminals. Because of its common occurrence among criminals, tattooing has assumed a new and special anatomico-legal significance that calls for close and careful study. But first we must examine its frequency among normal individuals for the sake of comparison.

To do this, I will use data on 7,114 individuals: 4,380 were soldiers and 2,734 criminals, prostitutes, and criminal soldiers. For this information, I have to thank that valiant student of forensic medicine, Tarchini Bonfanti, as well as the illustrious Dr. Baroffio, Cavaliere Alborghetti of Bergamo, Professor Gamba of Turin, Dr. Soresina of Milan, and Professor De Amicis of Naples. Table 4 summarizes the results of the survey.

The figures indicate immediately that in Italy, as among savages, tattooing is infrequent among women. Among noncriminal men, the use of tattoos is decreasing, with rates ten times lower in 1873 than in 1863. On the other hand, the custom persists and indeed reaches enormous proportions among the criminal population, both military and nonmilitary, where among 1,432 individuals examined, 115 or 7.9 percent sported tattoos. The most common place for tattoos is the smooth part of the forearm, followed by the shoulder, the chest (sailors), and the fingers (miners), on which they take the form of a ring. Only men who had been to Oceania or were in prison had tattoos on their backs or pubic regions.

The symbols and meanings of tattoos are generally divisible into the categories of love, religion, war, and profession. Tattoos are external signs of beliefs and passions predominant among working-class men. After a careful study of the designs chosen by 102 criminals, I found

Table 4: Tattoos in Soldiers, Criminals, and Prostitutes

YEAR	GROUP (total number)	MEDICAL EXAMINER	PERCENTAGE WITH TATTOOS
1863	Soldiers (1147)	Dr. Lombroso	11.6
1873	Soldiers (2739)	Dr. Baroffio	1.4
	Criminal soldiers (150)	"	8.6
1872	Criminals (500)	Dr. Lombroso	6.0
1873	Criminals (134)	Dr. Alborghetti	15.0
	Criminals (650)	Dr. Tarchini	7.0
	Criminal women (300)	Dr. Gamba	1.6
1866–1873	Prostitutes (1000)	Dr. Soresina	—
1871	Prostitutes (small number)	—	a few
1874	Prostitutes (small number)	De Amicis	a few

Editors' note: In this eclectic table, Lombroso has combined studies covering different parts of Italy and different years.

that several not only appear frequently but also carry a particular significance. In 2 out of the 102 cases, tattoos marvelously reveal a nature that is violent, vindictive, or divided by conflicting intentions. For example, an old Piedmontese sailor, who had been a swindler and committed murder as part of a vendetta, had inscribed on his chest between two fists the sad phrase "I swear to revenge myself." A Venetian thief who was a recidivist bore the following lugubrious words on his chest: "I will come to a miserable end." It is said that criminals know their own fate and engrave it on their skin.

Other tattoos are obscene, either from their design or the region of the body where they appear. Only a few soldiers, mostly deserters released from prison, had obscene tattoos in the genital region. More significant results are obtained from my direct study of 102 tattooed criminals, of whom four had obscene tattoos.[c] One had a figure of a nude woman traced over the length of his penis. A second had the face of a woman drawn on the glans, in such a way that the woman's mouth was the penis's orifice; higher up on the penis was the Savoyard flag. A third had the initials of his lover on his penis; a fourth had a bouquet of flowers. All of this reveals not only a shamelessness but also insensitivity, given that the sexual organs are extremely sensitive to pain. Even savages avoid tattooing these areas.

The study of tattoos sometimes helps us track individuals to criminal

[c] Tardieu has written about a coach driver and an iron smith who had boots tattooed on their penises.

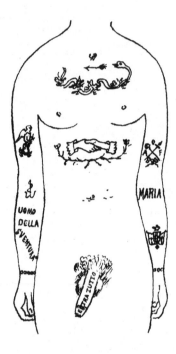

7 Tattoos of a Criminal Soldier
Editors' note: According to Lombroso, two tattoos on this Neapolitan soldier refer to homosexuality: the joined hands on his chest and the words on his penis reading, "It enters everywhere." The inscription on the soldier's right arm describes him as a "man of misfortune."
Source: Lombroso, *L'uomo delinquente*, edition 4.

organizations. Many members of the Camorra, a Neapolitan criminal organization, have a tarantula drawn on their arms; and three young arsonists from Milan sported tattoos with the same initials. Even tattoos that do not seem to have anything criminal about them and resemble those of farmers, shepherds, and sailors from the same region can be useful to the legal system and forensic medicine: they may reveal an individual's identity, his origins, and the important events of his life. Criminals, too, are aware of the advantages to the legal system offered by these involuntary revelations; thus the cleverest of them avoid tattoos or try to remove those they already have.

It would be interesting for anthropologists to ponder why such an apparently disadvantageous custom is maintained, given the discomfort and damage it causes. Here are some hypotheses:

—Religion, which tends to preserve ancient habits and customs, certainly perpetuates the practice of tattooing. Those who are devoted to particular saints believe that having their name inscribed on their flesh signifies their devotion and affection.

—A second reason is imitation.[18] Proof of this curious influence is
the fact that members of an entire regiment will often sport the
same design, such as a heart.

—Laziness also plays a part. For this reason tattoos are often found
on deserters, prisoners, and sailors. In one prison, I found that
twenty-five out of forty-one inmates had obtained their tattoos
while in custody. Idleness is more painful than pain itself.

—Equally if not more influential is vanity. Even those who are not
psychiatrists are aware of the way this powerful sentiment, found
at all social levels and possibly even among animals, can prompt
the most bizarre and damaging behavior. This is why savages
who walk around naked have designs on their chests, while those
who wear clothes choose to have tattoos in places that are visible
or easily revealed, such as the forearm, and more often on the
right forearm than on the left.

—Also influential is the sense of camaraderie, and perhaps even, as
the initials of those Milanese arsonists suggest, a sense of "sect."
I would not be surprised if some *camorristi* adopted, in addition
to tattoos of frogs or tarantulas, other primitive ornamentations
to distinguish their sect, such as wearing rings, pins, little chains,
or sporting a certain style of whiskers. African tribes distinguish
themselves by scarring their faces.

—Up to a certain point, noble human passions are also involved.
The rites of the paternal village, the image of the patron saint,
scenes of infancy, and depictions of distant friends—naturally
one does not want to forget these things. Tattoos bring
memories to life in the poor soldier's mind; the "prick of
remembrance" overcomes distance, deprivations, and dangers.

—The passion of love, or rather, eroticism, is also important, as
indicated by the obscene figures (4 out of 102 cases) or the
initials of lovers (10 out of 102 cases) found on our criminals,
and similar images on lesbians and prostitutes. Tribal women
tattoo themselves to show they are unmarried. In men, too,
tattoos often indicate virility. As Darwin puts it somewhat
exaggeratedly, tattoos are both a sign and a means of sexual
selection.[19]

Among Europeans, the most important reason for tattooing is atavism and that other form of atavism called traditionalism, both of which

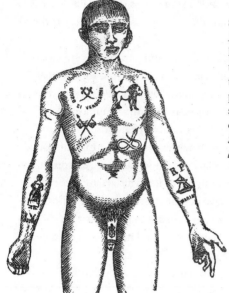

8 Tattoos of a Criminal Sailor
Editors' note: Incarcerated for homicide, this ex-sailor swears to avenge himself according to the words on his chest. His penis is decorated with a shield symbolizing Italy and the face of a woman.
Source: Lombroso, *L'uomo delinquente*, edition 4.

characterize primitive men and men living in a state of nature. There is not a single primitive tribe that does not use tattooing. It is only natural that a custom widespread among savages and prehistoric peoples would reappear among certain lower-class groups. One such group is sailors, who display the same temperament as savages with their violent passions, blunted sensitivity, puerile vanity, and extreme laziness. Sailors even adopt the habits, superstitions, and songs of primitive peoples. In their nudity, prostitutes, too, recall savage customs.

The foregoing should suffice to demonstrate to judges and practitioners of forensic medicine that tattoos can signify a previous incarceration. Criminals' predilection for this custom is sufficient to distinguish them from the insane. Both groups experience forced internment, strong emotions, and long periods of boredom. Although madmen resort to such strange pastimes as rolling stones, snipping their clothes and even their flesh, scribbling on walls, and filling entire reams of paper, they very rarely make designs on their skin. This is yet another proof of the influence of atavism on tattooing because madness is almost never a congenital illness and rarely atavistic.

Forensic medicine should recognize that in the case of the criminal man, who is in constant struggle against society, tattoos—like scars—are professional characteristics.

4

Emotions of Criminals

The unusual predilection of criminals for something as painful as tattooing suggests that they have less sensitivity to pain than ordinary men, a phenomenon that can also be observed in the insane, especially those with dementia. Except in cases of idiocy, what appears as insensitivity to pain is actually the dominance of certain passions. Thus lesbian prostitutes, to reach their lovers in hospital, use red-hot irons to give themselves blisters that resemble pustular eruptions. I once saw two murderers who had for a long time hated one another throw themselves at each other during exercise hour, remaining embroiled for some minutes, one biting the other's lip, the other tearing out the hair of his adversary. When they were finally separated, they were more concerned about their unfinished brawl than their wounds, which became seriously infected.

More generally, criminals exhibit a certain moral insensitivity. It is not so much that they lack all feelings, as bad novelists have led us to believe. But certainly the emotions that are most intense in ordinary men's hearts seem in the criminal man to be almost silent, especially after puberty. The first feeling to disappear is sympathy for the misfortunes of others, an emotion that is, according to some psychologists, profoundly rooted in human nature. The murderer Lacenaire confessed that he had never felt the slightest sense of regret seeing any cadaver except that of his cat: "The sight of agony has no effect on me whatsoever. I would kill a man as easily I would drink a glass of water."[20] Complete indifference to their victims and to the bloody traces of their crimes is a constant characteristic of all true criminals, one that distinguishes them from normal men.

An executioner, Pantoni, told me that nearly all robbers and murderers go to their death laughing. A thief from Voghera, shortly before his execution, ordered a boiled chicken and ate it with gusto. Another inmate wanted to choose his favorite among the three executioners and called him his "professor." While being taken to the gallows, the assassin Valle from Alessandria, who had killed two or three of his companions out of pure caprice, loudly sang the well-known song "It's Not True That Death Is the Worst of All Evils."

The criminal's insensitivity is further proved by the frequency with which an assassin's accomplices will return to murdering people just after he is put to death. Also instructive are the joking words that in criminal jargon are used to name the executioner and his instruments, as well as the tales that are told in prison, where hanging is the favorite theme.[d] This provides one of the strongest arguments for the abolition of the death penalty, which clearly dissuades only a very small number of these wretches from committing crimes. Instead, it may encourage crime thanks to that law of imitation that so dominates among the vulgar classes and to the horrendous prestige that accrues to the person of the condemned. His criminal companions are made envious by the lugubrious and solemn ritual of execution before a crowd of spectators.[21]

Insensitivity to their own and others' pain explains why some criminals can commit acts that seem to be extraordinarily courageous. Thus Holland, Doineau, Mottino, Fieschi, and Saint-Clair had previously won medals for valor on the battlefield. Coppa threw himself into the midst of a battalion firing his gun and came out unharmed. These apparent acts of courage are really only the effect of criminals' insensitivity and infantile impetuousness, which prevent them from recognizing even certain danger. It makes them blind when they have a goal or a passion to satisfy.

Insensitivity combined with precipitous passions explains the lack of logic in crimes and the disjuncture between the gravity of a deed and the motive. For example, a prisoner killed a fellow inmate because he snored too loudly and would not or could not stop (Lauvergne, p. 108). Another, from Alessandria, killed his fellow inmate because he would not polish his shoes. Such moral insensitivity among criminals explains a paradox: the frequent cruelty of criminals who at other times seem capable of kindness.

Criminals' feelings are not always completely gone; some may survive while others disappear. Troppman, a killer of women and children, cried on hearing the name of his mother. D'Avanzo, who roasted and ate a man's calf muscles, later wrote poetry. Immediately after commit-

---

[d] Fregier, *Des classes dangéreuses*, 1841, p. 111. In German slang, to be hanged is *Heimgangen*, going back home. In Italian there are various terms for being hanged, including to grimace or to squint.

ting murder, Feron ran to his girlfriend's children and gave them sweets. Holland confessed to a murder committed because he wanted to obtain money for his family, saying, "I did it for my poor child."

Parent-Duchatelet shows that while many prostitutes lose all ties to their own family, others use their ill-gotten gains to provide for their children, their parents, and even friends. They are excessively passionate about their lovers, so much so that even violence does not detach them. One unfortunate prostitute, after breaking her leg trying to escape her pimp's beatings, returned to him. Assaulted once again, she suffered a broken arm but lost nothing of her intense affection.

In most criminals, the nobler sentiments tend to be abnormal, excessive, and unstable. Mabille, to entertain a friend he had made one night in a restaurant, committed a murder. A certain Maggin said to me, "The cause of my crimes is that I fall into friendships too easily; I cannot see a companion offended without putting a hand on my dagger to revenge him."

A few tenacious passions dominate criminals in place of their absent or unstable social and family feelings. First among these is pride, or rather, an excessive sense of self-worth, which seems to grow in inverse proportion to merit. It is almost as if the psyche is dominated by the same law that governs reflex reactions, which grow stronger as the nervous system weakens. But in the case of criminals, this disequilibrium reaches gigantic proportions. The vanity of criminals exceeds that of artists, the literati, and flirtatious women. A death sentence did not worry Lacenaire nearly as much as criticism of his dreadful poetry and fear of public ridicule. As he put it, "I do not mind being hated, but do mind being mocked" for verses like the following:

The storm leaves a track
While the humble flower passes without a trace.

The most common motive for modern crimes is vanity, the need to shine in society, which is sadly known as "cutting a fine figure." At the Pallanza prison, a criminal told me, "I killed my sister-in-law because our family was too big, and it was thus difficult to make a show in the world." Denaud killed his wife, and his lover killed her husband, so that they could marry and save their reputation. When an infamous thief adopted a certain type of waistcoat and tie, his fellows imitated him, dressing themselves in the same style. Thus Inspector Vidocq found, among twenty-two thieves caught in one single day, twenty who wore the same color waistcoat.[22] They were vain about their strength, their looks, their courage, their ill-gotten and short-lived gains, and, most distressing of all, their ability to commit crimes.

Criminals resemble prostitutes, who always believe they belong to the highest grade of their profession. To prostitutes, the phrase "you are a one-lira woman" is a deep offense. Male inmates who have stolen thousands of lire laugh at petty thieves; and murderers consider themselves superior to thieves and swindlers.

The excessive vanity of criminals explains why they discuss their crimes before and after committing them, showing incredible lack of foresight and providing the justice system with the best possible weapon for finding and sentencing them. Shortly before killing his father, the patricide Marcellino said, "When my father returns from the fields, he will remain here forever." Berard, before going to commit the last of his crimes—the murder of three rich women—was heard to say: "I want to be connected to something big; oh, how I will be talked about!" But the clearest and most curious example of criminals' incredible vanity is a photograph discovered by the police in Ravenna showing three villains who, after having killed a companion, had themselves portrayed in the positions they had assumed while striking their blows. They felt the need to immortalize this strange moment at the risk of being reported and apprehended, which in fact happened.[e]

A natural consequence of criminals' limitless vanity and inordinate sense of self is an inclination toward revenge for even the pettiest motives, as in the example of the inmate who killed someone for refusing to polish his shoes. Prostitutes exhibit the same tendency. "They frequently become enraged for the smallest reason, for a comment about being ugly, for example. In this regard they are more childish than their own children. Prostitutes would consider themselves dishonored if they did not react" (Parent-Duchatelet, p.152). Such violent passions also lie behind the ferocity of ancient and savage peoples, although today they are so rare as to appear monstrous.

Once criminals have experienced the terrible pleasure of blood, violence becomes an uncontrollable addiction. Strangely, criminals are not ashamed of their bloodlust, but treat it with a sort of pride. Thus while he lay dying, Spadolino lamented having killed ninety-nine men instead of reaching a hundred.

[e] For this precious photograph, I owe thanks to Professor Magenta.

9 Group of Assassins from Ravenna
Editors' note: One of the few illustrations to appear in all
five editions of *Criminal Man*, this drawing shows a group
of murderers recreating the scene of their crime. In early
editions, this illustration did not include the small picture
of the same scene on the wall; Lombroso seems to have
altered the image in later editions to emphasize the role
of vanity in criminal psychology.
Source: Lombroso, *L'uomo delinquente*, edition 5 (*Atlante*).

Everyone agrees that the few violent women far exceed men in their
ferocity and cruelty. The brigand women of southern Italy and the
female revolutionaries of Paris invented unspeakable tortures. It was
women who sold the flesh of policemen; who forced a man to eat his
own roasted penis; and who threaded human bodies on a pike. Thus
Shakespeare depicts Lady Macbeth as more cruel and cold than her male
accomplice.

After the delights of taking revenge and satisfying his vanity, the
criminal finds no greater pleasures than those offered by drinking and
gambling. However, the passion for alcohol is very complex, being
both a cause and an effect of crime. Indeed, alcohol is a triple cause of
crime. First, the children of alcoholics often become criminals, and second, inebriation gives cowards the courage to undertake their dread-

ful deeds, as well as providing them with a future justification for their crimes. Furthermore, precocious drinking seduces the young into crime.[23] Third, the tavern is a common gathering place for accomplices, where they hatch their plots and spend the proceeds. For many it is their only home. The innkeeper is their banker, with whom criminals deposit their ill-gotten gains.

Few criminals fail to feel a lively passion for gambling, which explains a continual contradiction in the life of the malefactor: he greatly desires the belongings of others but at the same time squanders the money he has stolen, possibly because it was so easily acquired. Love of gambling also explains why most criminals end up poor despite possessing at times enormous sums.

Rarely does a male criminal feel true love for women. His is a carnal love, which almost always takes place in brothels (especially in London, where two-thirds of these are dens of criminals) and which develops at a very young age.[f] Prostitutes experience lesbian love, which distinguishes them from normal women, and they are passionate about flowers, dancing, and dining.

But the pleasures of gambling, eating, sex, and even revenge are nothing but intermediate steps to criminals' predominate passion, that of the orgy. Even though criminals shy away from regular society, they crave a kind of social life all their own, veritable orgies in which they enjoy the jubilant, tumultuous, riotous, and sensuous companionship of other offenders and even police spies.

I will not discuss criminals' many other passions, which vary according to their habits and intelligence. These range from the most terrible, such as pederasty, to the most noble, such as music; collecting books, paintings, and medals; and the enjoyment of flowers—a particular enthusiasm of the prostitute. One can find unusual emotions among criminals as among healthy people; what distinguishes criminal passions is instability, impetuousness, and often violence. In the quest to satisfy themselves, they give no thought to the consequences.

In many of these characteristics, criminals resemble the insane, who

[f] Of 3,287 homicides and assaults in Italy, 299 were caused by sexual jealousy and 47 for prostitution and loose behavior. Of 41,454 crimes, 1,499 involved illicit loves. In England, of 10,000 persons sentenced, 3,608 were prostitutes; in Italy, of 383 women sentenced, 12 were prostitutes. Of 208 crimes committed for reasons of love according to Descruret, 91 were for adultery, 96 for concubinage, and 13 for jealousy. Of 10,000 crimes of violence in France and England, 1,477 were for reasons of love (Guerry). Of 10,899 suicides in France, 981 were for love.

also exhibit not only violent and unstable passions but also insensitivity to pain, an exaggerated egotism, and (less frequently) a craving for alcohol. But the insane rarely show a predilection for gambling and orgies, and more than criminals, they will suddenly start to hate those who have hitherto been dearest to them. While the criminal cannot live without his companions and seeks them out even at his peril, the mad prefer to be alone, fleeing from every association with others. Plotting is as rare in the mental hospital as it is common in the prison.

In their emotional intensity, criminals closely resemble not the insane but savages. All travelers know that among the Negroes and savages of America, sensitivity to pain is so limited that the former laugh as they mutilate their hands to escape work, while the latter sing their tribe's praises while being burned alive. During puberty initiations, the young savages of America submit without complaint to cruel tortures that would kill a European. For example, they hang themselves upside down on butchers' hooks over dense columns of smoke. Such insensitivity encourages painful tattooing—something few Europeans can bear—and customs like cutting the lips and the fingers or pulling out teeth during funeral ceremonies.

Even moral sensitivity is weak or nonexistent among savages. The Caesars of the yellow races, called Tamerlanes, made their monuments out of pyramids of dried human heads. The emperor Nero was infamous for his barbarity, but even it paled in comparison to the cruel rites of the Chinese. Savages and criminals are further alike in the impetuosity and instability of their passions. Savages, as Lubbock tells us, have quick and violent emotions; while their strength and passions are those of adults, in character they are children. Similarly, Schaffhausen reports that "in many respects savages are like children: they feel strongly and think little; they love games, dancing and ornaments; and they are sometimes curious and timid. They are unaware of danger, but deep down they are cowards, vengeful and cruel in their vendettas."[9] A Cacique, returning from a failed hunting expedition, was greeted by his young son, who ran between his legs; to vent his rage, the father picked him up by the leg and dashed him against some rocks.

[9] *Uber den Zustand der Wilden*, 1868.

5

Criminals and Religion

Many would have us believe that criminals are completely irreligious—as if religion were the strongest brake on crime. It is true that some gang leaders and shameless criminals such as Lacenaire, Lemaire, Mandrin, Gasparone, and La Pommerais have found it convenient to liberate themselves from that last barrier against the unleashing of brutal passions.[h] But the majority of criminals are anything but atheist, although they have fashioned their own sensual and accommodating religion, which turns the God of peace and justice into a sort of benevolent guardian for criminals.

As the saying goes, every thief has his way of expressing religious devotion. I found that of 102 criminals with tattoos, 31 had religious symbols. In criminal jargon, God is *the first of May*, and the soul is *the perpetual*. This proves that they believe in God and the immortality of the soul.

Banda's gang had many amulets, while Caruso's group hung sacred images in the woods and in caves, lighting candles before them. Verzeni, who strangled three women, was one of the most assiduous parishioners at church and confession; he came from a family so religious that they were bigots. La Gala's companions, taken to prison in Pisa, obstinately refused to eat on Fridays during Lent; when the director asked why, they replied, "What do you take us for—unbelievers?"

According to Parent-Duchatelet, during orgies prostitutes often behave as if they were irreligious; however, close observation proves that they are not ungodly at heart. When one prostitute's son fell ill, she lit blessed candles to hasten his healing. In Paris, no prostitute will submit to medical examination on Fridays unless forced to. Italian statistics show that last year religious passion caused 40 crimes, while superstition caused 226.

[h] When the chief judge asked him why he went to church, Lemaire replied, "For amusement, as in the theater." Mandrin asked the priest who wanted to give him last rites how many taverns there were on the way to heaven, since he had only six lire to spend on the way. La Pommerais requested in her will that her son's education be free of religion and monastic superstitions.

Nevertheless, to deduce from these examples that contemporary religion provides an incentive to crime would be an impious exaggeration. It would be as absurd as arguing the opposite—that atheism or positivism causes crime. I emphasize this point because I know that many politicians, even if they are convinced of the truth of the positivist school, seek to stifle its teachings. They fear that positivism encourages communistic ideas and, even worse, criminal behavior. In fact, if one looks at the evidence, the opposite is true.[24]

6

Intelligence and Education of Criminals

If it were possible to measure the average intellectual capacity of criminals with the same accuracy with which we measure their cranial capacity, I am sure the results would be identical. The average would be lower than normal.[i] It is not the case, as Thomson claims, that many criminals are weak-minded, insane, or imbecilic (he found 2 percent insane and 12 percent imbecilic). Yet even in criminals of genius, there is an aspect in which the intellect is defective: they do not have the mental energy for continuous and diligent labor. This may be why they idealize a life free of work. Perhaps because of mental laziness, all criminals, as court records reveal, performed poorly in school—even crafty lawbreakers such as Verzeni, Agnoletti, Bourse, Raymond, Donon, and Benoist.

Criminals are generally very illogical and always imprudent. However able they may be, they bring to their crimes the lack of foresight that is part of the criminal character. Powerful and violent passions cloud their judgment; and the pleasure of committing a crime and telling others about it enables the law to catch up with them easily. Rognoni killed his brother and made up an alibi, but forgot to wash the blood stains from his clothing. The light that he left on while carrying out the murder may have alerted the neighbors or the police.

Specialists in Crime

Many criminals seem to have extraordinary abilities. Yet when we look more closely, the marvel diminishes. They succeed so well because they

[i] In Europe, only the Spanish have attempted to conduct research on criminal intelligence; in one study of 23,600 criminals, only 67.54 percent had normal intelligence; 10.17 percent were barely normal; 18.8 percent had low intelligence; 0.75 percent had very low intelligence; and, in 2.71 percent of the cases, the intelligence was unknown. It is unclear what criteria were used for such a difficult investigation (Legoyt, *E. de Statist.comparée*, 1864).

always repeat the same acts; even idiots, repeating a movement continuously, can seem skilled.

Pederasts, who are often very cultured and intelligent (office workers, teachers), have a strange need to associate with their own kind.[j] They form a sort of fraternity in which they recognize each other at a mere glance, even in foreign lands. Without the evidence revealed by Casper and Tardieu,[k] I would not be able to understand, or even believe, that such unmentionable love could be mixed with romanticism or mysticism.[25] Yet despite this, pederasts rarely focus on one individual but rather go after many, almost simultaneously. Less strange is the way these offenders, if from higher social classes, love women's work and clothes. They go out in public laden with jewels, their necks exposed and their hair curled. Combining wicked habits with exquisite taste in the arts, they collect paintings, flowers, statues, and perfumes, thus atavistically reverting to both the vices and the aesthetic refinement of ancient Greece.

Thieves, like prostitutes, covet bright-colored clothes, necklaces, chains, and even earrings. They are the most ignorant and gullible of the criminal species.[26] Almost always nervous about being caught, they talk nonsensically and constantly change the subject. Assuming that those who speak their jargon are worthy colleagues, they make friends hastily. They sometimes feign romantic love, but prefer prostitutes, their natural allies.

Murderers affect gentle, compassionate manners and a calm air among those they do not know. While they are not great wine drinkers, they love gambling and sex. With one another they act audaciously, speaking with arrogance and pride of their crimes, which require daring and physical strength rather than intelligence. What appears in them to be great skill is for the most part merely the result of repeating the same act.

---

[j] Livi points out that Dante, in Canto XV of the *Inferno*, speaking of sodomites, says: In sum, know that they [pederasts] were all clerics / And well-known men of letters . . .

[k] Tardieu quotes one male homosexual's confession: "How to explain the delicious shudder of the senses when I heard his voice; my happiness when I caught his gaze? His every word sung like a melody" (*Et. Med. Legale sur les attentats aux moeurs*. Paris, 1873).

Criminals of Genius

It cannot be denied that from time to time there have been criminals who are true geniuses—creators of new forms of crime, inventors of evil. Among these was certainly Vidocq, who as a criminal managed to escape the police nearly twenty times and later as a police inspector to consign several hundred other criminals to the justice system. In his *Memoirs*, he revealed the true psychology of crime. Another was Cagliostoro, who robbed and tricked royalty, very nearly passing himself off as an inspired prophet. In general, however, even these brilliant criminals lack the foresight to complete their crimes.

Learned Criminals

It is pleasing to note that few criminals come from the world of science. But this is not really surprising, since men who breathe the serene air of science and labor in search of truth are able to subdue their brutish passions and avoid the tortuous, arid path of crime. Moreover, they realize more clearly than others that crime is not only unjust and illogical but also fruitless, always returning to haunt the criminal himself.

Criminality among writers and artists presents a less favorable picture. Many of them are ruled by the passions, which provide a potent source of inspiration. Their feelings are less controlled by criteria of truth and the rigorous application of logic than in the case of scientists. Thus among criminals we have to list Bonfadìo, the philosopher Rousseau, the libertine Aretino, Ceresa, Brunetto Latini, Franco, and perhaps Foscolo and the rakish poet Byron.[27] In ancient times and in primitive countries, brigandage and poetry went hand in hand. Three great Arab poets, Soleik, Schanfa, and Mostareb, were also great thieves, just as in the Middle Ages Kaleiva Peag, Helmbrecht, and Robin Hood were simultaneously great brigands and great poets.

Artists are even more inclined than writers to crime, especially crimes of blood inspired by love and professional jealousy. It is enough to remember the life of the sculptor Cellini, who murdered more than once and perhaps also stole. Andrea del Castagno assaulted Domenico Veneziano for stealing the secret of oil painting. Other examples include the painter Filippo Lippi, who kidnapped and married a young

Table 5: Literacy in Male and Female Recidivists

	PERCENTAGE OF MALE RECIDIVISTS	PERCENTAGE OF FEMALE RECIDIVISTS
are illiterate	23	13
can read	40	43
can read and write	35	51
can read, write, and count	28	2
have advanced schooling	29	0

Editors' note: Neither column adds to 100 percent. Lombroso's conclusion that education does not promote honesty seems to be drawn from statistics in this table showing that most criminals are not entirely illiterate.

nun; Andrea del Sarto, a swindler; and the murderers Caravaggio and Lebrun.

Illiterate Criminals

If we descend from the effects of higher education to primary instruction, more typical of the population in general, the results are not very encouraging. In France, the most backward, central provinces report low levels of crimes against persons and property, while the more cultured departments in the northeast have the highest numbers of property crime.

The study of recidivists clearly reveals the weak effects of education on criminals, as shown in table 5. The simple recognition of a letter or knowledge of recent developments in technology and science do not add a jot to morality. Education can even become an instrument of harm, creating new crimes which are harder for the law to detect and making the weapons used by criminals sharper and more deadly. Participants in the Paris Commune employed petroleum. The Venetian criminal Fangin used his knowledge of the telegraph to send letters in code to his comrades, indicating which stagecoach to raid. All criminals avidly read about the trials of their companions in order to learn new methods.

At times, education can be an incentive to evil by promoting new needs and desires in those unable to satisfy them. School also provides criminals with new contacts. Nevertheless, Italian statistics from 1862–72 shown in table 6 illustrate that education is not as fatal as it first appeared. In the first years covered by the table, soldiers had higher illit-

Table 6: Illiteracy in Criminals and Soldiers

	ILLITERACY IN CRIMINALS (percentage)	ILLITERACY IN SOLDIERS (percentage)
1862	60.57	64.32
1863	62.50	65.46
1864	58.20	65.10
1865	56.38	64.27
1869	64.00	60.49
1871	75.00 (regular prisoners)	56.74
1871	50.00 (forced-labor prisoners)	56.74
1872	79.00 (regular prisoners)	56.53
1872	78.00 (forced-labor prisoners)	56.53

Source: Bargoni, *Sull'istruzione obbligatoria*, Firenze, 1865; Torre, *Relaz. sulle leve in Italia*, 1869, 71–72; Cardon, *Statistica delle Carceri*, Roma, 1872–73.

Editors' note: Lombroso gives two sets of statistics for the years 1871 and 1872; the first is for inmates of regular prisons and the second is for criminals convicted of especially serious crimes who were sent to hard-labor camps. Lombroso's text reports that the soldiers had all been recently drafted for required military service and were twenty years old, but gives no information on the age of the criminals.

eracy rates than criminals. Their illiteracy rates fell as education spread in Italy, but the illiteracy rates of criminals increased, which shows that better educated individuals were not swelling the ranks of criminals.

There is probably a point up to which education favors crime, after which it could serve as an antidote. Where education is widespread, the number of educated criminals increases, but the number of illiterate criminals rises even more. This implies that lawbreaking is becoming less frequent in the middle classes. In sum, it is not possible to say that education decreases crime, nor can it be said that it increases it. When education is spread through all classes, it is in fact beneficial, reducing crimes among those with middling education.

7

Jargon

One unusual characteristic of recidivist criminals, when they form organizations in big cities, is the use of an almost private language. Its general sounds, grammar, syntax, and idiom remain standard, but its lexicon differs completely. These mutations occur in different ways.[l] The most common and yet the most curious innovation, one that suggests a relationship between criminal jargon and primitive tongues, is that of naming something according to its attributes. For example, a goat becomes a *jumper*, while death is called the *thin*, *raw*, or *certain one*. Like savages, criminals create many words by onomatopoeia, as in *tap* for stamp, *tuff* for pistol, and *tic* for watch. The strangest aspect of criminal jargon is its retention of archaic words that have been completely lost from living speech. Examples include *arton* for bread, *lenza* for water, *strocca* for prostitute (in Calabria), and *marcone* for pimp.

Another intriguing characteristic of criminal jargon is its widespread use. While every Italian region has its own dialect, and a Calabrian would not be able to understand the dialect of a Lombard, thieves from Calabria use the same jargon as those from Lombardy. Thus both refer to wine as *chiaro*, a pocket as *berta*, a fig as *taschi*, a shirt as *lima*, and meat as *crea*.[m] Similarly, criminal jargon in Marseille is the same as that in Paris.

Everyone explains the origins of criminal jargon in terms of the need to escape the notice of police. Certainly this is the primary reason, especially for the frequent inversions of words and substitution of nouns for pronouns, such as *mother* for *I*. But this is not the only reason for jargon, for it is also used in poetry, which seeks to attract rather than deflect attention. Even the police use jargon, as do criminals within their own

[l] In this chapter I have summarized Ascoli's superb pages in *Studj critici sui Gerghi*, 1861 as well as Biondelli, *Studj sulla lingua furbesca*, 1846; Pott, *Zigeuner*, Halle, 1844; and Avè-Lemant, *Rotwelsche Studien*, 1858. On my own I have carried out only brief studies of jargon in Calabria and at Lago Maggiore. I consulted the *Trattato dei Bianti* (Italia, tip. di Didot, 1828) for historical jargon and Pitrè's *Canti siculi* for Sicilian jargon.

[m] See C. Lombroso, *Tre mesi in Calabria*, 1861.

families. The tendency to invent a private language increases among individuals who perform the same work, especially if it is marginal. Jargon is popular among those who move from place to place or are in some way restricted in relation to the broader public. In such cases, it confirms a sense of belonging and impedes surveillance by outsiders.

Why would there *not* be a need for a special language among groups with strange habits and with so many people to fear and to trick! People belonging to these groups always gather in the same places such as prisons, brothels, and taverns, and mix freely only with those of the same tendencies. Among themselves, they fraternize with an amazing ease, indeed finding in jargon, as Vidocq showed so well, a means of recognition, a kind of secret password.

The most plausible explanation of jargon is atavism. Criminals speak differently because they feel differently; they speak like savages because they are savages, living amidst the very flower of European civilization.

8

Criminal Literature

Just as they have their own jargon, criminals have their own special literature. Originating in prison, it is the product of long hours of indolence and uncontrolled passions. Here is an example:

Prison, my life, sweet, happy!
How I love being inside you!
Only crazy heads speak ill of it,
Or think it causes loss of peace.
Here you only find brothers and friends,
Money, food and serene peace;
Outside one is always among enemies,
And if you can't work, you die of hunger.

The habitual ne're-do-well clearly finds a natural nest in prison! But not all feelings have been extinguished in these unfortunates. Often memories of friends or a distant mother overcome their impulses toward cupidity and revenge. Then their poetry grows powerful and rich with the sweet fragrance of love—a surprise from such pens.

From the flats of the Vicaria prison,
She signals with little hands;
I see that she is my mama
And that her eyes are two little fountains.
Mother, only you think of me,
I am in the midst of evil Christians . . .
We are condemned to hell
And you, mother, are outside crying.

There are others of such exquisite delicacy that they would not seem unworthy of Petrarch, the troubadour of Laura;[28] for example:

When I saw you and heard you speak
The blood froze in my veins
And my heart wanted to escape from my breast. . . .

> Every word when she speaks
> Attracts, ties, pierces, nay, wounds.

Most prison literature is in verse, written by criminals themselves. They love the poetic form, which responds to their boiling passions and enables them to depict themselves and their suffering with extraordinary eloquence.

9

Insanity and Crime

Few would doubt that crime is often caused by cerebral afflictions and, above all, madness. Many well-known criminals, including Verger, Villet, and Schults, not only had insane relatives but themselves exhibited signs of madness. In a sample of 290 criminals, I found 3 with epilepsy, 2 with imbecility, 4 with partial paralysis, 1 with delirium tremens, 3 with facial convulsions, 4 with continual headaches, and 4 in a full state of insanity. In all, those with severe neuropathic diseases amounted to 7.2 percent of the sample; but the true level would be higher had I included the 11 percent with degeneracy of the temple arteries and the 3 percent with unequal pupil size (often an indication of incipient paralysis).

In a group of 266 chronically ill criminals, Dr. Virgilio found 16 percent afflicted by serious neuropathic disease; among these, 3.62 percent were mad and 4.6 percent had epilepsy. To these should be added another 13 percent with congenital abnormalities of the nervous system —such as deaf-mutes (1.3 percent), stutterers (4.1 percent), and semi-cretins and imbeciles (4.8 percent)—not to mention those with loco-moter ataxy (1.45 percent), hemiplegia (1.8 percent), ballism or muscular spasms (38 percent), and palsy with tremors (1.45 percent).[n]

Much the same has been found with prostitutes. Among 3,041 prostitutes, Parent-Duchelet found 32 epileptics. In only four years, Esquirol identified 105 insane prostitutes, most of them young. Of these, 43 were maniacal, 36 melancholic, 10 suicidal, 18 demented, and 13 alcoholic.[29]

The same factors create a predisposition to both crime and madness: civilization, celibacy, a hot climate, being male, living in an urban area, and working at certain jobs (shoemaker, cook, domestic servant, and, perhaps, soldier). Many criminals have insane relatives; and in many the tendency to crime or madness is provoked by trauma, anomalies of the head, and liquor. Meteorological conditions, especially heat, influence

[n] Virgilio, *Saggio di ricerche sulla natura morbosa del delitto*, Rome, 1874.

both murderers and the mad. Thomson has noted that both criminals and the insane tend to succumb to illnesses like meningitis, softening of the brain, and sleepwalking. Moreover, many of the insane present the same physical deformities as criminals: abnormal ears, scanty beards, filmy and wandering eyes, darkened skin, headaches, and arrested physical development. Like the insane, some criminals are completely insensitive to pain; and members of both group exhibit emotional imbalance, manifesting great affection for their friends, children, or a lover, but very little for their family.

But the opposite is also true. Criminals and the mad frequently lack affection entirely, showing neither pity nor benevolence nor remorse. They are capable of eating and dancing near the cadaver of their victim, all the while boasting of their crime. In addition, they manifest little affection for their companions.

For some criminals, carrying out their misdeeds assumes the form of impulsive mania. The opposite also happens: certain mad people premeditate and dissimulate like criminals.

> —Denham, an inmate on the hulks, confessed that he had an irresistible passion for theft: "For me not stealing would be like ceasing to live. Robbery is a passion which burns like love, and when my blood boils in my head and my fingers, I almost believe I could steal myself from me, if only I could." He even stole rings, nails, and the copper sheets from his galley ship. He himself decided the number of lashes he should receive as punishment—and then began to steal again immediately afterward (Lauvergne, *Les forçats*, p. 358).
> —Two individuals were found dead in Strasbourg for no apparent reason. Some years later the Abbot Trenk was arrested and confessed to having killed them for the mere pleasure of seeing them die. From the time of his youth, he had taken children into the forest, where he hanged and burned them (Gall).[30]
> —Jaenneret, who poisoned nine women friends, cried after they died and kept locks of their hair. Several of her relatives were suicidal or insane. She suffered from hysteria and for no reason had cauterized her vagina and spine with a red-hot poker. She felt a very strong need to take the same poison with which she had killed her friends.
> —The Marquis de Sade enjoyed making prostitutes undress,

beating them, and then tending to their wounds. He became a
sort of apostle for his ideal of mixing lust with violence.

Who can say at what point these are illnesses or criminal passions?

Criminals, like the insane, often lack prudence, considering it impossible that the law will ever catch them. They threaten those they want to kill, do not think of the future, and show no remorse. Pushed to crime by an impulse unique to them, they repeat their criminal acts with a strange uniformity. On the other hand, some mad people are capable of great foresight and subtle premeditation.° They can collude with others to commit crime and prepare alibis, and they know what is punishable. They flee after the crime, deny their guilt in court, and even simulate madness.[31]

Verzeni, who liked to touch women's necks, strangled them for sexual pleasure, eviscerated their bodies, and sucked their still-warm blood. Creating alibis for himself and accusing others of his crimes, he denied his guilt for years. He was afflicted with cerebral atrophy and had relatives with pellagra and cretinism.[32]

There are cases in which madness is simply a criminal tendency, a lack of any sense of morality. The English call this moral insanity.[33] In general, victims of moral insanity are born to mad or neuropathic parents, suffer nervous disease or hallucinations beginning in childhood, and experience emotions in a bizarre way. They hate and sometimes kill their own children or fathers for the slightest reason. Not only do they commit crimes without feeling any remorse, they say so. They are amazed to discover that others have feelings. Nevertheless, even in childhood they are precociously intelligent and unusually active.

Cases of criminal insanity create a quandary for judges because the law offers no guidance. Judges sometimes act too leniently, acquitting or reducing the sentence; more frequently, they punish too harshly, sometimes applying the death penalty. Doctors and psychiatrists are similarly perplexed.

If there is a line between crime and madness, it is a subtle division that is often not perceived until it is too late, after justice has been handed down, or when there is no remedy for the harm. In some cases there is no dividing line at all, since the distinction between crime and

° "The mere fact of having premeditated a crime seems to be in formal contradiction with madness. Nothing is more false." Tardieu, p. 50, *De la folie*, 1872.

madness is something constructed not by nature but by society. This is why we must establish criminal insane asylums; they are the only solution to the eternal conflict between justice and public security.[34]

Nearly every type of mental abnormality contributes in some way to criminality and, as the statistician Messedaglia observes, in fact determines the particular kind of crime that is committed.[35] Thus those suffering from epilepsy, alcoholism, and pellagra tend to impromptu murder and motiveless suicide. Alcoholics are also inclined to theft. Female maniacs who are prepubescent, amenorrheic, or pregnant manifest a particular tendency toward arson and sometimes bloody crimes of passion or, in the case of pregnant women, theft. The melancholic and the monomaniacal tend toward parricide, especially if they are hallucinating. Senile and palsied criminals often exhibit sexual tendencies inappropriate for their age, including homosexuality. Hysterical women prefer theft, calumny, and poisoning. When criminal acts result from insanity, they are nearly always preceded by physical phenomena such as headaches, diarrhea, hemorrhoids, menopause, insomnia, and dyspepsia.

Mentally ill criminals sometimes simulate madness at the suggestion of others, but they are seldom convincing since they try to imitate insane rages or complete imbecility. Like true criminals, they feel no remorse; but they confess everything, while true criminals hide it. And while criminals know their behavior is loathsome to the general public, the mentally ill are seldom capable of making that realization.

Insane criminals often overlook opportunities to hide evidence or evade discovery. They may leave the poison in the room with their victim, sign an obviously false signature, or let themselves be seen with the stolen object. Incapable of friendship, they tend to live isolated, quiet lives and never confide in others, while true criminals plot together, especially in prison. Both groups display indifference to their crimes, but the insane are indifferent even toward their punishments. For this reason they often irritate judges.

Instead of trying to hide their misdeeds, mad criminals chat about them with pleasure and describe them in their autobiographies. This is not because they are impudent or filled with false pride, but because they are confident of their innocence, believing themselves to have acted in self-defense and even to have behaved meritoriously.

10

Organized Crime

Organized crime is one of the most important phenomena in the realm of illegality because it reveals the powerful effects of association.[p] Why does the union of perverse souls generate an intensification of wickedness that would be repugnant to individuals acting alone? Why does it revive savage tendencies and, reinforcing them with group discipline, stimulate atrocities? Unfortunately for us in Italy, these burning questions are often intertwined with political issues.[36]

The attributes of members of organized crime correspond, unsurprisingly, to those of the majority of criminals. Men outnumber women, though there are exceptional cases of female leaders, such as Luigia Bouviers, who in 1828 led a band of about forty thieves. Groups of female robbers are rare. I know of only one, led by the ex–tavern keeper Lina Mondor and composed of women who were both thieves and prostitutes. Women usually prefer domestic crimes, but there have been associations of female poisoners in both Paris and Rome. Such women then became members of larger groups of criminals, which they join as receivers of stolen goods, lookouts, or lovers.

Organized criminals are almost always young. Among nine hundred brigands in the southern Italian regions of Basilicata and Capitanata, six hundred were less than twenty-five years old (Pani-Rossi). Nearly all are unmarried, and many are orphans. They tend to be illiterate. Often former soldiers, they routinely employ brutality and weapons in their work as butchers, peasants, and shepherds.

[p] Little work has been done in Italy on organized crime, with the following important exceptions: Tommasi-Crudeli, *La Sicilia nel 1871*, Firenze; Monnier, *La Camorra*, Firenze, 1872; idem *Notizie storiche sul brigantaggio*; Cantelli, *Documenti relativi al progetto di legge di pubblica sicurezza in Sicilia*, Roma, 1875; Giuseppe Ciotti, *La Sicilia e l'inchiesta parlamentare*, Palermo 1867; Tajani, *Discorso sull'amministrazione*, Palermo 1860; Avv. Locatelli, *Il Brigantaggio e la mafia. Perseveranza*, Maggio 1875; V. Maggiorani, *Sugli ultimi rivolgimenti di Sicilia*, 1861; Ajello, *Il processo Pugliesi*, Palermo, 1868; Du Camp, *Naples sous Victor Emanual. Revue des Deux Mondes*, 1862; N. N., *Resoconto del processo contro Pascucci e Bianconi*, Ravenna, 1874; Saint-Jorioz, *Il Brigantaggio nelle provincie napolitane*, 1864; Pani-Rossi, *Basilicata*, 1868; Verrua, *Processo Tronco*, 1865; Id. *La Banca*, 1864; Massari, *Relazione della Commissione d'inchiesta*, 1863.

Many criminal groups, even though they are enemies of society, form their own unique type of social organism. Nearly all have a leader invested with dictatorial power that, as in savage tribes, derives more from his own personal qualities than from the acquiescence of his followers. All criminal bands have external associates or protectors in case of danger. Very large groups sometimes institute a true division of labor, with members who function as executioner, teacher, secretary, traveling representative, even curate or surgeon. All criminal organizations follow specific codes or rituals that are impersonal but develop spontaneously. Even if they are not written, these rules are followed to the letter.

Camorra

The most highly developed form of criminal organization is the Camorra, which dominates Naples and the surrounding area. Small independent groups of *camorristi* form wherever a certain number of prisoners or ex-prisoners congregate. These groups are ruled through a hierarchical structure. For example, *camorristi* in the prisons of Naples are subordinated to those in the penitentiary of Castel Capuano, who in turn are subordinated to those in the hard-labor camp of Procida. Each group has various ranks. The aspiring little boy does not reach the next level, *picciotto di sgarro*, until he has proved his courage and capacity for secrecy by wounding or killing someone in obedience to the sect.

Camorristi are divided into ordinary members, on the one hand, and proprietors (the veterans, the sect's senators), on the other. They elect a leader from among the most courageous or powerful. Called *Masto*, *Maestro*, or simply *Sì*, the leader distributes the *camorra* or *barattolo* every Sunday. These are the names given to the money extorted from gambling dens, brothels, watermelon peddlers, newspaper vendors, transporters, beggars, and even parishioners at mass. Prisons, the birthplace of the Camorra, provide the most reliable profits. As soon as a wretch enters prison, he has to pay the so-called oil for the Madonna, giving over a tenth of everything he has to the Camorra. He has to pay to drink, to eat, to gamble, to buy, to sell—even to sleep in a slightly better bed. The poorest inmates are ruined by the Camorra. They are forced to sell half their rations or their few clothes for a smoke or a game

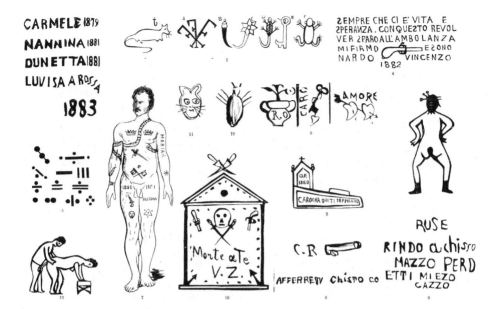

10 Tattoos of *Camorristi*

Editors' note: Lombroso believed that tattoos could help police identify members of organized crime. For example, the drawings at the top of animals and keys symbolize jargon used by *camorristi* and the lines and points to the left indicate the ranks of power.

Source: Lombroso, *Der Verbrecher* (*Atlas*). Photo courtesy of the Lloyd Sealy Library, John Jay College of Criminal Justice.

of chance. Even if they do not want to gamble they are forced to, because gaming provides the main earnings of the Camorra, who collect from both sides.

The *camorrista* has become a natural judge for the lower classes, especially when there are gambling disputes or fights. He maintains order in brothels and prisons, "protecting" those who pay a kickback. He serves, in his way, as a sort of savings bank. From the fees extorted from prisoners, he creates a reserve fund which is used to support victims who have lost everything. This system subjects the victim to even tighter control. The *camorrista* is also a type of middleman for small business: after swindling the wholesale merchant, he turns around and becomes his policeman, making sure that the retail peddlers repay the wholesaler for the merchandise.

Mafia

A variant of the ancient Camorra is a group variously called the *bonachi* (because of their smocks), the *sgaraglioni*, or the *spadajuoli*, but now labeled *mafiosi* after the title of a recent and popular play by Rissotto. The Mafia differs from the Camorra perhaps mainly in its ability to keep secrets, an attribute of the Semitic race.[q] Members faithfully adhere to the code of *omertà*, or silence, which was first described by Tommasi-Crudeli and Maggiorani and is often reflected in popular proverbs.[r] These are its main articles of faith:

—absolute silence about the crimes carried out by others;
—an obligation to give false testimony to erase evidence;
—protection for the rich in return for payment;
—defiance of public authority at all times by carrying prohibited arms, challenging others to duels on the most frivolous pretexts, and punishing infidelity with stabbings;
—revenge for any slight of honor, even by those most dear.

Those who fall short of this code are declared *infame*, or infamous, and are killed shortly afterward, even in prison where, if there are no weapons, the victim is drowned in a bucket of excrement.

In essence, the Camorra and the Mafia are nothing but variations on the old theme of brigandage. This is made clear by the fact that both *camorristi* and *mafiosi* have the characteristics of common criminals. For example, they love to go around laden with rings and in their own sort of uniform—a characteristic of thieves. Like other criminals, they have their own jargon; for example, the *camorrista* uses *dormente* for dead, *gatti*, *neri*, and *sorci* for police patrol, *asparagio* for gendarme, *tre alsange* for inspector, *ruffo* and *brutto* for a stolen object, *graffa* for receiver,

[q] Du Camp pointed out that in France, Jewish criminals' ability to keep secrets distinguished them from non-Jews. [In the text, Lombroso is referring to the supposed qualities of the Arabs who conquered Sicily in the Middle Ages. Because Arabs and Jews both speak Semitic languages, Lombroso considered them branches of the same Semitic "race."—Eds.]

[r] These proverbs (cited in Tommasi-Crudeli's *La Sicilia*, 1871, p. 66) include: "When a man is dead, one must think of him as alive"; "Testimony is a good thing as long as it does no harm to the next person"; "If someone takes your bread, you take his life"; and "First the weapons, then the wife." According to Vincenzo Maggiorani, *mafiosi* acquired their name before 1860, but it initially meant "arrogant" rather than criminal.

rubino for eye, *palo* for spy, *tic-tac* for revolver, *martino* for knife, and *cassa* for chest. In fact, the last three are common expressions in criminal jargon throughout Italy.

Like most criminal groups, the Mafia and the Camorra have their headquarters in prisons. They are implacable toward their enemies. It is said that one *mafioso*, to revenge a joke played on him by someone stronger, stewed with hatred for fifteen years until the joker happened to be condemned to death. The offended man then made a special request to the Court of Naples to be the executioner. When another *mafioso*, although dying of tuberculosis, heard that a companion had spoken ill of him, he jumped up from his bed, ran to the tavern, and killed him. Shortly afterward, exhausted by this effort, he himself died (Monnier, op. cit).

Anyone who has seen a true *camorrista*, with his muscles of iron, his warlike scowl, and his harsh pronunciation as he rolls his *rr*s, immediately notes the contrast between him and the generally flabby population with its soft accent and mild manners. It was inevitable that a diseased phenomenon like the Camorra would develop from the disequilibrium between a few energetic, robust individuals and the docile and soft multitudes. The *camorrista* himself rises above the others involuntarily. The Camorra is thus an expression of natural arrogance on the part of those who feel strong in the midst of the masses who feel weak. The Camorra maintains its power more by fear than by force.

Prisons and Organized Crime

The breeding grounds for organized crime are those prisons that do not isolate inmates in separate cells. Nearly all the leaders of criminal gangs (Maino, Lombardo, La Gala, Lacenaire, Souflard, Harduin) were escapees from prison and chose their accomplices from incarcerated companions who had exhibited particular audacity or ferocity.

The origins of the Camorra lie in the prisons themselves. At first the Camorra was a problem that did not spill outside the penitentiary, but when King Ferdinand of Naples pardoned many galley prisoners in 1830, they transferred their prison profits and habits to the outside world (Monnier, p. 58). For many years, the Camorra has chosen its chiefs from inmates of the Vicaria prison, and free *camorristi* would take no major decisions without consulting them.

None of this should be surprising. Let us remember the lugubrious verses of the Palermo criminal: "Prison is a blessing sent from on high, guiding us to companions and places of crime." Although imprisonment was devised to protect society, it actually provides inmates with introductions to accomplices and instruction in crime.

Race, Heredity, and Organized Crime

Race shapes criminal organizations. Both Bedouins and Gypsies can be considered races of organized criminals. The same seems to apply to Negroes in the United States (according to A. Maury), and to Albanians, Greeks, and sometimes the indigenous people of southern Italy. The inhabitants of Palermo, which is the center of the Mafia, are descended from the ancient bodyguards of the nobles (according to Villari) and, even further back, from the rapacious Arab conquerors of Sicily who were related to the Bedouins.

Questions of race lead to the issue of heredity. Harris (*Atl. Montl.*, 1875) was unable to explain why a town in the Hudson River area of New York produced an extraordinary number of criminals, nearly all of whom had the same name.[37] He set about studying the parish registers of the area and discovered that a large number of those concerned were offspring of a certain Margaret, an infamous woman who had lived about two centuries earlier. Among nine hundred of her descendants, two hundred were criminals and another two hundred insane or vagabonds. Among the Camorra, many of the famous members are brothers, for example the Borellis. Also well known are the seven Mazzardi brothers from Cannero, the Mansi brothers of Cerro, the Vadarelli brothers, and the La Gala brothers.

This explains why in a given village there may be more criminals than in another. All it takes is the survival of one family descended from a wicked progenitor, and the whole place will be corrupted. Up to a certain point, this justifies the barbarous practice of the ancients and savages who punished the innocent relatives of guilty criminals.

11

Atavism and Punishment

Those who have read this far should now be persuaded that criminals resemble savages and the colored races. These three groups have many characteristics in common, including thinness of body hair, low degrees of strength and below-average weight, small cranial capacities, sloping foreheads, and swollen sinuses. Members of both groups frequently have sutures of the central brow ridge, precocious synostes or disarticulation of the frontal bones, upwardly arching temporal bones, sutural simplicity, thick skulls, overdeveloped jaws and cheekbones, oblique eyes, dark skin, thick and curly hair, and jug ears. Among habitual criminals as among savages, we find less sexual differentiation than between normal men and women. In addition, in both we find insensitivity to pain, lack of moral sense, revulsion for work, absence of remorse, lack of foresight (although this can at times appear to be courage), vanity, superstitiousness, self-importance, and, finally, an underdeveloped concept of divinity and morality.

These facts clearly prove that the most horrendous and inhuman crimes have a biological, atavistic origin in those animalistic instincts that, although smoothed over by education, the family, and fear of punishment, resurface instantly under given circumstances. These immediate causes include illness, the weather, bad examples, and a sort of spermatic inebriation induced by excessive continence. This last factor explains why criminal behavior is common at the time of puberty in savage individuals or in those forced into a solitary or celibate life, such as priests, shepherds, and soldiers.[s]

If the concept of atavism helps us understand the inefficacy of punishment, so, too, does the statistical regularity of crime rates. Crimes against persons oscillate the most, yet even they vary by just a fraction from year to year (A. Maury and Guerry).[38] Certain crimes predomi-

---

[s] The criminal Legier was a shepherd who led an isolated life in the cliffs and was forced to be celibate for a long period of time. Mongrat, Ceresa, and Lacollange were priests, and Bertrand was a soldier (see *Verzeni e Agnoletti*, op. cit.).

nate in particular months, corresponding to changes in temperature or the price of certain foodstuffs. For example, libidinous crimes peak in June and July, poisonings in May, and thefts and forgeries in January. As Maury observes, unvarying natural laws govern society more profoundly than written legislation.

In sum, statistics as well as anthropological observation indicate that crime is a natural phenomenon—one that some philosophers would deem as necessary as birth, death, and conception.

Some ask, "But what right do you have to inflict punishment if you deny legal responsibility?" (Caro, op. cit.) I cannot forget how one venerable thinker, scratching his head as he read these pages, asked me, "Where are you going with this theory? Perhaps we should allow ourselves to be preyed on and killed by gangs of ruffians, because they may be unaware of doing harm?" I responded that nothing is more illogical than that which tries to be too logical. Nothing is less prudent than the attempt to carry theories to conclusions that could disrupt society. A doctor at the sickbed may feel confident about a certain procedure and yet hesitate to use it in the face of grave illness. Similarly, the lover of humanity would only prove the uselessness of science if he attempted dangerous innovations.[39]

Fortunately, my scientific findings, far from making war on social order, reinforce it. Crime is necessary, but so is defense against it, and thus punishment. When we justify punishment in terms of social defense, it becomes more logical and effective.

At one time, punishment itself was atavistic. It sought nothing beyond compensation or revenge.[t] Even in the present we have not lost that primitive instinct for revenge; we try to match the punishment to the horror of the crime or to the indignation it arouses in us. We cry out, scandalized, against those who confess to criminal activity. And all too often, public officials forget their abstract theories about the need to mitigate punishment by loudly demanding social revenge. Yet these same men condemn punitive sentencing as a holy abomination when they write books on criminal law or sit in Parliament. And where is the logic in the theory just now coming back into vogue which seeks to link

[t] In the *Iliad*, Achilles cut the throats of twelve Trojans in repayment for the murder of Patroclus. Compensation is received, Ajax tells us, for the murder of a brother or a son. When the murderer has paid, the one compensated renounces any feeling of resentment. IX, 632. Among the Franks, the fine for a murder was two hundred coins; thefts were recompensed in a similar way. Servants lost their lives for a crime that would cost free men forty-five coins (Del Giudice, *La vendetta nel diritto longobardo*, Milan, 1876).

punishment to reform of the criminal?[40] It is well known that among true criminals, successful reform is always, or nearly always, the exception, while recidivism is the rule. Moreover, prisons—unless they have isolation cells, which are usually too expensive—worsen the problem by serving as schools of evil.

I do not agree with those famous jurists who argue that all offenders should go to prison because they freely chose to break the law.[u] However, if anyone argues that offenders should be incarcerated to protect society, then I agree. That is the theory of social defense.

[u] V. Buccellati, *Sopra i principj di diritto penale*, 1865, Milano; *Allgemeine Deutsche Strafrechtszeitung*, Febbrajo, fasc. 2. 1866; Carrara, *Cardini della scienza penale italiana*, 1875.

EDITION TWO

1878

Editors' Foreword

Lombroso published a revised version of *Criminal Man* in 1878, only two years after the appearance of the original edition. In his preface, he announces that this second edition constitutes almost a new book because of its expanded length and coverage of such additional topics as suicide, recidivism, and criminal handwriting. This claim is exaggerated since the second edition, like all subsequent editions, retains many of the original chapters intact. However, Lombroso does include much new material here and, perhaps most important, defines a new category of offender, the criminal of passion. Driven by uncontrollable emotion, the criminal of passion is a normal individual who commits murder or other offenses in the name of love, politics, or honor. With the addition of the criminal of passion, edition 2 marks the beginning of Lombroso's construction of a typology of criminals, a classification system that he continues to elaborate in the subsequent editions. This classification remains simple in edition 2, where he continues to label all other types of offenders simply as criminals.[1]

Lombroso mentions the topic of the etiology of crime in the first edition, but he greatly expands the treatment of the subject in edition 2. In a discussion ranging from the weather to sexuality to imitation, Lombroso demonstrates his belief in the multicausal nature of crime. His analysis points to a curious but complex mixture of causal factors including inborn characteristics (race, age, and sex) and social conditions (moral upbringing, the availability of alcohol). His discussion of heredity as a mechanism that multiplies criminal tendencies—as exemplified most notoriously in the Juke family studied by Richard Dugdale—presages his emphasis on the moral insanity of children in edition 3. That one drunkard, Max Juke, could produce two hundred criminals and even more vagabonds and prostitutes over only five generations offers a clear warning, according to Lombroso, of the necessity of identifying dangerous individuals. Lombroso also emphasizes the role of race in predicting criminal behavior, pointing to Africans, southern Italians with Arab blood, and "Gypsies" as atavistic and immoral races. He contrasts these groups with Jews (his own religious group), whose lawbreaking he attributes to disadvantageous social circumstances.

Another topic that receives lengthy treatment in edition 2 is penal policy for the prevention and punishment of crime. Lombroso's discussion of new policing techniques and innovative types of prisons draws on his wide-ranging knowledge of developments in the rest of Europe and the United States while demonstrating his commitment to applying positivist criminology to the pressing issues of his day. Praising the use of forensic photography by police to identify lawbreakers, he recommends international police cooperation on the model of today's modern Interpol. Although he believes that crime prevention should start with children, he criticizes the reformatories of his era for mixing depraved with honest youth and therefore spreading the infection of immorality. Lombroso extends his critique of reformatories to prisons, arguing that only the cellular and Irish systems have the potential to reform less dangerous offenders. Atavistic criminals, on the other hand, should face perpetual incarceration in special prisons for incorrigibles, which Lombroso advocates as a civilized alternative to the death penalty. He extends his plea for the individualization of punishment — sentencing based not on the severity of the crime but on the dangerousness of the criminal — to insane criminals by recommending the establishment of criminal insane asylums.

Lombroso ends the second edition with a long appendix of transcripts of medical and psychological examinations of convicted criminals by criminal anthropologists. In his preface, Lombroso explains that these clinical studies will demonstrate to both legal practitioners and readers the practical applications of positivist theory. We include two of these transcripts at the end of this edition.

Author's Preface

My laborious efforts of many years to study crime from an anthropological perspective have met with a success that exceeded their merits and my own expectations. Within a few months, my book *Criminal Man* was sold out, despite having no great literary virtues and being almost strictly a theoretical work. From a scientific point of view, it was marred by defects that can be excused only by those who have followed lonely paths into little-known fields of research. I have therefore undertaken to present a revised version, which, because of the many additions and emendations, is more like a new work than simply a second edition. Particularly noteworthy is its practical approach to the crime question and its recommendations for penal policy.

I have expanded certain topics hardly mentioned in the first edition such as suicide among criminals, recidivism, reformatories, the handwriting of criminals, heredity, and crimes of passion. I did so to respond to the justified criticisms of renowned scholars in the field, namely Holtzendorf, Hofmann, Maury, Calucci, Ziliotto, Morselli, Pitrè, Raggi, Lucchini, Roggero, Beltrani-Scalia, and Tamburini. I am grateful to them all for their suggestions.

However, I have not been able to respond to every criticism, such as to the call for more statistical data. This is more easily requested than provided, especially as it was neither simple nor even possible to find large numbers of recidivist forgers and arsonists, and above all female criminals. But however scant my data, I am confident that they support conclusions that are firmer than the superficial observations and a priori assumptions that have hitherto dominated this field without even being challenged.

Less still have I accepted criticism of my overexuberant use of facts and figures, which may cause the less attentive to lose the thread of my argument. Cutting back on the data would have meant falling short of the positivist method, an approach which, in such a contentious field, has the advantage of showing the evidence for my conclusions. My data also provide others with material for correcting and improving my theories.

One point raised against me seems entirely unfounded: that of taking insufficient account of criminal psychology. My book is nothing if not a tract on the criminal mind, based on an examination of facts. Criminal psychology involves the study of the passions, writings, jargon, religion, morality, education, and mental illnesses of offenders, as well as of the influences of history, climate, hereditary, and nutrition on crime. The anatomical section of the first edition, targeted by certain critics, constituted merely an appendix to psychology, which even in the case of healthy subjects must be grounded on a strong anatomical base if it is not to lose itself among the clouds.

Several critics, observing my comparisons between criminals and certain categories of the mentally ill, accused me of confusing the two. I could have replied that there is an enormous difference between analogy and identity. Only the ignorant and malevolent would accuse me of equating the madman with the genius simply because I note similarities between them. I neither created nor even searched for points of comparison between criminals and the insane; they appeared spontaneously. Nevertheless, I often found differences, establishing a positivist rather than merely hypothetical basis for distinguishing the madman from the criminal.

To prove my conclusions and demonstrate the practical and immediate application of my theories, I have added appendices on forensic examinations carried out by myself and other advocates of experimental psychiatry on criminals, the criminally insane, and cases that lie in between. The transcripts of these examinations provide new raw material for theoretical study and abundant useful information for legal practitioners. When discussing important and controversial trials, lawyers are always eager to know what has been said about similar cases. From these forensic examinations, the reader will come to understand the advantages of the positivist method. Not withstanding pain and struggle, I was the first to apply this method to the study of mental illness in Italy.[a]

Finally, I do not claim to have completed my task. Nevertheless, I hope my efforts will suffice to show the usefulness of the new scientific avenue opened to penologists by my school. Legal experts will be finally won over, but only after this new approach has been seriously examined and subjected to rigorous proof, as I have done here.

[a] See C. Lombroso, *Medicina legale dell'alienazione mentale studiata col metodo sperimentale*, Padova, 1865; Lombroso, *Klinische Beiträge zur Psychiatrie*, 1870, Leipzig.

12

Suicide among Criminals

A phenomenon of such frequency among inmates as to be practically a criminal characteristic is that of suicide (Morselli, *Del suicidio dei delinquenti*, 1877). Suicide among criminals follows patterns similar to those observed in the general population. That is, suicides tend to occur in summer and to be committed by individuals who are male, single or widowed, and between the ages of twenty-one to thirty.[b] Where we find a marked difference between the groups is in suicide rates. In Italy, for example, prison inmates kill themselves at the rate of 17 per 100,000 as opposed to a rate of .62 per 100,000 for the general population.

This high frequency of suicide among inmates cannot simply be attributed to the horror of being sentenced, the pain of long imprisonment, or the deprivation of companionship. Suicide is not necessarily more prevalent in cellular prisons than in other types of prisons; certainly, it is not widespread in cellular prisons for minors.[c] We must also note that suicide rates are higher among criminals awaiting trial (who constitute 38 percent of all prisoners in Italy) and among pris-

---

[b] In Italy between 1866 and 1874, only three female inmates committed suicide (a rate of fewer than one per five thousand). Of all prisoners who committed suicide in these years, 62 percent were single or widow(er)s, 16 percent married, and another 17 percent married with children. The age of inmates who committed suicide was as follows:

AGE	PERCENTAGE IN 1866–1872	PERCENTAGE IN 1873
21–30	40	38
31–40	33	24
41–50	10	18
51–60	1.6	9
Above 60	2.2	–

[The columns in this table do not total 100 percent. We have eliminated an additional table on international suicide rates from the original footnote. — Eds.]

[c] The preferred method of suicide in Italian prisons is: hanging 101; jumping 25; wounding 19; slitting veins 9; fasting 9; poisoning 9; asphyxiation 1. [Lombroso does not give a date for these statistics. We have eliminated additional data on suicide across Europe from this footnote. — Eds.]

11, 12, and 13 Water Jug:
Effects of Cellular Imprisonment
Editors' note: On this water jug, an inmate
of a cellular prison predicts his suicide in
the following doggerel: Hope is a chimera
/ The world is an empire ruled by Egoism /
God . . . Religion! Justice! Grand words! /
I ask pardon of those who love me / I give
pardon to those who wish me wrong / Tired
of suffering, I have decided to die! / Better
death than the life of a slave on a crooked
path . . . .
Source: Photo courtesy of the Museo
Lombroso (Turin).

Table 7: Homicide and Suicide in Italy, 1870–71

REGION OR CITY	HOMICIDES	SUICIDES	REGION OR CITY	HOMICIDES	SUICIDES
Mantua	6	19	Caserta	126	1
Veneto	92	179	Campania	909	36
Liguria	57	101	Puglia	298	45
Bologna	23	29	Basilicata	139	9
Florence	23	40	Calabria	464	22
Marches	145	66	Sardinia	201	19
Abruzzi	459	36	Palermo	160	13
Naples	227	19	Sicily	880	85

Source: *Statistica delle morti violente*, 1872

Editors' note: We have rearranged the list of regions and cities to read from north to south. Lombroso is trying to show that suicide and homicide occur in inverse proportions, with suicide predominating in northern Italy and homicide in southern Italy. Lombroso has not used consistent geographical units in this table but instead mixes totals for regions (like Sicily) with those for cities within these regions (Palermo).

oners during their first months of incarceration than for long-term inmates.[2] Evidently the high frequency of suicides among criminals in the first months in prison, or even before sentencing, relates to their insensitivity and lack of instinct for self-preservation. Since they have little foresight and patience, they prefer quick but intense suffering to a lesser pain endured for a long period. For this reason, they find death an easier solution than long-term deprivation of their momentary passions.

For some criminals, then, suicide is a safety valve against the prospect of long-term deprivation. For others, it is part of the same tendency that led them to crime. And for yet others, it is a sort of instrument of "rehabilitation" after the crime, a way of requesting pardon from others and from oneself. It demonstrates the irresistible violence of the passions that drive criminals, or the weight of their remorse.

The close relationship between crime and suicide is demonstrated by the confession of the killer Lacenaire. In his words, "There came a day when I had no alternative but crime or suicide. I wondered whether I was a victim of myself or of society. Once I decided it was society, I struck back."

Social statistics show an inverse ratio between violent crimes and suicides (Oettingen). As table 7 shows, the latter are rare in hot climates, while the former are more numerous in warm areas such as Spain, Corsica, and the southern and island provinces of Italy. The opposite occurs in northern and central Italy, where it might be said that many murders are forestalled by suicide. The same inverse ratio can generally be found in more civilized countries and epochs, where suicides increase in line with cultural progress.[3]

Suicide-homicides, or rather double suicides, are essentially crimes of passion. They are the culmination of great paroxysms of love among the young and unmarried, especially soldiers. Lieutenant C. and the prostitute Q., being unable to marry respectably yet not wanting to separate, killed themselves in Bologna. In an extremely moving case from France, in 1835 the health official Bancal returned from a long expedition to find his lover married and mother of a child. Their love reflowered but could not continue honorably, leading the couple to commit a double suicide that took days to prepare. Bancal survived and tried twice more to kill himself.

Suicide is easier for criminals of passion than for common criminals. It is even easier for the criminally insane. This is natural, because suicide is common among the mad (about one fifth of whom kill themselves) and among criminals. Thus it stands to reason that it would occur frequently among those who are both, especially if they are driven by strong passion.

13

Criminals of Passion

There is one category of crime on which I cannot dwell for too long since it falls outside the scope of this work.[4] It is that of the so-called crimes of passion, which might be better labeled crimes of impulse, since all crimes flow from the violence of certain emotions. But while in the true criminal the passionate impulse is neither spontaneous nor unique, the type of crime under consideration here is different. Crimes of passion are very rare: in Prussia, Pennsylvania, and Switzerland the rate is thought to be about 5 to 6 percent of all cases.[d] According to Bittinger, "the ratio of crimes of passion to premeditated crimes is 1:27. The ratio of crimes of evil passions to crimes of innocuous passions is 1:50" (*Crimes of Passion*, 1872).

These offenses involve people of full-blooded or nervous temperament. Unlike the apathetic common criminal, the criminal by passion displays exaggerated sensitivity and excessive affections. Quadi, having overheard words suggesting that his lover was completely depraved, rushed to a shopkeeper and begged him to chop off his ear. When the shopkeeper refused, he cut it off himself. This act reproduced the tendency of savages to use tropes and symbols in which the part stands for the whole and the sense organ signifies the sensation. When I examined Quadi twenty years later, despite the fact that he was now married and a father, the mere mention of the other woman made him delirious. Similarly, the political criminal Sand had been a patriot since his boyhood.[5] Nation and liberty became the only ideas that could animate him.

When arrested, criminals by passion, far from showing that apathy or reserve typical of assassins, are rather extremely, almost insanely, emotional. They appear to have been so even before committing their crimes. Most crimes of passion are committed by young people. Before their crimes, these wretches are known for honorable conduct. Curti, for example, financially supported his three brothers. Sand lived and

---

[d] B. Scalia, *Sulla Riforma penitenziaria in Europa*, 1874.

died like a saint, and people referred to the place of his execution as the spot "where Sand went to heaven" (*Sands Himmelfartsweise*).

As soon as they have committed their crime and satisfied their passionate impulse, nearly all criminals of this sort experience a fierce reaction; they repent bitterly and commit suicide or attempt it. Cipriani, who killed his wife when he found her committing adultery, threw himself out of the window. Sand, too, even though he considered his murder of Kotzebue a holy act, immediately afterward stabbed himself twice in the chest and turned himself in to police. Thus, unlike common criminals, offenders of this type do not create alibis to hide their crimes. They enjoy confessing to judge and jury, for it soothes the pain of their remorse. Crimes of religious and political passion are the only ones that evoke little remorse in their authors, who believe, like Sand and Orsini, that they have carried out their duty.[6] In prisons, criminals of passion, or rather of impulse, are the only inmates who undergo complete reformation—up to 100 percent according to Swedish and Prussian statistics.

The passions that feed crimes of impulse are not those that rise gradually from within and can more or less be controlled, such as avarice or ambition. They are those that explode unforeseen, like rage, love, or offended honor—passions that are generous and often sublime. Conversely, the passions that predominate among common criminals are ignoble and primitive, such as revenge, cupidity, lust, and alcoholic rage.

While the motive for crime is weak in the genuine criminal, in the case of crimes of passion the cause is proportionate in strength to the crime. Orsini and Sand felt an intense love for their countries and hoped to render a great service by killing men whom they considered their nations' worst enemies. Bounin heard his wife betraying him at the foot of his bed while she believed him to be asleep, telling her paramour how she wished her husband would die. Enraged, he leaped up, trampled on her, and attacked the paramour.

To such cases should be added infanticides, which are often committed from an exaggerated sense of honor and whose ultimate cause is the infamy our society attaches to unwed motherhood. As confessions indicate, women who commit infanticide are rarely recidivists and often come from completely honest backgrounds. They usually act without premeditation, without accomplices, without proper instruments, and in a state of delirium. In penal colonies, they often make very good wives, unlike female thieves, assassins, and swindlers (Cère, *Les populations dangereuses*, Paris, 1872).[7]

Crimes of passion are also widespread among people who live in something close to a savage state. Familiar with the knife and vendetta, such people take seriously even slight offenses to honor. This has been observed in Sardinia and Corsica, where the smallest provocation—a refusal of marriage or a report of a theft—can end in pistol shots. Revenge is considered necessary against the perpetrators and their relations, not excluding women and even priests. In such cases, even murder assumes the character of a crime of passion because it is nearly always carried out in broad daylight; without ambush, accomplices, or a plan; never with poison or for material gain; and often by people who until that moment had lived honorable lives. Thus in Corsica, out of every one hundred crimes, seventy-seven were committed against persons (Riboquel, *Crimes commis dans la Corse*, 1842, Paris).

14

Recidivism, Morality, and Remorse

Recidivism

Crime statistics unanimously demonstrate that the proportion of recidivists among criminals is increasing. In France in 1826, recidivists
constituted a mere 10 percent of criminals; by 1850, this had increased
to 28 percent. And in 1867—that is, seventeen years after the establishment of judicial record offices—the proportion of recidivists reached 42
percent (Yvernes, *De la récidive*, Paris, 1874). In England in 1871, out of
160,934 arrested persons, 37,884 were recidivists, as shown in table 8.

No prison system is immune from recidivism; in fact, penitentiaries
are the main cause of the phenomenon. At Clairvaux prison, according to Bretignères De Courtelles, 506 recidivist thieves and vagabonds
committed their offenses simply to procure an easy life in prison. In
addition, out of 115 prisoners, 17 declared that they had taken no precautions in committing their crime because they needed to have a stay
of at least one or two years in prison to restore their health, which had
been ruined by orgies. He continues that recidivists reenter prison with
the same contentment as their own homes, and that comrades greet
them as "travelers" (*Les condamnés et les prisons*. Paris, 1838).

If prisons do not reduce recidivism, education has an even smaller
effect. While superficial investigators often claim that education is a
panacea for crime, it is in fact one of the causes of recidivism, or at
least one of its indirect causes. Those who, like Locatelli, investigate the
pernicious effects of education more closely, find that in prison criminals learn how to commit crimes more effectively and less dangerously
than on the outside. Learning the crafts of iron mongering, calligra-
phy, and printing in prison, the molester becomes a forger, the thief
a swindler or counterfeiter, and so on. But learning such skills brings
about no psychological or anatomical change in these criminals. Maudsley writes that the true thief is born a thief, rather than becoming one,
just as the poet is born a poet.[8] How can one expect to reform that
which has been created over several generations! He cites Chesterton,

Table 8: Recidivism in England, 1871

NUMBER OF PREVIOUS CONVICTIONS	NUMBER OF OF CRIMINALS	NUMBER OF PREVIOUS CONVICTIONS	NUMBER OF CRIMINALS
1	21,803	5	3,042
2	10,147	6–7	3,883
3	5,640	7–10	3,341
4	4,350	10+	3,678

Editors' note: According to Lombroso's text introducing this table, the total number of individuals arrested in England in 1871 was 160,934, of whom 37,884 were recidivists. The number of recidivists in this table, however, totals 55,884. In addition, Lombroso overlaps two categories: those offenders with six to seven convictions and those with seven to ten.

who heard thieves in prison declare that even if they became million-aires, they would continue to rob. Nine-tenths of criminals are like that (*Responsability*, 1873).

Morality of Criminals

Because the majority of criminals lack any moral sense, they fail to understand the immorality of crime. In French criminal jargon, the conscience is *the mute*; the thief, a *friend*; and robbery *serving* or *working*. A Milanese thief told me, "I don't rob, I merely relieve the rich of their excess; in any case, don't shopkeepers and lawyers rob? Why then do you accuse only me and not them?"

One often hears of remorse among criminals, and until a few years ago the penal system's point of departure was the criminal's repentance. But those who have worked among these wretches, even for a short time, soon realize that they are far from remorseful. According to Elam and Tocqueville, the worst offenders are those who behave best in prison; being cleverer than others, they dissimulate honesty in order to be well treated.[9] English prison wardens say it is easier to transform a dog into a wolf than a thief into a gentleman.

If we now compare the morality of criminals with that of the insane, we find curious differences and similarities. Few of the insane are born wicked or immoral; rather, they become so after an illness changes or modifies their character. Like the criminal, the madman rarely feels remorse; instead, he boasts of his misdeeds or at least says he felt forced to commit the crime despite himself. Yet as soon as he has committed a crime, he reacquires his lucidity and sense of what is right. Then he gives himself up to the courts, not with the cynicism of the criminal, but with the attitude of a repenting sinner.

The savage man, on the other hand, feels no remorse whatever. In fact, he is proud of his misdeeds; justice for him is synonymous with revenge and the use of force. In classical Latin, *latrocinio* (larceny) meant "militia." Among the Gauls (Caesar, *De Bello G.*, xi), acts of theft committed outside the city walls were completely blameless. Even now in Albania, homicide is not a crime because strong means just, and weak means bad.

Cannibalism is common among savages. In Australia, Obfield found no graves of women and concluded that fathers or husbands killed them before they got too thin or too old and thus less appetizing. In the Peruvian language, *mirca* means to eat one's own father or mother; in their mythology, there was a cannibalistic parricide god, *mircik-coyllon*.[e]

[e] See Lombroso, *L'Uomo bianco e l'uomo di colore*, 1870, Padova.

15

Handwriting of Criminals

Since we usually attribute little value to everyday phenomena, the idea that a man's handwriting can provide clues to his psychological state may seem useless and even bizarre. Everyone admits that gestures, tone of voice, and pronunciation provide clues to psychological disturbances, but few have read the numerous works that currently treat the interpretation of handwriting (Bovary, *Graphologie*, 1876; Adolfo Heuze, *Chirogrammatomanzia*, Leipzig, 1862; and Dubarolles, *Les mystères de l'écriture*, 1872). Gestures and speech are momentary, while examples of handwriting survive long after their creation, sometimes for centuries.

I know full well that copious data is needed to prove my argument that criminals can be diagnosed by their handwriting. Therefore my illustrious friend Alfredo Maury, director of the Archives of France, provided me with the signatures of certain well-known French criminals. Similarly, Beltrani-Scalia, who has turned penology into a veritable science, furnished me with the signatures of several hundred Italian prisoners.[10] Other handwriting samples were given to me by the honorable Lucini, the king's agent in Pavia, and Costa, director of the prison in Turin.

Totaling 407, the signatures I have collected fall mainly into two clearly defined groups. Only the signatures of semi-illiterate criminals, who include some of our most famous brigands, retain a childish character and are not easy to categorize. The first group is made up of signatures of murderers, highway robbers, and brigands, who generally elongate their letters, adding curves to the upper and lower extensions. In many of the signatures, the cross of the "t" is very clear or elongated, as also found in the script of soldiers and other particularly energetic people; in a few other cases the letters have acute angles and flourishes. The signatures of this first group are further distinguished by their extraordinary curlicues and arabesques. This is proved by the signature of Desrues, an extremely ferocious poisoner and forger, as well as those of the murderers Carrier and Vidocq.

The handwriting of a subgroup of murderers, headed by Lacenaire

14 Handwriting of Criminals
Editors' note: Lombroso collected these signatures of famous criminals—including Vidocq (no. 48), Passanante (no. 68), and Robespierre (no. 83)—to prove that handwriting provides a clue to criminality. The letters following each number refer to types of crime (*o* for homicide, *b* for brigand, *l* for thief, etc.).
Source: Lombroso, *L'uomo delinquente*, edition 4.

and Cosimi, have letters that lack flourishes in their vertical extensions. Letters in this subgroup are all slightly distant from each other, a little squashed and rounded. Despite their young age (from thirty to thirty-six years), many of these murderers show traces of a trembling hand, which is perhaps a sign of alcoholism or nervous diseases. Only thirty-six of ninety signatures in the first group lacked these peculiar characteristics, showing handwriting that is completely normal.

The second group of signatures, belonging mostly to thieves, is distinct from that of highway robbers and lacks emphatic verticals. In general, the letters are soft and ill-formed, and the signatures are clear and easy to read. This kind of writing is similar to that of women and indeed to normal handwriting. In addition to these characteristics and a slight tremble, the handwriting of a certain type of thief—such as Cartouche—has a sort of hook and curvature to practically every letter, which reminds us of the particular configuration of their fingers; similar hooks and curves are also found in the writing of other thieves. Out of 106 examples of thieves' writing, only 12 lacked these anomalous characteristics.

The writing of female murderers is very similar to that of male assassins (like Trossarello), and in general their writing tends toward the virile, a characteristic also found among honest but energetic women. Raffaella Amato, convicted of murder, was actually a male though people thought her a woman due to her hypospadias or congenital malformation of the urethra.[11] The letters of her writing were particularly virile.

16

Etiology of Crime
WEATHER AND RACE

An etiology can be established for crime just as it can for illness, and possibly more easily. Cholera, typhoid, and tuberculosis all originate from specific causes, but who can deny that they are also influenced by broader meteorological, hygienic, individual, and psychological factors? Similarly, crime is rooted in multiple causes, many of them intertwined. We need to consider the causes of crime one by one, as with any other human phenomenon.

Influence of Weather

One of the determining causes of crime, albeit an indirect and external factor, is the weather, particularly heat. According to Guerry, in England murders occur most frequently during the hottest months, as shown in table 9; I have here added comparable figures for Italy.

Inversely, crimes against property dominate in the winter months. For example, theft and forgery rise in January because as needs increase, the means of satisfying them decrease. Crime rates vary little in other seasons. The influence of heat explains why crimes against persons occur more often in southern areas, at least in France and Italy, than in the northern and central areas.[12] In their sensitivity to heat, criminals resemble the insane. Admissions to both prisons and mental asylums reach their highest levels in the hottest months.[f]

Influence of Race

The notion of crime is indistinct among the savage races, so much so that one suspects it was entirely lacking in primitive man. Many tribes

[f] See C. Lombroso, *Pensiero e meteore*, Milan, Dumolard, 1878.

Table 9: Climate and Violent Crime in England and Italy

MONTH	ENGLAND (Murders, 1834–1856)	ITALY (Violent Crime, 1869)
July	1,043	307
June	1,071	301
August	928	343
May	842	288
February	701	254
March	681	273
December	651	236
January	605	237

have a relative morality, one all their own, which they apply in their own way and from which they derive their first notions of crime. Among the Yuris of America, respect for property is so great that a string suffices to mark boundaries. The Koriaks and the Mbayá punish murder committed within the tribe, though they do not consider murder a crime when it is committed outside the tribal confines. Without such a rule, the tribe would lose its cohesiveness and dissolve.

However, some tribes have no morality at all. In the Caramansa region of Africa, the Balanti hunt and pillage, stealing from other tribes and killing those who steal from them (*Revue d'Anthropologie*, 1874). In India the Zacka-Khail tribes are professional thieves. When a male child is born, they bless it by passing it through a breach in the wall of his house and chanting three times: "Be a thief." On the other hand, the Korubar are famous for their sincerity. They never lie. Rather than rob, they would let themselves die of hunger (Taylor, *Sociétés primitives*, Paris, 1874).

These cases suggest that race must be an influence on crime. Yet documentation is scarce and uncertain for the uncivilized world. In Italy the descendants of Albanians are renowned for brigandage. In all regions of Italy, certain villages are known for having supplied an uninterrupted stream of criminals. In Liguria, for example, Lerici is well known for its swindlers and Campofreddo and Masson for its murderers. In Pergola near Pistoia, "Pergolino" has become a synonym for thief. Near Pesaro, Sant'Andrea in Villis and Ferreto are notorious for murder by men and petty theft by women.

In Sicily, brigandage is concentrated in the famous valley around

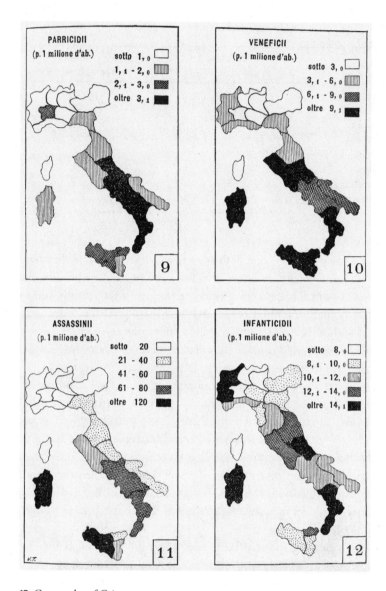

15 Geography of Crime

Editors' note: Drawn from Ferri's book on homicide, these maps purport to show that murder (no. 11), parricide (no. 9), and poisoning (no. 10) predominated in southern Italy, which Lombroso considered racially inferior to the north. Infanticide (no. 12) offered an exception because, according to criminal anthropology, its roots lay in social conditions rather than in heredity. The darker areas of the maps indicate higher rates of crime. *Source*: Lombroso, *L'uomo delinquente*, edition 5 (*Atlante*). Photo courtesy of the New York Library of Medicine.

Fig. 19. Tipo di razza inferiore - Parricida.

Fig. 22. Tipo criminale comune - Associazione di malfattori.

Fig. 20. Tipo di razza inferiore - Ladro abituale.

Fig. 23. Tipo comune di ladro - Ladro abituale.

Fig. 21. Tipo di razza inferiore - Ladro abituale e feritore.

Fig. 24. Tipo comune di ladro (degenerato) - Borsaiuolo.

16 Types of Killers and Thieves

Editors' note: According to Lombroso's labels, these photos illustrate two types of offenders: racially inferior criminals in the left-hand column and common criminals in the right-hand column. He points out biological anomalies in each face like the huge jaw and thick hair of the habitual criminal in photo no. 20 and the jug ears and thin lips of the brigand in photo no. 22.

Source: Lombroso, *Der Verbrecher* (*Atlas*). Photo courtesy of the Lloyd Sealy Library, John Jay College of Criminal Justice.

Palermo, where the rapacious Berber and Semite tribes had their earliest and longest-lasting settlements and where anatomical types, customs, politics, and morality retain a clear Arab imprint.[9] The Arabs are a race of greedy conquerors who are hospitable but cruel, intelligent but superstitious, and always restlessly in movement. Their blood must play a role in fomenting spontaneous and implacable insurrections and perpetuating brigandage. In Sicily today, following the tradition of the original Arab settlers, both uprisings and brigandage are intertwined with politics. Brigandage provokes neither horror nor revulsion in people of this area as it would in groups with a greater proportion of Aryan blood. It is difficult to offer precise statistics on these racial influences, partly because crime has complex causes. Furthermore, even differences within Sicily may depend less on ethnicity than on variations in standards of living, climate, and levels of culture.

On the other hand, race clearly influences crime among Jews and Gypsies, although in opposite directions. According to statistics, in some countries the level of Jewish criminality is lower than that of their fellow citizens. The rates would be lower still if Jews did not gravitate toward professions like shopkeeping and manufacturing, which have very high levels of criminality among all population groups. In Bavaria, only 1 out of 315 convicted criminals is Jewish compared to 1 out of 265 for Catholics. In Baden, for every 100 Christian criminals, there are but 63.6 Jewish criminals (Oettingen, p. 844).

Even more distinctive than the low numbers of Jewish criminals are the types of crime they commit. Among Jews as among Gypsies, crime takes a hereditary form. In France, for example, entire generations of swindlers and thieves can be found among those with Jewish names such as Cerfbeer, Salomon, Levi, Blum, and Klei, but few Jews are found guilty of murder. In Prussia, Jews are commonly charged with forgery, calumny, and especially receiving stolen goods. Because the thief often adopts the vocabulary of receivers, many Jewish words have entered criminal jargon in England and Germany.

The same reasons lie behind the Jewish involvement in the crime of receiving stolen property and in the grimy profession of usury: ava-

[9] Tommasi-Crudeli writes of the Sicilian Arabs (*La Sicilia*, Firenze, 1871): "They are sober, patient, and persevering; they have strong friendships; they have an instinct for using silent and hidden ways to obtain their purpose. Hospitable but rapacious, the lower classes are superstitious and the upper classes are haughty. The word 'scoundrel' loses its meaning in Sicily, where it merely indicates something like having blood in ones veins. To report a murder is to fall short of the code of honesty."

rice for gold, desperate poverty, exclusion from jobs and public assistance, and a need for protection against persecution. Perhaps it was to avoid being massacred that Jews decided to become accomplices to feudal lords as receivers of stolen goods. But if this is true, it is surprising that Jewish crime rates are not higher. Instead, they began to decrease as soon as political life was opened to Jews.[13]

The same cannot be said of lawbreaking by Gypsies, who epitomize a thoroughly criminal race, with all its passions and vices. According to Grelmann, Gypsies have a horror of anything that requires the slightest effort.[h] They prefer to suffer hunger and misery rather than to subject themselves to any sort of continuous work, and they want only the minimum they need for survival. They are deceitful with one another, ungrateful, cruel, and, at the same time, cowardly. For this reason, there is a proverb in Transylvania according to which fifty Gypsies can be put to flight by a wet rag. When they were drafted into the Austrian army, they made a poor showing. They are extremely vengeful. A Gypsy who had been struck by his employer got revenge by carrying him to a cave, stitching him into a skin, and adding the most disgusting substances till he died of gangrene.

Gypsies have the same lack of foresight as savages and criminals. Lovers of orgies and noise, in the market they make a great hubbub. Ferocious, they kill for money without remorse. Years ago, they were suspected of cannibalism. The women are able thieves and train the children. Gypsies poison farm animals with powders and then either claim to heal them or try to buy the meat cheaply. In Turkey they prostitute themselves.

[h] *Histoire des Bohémiens*, Paris, 1837; Predari, *Sugli Zingari*, Milan, 1871; Pott, *Zigeuner*, Halle, 1844; and Vidocq, op. cit., p. 330.

17

Etiology of Crime
CIVILIZATION, ALCOHOL,
AND HEREDITY

Civilization

Among many social questions, one in particular demands an answer: How does civilization affect crime and insanity? Bare numbers seem to answer the question, because most years show a disproportionately large increase in rates of both criminality and madness.[i] But as Messedaglia has appropriately pointed out, a great probability of error arises from trying to resolve complex problems by simple numbers.

Civilization and barbarism have, in Messedaglia's apt phrase, their own characteristic crimes. Barbarism encourages bloody crimes by deadening moral sensitivity and revulsion against murder, which instead is regarded as heroic. Revenge is a duty, and might makes right. Criminal associations flourish in barbaric societies, as do religious manias among the mad. Yet the closely knit families, lack of sexual stimuli, and absence of acquisitiveness typical of savage society means that parricide, infanticide, and theft are less common than today. In contrast, the progress of civilization multiplies needs and wants by a hundredfold, and wealth stimulates the senses. Civilization thus increases rates

[i] In France, the ratio of indicted persons to the population in general was 1:100 in 1826–1837; by 1868, this ratio had grown to 1:55 (Dufau, *Traité de statist.*, 1840; Block, *L'Europe politique*, 1870). The statistics for Austria are as follows (Messedaglia, op. cit):

YEAR	RATE OF CONVICTED CRIMINALS	RATE OF INDICTED CRIMINALS
1856	1:1,238 inhabitants	1:832 inhabitants
1857	1:1,191 "	1:813 "
1860	1:1,261 "	1:933 "
1861	1:1,178 "	1:808 "
1862	1:1,082 "	1:749 "

[We have cut additional data on England. — Eds.]

of alcoholism and progressive paralysis in the madhouses, and it fills the prisons with offenders against property and public morality.[j]

Thanks to railways and the concentration of commerce and government, cities continue to expand. Criminals tend to gather in urban centers, which offer greater profits and more anonymity than rural areas. As long as individuals live in isolation, the primitive instincts of theft, murder, and lust remain embryonic, especially if tempered by education. But these instincts increase exponentially on contact with others.

Civilization encourages certain crimes and mental illnesses (palsy, alcoholism) by encouraging the use of stimulants that were hardly known to primitive man. So great is the craving of civilized society for stimulants that nowadays in England and America the abuse of opium and ether has been added to that of alcohol and tobacco. In France, the consumption of distilled spirits has increased from eight liters a year per capita in 1840 to thirty liters in 1870 (Lemarque, *La réhabilitation*, 1877).

Every day civilization introduces new crimes that while less terrible than the crimes of antiquity, are no less damaging. In London, the thief substitutes shrewdness for violence; deft larceny for forced entry; and blackmail and newspaper swindles for burglary (*Quart. Rev.*, 1871). Murder with the aim of collecting life insurance exemplifies a new form of crime, this one committed mainly by doctors. Because the symptoms of arsenic poisoning are similar to those of cholera, physicians in Magdeburg and Munich poisoned many patients during a cholera epidemic, after having taken out life insurance on them (Pettenkoffer, *Théorie des Cholera*, 1871).

But we should not curse progress because while civilization temporarily increases crime, it also mitigates its severity. Furthermore, civilization has already started curing the plagues it has caused with asylums for the criminally insane, cellular prisons, industrial factories, the savings banks available at post offices and workshops, and charitable organizations that protect homeless children, thus preventing crime practically from the cradle.

Comparing annual crime rates in Germany with the prices of staple foods, we see that food is perhaps more important than civilization in the etiology of crime. As shown in table 10, property crime de-

---

[j] At Bicêtre there were only nine cases of progressive paralysis in 1818–1819; there were thirty-four in 1848–1849. [Bicêtre was a well-known Parisian insane asylum. —Eds.]

Table 10: Price of Food and Types of Crime in Germany

YEAR	RAPE	ARSON	PROPERTY CRIME	VIOLENT CRIME	PRICE OF GRAIN AND POTATOES
1854	2.26	0.43	88.41	8.90	217.1
1855	2.57	0.46	88.93	8.04	252.3
1856	2.65	0.43	87.60	9.32	203.3
1857	4.14	0.53	81.52	13.81	156.3
1858	4.45	0.60	77.92	17.03	149.3
1859	4.68	0.52	78.19	16.63	150.6

Editors' note: Lombroso does not explain how he measured the price of food; his figures for crime seem to be percentages because they add across to 100.

creases when grain is affordable, while violent crime increases, particularly rape. Lack of food depresses the sexual appetite, while abundance increases it. On the other hand, the lack of staple foods stimulates theft, while their abundance makes stealing less necessary.

Alcohol

Like hashish and opium, distilled alcohol stimulates the brain perversely, provoking a tendency to crime and suicide. It also leads to incurable diseases like creeping paralysis and narcotic addiction. Even worse is wine. Habitual wine drinkers are immoral and produce criminal, insane, or precociously libidinous offspring, as I will show with the story of the Juke family (*Ann. Med. Psyc.*, 1877). Even an isolated incident of acute drunkenness can give rise to crimes: according to Gall, the brigand Petri felt the need to kill as soon as he had a drink, while drunkenness provoked blood lust in a woman in Berlin.

Bertrand found four to six drunkards among every one hundred English criminals. In 1857 in England, there were 403 arrests for drunkenness for every 100,000 inhabitants. In 1863, this rose to 450 and in 1865, to 503 (*Journal of Stats. soc*, 1868, folio 157). While under the influence of alcohol, English offenders committed 111,465 crimes in 1867–68, a figure which rose to 151,054 in 1871–72 (Lemarque, *La Réhabilitation*, 1877). In Holland, four-fifths of all crimes have been attributed to drink; more precisely, alcohol accounts for seven-eighths of all fights and misdemeanors, three-fourths of all violent crimes, and one-fourth of all property offenses (*Essai sur l'intemp.*, Paris, 1871).

Heredity

Official Italian statistics for 1871–72 reveal that of 2,800 juvenile delinquents, 6.4 percent had drunken parents. Most had drunken fathers (5.3 percent), fewer drunken mothers (1.7 percent), and very few both (0.4 percent). These figures indicate the importance of heredity in crime. But parental alcoholism is not the only factor that produces criminal tendencies in children, for criminality itself is hereditary.

I studied a boy in the Pavia prison who had pronounced prognathism, thick hair, strabismus, and a feminine physiognomy.[14] At the age of twelve he had committed murder and subsequently been imprisoned for theft six times. He had two brothers who were thieves, a mother who received stolen goods, and two sisters who were prostitutes.

Of 3,580 criminal minors in Mettray,[15] 707 were children of convicted criminals and 308 offspring of parents living in concubinage (Barce, op.cit.). Italian statistics show that in 1871–72, 3 percent of juvenile delinquents had a parent in prison. They also confirm Virgilio's findings that 28 percent of minors convicted of crime come from families of questionable reputation and 26 percent from families with undoubtedly bad reputations.

The ferocious Galetto of Marseille was the grandson of Orsolano, the cannibal-rapist; Dumollard was the son of an assassin; Patetot had murderers among his grandfathers and great-grandfathers; Papa, Crocco, and Serravalle had grandfathers who had served time; and both the father and grandfather of Cavalante had prison records. The Cornu family was filled with murderers from father to son, as were the Verdures, the Cerfbeers, and the Nathans, who on one particular day had fourteen family members in the same prison.[16] Mocc . . . , who poisoned her husband and committed adultery shamelessly, was the offspring of an incestuous relationship.

After examining 109 criminals, Thomson found that 50 were related and 8 were members of a single family headed by a recidivist criminal. He identified 3 brothers and 2 sisters who were thieves and whose father, uncles, aunts, and cousins were assassins. Further proof of the heredity of crime comes from Despine's report on the genealogy of Lemaire and Chretien, which I will summarize in table 11 so that you will understand it at a glance.[17]

The most important proof of the heredity of crime and its relation-

Table 11: Chretien-Lemaire Family Tree

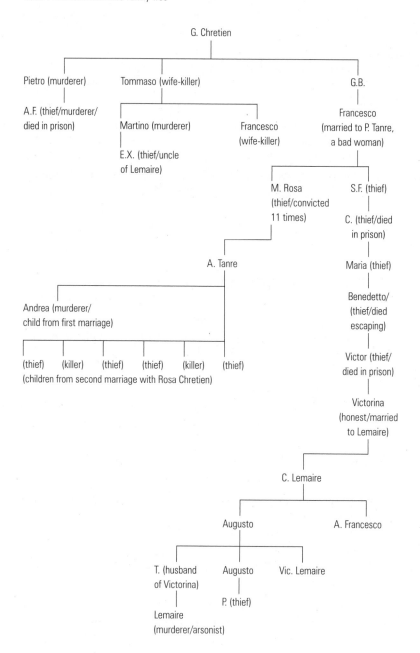

ship to mental illness and prostitution is Dugdale's unique study of the Juke family, whose name has become synonymous with *criminal* in America.[k] The source of this wretched progeny was one Max Juke, a hunter and fisherman, drunkard and seducer who was born about 1720 and became blind in his old age. His descendants now number about 540 legitimate and 169 illegitimate offspring. Unable to trace all branches of the family, Dugdale followed the offspring of five daughters (three of whom were prostitutes before marrying) and various collateral branches for seven generations. Strangely, criminals barely appeared in the second Juke generation, but then they multiplied to twenty-nine in the fourth and sixty in the fifth generations.[l] Similarly, the number of prostitutes grew from fourteen to thirty-five to eighty, and that of vagabonds from eleven to fifty-six to seventy-four. These numbers fell in the sixth and seventh generations because nature, the source of deformity as of crime, put an end to the problem through sterility. The number of sterile mothers grew from nine in the third generation to twenty-two in the fifth, while early deaths among the family's babies increased to three hundred in the later years.[18]

The following diagram, which gives the total numbers of Juke family members in all these categories, reveals a clear connection between prostitution, crime, and illness:

The Progenitor Max

77 criminals;[19]	128 prostitutes;	131 impotent, idiotic,
142 vagabonds	18 brothel owners;	or syphilitic offspring;
	91 illegitimate babies	46 sterile offspring

[k] *Thirteenth annual report of the executive committee of the Prison Association of New York, with accompanying documents, for the year 1874.* Transmitted to the legislature April 9, 1875 (Albany, Weed, Parsons and Company, 1875). I am grateful to my friend Beltrani-Scalia for this reference.

[l] Of the seventy-seven offenders among the Juke offspring, fifty-eight were male and nineteen female. They engaged in 106 forms of criminality including:

Misconduct:	51 instances, of which 38 were in the fifth generation	
Theft:	26 " " 10 " "	
Forgery/swindling:	3 " " 0 " "	
Robbery and murder	18 " " 8 " "	
Rape	8 " " 5 " "	

The propensity to crime in the Juke family tended to follow the male line. It was even more accentuated in the illegitimate lines, a phenomenon that recurred in all other areas of immorality as well. The following table compares thirty-eight illegitimate offspring of the fifth Juke generation with eighty-five legitimate offspring:

38 Illegitimate Offspring			85 Legitimate Offspring	
4 drunkards	11 beggars, idiots, or prostitutes	16 convicts (including 6 felons)	5 convicts	13 beggars or prostitutes

The figures for prostitution here underestimate the frequent eruption of sexual dissipation among women in the Juke family. They produced an enormous number of illegitimate children; sixty-seven women had syphilis and a larger number were immoral. Rates of female immorality rose from 60 percent in the first generation to 69 percent in the third, before declining to 48 percent in the fifth and 38 percent in the sixth. Overall, sexual depravity characterized 52.4 percent of the women descended in a direct line from Max Juke and 42 percent of the women descended in collateral lines.

Summarizing these data, Dugdale found that 200 criminals, 280 sick or impoverished individuals, and 90 prostitutes or women with venereal disease had descended from one drunkard. These numbers do not include 300 childhood mortalities, 400 men infected with syphilis, and 7 murder victims. Over seventy-five years this family cost the state over 1 million dollars.

18

Etiology of Crime
AGE, SEX, MORAL EDUCATION, GENITALS, AND IMITATION

Age

The influence of age on crime clearly differentiates criminals from the insane. Table 12 demonstrates that the largest number of criminals fall into the age bracket of twenty to thirty, while insane people are concentrated in the older age grouping of thirty to forty. After the age of forty, the numbers of the insane become at least double those for the normal and criminal populations. Meanwhile, the number of criminals continues to decrease until, after age fifty, it is less than half that of insane or normal individuals.

As adolescence ends, young men are instinctively drawn toward criminal acts to prove their virility. Manzoni expressed this well in his novel: "Gervaso, who by having participated in something tainted with crime, felt he had become a man like the others . . ." (Ch. XI).[20] All major criminals begin to display their tendencies in youth, often at the onset of puberty. This precocity, which distinguishes criminality from insanity, is further proof of the congenital nature of crime.

Sex

All statistics agree that the overall proportion of criminal women is low compared with criminal men, and lower still if we exclude the crime of infanticide. Women account for no more than 14 percent of convictions in Austria, 11 percent in Spain, and 8.2 percent in Italy. However, no matter how accurate these statistics are for serious crime, they are nevertheless misleading. In Italy, prostitutes are not considered criminals in the eyes of the law, but they are by public opinion. If we include prostitutes in our statistics, the crime rates of the two sexes become nearly

Table 12: Age of Normal, Insane, and Criminal Men

| AGE (years) | ITALIANS | | | ENGLISH | AUSTRIANS |
	Normal (percentage of 20,011)	Insane (percentage of 20,011)	Criminal (percentage of 26,500)	Criminal (percentage of 23,768)	Criminal (percentage of 12,786)
Under 20	43.55	6.18	12.9	25.10	10.4
20–30	17.01	2.34	45.7	42.40	42.6
30–40	14.32	26.21	28.8	16.80	27.07
40–50	10.67	22.91	11.6	8.40	12.1
50–60	7.89	14.02	3.8	4.20	5.9
60+	6.56	9.34	0.9	2.00	1.24

Source: Lolli, *Stat. del Manicomio di Imola*, Imola, 1874; Cardon, *Stat. delle Carceri*, Roma, 1871; Mayhew, op. cit.; and *Oesterr. Strafanst.*, Vienna, 1874.
Editors' note: Columns 2 and 3 do not add to 100 percent.

equal, with the weaker sex possibly predominating. According to Ryan and Talbot, in London one in seven women is a prostitute, and in Hamburg one in nine. In Italy, there are nine thousand known prostitutes, with a rate of eighteen to thirty-three per one thousand inhabitants in the major cities (Castiglioni, *Sulla prostituzione*, Roma, 1871).[21] Criminals and prostitutes share the same physical and moral characteristics, as well as a liking for one another.

In fact, law and statistics argue that a portion of prostitutes also commit other crimes. According to Guerry, in London 80 percent of all prostitutes less than thirty years of age are also criminals; as they grow older, this rate falls to 30 percent, and then 7 percent. Like prostitution, criminality is increasing among women with the progress of civilization, which makes them more like men. In London, women made up 18.8 percent of all criminals in 1834 and 25.7 percent in 1853. While the proportion of women among offenders is only 14 percent in Austria, it reaches 25 percent in the capital city.

Other strong arguments also suggest that statistics underestimate the number of female criminals. Crimes that come naturally to women —like receiving stolen goods, abortion, poisoning, and domestic theft —are among those least likely to come to light. To this can be added woman's notorious intensity and tenacity when she does commit a crime. Perversity in women, when it exists, usually expresses itself more strongly than in men. For instance, American women have shown themselves less susceptible to correction than men. Messedaglia showed

17 German and Italian Female Criminals
Editors' note: Lombroso believed that masculinity characterized the faces of female criminals of all nationalities.
Source: Lombroso, *L'uomo delinquente*, edition 4.

that among Austrians, female repeat offenders are more common than onetime offenders, while for males the numbers are equal.

Women naturally have their own criminal nature. According to Messedaglia, in the Austrian Empire women often commit abortion, bigamy, calumny, aiding and abetting crime, arson, and theft, but they rarely commit murder and counterfeiting. In France, the most common crimes for women are infanticide, abortion, poisoning, murdering relatives, mistreatment of babies, domestic theft, and arson. In England, women are increasingly involved in forgery, perjury, calumny, and, to a lesser extent, murder (Guerry, Quetelet).[22]

Quetelet wisely observes that women's lower rate of crime has less to do with purity of spirit than with the more protected lives women lead, which provide fewer opportunities for aggression and moral laxity. In addition, women are weaker than men and so less likely to be murderers. Poorly educated, they are less able to commit crimes that involve writing or forgery. On the other hand, women equal and sometimes surpass men in crimes within the household; thus women commit 91 percent of poisonings and 60 percent of domestic thefts. For every 1,250 abortions and infanticides committed by women, only 260 are committed by men. Moreover, crimes of prostitution outnumber men's offenses against morality. In civilized countries and epochs, women's crime increases and starts catching up with that of men, revealing a much greater similarity between the sexes than might have been expected.

Moral Education

The importance of early moral education for preventing crime is clear from the statistics on the growth of illegitimacy in advanced nations. In Prussia, the percentage of criminal men without legal fathers has risen from 3 percent in 1858 to 6 percent today; for criminal women, from 5 percent to 8 percent. In France, 60 percent of the 8,006 minors arrested in 1864 were bastards or orphans, and 38 percent were offspring of prostitutes or criminals. In Austria in 1873, 10 percent of male criminals and 21 percent of female criminals were illegitimate (Messedaglia, op. cit.). In Hamburg, 30 percent of prostitutes are descended from bastards (Hugel, op. cit.). In Paris, one-fifth of urban-born prostitutes and one-eighth of prostitutes from the countryside were illegitimate (Parent-Duchatelet, op. cit.). During one year in New York, police arrested 534 illegitimate children and 222 foundlings.

In Italy, 36 percent of recidivists are illegitimate or foundlings. As everyone knows, the most common name among the Neapolitan *camorristi* is Esposito, and many thieves from Lombardy and Bologna have the surname Colombo. These are surnames commonly given to foundlings.[23] Thus the majority of foundlings who escape death abandon themselves to crime. One influence here could be heredity, and it is no doubt augmented by the difficulty of making a living. But the greatest influence is the sense of abandonment. With no family name to defend, no brake for the passions, no guide to offer treasures of affection and sacrifices that would help develop the noble instincts and suppress the ignoble, foundlings are easy prey to temptation.

Among orphans and foundlings convicted of crime, girls predominate. This is the case even if we exclude data on prostitution. Oettingen established the following proportion: while women make up only one-sixth of all criminals, they make up three-fourths of all criminals who were foundlings. Girls, weaker and more passionate than boys, have a greater need of family support and discipline to stay on the path of righteousness. They stray much more easily than boys, usually in the wanton direction of prostitution. Here heredity is a factor: daughters born from an illicit liaison are more likely to show lascivious tendencies and to commit serious crimes than legitimate girls.

Bad example has a worse influence on a minor than the mere fact of abandonment. How can a child defend himself from harm when it visits him in rosy garb and, worse, carries the authority of relatives or teachers? V., the sister of thieves, was brought up as a male by her relatives; she took on a masculine appearance and handled knives skillfully. When arrested on the streets for stealing a cloak, she blamed her relatives.

The murderers and thieves of the Cornu family were raised by criminal relatives. Among the five siblings, only the youngest girl resisted a life of crime. But her relatives initiated her regardless, forcing her to carry the head of one of their victims for six miles in her apron. She completely lost any sense of remorse and became the fiercest of the entire gang, gleefully subjecting her victims to the cruelest tortures.

Genitals

It is said that enlargement of the liver has an influence on crimes of revenge. Similarly, hypertrophy of the genitals is probably one cause of rapes, murders, and arson. Virgilio reckons that 1.3 percent of the population has oversized genitals. One woman, convicted for violence against the husband who forced her to witness his lustful acts, had a clitoris double the normal size. All criminals, particularly thieves and murderers, show precocious development of the genitals. Some female thieves exhibit tendencies to prostitution as early as six to eight years old. At sixty-two years old, the criminal Boggia had numerous and very lively spermatozoa (Mantegazza, *Sui testicoli*, 1863). I have noticed that all great poisoners are exceptionally fertile or libidinous, like the murderers and criminals of the Juke family.

Casper found complete hypospadias and crookedness of the member in a habitual pederast; Hoffman identified the latter characteristic in another pederast.[24] According to Tardieu, hermaphrodites and those without testicles frequently commit crimes against nature (*Sur l'identité*, 1870). For them, this is a physiological phenomenon. According to Westphal, men with an appetite for crimes against nature display a moral, if not physical, femininity and experience inverted sexual impulses. In such cases, who can say where guilt begins? Perhaps hermaphroditism and hypospadias, just like microcephaly, are the results of partially arrested development of the central nervous system and thus indications of a lack of moral sense. This may explain why such individuals commit many sexual crimes.

Hoffman mentions a pseudo-hermaphrodite midwife who raped her patients during examinations. I know of a pseudo-hermaphrodite whose jealousy over lovers was so violent as to resemble crime. I also know of a case of complete hypospadias, Raffaella Amato, who was thought to be a woman for twenty-four years; he murdered the person who revealed his true sex and his impure love of a woman. As Hoffmann notes (*Ein Fall v. Pseudoermafroditismus*, 1877, Wien), pseudo-hermaphroditic criminals lack beards and thick hair, and they present a feminine appearance.

Arrested moral development also accounts in part for the frequency of precocious pederasty in prison. Among the young men of the Generala Reformatory in Turin, 3 percent confessed to having had sexual

18 and 19 Trococephalic Rapist from the Romagna (2 Versions)
Editors' note: These two portraits of the same rapist from different editions of *Criminal Man* show how Lombroso sometimes reconfigured his illustrations to bolster his theory of the born criminal. The face of the rapist, which presents unremarkable features in the drawing from edition 1, takes on a more sinister physiognomy in the etching from edition 4.
Source: Version 1 from Lombroso, *L'uomo delinquente*, Edition 1. Photo courtesy of the National Library of Medicine. Version 2 from Lombroso, *L'uomo delinquente*, edition 4.

relations with women before the age of fifteen. Pederasty, which is no longer quite so frequent because of continual nighttime surveillance, used to be extremely common there. It still flourishes in other reformatories, particularly those of Bosco Marengo and Testona, where the boys sleep in dormitories. The younger inmates attest to the obscene behavior of nefarious gangs of older boys, sometimes numbering thirty to forty.

Prison love, says Courtelles, is so alluring to some criminals that they commit new offenses just to rejoin the delectable company. Prostitutes do the same.

Imitation

In many cases, imitation is the main cause of crime and madness. In 1868 and 1872, after newspapers began to report the abandonment of infants, the number of foundlings in Marseille rose to eight per day (Despine). In Bergamo, a short time after Verzeni's trial, two more women were strangled. In 1851, a few days after a woman in New York killed her husband, three other women did likewise.

19

Prevention of Crime

The illusion that education and prison are panaceas for crime simply falls apart if we agree that crime is inevitable and caused mainly by organic factors, upbringing, or the environment. From this perspective, the growth of crime seems irremediable. Yet if we accept the reality of recidivism, which prevails in all penitentiary systems, we reach a point of departure for new therapies for crime. Instead of trying to cure crime, we must try to prevent it by neutralizing its causes.

Civilization

We must develop innovative defenses against the new weapons offered to criminals by urbanization and the developments of modern life. The English scholar Hill (*Criminal Capitalists*, 1872), a citizen of a country scrupulous about personal liberties, proposes spying, surveillance, and —in the great cities—occasional suppression of criminals' safe houses.[25] Americans use a more practical institution: security companies that protect against crime. They have introduced a telegraph alarm that signals the entrance of an intruder by means of a mechanism placed at the head of the bed. The turn of a key opens a channel of communication with the telegraph office, which sends assistance immediately.

England and Austria have introduced groups of detectives and *Vertraute* [confidants], who are true front-line soldiers against crime. Some work alone, disguising their true mission with false names and professional identities; others work in small groups but unknown to one another. Paid according to the importance of the arrest, they are true crime hunters. They catch criminals in the act, using trains, the telegraph, and detailed prison records of physiognomy, including the malefactor's immutable gaze.[m] Above all, they take advantage of a practice that has

---

[m] In Vienna in 1872, 150 *Vertraute* arrested 4,958 criminals in nine months. Of these, 1,426 were thieves and 472 swindlers (Haybenz, *Wiener Verbrechen* in *Deut. Rundschau*, 1875).

yet to arrive in Italy, but which is very useful: the taking of prisoners' photographs, which are then filed alphabetically with a short biography.[n]

One excellent idea is cooperation among nations in the arrest of criminals by creating uniform extradition treaties, as suggested by Guillar. A sort of international police should exchange photographs of those who commit crimes abroad or who, at the end of a prison sentence, migrate to a nearby country. Such an international record office would facilitate criminal identification (*Riv. de Disc. Carcer. Bullet. Internation.*, 1876).[26]

The photograph, the telegraph (particularly on trains), and indeed railways themselves provide means of neutralizing the new weapons of crime introduced by civilization. Some time ago the Germans began to publish information on criminals' physical characteristics, like height, and even photographs of criminals on the fourth page of popular newspapers. In this way the press, which in the past has fostered blackmail, trickery, and calumny, becomes a bulwark of social defense.

We must protect the minors, orphans, foundlings, and abandoned children who swarm the streets of the great cities, which constitute seedbeds of crime. We must prevent these children from being drawn to crime because the problem only gets worse when they are later exposed to others in prison. We can do this by improving and expanding foundling homes, orphanages, and schools for the young and derelict. Such children should be placed under continual surveillance until puberty and beyond, surveillance that forms a substitute for the family that has been materially and morally lost.

---

[n] These photographs are divided into ten categories. A very precise index provides a brief description of the deeds of each individual. A second photograph of each person in the album is attached to the relevant page. The categories are as follows:

(1.) Murderers, brigands, and arsonists; (2.) Thieves who resort to violence; (3.) Pickpockets; (4.) Swindlers; (5.) Tricksters who lure rustics to the city (*Bauernfänger*); (6.) Forgers; (7.) Sex offenders; (8.) Prostitutes who maintain relations with criminals or who are suspected of other crimes; (9.) Persons sought by the police of other cities of the kingdom, whose photographs have been sent to the capital; (10.) Foreigners sought by police of other nations.

Reformatories

There are 7,685 reformatories and other places for incarceration of youth in France, 3,770 in Italy, 1,473 in Belgium, 161 in Holland, and 2,400 in America. Studies have already shown the reasons for the ineffectiveness of these institutions, which were established more from a benevolent impulse than from an understanding of criminal man.

Anything that increases reciprocal contact increases criminality. This applies particularly to members of that age group that is no longer young enough to be corrected and molded yet still inclines to imitation. They are naturally drawn to evil because of the violence of their passions, their minimal education, and their lack of judgment. Where will this tendency lead in the absence of the preventive influence of the family? Reformatories seem to be all the more damaging when the number of inmates exceeds one hundred (and attempting to keep the number below that figure is uneconomical). At that point incarcerated boys cease to be individuals. They become, in bureaucratic jargon, a number, and they cannot be kept under surveillance or reformed by even the most able director. In effect, even well-conceived rules and regulations collide with the material impossibility of reform.

Men of extraordinary philanthropy and educational insight—such as Demetz, Ducci, Rey, Obermayer, Spagliardi, and Martelli—head certain outstanding juvenile reformatories, and their personalities make up for a great deal. But a state cannot base its planning on the abilities of exceptional men. Statistics from these same institutions prove their limitations.

Everyone has heard inflated praise for the rural reformatory of Mettray, which in the past reduced recidivism from 75 percent to 3.8 percent (see Despine). But according to recent statistics of Du Camp, Mettray's recidivism rate has risen to 33.3 percent. He blames this increase on boys from Paris who hate the countryside. Whatever the case may be, recidivism has increased even in this model reformatory, where groups or families of sixteen or seventeen inmates live in little houses, each with its own director.

In America, with its many reformatories, up to 33 percent of all inmates are recidivists. Even Tocqueville, who praised American reformatories as models of penal reform, admitted that 300 out of 519 young offenders were recidivists. Nearly all of them, particularly the young women, were devoted to theft and wine. Among 85 girls released from reformatories, only 37 had a record of good conduct and a mere 11 had excellent conduct. Out of 427 boys, 85 had displayed good conduct and 41 excellent conduct.

The idea that reformatories protect the young from bad influences is an illusion. While they do impede contact with vagabonds and slightly depraved companions on the outside, they house a far worse crowd that has already entered the web of the criminal justice system. Thus the young are subjected to an atmosphere of concentrated vice at an age when they are particularly susceptible to crime. Part of the problem is that virtually no reformatory separates individuals into cells at night or enforces silence. Both policies are difficult to implement in these partly educational, partly industrial institutions, and furthermore the inmates cunningly circumvent them. Minors coming from the country-side, where it is difficult to associate with criminals, will find all they need in the way of bad influence and will be exposed to a learning pro-cess that would otherwise never have taken place.

I speak not theoretically but from experience, having examined de-linquent youth both outside and inside reformatories. It might be ob-jected that my observations at just one or two institutions prove noth-ing—that they could be exceptional cases. Unfortunately, new studies that I carried out with Dr. Raseri and the lawyer Frisetti-Tancredi at the Generala Reformatory undermine this objection. We found that 40 percent of the inmates had tattoos, a clear indication of boredom and immorality. But impossible as it sounds, there is worse: they speak in a special jargon. They refer to meat as *cucurda* or *scoss*, to soup as *boba* or *galba*, to water as *lussa*, to cigars as *lucertole* or *busche*, to tobacco as *moro*, *gangher*, or *fanfaer*, to the guards as *gafu* or *bau*, to disciplinari-ans as *tola*, to masturbation as *vecia*, to the lawyer as *lo scuro*, to one thousand lire as a *gamba*, to one hundred lire as a *caviglia*, to ten lire as a *busca*, and to pederasty as *una presa di tobacco dell'abate*. All of this shows the evil spirit that prevails in reformatories. Reformatory riots are famous, especially the one in 1875 where the most courageous boys almost succeeded in escaping en masse. It was organized by a gang of the strongest and most astute inmates, known as the "Society of the Rope" because their sign was a cord stretched across their fist.

Eight percent of the young people we questioned at the Generala Reformatory showed no sign whatsoever of repenting the error of their ways or even their most serious crimes, including stabbing and repeated theft. They said that if other members of their age group had money for amusements, then they had the same right even if the money was obtained by robbery. One even added that *no crime whatever could compensate them for the harm they suffered in the reformatories.*

I am therefore opposed to reformatories, except those which separate inmates by class, age, habits, and degree of criminality, and that have at least nighttime cells. I would allow commitment only of those whose poverty barred them from admission to military schools. Well-to-do parents who wish to intern their children should be charged a hefty daily fee proportional to their income.[27] All inmates should be individually observed by well-trained instructors who would set an inspiring example. And instead of issuing numerous unhelpful rules against the stream of evil, reformatories need to study ways of identifying and reforming delinquent youth.

None of the above occurs in Italian reformatories, where for many years financial considerations and governmental narrow-mindedness have made such improvements impossible. Instead, we find overcrowding and thus contact between the various groups, fraud perpetuated by parents, and a lack of individual cells and workshops. This being the case, I believe it would be better to send young offenders to stay with moral and energetic rural families, who would isolate them from big-city corruption.

The question of how to provide for the large number of delinquent orphans and abandoned minors will inevitably be raised. In such cases private charity, or, better yet, state welfare, needs to take new forms.[28] We must abandon both the pious path of alms and the violent militarism of prisons and barracks; above all, we must turn our backs on the abstract moral approach, which has little to say to those inclined to crime and pays little attention to primary education. Instead, we need institutions of industry and cooperation that encourage respect of property, the love of work, and the sense of beauty. It would be useful to replace reformatories with industrial schools.

Ragged Schools

A useful institution is the Ragged School which provides clothing, a bit of food, and education, as well as nightly shelter for orphans and poor boys abandoned on the streets. The first such institution, which cost the government nothing, was founded in 1818 for a few ragged boys from the streets of London. By 1869 no fewer than 23,498 branches with 3,897,000 students were spread throughout the poorest districts of England, organized by industry.[0] They form an important link between the upper and lower classes: in one such school, a Chancellor of England gave literacy lessons every Sunday for thirty-four years. Some boys attend voluntarily, and others are brought there by the police. More than a few Ragged School children support themselves with their own work. For example, in 1860, the 368 shoe-shine boys each brought back to the school six pennies a day. In a measure worthy of imitation, negligent parents are obliged to pay for their offspring's detention in English Ragged Schools at the rate of one penny for every shilling of their salary. This way, they keep better watch over their children than here in Italy, where parents consider internment a right.

[0] V. Bertrand, *Essai sur l'intempérance*, 1875.

20

Penal Policy

Alternatives to Incarceration

In cases where the crime of a youth requires serious punishment, short periods of incarceration must be avoided. Prisons are schools for crime of the most damaging type. We should substitute corporal punishment for prison sentences whenever this can be tolerated by the sometimes absurdly delicate sensibilities of our culture. Other alternative punishments, which can be meted out in gradations, include food rationing, cold showers, forced labor, house arrest, exile to inhospitable countries, and (least severely) fines. England and Norway have just reintroduced the whip for minor offences. Tissot finds whipping beneficial because it is inexpensive and can be finely calibrated (op. c., p. 270).

Cellular Prisons

If a prison sentence is really necessary because of the gravity of the crime, contact among inmates must be avoided at all costs. This requires individual cells; although such cells have no intrinsic power to reform the criminal, they reduce the possibility of contamination.[29] They also impede the buildup of that kind of pressure that obliges the criminal to compete with the vices of his companions. The overall result, at least in some countries, is a reduction of the number of recidivists.[p]

However, the advantages of the cellular system are offset by its great costs, which prevent even the richest states from using it on a large scale. (Of France's 396 provincial prisons, 74 have no cellular separation of inmates and 166 have only incomplete separation.) The cellular system prevents criminals from getting worse but does not in itself improve them.

Psychology Applied to Prison Science

To make the prison a place where criminals are cured, we cannot simply depend on solitary confinement. We need to forget about improving literacy, which is almost always counterproductive because it provides a means of communication within the prison and new methods for committing crime outside. Instead, we must institute gymnastics and other obligatory labor to develop the physical and mental energy that is nearly always lacking in criminals. Even more important is the need to impart an understanding of useful trades—such as shopkeeping, agriculture, and mechanics—as they do, for example, in Swiss prisons. To these could be added an appreciation of design and color, which develops a sensitivity to beauty that is in turn linked to an understanding of what is good.

Even more important than molding prisoners' minds is developing their feelings. Here we need to remember, as Sollohub says, that virtue cannot be artificially manufactured. It derives more from men's interests and passions than from logic; man can divest himself of existence but not of the emotions. All people, especially the unhappy, need to have an interest and purpose in life. One can be insensitive to danger, fear, and even physical pain, but not to vanity, to the need to distinguish oneself from others, and above all to the lure of freedom. Sermons and lectures on abstract morality are useless; instead, inmates become interested in what is morally right through material advantages such as the graduated reduction of punishment. Vanity can be used as a lever. Promising results have been obtained with prizes and marks for good

[p] Rates of recidivism among inmates in different types of prisons are as follows:

PLACE	TYPE OF INSTITUTION	PERCENT OF RECIDIVIST INMATES
Switzerland	Irish system (Basel)	15–19
	Collective/Auburn system (St. Gallo)	19
	Collective/Auburn (Lucerne)	45
	Collective/Auburn (Argovia-Women)	50
	Irish system (Argovia-Men)	28
Baden	Cellular system	20
Sweden/Norway	Cellular system	28–38

[We have cut material in this footnote about suicide, a topic already discussed in Chapter 12.—Eds.]

behavior that allow promotion into privileged groups with permission
to grow beards, wear normal clothes, decorate one's cell with plants and
pictures, receive visitors, work for money, and, finally, breathe the air
of liberty during short periods of release.

Liberty is the prisoner's dream and constant preoccupation. When
inmates see an open and secure road to the outside, they follow it immediately. For release from prison, they will do what is right. And because repeated actions become second nature, they might even get used
to it. For this reason, we must abolish the right to pardon, which grants
release not for the merits of the receiver but through the grace of the
powerful.[30]

We can cure and educate criminals by action rather than words and
by encouraging good behavior rather than spouting theories. Certainly
criminals require more energetic discipline than other groups. Light
punishments that require constant repetition are more harmful than a
few more energetic reprimands. This is why the Auburn Penitentiary,
which retained the whip, had lower mortality rates than the Philadelphia prison, which abolished it.[31] But exaggerated use of force also does
more harm than good. Force may crush criminals and, instead of correcting them, induce anger and hypocrisy.

Think of criminals as overgrown children.[q] Morally ill, they must be
cured with care rather than with severity. Endowed with vengeful and
prickly natures, they view even a light punishment as unjust torture.
Even rigorous enforcement of silence has been known to injure prisoner morale.

Work must be the purpose and pastime of every prison. It will
awaken inmates' drowsy energies and prepare them for productive labor
after release. Work is also an instrument of prison discipline, and it com-
pensates the state for the costs of maintaining the inmates.[r] But job as-

[q] Miss Carpenter, who dedicated her whole life to criminals, said "they are big children whom society must govern as it governs children." [Mary Carpenter (1807–77), an English penal reformer, established a series of youth reformatories. – Eds.]

[r] As far as I know, only the prisons of Charlestown, Chatham, Portsmouth, and Alipore almost
covered administrative expenses with income from prison labor. In 1871–72, Chatham and Portsmouth
even made a profit of £17,759 (Du Cane, 1872). According to Garelli, our own prisons cost the state 32
million lire and earn only 1.5 million (Lezioni sulla riforma delle carceri, 1862). According to Nicotera's
report on the years 1874–75 (Sul lavoro dei detenuti, 1876), 32,178 Italian prisoners did no work at all,
and 38,407 worked in a variety of crafts. A quarter were weavers, a sixth were shoemakers, a tenth
farmers, a twentieth carpenters, and a fortieth salt-workers. In 1871, the Italian state received a profit

signments must be tailored to the strength and abilities of the prisoner. A weak, semiskilled inmate who makes a notable effort should be rewarded with at least a sentence reduction if not money. Likewise, the strong should be rewarded for their physical efforts. We must abolish the miserable position of prison contractor, who employs only those who exhibit physical ability, ignoring moral improvement.[32] In some countries, the prison contractor is even able to award pardons.

Graded Systems

At this point all will see the advantage of the Irish system, where prisoners initially live in isolated cells with miserable clothes, a vegetarian diet, and the monotonous task of unraveling threads. This period does not exceed nine months and can be reduced to eight. The prisoner then proceeds to a second stage of working with others on a daily basis under careful surveillance. This work is divided into four categories, each more privileged than the last. Progress is rewarded with badges of merit, which can be obtained through good work, assiduous study, and good behavior; demotion occurs though the opposite. This is a superb way of making coarse minds appreciate virtue. In the lowest category the cell door stays open all day and the work is either unrewarded or rewarded with but a penny; after the prisoner earns fifty-four badges, he passes to the next stage, in which he earns more money, receives instruction, and is put into contact with the public, and so on.

The results of this system, at least in Ireland, appear to have been stupendous. Since 1854, when the system was introduced, there has been a noteworthy reduction in crime, as shown in table 13. The Irish system favors the application of criminal psychology by permitting gradual movement toward complete liberty and turning the prisoner's perpetual dream into an instrument of discipline and correction. Moreover, it offers a way to overcome public resistance to the early release of prisoners.

To the gradation of punishment we should add *individualization* of punishment.[33] Specific methods should be applied to each individual

---

of 1,632,530 lire from prison labor, and inmates received 0.473 lire per day in wages. These wages are higher than in Belgium (0.266 lire), Hungary (0.218 lire), and Austria (0.407 lire). In Austria, a prisoner can be obliged to pay for his detention. In Bern, he must earn at least 75 cents a day before he can keep a portion. In France, he keeps one-third of his earnings.

Table 13: Number of Prisoners in Ireland

YEAR	NUMBER OF INMATES	NUMBER OF NEW ADMISSIONS
1854	3,933	710
1857	2,614	426
1860	1,631	331
1869	1,325	191
1870	1,236	245

case, just as the doctor prescribes different diets and treatments for different patients.

Prisons for Incorrigibles

Even the best possible prison system cannot completely eliminate recidivism. We need to establish institutions for those criminals who demonstrate a tendency to crime from childhood and have become continual repeat offenders, especially if they have no family (or an immoral family) or if they themselves request such treatment. Those deemed incorrigible should also display all the physical and mental characteristics typical of the true criminal. They should be sentenced to life imprisonment by a jury made up of the prison's director and doctors, as well as judges and members of the public.

These wretches should be held under a regime that is gentler than the normal prison, ideally on an island. They should work in the countryside, which is good both for their health and the state, especially if they work in harvesting teams as in Sweden (*Kronarbets*), under military discipline as road builders, or in land reclamation. They should be allowed to receive letters from relatives and to have a few hours a day for personal business; but they should be released only if they show exceptional improvement.

This type of life imprisonment can replace the death sentence, which public opinion, rightly or wrongly, wants removed from the penal code. Modern criminal anthropologists also oppose the death penalty.[5] The

---

[5] I do not intend to engage in debate over this controversial question. Unfortunately, the death sentence is written into the book of nature, as well as that of history. The death of a small number of criminals

establishment of prisons for incorrigibles would free up cells for less serious criminals, allowing the implementation of the cellular system in regular prisons on a much larger scale.[34] Prisons for incorrigibles would offer a place to hold in perpetuity those recidivistic offenders and members of criminal organizations who most threaten society. Such institutions for incorrigibles would also give us a way to purge regular prisons of the gangs that, by glorifying vice, stymie efforts at correction. Furthermore, they would gradually reduce that not inconsiderable proportion of criminality that stems from hereditary factors and the bad example of relatives. There would be a return to the process of natural selection that has produced not only our race but the very justice that gradually came to prevail with the elimination of the most violent.

The expense of maintaining prisoners for life would be significant, for many would refuse to work; and yet it would be lower than that incurred by society as a result of more crimes and more trials. The latter often cost fabulous sums. Thomson has calculated that 458 Scottish recidivists cost £132,000, of which £86,000 alone went into their trials—a truly princely sum!

Whether biologically abnormal or not, recidivists are harmful to themselves and their offspring. Life imprisonment for incorrigible criminals is not more unjust than internment of the insane in mental hospitals—and possibly more useful.

Criminal Insane Asylums

Another institution that I believe can balance the need for humane treatment and the demands of public security is the criminal insane asylum. We can debate theories of punishment endlessly, but at least all agree that many criminals are insane. In their case, liberty is dangerous, but prison would be unjust. Presently, we provide poorly for these cases with half measures that threaten both morality and public order.

---

is nothing compared with the slaughter of numerous young and vigorous soldiers on the battlefield. As the most secure method of social defense, it should certainly be permitted among uncivilized peoples, where prisons have little effect. But among civilized peoples that delicate sentiment which calls for the abolition of the death sentence is too widespread among the respectable classes to oppose. This is all the more so because in those rare cases in which an offender undergoes the death sentence with courage or even boldness, he encourages imitative crimes and creates a cult following among the lower classes. [The remainder of this footnote, dealing with other legal issues, has been cut. —Eds.]

20 Drawing by Sighetti Showing his Execution
Editors' note: In this example of prisoner art, the soldier Gustavo Seghetti
drew the scene of his future execution after absolution by a priest. Although
Lombroso ridiculed Seghetti's drawing as proof of criminals' vanity and
insensitivity to pain, he also admired the artistic composition, which was framed
by trees on each side and a balcony of spectators at the top.
Source: Lombroso, *Der Verbrecher* (*Atlas*). Photo courtesy of the Lloyd Sealy
Library, John Jay College of Criminal Justice.

Every day produces new cases in which it is difficult to decide whether the criminal impulse began in mental illness or inner perversity. Legislation fails to provide a middle road for judicial sentencing. Lacking an appropriate institution or even a relevant article of law, judges rule unjustly or imprudently.[t] When madness is obvious, they acquit or reduce the punishment. But just as often they convict, even applying the death sentence in cases in which the insanity is so obscure that psychiatrists alone can detect it.

Many will object that if we make allowance for the possibility of mental disease, we might end up punishing no one. But similar objections were once raised against those who opposed burning witches. In the case of insane criminals, one might repeat Montaigne's wise phrase that "in any case, roasting people alive is too high a price to pay for a doubt."[35] However, I am not advocating a sentimental pity that might threaten the well-being of others. Criminal insane asylums are more a precautionary than humanitarian measure. Although many insane criminals are now sentenced to prison, many are also imprudently acquitted. The new institutions would prevent dangerous people from reentering society before they are entirely cured.

---

[t] Article 95 of the criminal code provides for "custody" of up to twenty years in cases of criminal insanity, but this custody in fact constitutes punishment rather than treatment. Because appropriate establishments are lacking, judges in northern Italy hardly ever apply this provision to adults. [Lombroso implies that judges in northern Italy were more humane than those in the south, who did not hesitate to sentence insane criminals to custodial punishment. — Eds.]

Appendix 1

GIOVANNI CAVAGLIÀ
A Suicidal Murderer with Cranial Meningitis;
A Study by Dr. Fiore and Prof. Lombroso
(Laboratory of Legal Medicine and Psychiatry, Turin)[u]

On the night of 18 February of this year, the prisoner Giovanni Cavaglià, nicknamed *Il Fusil* [the Pistol], committed suicide in the jail of
Turin. A bricklayer from Santena, he was charged with murder for the
purpose of robbery.

Cavaglià was one of the most perfect examples of *criminal man*.
A youth aged twenty-four years, he displayed medium height (1.60
meters), a robust constitution, strong muscles, and a large thorax (with
a circumference of eighty-five centimeters). He had abundant, thick,
black hair; soft down on his face instead of a beard; a large snub nose
that pointed slightly to the right; and elongated jug ears [see figure 5.
—Eds.]. Employing threats and fraud, he had forced his brother to hand
over an inheritance of over one thousand lire; within a few days, he had
squandered it on dinners with his companions. When he was eighteen
years old, he wounded two of his aunts with a reaping hook because
they reproached him for bad behavior. As is customary among real
criminals, he boasted of his wicked actions and bragged to his friends
that *he had been in prison and did not fear the law*.

In August of last year, he was the guest of Gambro, a man of low
reputation. They seemed extremely intimate, even sharing a bed. Five
days later, a putrefying cadaver was found in a closet of the house of this
same Gambro. Naked and with the knees bound tightly with towels,
the dead body had eleven wounds lacerating and bruising the head and
several fractures of the skull. It was the dead body of Francesco Gam-

[u] All the facts for this study were drawn from the trial transcript given to us by the Honorable Torti
and from communications with the examining judge, the Honorable Millio.

21 and 22 Cavaglià's Water Jug
Editors' note: Lombroso believed
that criminals resembled "primitive" peoples in their preference
for expressing themselves in
pictures rather than words.
On this water jug, the criminal
Cavaglià depicts his murder of
Gambro and his intention to
hang himself on the hundredth
day of his imprisonment.
Source: Photo courtesy of the
Museo Lombroso (Turin).

bro, who had been murdered five days earlier, according to the autopsy report.

Once Cavaglià realized that he could not deny the crime, he began with singular indifference to recount the deed in great detail. During the interrogation, he denied factors that might have increased his punishment. Thus he claimed that he hit Gambro during a quarrel and not to rob him. The trial record, however, proves that they did not have a row, but that he murdered Gambro for profit at the moment when he was undressing for bed. During his confession, Cavaglià sometimes wept. Rather than the murder, putting Gambro in the closet was what he lamented, as if this was the most blameworthy aspect of his crime!

But Cavaglià had already decided to kill himself, on a precise day and time, with the same indifference with which he had murdered Gambro. Rather than upsetting him, the idea of suicide made him smile and perhaps explained his tranquil demeanor. In his cell, he patiently unraveled the covering on his mattress and skillfully wove the threads into a noose. On a piece of paper, he embroidered the following words: "I have spent 100 days in this cell, 100 daytimes and 100 nighttimes." Afterward he decorated his water jug with the story of his last days. Confessing both murder and suicide, he told the story in a mixture of words and pictures in a way that evoked the customs of savage peoples, whose language is too poor to clearly express complicated ideas.

At 11:30 the same night, the guards found Cavaglià swinging against the wall, hanging from a cord suspended from the window bars. They immediately cut the cord and laid him on the bed, but the body of Cavaglià was already a cadaver. He was clothed but without shoes. His skin was already cold and his limbs were becoming rigid, although his neck was still flexible. His penis, of medium size, lay flaccid on his abdomen and appeared wet from sperm.

The most interesting results of the autopsy, which was done immediately, concerned the brain and skull. The exterior brain covering, with its swollen blood vessels, was slightly dense. On both sides of Rolando's fissure, it adhered laterally to the underlying tissue for two centimeters; this adhesion, which was not new, also extended toward the back of the cranium for three centimeters. The circumvolutions of the brain appeared regular, although large, flat, and lacking deep furrows. The middle lobe of the cerebellum was enlarged; the left hemisphere was larger than the right and was cut in two by a small furrow running from the front to the back.

The skull was round and slightly asymmetrical, with delicate regular lines and a forehead flattened toward the top. The sutures were marked and notched. The bone was so thin that the skull resembled that of an old man. Parts of the forehead and occipital bones were nearly transparent, especially around the orbital arch and the median occipital fossetta. The bone measured only four millimeters on the forehead humps and less than one millimeter on the median occipital fossetta. The jaw was square, with large ascending apophesis and strong outlines of the muscles.

This case is important from many points of view, but primarily to prove the influence of heredity. Cavaglià's father, an alcoholic and spendthrift, wasted 134 lire on one dinner and died by drowning, probably by suicide. His mother had goiter and threw herself in a well after eight years of a desperately unhappy marriage. Cavaglià himself was an alcoholic, careless with money, goitrous, and suicidal.

Even more important, Cavaglià exhibited the anomalies and cerebral irregularities of the criminal man. These same features appear even more frequently in the insane. Nevertheless, his laziness, useless squandering of money, and drunkenness are best interpreted as signs of criminality rather than insanity.

Cavaglià also exhibited another characteristic of the criminal man: insensitivity toward himself and others. Before committing suicide, he cynically chewed tobacco, ate a large meal, and carefully drew the hieroglyphic designs on his water jug. This revealed his true nature as someone able to premeditate cruelty toward himself and others with cold cunning.

It is impossible not to connect his intellectual and moral perversion with the physical anomalies of his brain.

This relationship between psychological impairment and cerebral defects does not erase the need for punishment. Instead, it confirms that prisons for incorrigibles and asylums for the criminally insane should be brought from the margins to the center of our justice system.

New instruments like the ophthalmoscope and esthesiometer, and physiological tests of the muscles and urine, are promising to reveal the causes and symptoms of criminal behavior. When such tests verify cerebral anomalies in a defendant, he should not be held responsible even for crimes that disgust the public, but sent to a criminal insane asylum. But when tests cannot verify that a cerebral anomaly has caused a crime, then the law—which is based on tradition and public opinion—requires that he be classified as a real criminal type. Prisons for incorrigibles would be appropriate for these cases.

Appendix 2

A Medical Examination of Parricide and Insanity
by Prof. L Perotti and C. Lombroso

A young man Giovanni aged twenty-nine from Verolengo killed his father in April 1877. During a quarrel, he hit him with a reaping hook for economic gain. According to the mayor's report, Giovanni had a reputation for laziness and alcohol. He had continual rows with his father, whom he wanted to worm money out of for his whims. Neither he nor his parents had ever been diagnosed as insane.

After more questioning, however, the mayor admitted that the family had once included a woman of weak mind and a cousin who was a semicretin. Some of the townspeople considered Giovanni to be mad, while others thought him only lazy because he spent entire nights on the banks of the Po river without even fishing. His father tried to make him enter an insane asylum, but he refused.

Interview

PROFESSOR LOMBROSO: Has your head ever felt heavy?

YOUNG MAN: Yessir, especially in the months of June, July, and August, and particularly in the summer of 1875, when I took medicine. Then I fled from the house.

PL: Did you kill your father?

YM: I don't know; to tell the truth, I don't know.

PL: Are you crazy?

YM: (laughs and shrugs his shoulders) I believe myself to be wise.

PL: Why did you run away from home and rip your clothes?

YM: To be able to climb trees looking for dry wood. Otherwise, it was my father's fault. He was good in his youth, but became wicked when I was twenty. He taught me to fish when I was twelve to fourteen years old. (repeatedly jerks his head backwards) By the age of eighteen or twenty, I no longer listened to my father because I wanted to do my work well. My father didn't love me anymore; he always wanted me to do as he did. I left to fish and returned home *with a head heavy with water*.

PL: Why did you have water in your head?

YM: Because I stood so long in the Po river that water penetrated my body.

PL: Did your neighbors dislike you?

YM: My neighbors were malicious and said that I had *stinking breath*.

PL: What did you eat?

YM: Polenta, sometimes moldy and acidic.

PL: Did you have vertigo? Did the fields seem to spin around?

YM: I fell one time while harvesting cornstalks at the end of August and beginning of September. I think that my nose bled, and then I got up.

PL: The doctor said that you had a *liver rash*.

YM: Once when I had pain, they said it was *liver rash*; another time they peeled the skin off my face.

PL: Have you ever felt like a rock was in your stomach?

YM: Yes, but not this year or last year, but in 1875. One of my brothers had a similar problem and took purgatives several times a year.

PL: Do you ever have headaches?

YM: No, I feel lightheaded, *fresh as a rose*. I am often hungry, but if I eat even a bit of bread I feel a knot in my stomach.

PL: Did you kill your father?

YM: I would have to say yes, although really I'm not sure. I know that he was behind me stirring the polenta and that we argued. But I don't know if I hit him hard enough to kill him. (laughs)

PL: Do you regret it?

YM: No; it was my father who was threatening me. One holiday when he was going fishing, I overheard him say that I must disappear. They planned to lock me in a room where *I couldn't do my affairs* [go to the bathroom]. My father told my mother to give me all of the medicine, but out of goodness she gave me only one half. She threw away the rest, which became hard *as plaster on a wall*.

PL: Why didn't you get angry at the doctor rather than your father? It was the doctor who wrote the prescription.

YM: Oh no! The doctor was as good as my mother, or perhaps a little less good; he did it to please my father.

PL: Can't you see that you are alive and the others are dead?

YM: But it was *for love* that I ran away.

PL: Why were you angry at the parish priest?

YM: I wasn't angry at the priest but at the assistant priest, who once said from the pulpit that I had *stinking breath*.

PL: But it's not evil to have stinking breath.

YM: The assistant priest also told my neighbors that they didn't have to talk to me because of my *bad breath*.

DR. PEROTTI: Were you persuaded that your father instigated the authorities to make you disappear?

YM: Yessir.

DP: For what reason?

YM: They made sure to fill my stomach with filth so that I couldn't escape and would die. I've already said several times that things would go badly if I didn't kill them—my father and mother—and send them to the other world.

PL: And where will the person go who has killed them?

YM: To prison.

PL: And afterward?

YM: I will get out.

PL: But they could hang you!

YM: I know someone who killed a woman and served only five days in prison.

PL: But if you receive the death penalty, where will you go?

YM: I don't know.

PL: Will you go to hell?

YM: Those who repent are saved.

PL: How will you repent?

YM: I have already paid in my past life and by going to prison. If they let me out I'll leave.

Summary

From the evidence, we must conclude that the young man has been mentally ill for many years. More specifically, he exhibits a persecution complex accompanied by acoustic hallucinations and impulsive mania probably caused by pellagra.

Despite the protestations of the mayor, our physical and psychological examination demonstrated preexisting mental illness. Symptoms that differentiated him from normal men included defects of the skin and skull, anomalies of the brain and the extremities, and an unusual tactile insensitivity to pain.

Furthermore, his writings and conversation demonstrate a medical history of insanity. Both exhibit a preoccupation with supposed persecution by his father, which shows a loss of feelings and preexisting hallucinations. Unlike common criminals, he does not hide his crime or his insanity. Rather than pretending to show remorse, he instead laughs at the mention of his fathers' murder.

Etiology

Our interview and other data indicate the causes of his mental illness. He had insane relatives, and, in fact, the anomalies in his joints, ears, and skull indicate a hereditary form of mental illness.

He also ate moldy polenta for many years, something that recent studies have incontrovertibly shown to cause pellagra. This disease affects the brain, causing impulsive behavior and a complete loss of affections.[v]

Therefore, the young man was probably mentally ill for the past three years and most severely at the moment at which he committed parricide. He continues to exhibit a chronic state of madness.

[v] Lombroso, *Studi clinici sulla pellagra*, 1872; *Sui veleni del mais*, 1878, Bologna.

EDITION THREE

1884

Editors' Foreword

The third edition of *Criminal Man*, published in 1884, reconfigures the second edition of six years earlier and adds significant new concepts. Employing the phrase *born criminal* for the first time, Lombroso analyzes the craniums, physiognomy, and psychology of this type of offender. New chapters trace "the embryology of crime" to plants, animals, primitive peoples, and finally children, systematically establishing the Darwinist framework of criminal anthropology. Drawing on the writings of botanists and biologists, Lombroso seeks to demonstrate that crime is a natural and eternal aspect of human society by tracing its origins to organisms whose behavior is instinctual, not willed. Through bizarre descriptions of carnivorous plants, murderous bees, and thievish cats, he paints a vivid picture of the criminal roots of civilized society.

Moving up the evolutionary scale, Lombroso draws parallels between the psychology of what he terms "savages" and modern born criminals, who favor violence in the case of men and prostitution in the case of women. Yet he concedes that even primitive peoples became less violent over time and that their code of revenge evolved into more humane forms of punishment. Lombroso tells a fascinating but sometimes contradictory story that locates the origins of modern monogamous marriage in primitive licentiousness and traces the roots of contemporary penal law to ancient customs of vendetta and theft.

Lombroso ends this exploration of the roots of atavism with a chapter on the inherent criminality of children. His surprising equation of children with savages draws on the widespread belief among late-nineteenth-century scientists that individuals replicate the evolution of the species in their development from fetus to adulthood. Children thus share abnormal physical traits and psychological tendencies toward lying, cruelty, vanity, and obscenity with both primitive peoples and born criminals. Through good upbringing and moral education, most children lose these atavistic traits and become normal adults.

Lombroso uses his chapter on children to introduce the concept of moral insanity—the condition of an individual who, like a child, is rational but lacks a sense of morality. Widely accepted among nine-teenth-century psychiatrists, the concept of moral insanity assumes a prominent place in Lombroso's theory in this third edition. He demon-strates resemblances between the morally insane and born criminals in their cranial deformations, abnormal physiognomy, abundant tattoos, peculiar sexuality, and psychological anomalies. By the end of this edi-tion, moral insanity takes its place beside atavism as a major determi-nant of criminal behavior.

In another notable addition, Lombroso includes a chapter with pho-tographs to bolster his claim of a distinctive criminal physiognomy. He expects that readers, by contemplating a series of multiple photographs, will be able to spot the born criminals among the rogues' gallery (see figure 28). To assist in this identification process, he points out the born criminal's physical anomalies such as large jaws, a shifty gaze, and jug ears. Lombroso's excursion into photography forms part of a broader movement on his part toward using pictures—of criminal craniums, physiognomy, tattoos, and artwork—in the successive editions, culmi-nating in the separate *Atlas* of illustrations appended to the final edi-tion.

Lombroso ends the third edition with an admission that he must listen to his critics and add disease to atavism as a cause of physical and psychological anomalies, and therefore of crime. Unlike atavism, which constitutes an inborn condition, disease may attack the brain or nervous system of an individual at any time from conception to death. Lombroso finds the idea of arrested development more plausible than that of degeneration as an explanation for the way in which illness may lead to psychological disorders—including moral insanity—and finally criminality. However, although he gives disease a place in the etiology of crime, Lombroso nevertheless concludes this edition with a ringing defense of atavism as the outstanding cause of innate criminality and the most enduring characteristic of the born criminal.

Author's Preface

This work constitutes the first attempt to understand criminal man in an anthropological way. In earlier editions, its lacunae were greater than its discoveries, and it was often based on unreliable statistics. I was too preoccupied with the born criminal, whom I came across frequently in prisons, and I ignored the less obvious but much more frequent forms of the criminal who is closer to normal man. Although incomplete on all counts, the second edition had greater success than it deserved and more recognition than any scholar could expect in this country, which is apathetic toward scientific ideals. In particular, our law schools, with their traditional emphasis on rhetoric and metaphysics, have resisted naturalistic theories of crime.[1]

But like the humble insect that spreads fertile pollen, this book has germinated a seed that has born fruit. It has given rise to a new school of thought, led in Germany by Liszt and Kraepelin, Benedikt, Flesch, and Baer; in Spain by Pulido and Zanches; in Russia by Drill, Kowaleski, and Danillo; in France by Manouvrier, Tarde, le Bon, Lacassagne, and above all Maxime Du Camp; in Belgium by Heger, Albrecht, and Prins; in Hungary by Lenhossek, and Schwartze; in England by Clarck, Maudsley, Mayhew, and Thomson; in Italy by Laschi, Pugliese, Berenini, De Renzis, Riccardi, Cantarano, Majno, Sergi, Tammeo, Seppilli, Tamburini, Tamassia, Cosenza, Barzillai, Marro, Virgilio, Morselli, Garofalo, Puglia, Ferri and above all Beltrani-Scalia.[2] All of these scholars have pointed out and often filled the many lacunae of my original conception and have developed legal applications for my ideas.

Thanks to them, for the first time I have distinguished between the born criminal and the occasional criminal, the madman and the alcoholic. Thanks to them I have been able to extend my inquiries to primordial forms of crime among savages, children, and animals. By expanding my studies of the anatomy and physiology of criminals to include anomalies in sensitivity, in the vascular system, and in reflex reactions, I have been able to explain the paradoxical appearance of normality among those who had been abnormal from birth. And thus I have been able to demonstrate the relationship between morbidity and atavism in such individuals, fusing the concepts of born criminality and moral insanity.

If my work found good fortune in its advocates and collaborators, this was no less the case in its adversaries, venerable as they are for both wisdom and honesty (such as Calucci senior, Messedaglia, Oettingen, Brusca, Bucellati, Orano, Guerini, Lucchini, and Ungern-Sternberg).[3] It would be irreverent to ignore their criticisms.

These distinguished figures have said to me: "You too often draw deductions from isolated facts; if for example someone has an asymmetric cranium or a jug ear, you immediately assume the presence of madness or criminality, even though there is no clear relationship between the two things." Now, physical anomalies do not simply appear for no reason, especially in cases of arrested development. Although regressive anomalies tend to appear in clusters, experience has shown that individuals with even a single anomaly may display profound moral maladjustment. I have not made such deductions a priori but after finding abnormalities in a large proportion of criminals compared with normal individuals. I consider isolated anomalies to be but a clue, a hint, like a musical note, which cannot form a melody unless found together with other physical or moral notes. The fact that someone has committed a crime or is under investigation for one should count for something. In this edition, I have taken great care to establish the ensemble of anomalies that constitute the criminal type, which the reader can verify for himself by having the facts at hand.

Having seen how critics particularly appreciated those parts of the second edition where the documentation of my assertions was most complete, I have expanded this procedure in the third edition. Being more concerned about the benefits of information than the reader's possible boredom, I have provided the maximum number of proofs for each conclusion. For example, a photograph of the three criminals from Ravenna reenacting their crime, which I obtained through semi-official channels, caused a recent sensation.[4] Yet I could give enough other evidence of the vanity of criminals to erase doubt even among my most malevolent critics.

Nevertheless, many object, "How can you speak of the criminal type when your own findings show that 60 percent of criminals are indistinguishable from normal men?" Apart from the fact that 40 percent is a proportion that deserves consideration, there is an almost imperceptible boundary between the two categories, even in animal and plant species. This is more so the case among humans, where individual variability increases in direct relation to the progress of civilization, so that the complete criminal type almost disappears.[5] Among one hundred Italians, for example, it would be hard to find five who perfectly represent the Italian "type." Most represent only a partial type, but their Italian characteristics suddenly jump into relief in a comparison with foreigners. It would not occur to anyone to deny the existence of the Italian type, and even less the Mongol type.

Like Turati (*Archivio*, III), I find it strange that this new school of criminal anthropology is accused of including members from outside the field of law.[6] Those who complain that doctors have created forensic medicine or that anthropologists have applied their discipline to legal questions forget that scientists created the chemical industry and mechanics invented hydraulics.

More than a few jurists have reproved me for reducing criminal law to a mere chapter of psychiatry and of subverting the entire system of courts and prisons! There is a little bit of truth to this because the preventive measures I advocate will keep occasional criminals out of the legal system.[7] But nothing will change for born criminals under my proposals, except that life sentences will increase the sense of community safety. These will be served in institutions for incorrigibles that will be prisons in everything but name.

To the serious objections leveled by rigorous scholars we must add one that seems imprecise, intangible, and less worthy of discussion— and yet, because it has become a popular "legend," is also the most dangerous. The legend claims that I wish to undermine criminal law, giving liberty to all rascals and undermining the principle of free will.[a] I would respond that while we may deny individual responsibility, for it we substitute social responsibility, which is much more exacting and severe. While we may reject the legal responsibility of criminals, we do so not to reduce their punishment, but rather to increase the length of their detention.

[a] It is curious that a similar legend was created against Beccaria. [In his famous eighteenth-century treatise, Beccaria strongly supported preventive measures—education, fair and comprehensible law codes, and swift and certain punishment—to reduce rates of crime; he also recommended mild punishments for less serious crimes. For Lombroso, it appears curious that both he and Beccaria face accusations of being soft on crime because Lombroso's positivist school made its reputation by attacking most other tenets of the classical school associated with Beccaria.—Eds.]

This study can have broad application even in legal doctrine. My theory replaces the ecclesiastical notion of sin with the law of social defense, and the idea of free will with that of the dangerousness of the criminal. It thus offers a stable foundation for a new philosophy of criminal punishment.

21

Crime and Inferior Organisms

Crime among Plants and Animals

Espinas applied the study of zoology to the sociological sciences, Cognetti to economics, and Houzeau to psychology. Therefore it was natural for me to make zoology the foundation of the new school of criminal anthropology, which relies so much on the modern theory of evolution. My first publication to do so was quickly followed by an article by Lacassagne and then a full-scale study by Ferri.[b]

Who is unfamiliar with the fascinating descriptions of insectivorous plants by Darwin, Drude, Rees, and Will?[c] No fewer than eleven species of droseraceae, four of saracenaceae, five of nepenthaceae, eleven of utricolaria, not to mention the *Cephalotus follicularis*, commit true murders of insects. When an insect, however small, lands on the leafy disc of the drosera (and indeed this seems not to happen by chance, since certain leaf secretions attract it), it is immediately enfolded and compressed by numerous tentacles, about 192 per leaf, which surround it in ten seconds. They release the victim once dead and partially digested, thanks

---

[b] Brehm, *La vita degli animali*, Torino, 1872–1875; Pierquin, *Traité de la folie des animaux et de ses rapports avec celle de l'homme et les législations actuelles*, Paris, 1839; Büchner, *La vie psychique des bêtes*, Paris, 1881; Boccardo, *L'animale e l'uomo*. Prefazione al vii volume della *Bibl. Dell'Economista*, ii serie, Torino, 1882; Lioy, *In montagna*, Bologna, 1880; Darwin, *Sulla origine della specie per elezione naturale*, Torino, 1875; Id., *L'origine dell'uomo e la scelta in rapporto col sesso*, Torino, 1882; Lombroso, *Archivio di psichiatria*, Torino, 1881, vol. ii. Fasc. iv, *Il delitto negli animali*; Lessona, *Dell'esterna conformazione del cavallo*, Torino, 1829; Rodet, *Notions élémentaires de vétérinaire militaire*, Paris, 1847; Houzeau, *Études sur les facultés mentales des animaux comparées à celle de l'homme*, Mons, 1872, 2 vol.; Espinas, *Des sociétés animales, étude de psychologie comparée*, Paris, 1878, ii edit.; Lacassagne, *De la criminalité chez les animaux*, nella *Revue scientifique*, 14 January 1882; Id., Lyon, 1882, p. 32; Rousse, *Instinct des animaux*, Paris, 1835; Roberts, *Les animaux domestiques*, Bruxelles, 1837; Id., *Les animaux sauvages*, 1831; Romanes, *Animal intelligence*, Londra, 1882; Camerano, *Scelta sessuale degli anfibi anuri*, 1882; and Ferri, *Dell'omicidio*, 1884.

[c] Darwin, *Insectivorous plants*, 1880; D. O. Drude, *Die Insektenfressenders Pflanzen*, nell'*Handbuch der Botanik herausgegeben*, von Prof. Schenk, Breslau, 1881; F. Cohn, *Beiträge zur Biologie der Pflanzen*, Bd. ii, Heft. i; and Rees und Will, *Botanische Zeitung*, 1875.

to an acid that is similar to our own pepsin. According to Darwin, this acid causes the tentacles to move in the same way that reflexes work in animals. The *Genlisea ornata* catches insects in exactly the same way as fishermen use traps for eels.

These examples show the dawn of criminality. They establish that premeditation, ambush, killing for greed, and, to a certain extent, decision-making (refusal to kill insects that are too small) are derived completely from histology or the microstructure of organic tissue — and not from an alleged will.

The comparison of human crimes to those of lower organisms becomes much clearer when we consider the zoological world. For murder alone Ferri (o. c.) has been able to distinguish no fewer than twenty-two types among animals, many analogous to crimes in our own penal code. The first type, killing for food, is so common that it is not worth giving examples; it corresponds to human crimes rooted in hunger or indigence. Among horses, bulls, and deer, fighting and killing for control of the group are equivalent to human crimes of ambition. For example, the *Gorilla gina* have only one leader, an adult male, who proves his strength by killing male rivals. Moreover, Tarpan wild horses, found in Russia, fight tenaciously for leadership (Ferri, o. c.).

Killing for Sexual Access to Females. Relentless struggles by males to dominate females and satisfy the reproductive instinct are common among all animals that reproduce sexually. This struggle has given rise to the Darwinian theory of sexual selection (Ferri, o. c.). With love comes jealousy and hatred of rivals. Bitter tensions are fought out, and even the timid become aggressive. Lions, tigers, jaguars, and leopards are particularly formidable in sexual struggles. The deer of Virginia are so violent that they spend all day fighting, and sometimes two adversaries get their horns so entangled that they cannot separate and thus die.

Killing in Defense. Bees do not admit foreign bees into their hives. When an apiarist placed a newcomer among the bees that guarded the entry of a hive, the guards fell on the intruder, killed it, and threw it out.

Killing for greed. The wars undertaken by Amazonian ants in order to obtain the highest possible number of larvae of slave ants, which they then raise in their own nests, are ferocious and deadly. Mexican honey

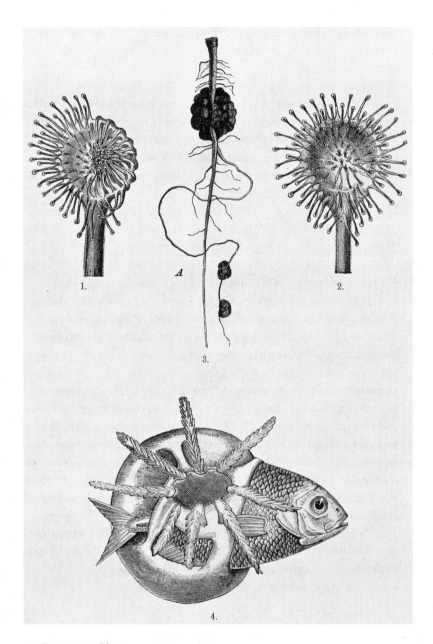

23 Carnivorous Plants

Editors' note: For Lombroso, crime was a natural phenomenon whose atavistic roots can be traced back to aggressive and immoral behavior in animals and even insectivorous plants.

Source: Lombroso, *L'uomo delinquente*, edition 5 *(Atlante)*. Photo courtesy of the New York Library of Medicine.

ants, to give another example, will eviscerate their companions to eat the honey they have accumulated.

Killing in War. Everyone knows that many animals, even those of the same species, go to war with one another, not for survival but to kill for the sake of killing. Sometimes these struggles are external wars, which arise when nests are in close proximity; but civil wars, too, can break out, during which a faction seeks to eject its adversaries from the nest. At the level of personal battle, the struggles are cruel and intense. Sometimes prisoners are taken to the victors' nest and put to work as slaves. When the surrounding terrain is strewn with corpses, each side carries away its dead. Among termites, a special caste of warriors is dedicated entirely to war.

Simple Cannibalism. Notwithstanding the famous saying to the contrary, wolves do eat each other.[8] When voles fall into a trap, they devour one another; and the same is true of mice. Frog tadpoles eat each other; and pike are known for their voracious cannibalism. Two crickets placed in a cage will consume one another.

Cannibalism with Infanticide and Parricide. The study of animals contradicts sentimental cant about bonds of blood and innate maternal and filial affection, as noted by Houzeau and Ferri (op. c.). The female crocodile will sometimes eat those of her young that do not learn how to swim. In many animal species, as in barbarous tribes, physical imperfections give rise to shame and contempt. I once observed a hen abandon the nest, leading away healthy offspring and leaving the deformed chicks to die.

When female Amazonian monkeys tire of carrying their young, they occasionally eat their heads or dash them against a tree. Cannibalism with parricide occurs among wolves, "whose young often eat each other, and sometimes even their mother" (Brehm).[9]

Universality of Crime

Can we seriously declare these animal killings to be crimes? Is *crime* the correct label for organized theft among monkeys, domestic theft among cats and monkeys, abduction of minors among ants, and child abandonment among cuckoos who lay their eggs in other birds' nests? Are these actions crimes or simply the necessary effects of heredity—an organic structure imposed by competition for survival, by sexual selection, by the social necessity to quell discord, or by the need for food among voracious animals? These examples underline the absurdity of a concept of justice based on free will and explain why we find criminal tendencies among all creatures, even within the most civilized races.[10] Ancient people were probably right to convict and punish animals that behaved dangerously or mutilated sacred objects.[d]

Cranial Abnormalities in Animals. Among domesticated and docile species of animals, criminal tendencies are usually the result of congenital cerebral alterations. This is how veterinarians explain the fact that some military horses resist discipline, defy commands, and retain for months a lively memory of anyone who has struck them. Such horses, if they are stallions, are aggressive and proud, with a tendency to kick their fellow beasts on the sly; if they are gelded, they are voracious and bad-tempered. Veterinarians are so certain that these depraved instincts are related to cerebral anomalies that they diagnose problem cases by studying the form of the skull, looking for a narrow, receding forehead or noting a harelip.

Killing for Love. Impulsive crimes among animals, as among humans, are frequently prompted by love. Usually prudent, elephants in love can become enraged over the tiniest matter. Among polygamous fowl, the need to reproduce so overwhelms other needs and feelings that they seem to become deaf and blind, and even attack men (Brehm, 329). Even adultery is not absent in the animal realm, where it is often followed by murder of the original mate. The apparently innocent female dove is often adulterous, jealous, and cruel to her mate, hiding food

---

[d] Mosaic law (Exodus, xxi) prescribed the stoning of any ox that killed a man, and if this occurred more than once, its owner. In medieval times, animals that killed or harmed crops were convicted (Lacassagne, op. cit.). Under Francis I, however, these animals were assigned a lawyer to defend them. In 1356, a sow that had eaten a child was condemned to death at the hand of the executioner at Falaise. The bishop of Autun excommunicated rats that had gnawed sacred objects. Benoist Saint-Prix listed eighty similar excommunications beginning with that of an ass and ending with that of a cricket. [We have cut some further examples of animal trials.—Eds.]

under her wings. A male dove, if his mate is removed from the dove-cote, abducts the female mate of another dove.

Agglomerations. Here we note another parallel in the cause of crime among animals and men: the stimulus to crime by large groups. Thus sodomy, which never occurs in small stables, becomes common in large herds (Scarcey). Unsatisfied love leads to crimes against nature among sociable animals such as horses and cattle, wasps and bees, and domestic chickens. In Egypt, Lessona observed frequent acts of sodomy among male donkeys that were separated at night from the females.

Organized Crime among Animals. The germ of that truly human be-havior, organized crime, can be observed among domestic animals and in creatures that live in large groups. Admiral Sullivan told Darwin about having taken a young English stallion and eight mares to the Falkland Islands. There they encountered two combative wild stallions, each leading a small herd of horses. Each wild stallion tried individu-ally to defeat the English stallion and steal his mares. Unable to succeed alone, they joined forces and won as a team.

Theft. The monkey is a true pickpocket. While being petted or stroked, it reaches into pockets, steals without being noticed, and hides the booty in curtains or bedclothes, much as servants do (Brehm). Al-though the bee is the most diligent of creatures, bit by bit some swarms become thievish, eventually turning into habitual criminals.

Alcoholism. The use of alcohol or other substances that irritate the nerve cells is as common a cause of crime among animals as among men. Intel-ligent creatures like the thieving bees mentioned above enjoy these sub-stances most. Like humans, bees quickly acquire a taste for drink, which causes them to become excited, inebriated, and incapable of work.

Abyssinian shepherds noticed that after their goats ate perfumed berries from certain mountain bushes, they became livelier, frolicked among the rocks, and sometimes got onto fierce fights. When a shep-herd tasted the berry, he discovered it to be coffee (Houszeau, 11).

Physiognomy of Animals. The most ferocious animals are physiognomi-cally close to the born criminal; tigers and hyenas have bloodshot gray

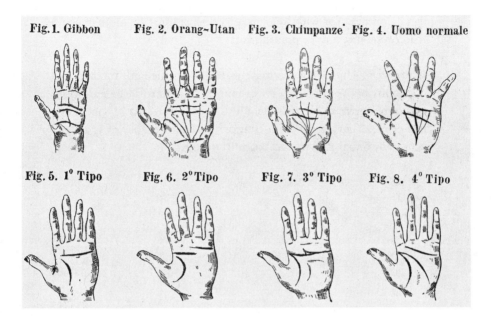

Fig. 1. Gibbon   **Fig. 2. Orang-Utan**   **Fig. 3. Chimpanze'**   **Fig. 4. Uomo normale**

Fig. 5. 1° Tipo   **Fig. 6. 2° Tipo**   **Fig. 7. 3° Tipo**   **Fig. 8. 4° Tipo**

24 Anomalies of the Palm in Monkeys, a Normal Man, and Criminals
Editors' note: Lombroso used an evolutionary framework to argue that biological anomalies in criminals resembled the physical traits of animals. Here he compares the palms of apes and monkeys (nos. 1–3), a normal man (no. 4), and criminals (nos. 5–8).
Source: Lombroso, *L'uomo delinquente*, Edition 5 (*Atlante*). Photo courtesy of the New York Library of Medicine.

eyes identical to those of assassins. Brehm notes that "birds of prey, including hawks, have a short curving beak with a sharp tooth on the upper jaw and *an eye socket filled with blood*" (as Tamassia found in criminals). It is impossible to study the physiognomy of insects because of the immobility of their faces; however, the strength of their jaws shows that they are carnivorous predators.

Punishment and Penal Substitutes. Punishment modifies some but not all criminalistic habits among animals. We attempt to instill morality in animals, using both harsh and subtle means to gain the best result with the least effort. With domestic animals, the best results are often obtained through kind treatment rather than torture and through indirect measures that appeal to their vanity or greed. Ferri has already lucidly proven that with humans, penal substitutes are more effective than brutal methods of punishment.

However much one tries to make distinctions, one finds fundamental continuity between criminality in animals and humans; the transitions are so minute as to be invisible. How, then, can we avoid concluding that crime, from its first manifestations in the lower species, is a product of any organism's physical constitution?[e]

[e] See Vignoli, T. *Della legge fondamentale dell'intelligenza nel regno animale*. Dumolard, Bibl. Intern., Milan, 1880.

22

Crime and Prostitution among Savages

In studying crime among savages, our earliest human ancestors, we face the same difficulties that we encountered in the animal kingdom. Here, as with animals, crime is not the exception but almost a general rule. This is why so few have understood the behavior of savages to be criminal or recognized in it the origin of modern criminality.[11]

Crimes of Lust

Immodesty. Ancient and primitive peoples had almost no sense of shame and found nothing offensive about copulation. Spartan girls frequently appeared nude in public among young men (Plutarch).

During the festival of Phallefore in Greece, girls formed a procession carrying an enormous phallus rising out of a sacred vessel and decorated with flowers. Made of fig wood covered with red leather, it was inserted by the Itifalli priests between their thighs so that it seemed to emerge from their bodies (Aristophanes, v. 537).

Civil Prostitution. Originally, marriage did not exist, and prostitution was the rule.[12] The Honomas often exchange female partners, and the women are obliged to offer themselves to relatives (Hartmann). Among the savages of California, there is no such word as *marriage*; jealousy occurs only when a woman gives herself to someone in another tribe.

Tibetan girls wear rings around their necks—gifts from their sexual partners. The more rings they have, the more famous are their weddings. Among the Andamans and also in some Californian tribes, women belong to all the men of the tribe, and to resist even one of them would be a grave crime. Sometimes temporary unions are formed, especially during pregnancy. These end when women start nursing, but it was from such temporary unions that marriage eventually evolved.

Hospitable Prostitution. Primitive people viewed prostitution as one of the obligations of hospitality. The custom of offering one's wife to a guest has been found in Ceylon, Greenland, the Canary Islands, and Tahiti; in these lands, for a visitor to refuse a girl was considered offensive. One chief told a scandalized priest that he could not imagine a religion that prohibited an innocent pleasure that provides a service to the country by producing a new being (Radiquet, o.c.).

Male Bestiality and Prostitution. There is worse. In some lands, men practice sodomy without the slightest sign of embarrassment. According to Bourgarel (*Des races de l'Océanie*, II, 389), men in New Caledonia gather together for lustful purposes. Ancient Mexicans held gatherings where male prostitutes dressed as women (Diaz, *Histoire de la conquête de la Nouvelle Espagne*, II, 594). The Normans, according to a complaint made in 1117 by the Abbot of Clairvaux, replicated biblical Sodom by practicing pederasty wherever they went.

The terms *far la corna, far becco*, and *cervo—kèren* in Hebrew, *hornerträger* in German—are used to taunt husbands.[13] Such phrases lead one to suspect that our ancestors shamelessly had sexual intercourse with animals, as men do today in Finland with reindeer when they are away from women for several months at a time.

Religious Prostitution. Religion sanctified and perpetuated ancient forms of promiscuity through sacred prostitution, which was widespread in antiquity and can still be found today in India. Cheops financed his pyramid mainly by prostituting his daughters, who in turn built their own pyramid by requiring each lover to furnish a stone (Herodotus, II, c. 126). Even now large numbers of prostitutes in India ply their trade in temples to which they contribute their profits.

Polyandry. To get from promiscuous love to monogamy, man passed through various stages of sexual behavior that today would be considered crimes, including polyandry, incest, and—worse—rape and abduction.

Among the Toda, a woman becomes the wife of all her husband's younger brothers and of the husbands of his sisters. The eldest brother is considered the father of the first male child, the second brother of the second male child, and so on down the line (Shortt, o. c., 240). Similarly, Singalese women are wives to all the brothers in a single family. Here we see promiscuity moving from the tribe to the narrower confines of the family. The family can thus be viewed as a stepping-stone to morality since it denies the broader group its former right of access to all women.

Abduction and Rape. The custom that more than any other pushed promiscuous love in the direction of monogamous marriage was abduction followed by violent rape. In Australia, the groom still waits for a woman behind a hedge, hits her with a club, transports her to his hut, and then rapes her (Dumont D'Urville, 11, 357). Or, helped by his friends, he enters her dwelling, frightens and beats her relatives, and overpowers the girl with the aid of his truncheon (Letourneau). This type of abduction was practiced by the Arawaks, the Fuegians, and the ancient Russians, Lithuanians, Poles, and Chinese. Traces of it remained in the well-known nuptial rites of the ancient Romans (De Gubernatis, *Riti nuziali*, Milan, 1878).

In a later period, relatives who lost their female property received financial compensation. When women became property through sale or abduction, society began to regulate their purchase and access, right down to such details as the making of loans and payment of restitution to their fathers.

Homicide[f]

A disproportionate increase in population relative to the food supply is a grave and continual danger for primitive peoples. This explains their attitudes toward killing and its high incidence among them. They murder one another with impunity for religious reasons or merely for glory.

Abortion. A type of preventive murder, abortion is unknown among animals in its conscious and therefore criminal form. But it is common among primitive peoples. Among the Tasmanians, women prefer to become mothers only after several years of marriage to keep their bodies fresh. For this reason, they provoke abortion with very archaic

[f] I have summarized here the wonderful chapters by Ferri in *Omicidio* and of Letourneau, *Sociologie*, p. 145 and p. 132 et seq. [Lombroso's inconsistent use of quotation marks in this section make it impossible to identify the exact contributions of Ferri and Letourneau. We have therefore eliminated the quotation marks.—Eds.]

means such as repeated blows to the stomach. In New Caledonia, eating green bananas with the aim of inducing abortion happens frequently and carries no blame.

Infanticide. Among savages, infanticide is more common than abortion because the latter is more dangerous, more difficult, and requires more foresight. As a rule, the firstborn will escape infanticide. Moreover, girls are killed more often than boys (Letourneau, p. 134). The Australian has few scruples about killing an infant if it is a girl or if the delivery is laborious. As Marco Polo recounted, infanticide constituted a form of violent birth control in Japan and China. Southern African tribesmen use their children as bait in lion traps, and in certain regions of Australia, people kill babies to use their fat on fishhooks. A pregnant Australian savage told Grant that she intended to kill her child to avoid the labor of feeding him.

Killing of the Elderly, Women, and the Infirm. In the animal world, overpopulation results in the abandonment and killing of those unable to work. Savage tribes have inherited this instinct, so that children and wise men continue to murder the infirm with the full consent of those sacrificed, even where the need no longer exists.

In the past, the Sioux and other tribes of the Missouri Valley habitually abandoned those who were too old or infirm to keep up with the camp during the hunt. The Itonamos of South America strangle their sick members. During famines, the savages of Tiera del Fuego kill not only their elderly parents but all old women, whom they view as less useful than domestic animals. According to Suetonius, the Romans left their sick slaves on an island in the Tiber, and the Spartans exposed their deformed infants.

Murder for Sacrifice. Human sacrifice was practiced by almost all barbarous peoples, even the Aryans, Greeks, Latins, and Celts. This practice reached the height of cruelty among the black tribes of Guinea and in certain ancient civilizations of the Americas like Mexico.

The Bible mentions human sacrifices among the Jews, including the killing of Isaac and the daughter of Jephtah. As Spencer has shown, circumcision among Jews is a vestige of human sacrifice reduced to an absolute minimum (*Revue philosophique*, 1878).

25 Types of African Criminals
Editors' note: Lombroso held that these African faces were "savage" and therefore models for the atavistic born criminal.
Source: Lombroso, *Der Verbrecher* (*Atlas*). Photo courtesy of the Lloyd Sealy Library, John Jay College of Criminal Justice.

Murder for Brutal Wickedness. While most murders are caused by a motive, such as religious belief, jealousy, or revenge, others have no clear cause. Called murders "with no apparent motive" by Romagnosi, they are rare among civilized peoples except in abnormal or pathological cases. However, they are much more frequent among savages, who have less regard for human life, especially the lives of subjects ruled by chiefs and priests (Ferri, o. c.).

In Asia, the Turkmen are true predators. They pounce on peasants, enjoying their deaths, and kill their own women, children, and servants for the slightest reasons. The indigenous tribes of the Americas are ferocious, as exemplified by the infamous ways in which the Redskins and Brazilian Indians make prisoners suffer.

Murder for Blood Feud. In former times, the desire for admiration, together with fear of ridicule, turned blood feud into a veritable religion. Tribal opinion made blood vendetta a duty. Tribes applauded any man who revenged the killing of his relative.

Cannibalism. Cannibalism, the highest grade of human ferocity, was born of the need for nutrition. It was perpetuated by religion, frenzy of combat, and horrendous greed, especially on islands. Its grotesqueness erases the distinction between man and beast (Ferri).

De Mortillet has recently contested the assertion that cannibalism was practiced in prehistoric Europe. But paleontologists from Spring onwards have gathered so much evidence that few such doubts remain. This evidence, summarized most recently by De Nadaillac (op. cit. 11, 206 et seq.), leads to the conclusion that "there is no race, no people, no important geographical group of humanity that has not practiced cannibalism or human sacrifice. Black, brown, yellow, and white; European, Asiatic, African, American, Australian, and Polynesian; Aryans, Semites, and Hamites have all, without exception, sacrificed and devoured their fellow men. Remnants of broken and gnawed bones speak in the absence of historical documents."

There is even a tradition of cannibalism among the superior races, Mongol and white. The Bible refers to cannibalism (Deuteronomy, ch. VIII, v. 53; Jeremiah, ch. XIX, v. 9), as does Homer's *Odyssey* (ch. IX, v. 287–293, c. V, v. 116–124). According to Strabo, the ancient Irish—who were more savage than the neighboring Britons—considered it an honor to eat their parents after they died (*Geogr.*, I. iv).

Religious cannibalism and human sacrifice reached the acme of cruelty in Mexico. They placed the victim on the sacrificial stone, and the chief priest rapidly opened the victim's chest with a stone knife. He plucked out his heart, offering it to the sun, or less often, the moon. Only elderly high priests were allowed to eat it. The body was then thrown down the steps to the praying masses, who devoured it.

Cannibalism is an inveterate habit among the Fijians, who love human flesh so much that they can give no higher praise to a dish than to say it is as tender as a dead man. Furthermore, the delicacy of their taste is such that they disdain the flesh of whites, prefer the flesh of women to that of men, and consider the forearm and thigh the tastiest parts. Only men are allowed to eat human flesh, women being deemed unworthy of such a treat.

Psychologically and legally, then, primitive man was the complete opposite of civilized humanity. Yet because nothing is immobile in nature, we can discern a double evolutionary process among savages. First, they gradually become less ferocious, and second, they develop the germs of moral sentiment and the institutions of justice. We can observe this in the historical evolution of murder (Ferri).

Although my discussion of homicides has contrasted primitive with civilized man, even among savages the most repugnant forms of murder tend to decrease in number and disappear. Homicide motivated by the desire for fame or by simple brutality has become less frequent. The same is true of cannibalism motivated by war or greed. Religiously inspired cannibalism persisted longer, but it gradually dwindled from consumption of the whole body to consumption of certain parts. Then cannibalism was replaced by animal sacrifice and finally by sacrifice of representative figures (among the Mexicans, the image of the god Quetzalcoatl, made of blood and flour; among the Chinese, paper figurines burned in ceremony; among the Romans, statuettes known as *oscilla*). The Catholic wafer, as Waitz and Vogt have noted, is the ultimate, unconscious vestige of cannibalism (Ferri).

Crimes against Custom: The True Crimes of Savages

Now we can define the nature of crime among primitives: they punish few immoral acts, with most violations not being recognized as crimes until later in history. That which for us is a crime often seemed nothing to savages. On the other hand, acts that seemed terrible to them are insignificant to us. These are offenses against custom and religion, which, given the general tendency of religion to perpetuate customs, end up being one and the same.

Thus in Australia the flesh of the emu is prohibited to all but the elders and chiefs. If a young and honest man, falling prey to temptation, eats an emu after killing it, he is seized by such remorse and melancholy that he begs to be punished (Stuart, *Histoire universelle des voyages*, 43). Similar guilt is felt by the Hindu who drinks beer reserved for the Brahmin; by the Jew who eats pork; and by the Chinese woman who feels no shame at prostitution but is embarrassed to show her feet.

Savage or primitive peoples, because they have a lower level of mental activity than civilized peoples, react violently against novelty. Thus they look with deep suspicion on inventors of new things and initiators of new ideas.

23

Origins of Punishment[g]

Punishments were initially acts of personal retaliation and only later became public measures to suppress lawbreaking. At the beginning, primitive people had no concept of crime and therefore none of punishment to protect society. They not only recognized the legitimacy of revenge but considered it a duty; these acts of vendetta constituted the first stage of punishment.[14] Groups rebelled against the strongest and most dominant members, and if the rebels triumphed, their crime became an instrument of morality. Rather than bringing justice, however, revenge involved brutality and, what is worse, varied in strength according to the vulnerability of the victim and his friends. In homicide cases, revenge demanded death or retaliation ("a tooth for a tooth" from Deuter., 19), while for purse-snatching it demanded mutilation of the fingers or return of stolen objects. This type of simplistic revenge still appears among our own children who are not content unless they retaliate against slaps proportionately. Indeed, they often hit the other person exactly where they were hit themselves.

Punishment of Homicide and Theft

Since human life has little value among primitive peoples, killing provokes almost no reaction. It is considered a grave crime only when

[g] Alb. Du Boys, *Histoire du droit criminel des peuples anciens*, Paris, 1845; Id., *Histoire du droit criminel des peuples modernes*, tom. i, Paris, 1854; T. Thonissen, *Etudes sur l'organisation judiciare, le droit pénal et la procédure criminelle de l'Egypte ancienne*, Bruxelles, 1868; Id., *Études sur l'histoire du droit criminel des peuples anciens, Inde Brahminique, Egypte, Indée*, 2 vol., Bruxelles, 1869; T. Tissot, *Le droit pénal*, ii édit., tom. i, ch. xxvii, Paris, 1880; Fr. V. Holtzendorff, *Handbuch des Deutsch. Strafrecht*, B. I, § 9 e segg., Berlin, 1871; P. Del Giudice, *La vendetta nel diritto longobardo*, nell'*Archivio storico-lombardo*, 1875, p. 217; A. Pertile, *Storia del diritto italiano*, vol. v, Padova, 1877; A. Andreozzi, *Le leggi penali degli antichi Cinesi*, Firenze, 1878; Fulci, *Sull'evoluzione dell diritto penale*, 1883; Puglia, *Sull'evoluzione del diritto penale*, Messina, 1882; Ferri, *Sull'omicidio*, Bologna, 1883; Wiarda, *Geschichte und ausleg. der Salische Geschetze*, 1801; Bar, *Deutsch. Strafrecht*, 1882; Zastrow, *Zur Strafrecht Stell. der Sclaven*, 1878; and Waitz, *Deutsch. Verfassungsgeschichte*, 1880.

perpetrated by members of another tribe or against a chief or priest, who represent God on earth. Conversely, homicide is never considered serious if committed by the chief or the priest. After killing a slave, a Kimbunda expiated his crime by sacrificing an ox, the blood of which cleansed the spilling of the slave's blood. For the death of a lower-caste Sudra, a Brahmin had to pay a fine no more than that for the killing of a cat, and he could steal the money.

With the growth of despotism and armies, chiefs turned themselves into proprietors of the whole tribe. Thefts from chiefs became a major crime, as did adultery with a chief's wife. Thus the notion of punishment was first applied by chiefs, only later being extended to the full tribe. Primitive people viewed theft as more serious than murder because the latter did not endanger the property of the chief. In Africa, the Kafri punish theft with fines and even with death. The same applies to adultery, which is regarded as a form of theft. On the other hand, human life is barely protected at all. "A husband may kill his wife for the pettiest of reasons" (Letourneau).

Transformation of Punishment: Duels

In the beginning, vendetta and punishment were intertwined. A chain reaction of vendettas would have led to the extinction of the tribe; thus vendettas had to be regulated. They became less ferocious and somewhat systematic, a sort of rite that mattered enormously to primitive peoples.

Early punishment assumed the form of a struggle: a duel or even the semblance of battle.[h] For such events, tribes gave advance notice and provided adversaries with weapons. At a signal, the adversaries drew their arrows; after a certain number of deaths, they shook hands and finished up with a dance (Hovelaque, p. 108). Alternatively, the combatants faced each other in rows and threw javelins. The first legalized punishments took the form of duels or battles involving many people against the person considered guilty. These struggles later developed into legal rituals.

[h] It is worth noting that Vanicek, o. c., derives *bellum* [war] from *duellum* [duel].

Amends and Restitution

As human nature became more refined and life and property assumed more value, material compensation began to replace personal violence. Compensation followed the same norms as the vendetta, varying according to the social class of the offender and the offended.

Among the Ashanti, thieves were subject to a fine. If the thief could not be found, his relatives or village had to pay. In Tibet, too, relatives were responsible for a thief's fine. The Koran specifies payment of twenty camels for a murder. In the Bible, he who steals an ox has to give back five if he has already killed it, two if it is still alive. Anyone striking a pregnant woman pays compensation to her husband; if the assailant kills her, he himself is killed. A man who rapes a virgin is fined fifty coins and is forced to marry her (Deut., XIII).

Self-interest and necessity explain changes in punishment. Commercial peoples had to renounce old-fashioned pillage so that trade would not be interrupted. Little by little, they became less violent.

The main force behind the evolution of punishment was the growth of wealth and the possession of property, which encouraged the calculation of compensation in proportion to the level of harm or loss. This in turn increased the power of chiefs, who had to determine these levels and settle on the punishment. Once compensation had replaced vendetta and murder, the intervention of a third party representing legal authority was a natural next step. Eventually the new system was extended to all crimes, which were now adjudicated according to the concept of measurable harm.

Religion

In addition to the chief, those most interested in repressing crime have been the Priest, Koen, Tabib, and Nigrata—and of course witch doctors and fortune-tellers. Religious leaders, sometimes in alliance with chiefs, focused on sins and violations of sacred rituals that we would consider today simply superstitions. In addition, they used every disaster, death, and season of the year as a pretext for punishing some sin, identifying a victim, and persecuting real or imagined culprits, in this way increasing their power. In the midst of so much injustice, sometimes they even caught a real criminal.

Medieval punishments included trials of fire, water, the rod, and the stake. In the trial of cold water, the accused had to jump into a lake that had been blessed with offerings. He was considered guilty if he floated and innocent if he sank, in which case he would be pulled out by ropes. Servants were commonly subjected to the trial of boiling water, in which the accused was forced to grab something from the bottom of a pan of water on the fire. He was found innocent if his arm came out unharmed, something that occurred very rarely.

According to Du Boys (o. c.), murder among the Germans gradually diminished thanks to the cult of the goddess Freya. During her festivals, enemies and adversaries declared a truce, a period of peace that was also extended to the weak—women and children—by the strong. These truces encouraged the spontaneous organization of fairs and markets, which became permanent as safety increased. Anyone who broke Freya's truce was put to death. Thus religion, intertwined with commerce, contributed to the diminution of crime.

In sum, religion gradually extended its mission from protecting the self-interest of the few to protecting the interest of many. While encouraging superstition, it also established the ideas of morality, guilt, and punishment. By restraining physical force, it enabled the human race to shape itself into a true social organism.

Conclusion

Crime gave birth to morality and punishment—an audacious conclusion, but one that becomes plausible when we consider the following factors. It was vendetta that first encouraged the punishment of crime. Incest, polyandry, and polygamy eventually caused sexual promiscuity to disappear. The origins of these sexual practices lay less in a scarcity of women than in the chief's predilection for a given female. Rape became a crime against the wife of a chief before it was a crime against other women. Punishment for theft started to appear after conquests by strong chiefs who wanted to conserve their possessions. Thus justice had its roots in the punishment of theft and rape.

The impure origins of law serve to explain its unequal application from person to person and, worse, from class to class. Judges and law professors proclaim the universality of the laws of justice, yet poor men —unless by accident or pardon—enjoy no real justice compared with the rich, who find ways of escaping or reducing their sentences. The origins of justice often lay in the caprice of kings or priests or in popular anger, a fact that helps explain the perpetuation of the absurd and atavistic practice of royal pardon. It also explains why we are not yet liberated from the jury, another institution that is atavistic in its ineffectiveness and corruptibility.[15]

24

Moral Insanity and Crime among Children

The seeds of moral insanity and criminality are found in man's early life. This fact has escaped most observers—aside from Moreau, Perez, and Bain—precisely because of its simplicity and ubiquity. Just as the fetus shows deformities that in the adult would be considered monstrosities, so, too, does the child lack moral sense.[16] When adults possess the following impetuous passions of children, psychiatrists call them moral madmen, and we call them born criminals.[17]

Anger. Perez has shown the frequency and precocity of rage in children. "In the first two months the infant demonstrates true excesses of rage by moving his eyebrows and hands when he is to be bathed or has an object taken away. By the age of one, the strength of his anger causes him to hit people and to break plates and throw them at people he does not like. Children resemble savages, like the Dakota Indians, who become wild when they kill bison, or the Fijians, who are extremely excitable for short periods."[i] Anger is thus a human emotion present from infancy which can be controlled but not extinguished.

Desire for Revenge. Children frequently show a desire for revenge. Even at the age of seven or eight months, a child may scratch his nurse when she withdraws her breast and return the slaps he receives. I knew a boy, slightly backward and hydrocephalic, who became irritated at the slightest scolding right up to the age of six years old. If he could hit the person who had irritated him, he felt better; if not, he shouted and bit his own hands, just as caged bears do when threatened from the outside.

Jealousy. Fits of jealousy are common among all animals and occur in even the calmest men: one day jealousy may explode like a fire, and

---

[i] Perez, *Psychologie de l'enfant*, ii ed., 1882.

another it may hide among the embers. Children who become jealous through love or possessiveness react violently. Most children prefer breaking a toy to giving it to someone else. A three-year-old boy evinced great pleasure at the idea of a new sister, but when he saw her being cuddled asked whether she would die soon. I have seen similar sentiments develop in the first month, even in the first days after birth, as in the case of an infant girl who refused to suckle if she saw her twin sister at the other breast. They had to be separated.

Lying. Montaigne has observed that lies and obstinacy grow in proportion to children's bodies. Along the same lines, Bourdin writes that all children are liars, particularly foundlings, who lie for fun. Children may lie to obtain that which has been prohibited or to avoid punishment. Sometimes they lie to obtain more candy, pretending not to have eaten it already, or to give the impression of great pain after they fall down. Or they lie out of laziness (for example, not wanting to go somewhere, they pretend to be ill). I myself remember using this method to avoid a particularly boring arithmetic lesson—I was about five or six years old—and successfully tricking the doctor called to examine me. At the age of three or four, children begin to lie out of fear of being punished, provoked by the manner in which we interrogate them and await their reply. And often they simply lie for fun or to satisfy their vanity.

One reason children lie is their impulsiveness and undeveloped or incomplete sense of the truth. Like savages and criminals, they easily alter the truth, dissimulating in ways that we would not believe possible among more mature individuals. A few days after overhearing her adoptive mother describe a scandalous crime reported in the newspaper, a girl of five or six pretended to have been raped by her father and grandfather. During the subsequent trial, a medical examination showed the rape to be pure fantasy. The girl's only motive had been to make the newspapers write about her (Bourdin, o. c.).

Lack of Moral Sense. Children lack any sense of morality in the first months and even the first year of their lives. Good and evil for them is that which is permitted or prohibited by their parents. On their own, they have no sense of what is bad; only when they have been punished and told what is wrong do they start to develop a sense of justice and property. The first sign of a moral sense comes when they register a certain tone of their parents' voice, understand the meaning of reprimand, and begin to obey out of fear or habit.

Self-interest, strong feeling, the development of the intelligence, and reflection teach the child the difference between good and evil. The most effective means of instruction are kindness, good examples, and inculcation of fear of reprimand. These approaches help mold the child's moral conscience. He will be more or less inclined to develop it according to his own capacity and circumstances (Perez, o. c.).

Lack of Affection.   Children also lack any innate sense of affection. They are attracted by pretty faces or by things that give them pleasure, including small animals that can be tormented, and they dislike things that are unfamiliar or frightening. But they do not feel affection, and even at the age of seven, children can forget a mother whom they seemed to adore. One child of four lost his closest friend. The friend's father took him in his arms, but the child immediately pushed away and said, "Now that Pietro is dead, you'll give me his horse and his tambourine, won't you?"

When you believe they love you, you discover that children are just like prostitutes. They adore you for the benefits they receive and stop loving when they have no further hope of gain. There are some exceptions: you my angel were among them, with your sweet lively eyes that still look out at me from the grave; you seemed only to enjoy the pleasure felt by others![18] But the exceptional cases, like the few noble savages, prove the rule. Precocious emergence of affection in children prevents the proper development of a healthy physical constitution. Thus affectionate children are all too often taken from us. Unfortunately!

Cruelty.   La Fontaine, that skilled student of human nature, declared of childhood: "This age has no pity."[19] Cruelty, in fact, is one of the most common characteristics of children. There is hardly a boy who does not bully those who are weaker, as Broussais has observed (*Irritation et folie*, p. 20). In general, the child prefers bad to good. He is more cruel than kind because he experiences strong emotions and has a sense of unlimited power. Thus we see him deriving great pleasure from breaking inanimate objects. He loves stabbing animals, drowning flies, hitting his dog, and suffocating sparrows. Sometimes children dip cockroaches in hot wax to make them into kites or dress them as soldiers, prolonging their agony for months on end. One authority tells us that it was a lad who invented wicker cages, traps, and nets for butter-flies, while another reports having seen mischievous rascals batting a poor guinea pig back and forth with their rackets (Blatin, *Nos cruautés envers les animaux*, p. 414).

Indolence and Laziness. Another characteristic that the child shares with the born criminal is intellectual laziness. Children flee from continuous work and from any task that fails to appeal to them. Sometimes their intellectual laziness is exacerbated by a true muscular laziness, as when they wet their beds to avoid getting up. Yet paradoxically, they also love motion and new toys. They like to be surrounded by friends, although they are not particularly affectionate, and to make a racket. Their revels often occur, as meteorologists have noted, the day before a thunder-storm and in the presence of elderly people, cretins, or anyone weaker than themselves. As with criminals, liveliness coexists with their essen-tial laziness; children, too, become active only when they can gain plea-sure easily and quickly.

Jargon. Like criminals, children develop a type of jargon, using hand signs in order to avoid detection by adults. I have noticed such jargon in many schools among boys aged seven to twelve.

Vanity. Excessive vanity—the foundation of megalomania and inborn criminality—is one of children's outstanding characteristics. In two families in which the parents taught the principles of equality, the chil-dren displayed all the pretensions of class snobbery. At the age of three, they treated the poor with disdain, while at the same time they behaved respectfully to the children of rich and titled families. One sees the same tendency among animals, as when a household dog torments strays.

Alcoholism, Gambling, and Obscene Tendencies. Upper-class people have no idea of children's passion for alcohol. But at lower levels of society, even suckling infants drink wines and liqueurs with relish, and their parents laugh to see them collapse from inebriation (Moreau, p. 115). Many prisoners have told me that they were given drink as children. The passion for gambling is also characteristic of children, but it is not necessary to dwell on it.

There is no lack of obscene tendencies among children three or four years old, however incomplete the development of their sexual organs. In every nursery school I have visited, the teacher has pointed out one or two male children who are dedicated masturbators. Anomalous and monstrous sexual tendencies, like criminal behavior, begin in childhood.

These facts provide a natural explanation for why moral insanity originates spontaneously among savages and children: it flows from lack of self-control.[20] Education alone cannot rescue children from moral insanity. As Campagne writes in his *Folie raisonnante*, children who are insensitive to both praise and blame may be afflicted with moral insanity. Indifferent to the difficulties their behavior causes for their families, they remain undisciplined, careless, and riotous. Laziness, masturbation, self-indulgence, and overexcitement are typical of that particular exaltation which is known as moral insanity, "reasoning madness," or madness without delirium. Laziness in these children is coupled with unlimited temerity; at the slightest reprimand they shout, smash everything in sight, and strike anyone within reach.

Because moral insanity is both a trait of children and the equivalent of criminality, we can see why great criminals reveal their tendencies at an early age. Starting in childhood, Lafarge took great pleasure in strangling chickens. By the age of nine, the brigand B. was a thief and rapist; at the age of eleven, Lasagna nailed oxen's tongues to benches. Again demonstrating the links between childhood and criminality, Roussel observes in his wonderful *Inchiesta sui minorenni* (1883) that large numbers of French prostitutes are under the age of legal maturity; for example, 1,500 out of 2,582 prostitutes arrested in 1877 were minors.

Case Studies

We now see why the crime rate is anything but low among children. Thirteen-year-old B. A. stabbed and killed a companion who would not turn over his gambling winnings. B. A. was brachycephalic with a pointed skull, a high cephalic index of eighty-seven, oblique eyes, protruding cheekbones, voluminous jaws, and jug ears. At the age of twelve he already frequented brothels. His brother was convicted six times for theft, his sister was a prostitute, and their mother was a criminal. Although B. A. believed in God and went to church, he said nothing to his confessor about his crime. As a child, B. A. had been struck on the head, a trauma that took a long time to heal. Predictably, he was the offspring of neurotics. His mother suffered from migraines, his sister was

4. William Bender, figlio di madre onesta ma con un fratello ladro:
faceva parte di un'associazione di piccoli malfattori.

5. Tom Wellington,
prima vagabondo per le strade di Londra, ora laborioso fattore nel Canadà.

26 Before-and-After Pictures of Vicious and Criminal Boys
Editors' note: For Lombroso, these pictures illustrate the merits of the
English approach to juvenile delinquency, which had reformed William
Bender (no. 4), a former gang member, and Tom Wellington (no. 5), a
London vagabond who later became an industrious immigrant to Canada.
Source: Lombroso, *L'uomo delinquente*, edition 5 (*Atlante*). Photo
courtesy of the New York Library of Medicine.

hysterical, his grandfather died of financial anxieties, his grandmother died of poisoning, a cousin was a semi-imbecile, and a brother stuttered.

Sexual aberrations appear early in children. I have already established (*L'amore dei pazzi*, 1881) that all monstrous forms of sexuality (except those due to decrepitude) begin at the prepubescent stage, and that they are accompanied by criminal tendencies. Such was the case with Bor . . . , a thief who had continual erections from the age of nine years old. He was so oversexed that the sight of white sheets drying in the breeze drove him to rape. These strange symptoms started to appear at the age of three or four, when he saw his school companions with white smocks over their uniforms. The gentle rustle of white linen aroused him like the touch of a woman. This fetish for white linen cloth caused him to commit rapes and steal in order to pay prostitutes.

Zambaco (*Encephale*, n. 1–2, 1882) describes another strange case, that of a girl seized by onanistic and criminalistic passions. At as early as five years old she showed tendencies to theft, even stealing objects that she could have obtained for nothing, and obstinately denied those thefts. By the time the girl was nine, excessive masturbation caused swelling of her vulva. Whipping did not cure her, but rather made her stupid, mendacious, and wicked. Equally useless was the straitjacket and cold-water treatment with which she at first tried to calm herself. The upper half of her body lost weight, but the lower half grew. She touched herself in front of everyone, asking "Why should I deny myself such an innocent pleasure?" but then adding, "I know it's dirty, but I can't stop." Occasionally she repented when she saw her mother's tears, but then she took it up again. While a priest was in the process of warning her against it, she masturbated herself with her petticoat. They tried applying a flame to her clitoris, but even that did not help.

Clearly these are cases of insanity and, when the subjects become adults, of absolute criminality. They demonstrate the difficulty of differentiating between criminality and moral insanity in childhood.

Anthropometric Statistics on Childhood Criminality

A few anecdotes are insufficient to demonstrate that criminality among children is equal to that of adults. Thus through research in reformatories and nursery schools, we tried to discover if young criminals show the same physical anomalies as adult offenders.

Of seventy-nine children in one reformatory, forty were thieves, twenty-seven rebels or vagabonds, and seven murderers (the crimes of the remaining three were unknown).[21] Forty-seven of the children, or 59 percent, exhibited three or more anomalies, making them equivalent to born criminals. Of the forty young thieves, twenty-seven (67 percent) exhibited the true criminal type characterized by jug ears, low forehead, plagiocephaly or protuberances on the sides of the skull, large jaw, facial asymmetry, and fuzz on the forehead. Ninety-one percent of the children exhibited at least one anomaly, a proportion equal to that of adult criminals. Similarly, the reformatory children showed the same rates of hereditary alcoholism, madness, and criminality as adult criminals.

For a control group, we selected a sample of noncriminal nursery school children.[22] Table 14 shows that all children display large numbers of physical anomalies, although we must recognize that most of these will disappear with time. Almost one-half of the children, more exactly 44 percent, manifested such abnormal moral behavior—including excessive irascibility, tendency to vagabondage, persistent lying, bizarre habits, restlessness, and a propensity to tear their clothes—that their teachers singled them out as semi-insane. Seventeen percent of the total had already shown such criminal proclivities as thievishness and lasciviousness.

In the same sample, abnormal physical characteristics showed up among 69 percent of immoral children, but among only 30 percent of moral children. The difference is even more striking in the case of the semidelinquent children like the masturbators and thieves, of whom 72 percent and 83 percent, respectively, displayed physical anomalies. The most frequent physical abnormalities were:

an aged physiognomy (8 cases)

large jaw (8 cases)

protruding sutures (6 cases)

plagiocephaly (6 cases)

asymmetrical and stunted face
   (6 cases)

enlarged sinuses (6 cases)

prognathism (4 cases)

low, flattened forehead (4 cases)

trococephaly or round head (3 cases)

fuzz on the forehead (3 cases)

underdevelopment (2 cases)

shifty gaze (2 cases)

jug ears (2 cases)

Table 14: Anomalies in 160 Nursery School Children

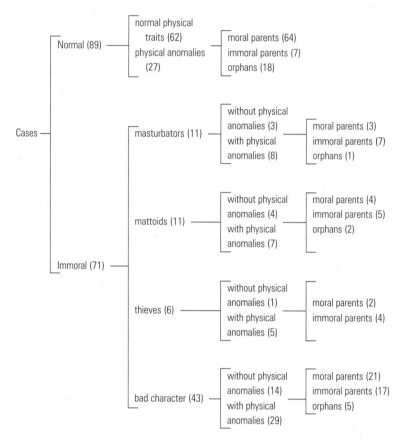

Editors' note: Lombroso defined a mattoid as semi-criminal inspired by idealistic but delusional ideals.

In addition, there was one case each of prominent cheekbones, a large head, and a deformed mouth. Eight children displayed three physical abnormalities and therefore resembled the born criminal.

We can conclude that abnormalities of moral character, which in an adult would constitute criminality, appear in greater proportions in the child. However, these abnormalities tend to disappear with proper education. Otherwise, it would not be possible to explain the lower proportion of criminal types among adults, even after taking into account child mortality and the proportion of criminal adults who escape arrest.

Preventive Measures for Childhood Crime

A certain proportion of criminals exhibits immoral tendencies from birth, whether or not these tendencies are inherited. In many cases good education has no influence whatsoever, while in others its benefits are clear. Only education can explain the normal metamorphoses in most children away from their criminal tendencies.

By education we do not mean the theoretical instruction in literature, rhetoric, and ethics that rarely does any good, even among adults. Still less do we mean coercion, which creates hypocrites and, rather than turning vice into virtue, turns vice into more vice. Rather, education means the substitution of new habits for those that caused depraved behavior. These new habits can be formed by imitation while living with honest people.

Better than punishment in the training of children are preventive measures such as good air, light and space, a diet of vegetables rather than meat, avoidance of alcohol, and sexual abstinence. Jealousies that lead to impulsive violence must be discouraged; precocious pride must be reigned in; the intellect must be cultivated through the senses; and the heart must be trained through the intellect.

Because alcoholics and offenders beget criminal children, we must prevent them from procreating by prohibiting sexual intercourse. This constitutes the only possible preventive measure against born criminals, who are not susceptible to reform.

25

Anomalies of the Brain and Internal Organs

Convolutions of the Brain. Many authors have hoped to find the secret of criminal tendencies in anomalies of the convolutions or ridges of the brain. While rejecting the exaggerations of phrenologist Gall, some scientists today continue to assert claims about anomalous brain convolutions as true. They have noted that Guiteau had gaps between the central and lateral solci, as well as between the transverse occipital and intraparietal solci.[23] In the right hemisphere of his brain, the parietal lobe was atrophied, the paracentral lobe extremely small, and the postcentral convolution shrunk by a quarter (Mendel, *Nevrolog. Centralbl.*, 1882).

In the brains of eleven criminals, Hanot found four with double forehead convolutions (*Gaz. Medic.*, 1880). Benedikt tried to turn such observations into a natural law in his celebrated study (*Anatomische Studien an Verbrecher Gehirnen*, Vienna, 1879), arguing that criminals are distinguished by more frequent confluent brain fissures.

Although it would be premature to conclude with certainty that the cerebral convolutions of criminals have specific abnormalities, it is undeniable that atypia or cellular abnormality is frequent among them. Atypia harks back to a characteristic of inferior animals and sometimes of the embryo (Flesch).[i]

Histology. Fewer doubts remain about the frequency of pathological anomalies in the brain tissues of criminals, for these appear every time a criminal is autopsied. The histological examination of Guiteau carried out by Arnold and MacDonald revealed that the perivascular lymphatic

---

[i] Flesch has promised to send me the final results of his examination of sixty criminal brains, which I will publish in the second volume of this edition. In his preliminary study, Flesch found two types of abnormalities in criminals' brain convolutions. The first, which is not even found in animals, includes transverse ridges of the frontal lobe so pronounced that it was impossible to see the longitudinal ridges. The second type consists of anomalies that are found in lower animals, such as the separation of the calcerine fissure from the occipital fissure, a lateral fossetta that remains open, and the frequent formation of an operculum on the occipital lobe.

Guiteau.

27 Guiteau
Editors' note: Based on this etching
and medical reports, Lombroso
diagnosed Charles Guiteau, who
assassinated president James Garfield in 1881, as morally insane.
Source: Lombroso, *L'uomo delinquente*, edition 4.

spaces were filled with pigmented granular masses, the residues of leak-
ing blood vessels; in addition, the surrounding cells were filled with
lymphoid elements. At many points the capillaries had a gray substance
that was becoming granular as it degenerated.

Table 15 displays the results of a careful scientific study by Flesch
of twenty-eight criminal brains. This long list of anomalies shows that
criminals equal the insane in diseases of the brain, sometimes even ex-
ceeding them. The symptoms of these grave internal abnormalities,
however, are often overlooked, even by specialists.

In his observations on the development and gradual multiplication
of the centers of voluntary movement in the brain's cortical substance,
Soltmann has shown that the human brain may undergo profound
alterations over a lifetime without manifesting symptoms of illness. His
experiments on newborn rabbits and dogs show that immediately after
birth, electrical impulses applied to the cerebral cortex do not yet cause
movement. Cortical centers develop gradually during the first sixteen
days, affecting different groups of muscles. A lack of these centers in
the first period of life explains why early cerebral illnesses may remain
latent.[k] If development is arrested in an area of the cerebral hemispheres

[k] Soltmann, *Experimentelle Studien über die Functionen des Grosshirns der Neugeboren* (Jahres-
ber: f. Kinderheilk., ix, 1875); and Raseri, *Sui crani veneti* (Dalle, *Memorie del Laboratorio di Medicina
legale di Torino*, 1878).

Table 15: Brain Anomalies in Twenty-eight Criminals

TYPE OF ANOMALY	NUMBER OF ANOMALIES
Adherences of the inner brain cover to the cortex	4
Adherences of the outer brain cover to the skull bone	6
Bleeding internal pachymeningitis	2
Cranial pachymeningitis	8
Leptomeningitis in youth aged 21, 27, 29, and 36	14
Tubercular meningitis of the skull base	1
Edema of the outer brain cover	7
Atheroma of the basilar arteries	8
Hemorraging spinal meningitis	1
Edema of the brain	1
Atrophy of the gray matter	1
Cerebral hemorrhage	3

during this period, the multiplication of the centers regulating the various functions cannot take place.

Heart and Blood Vessels. Flesch's research has revealed another fact that was hitherto unknown: criminals exhibit many anomalies of the internal organs and blood vessels, some of which are inborn. These outnumber the congenital abnormalities of the blood vessels and heart found in the insane. In fourteen autopsies, I found nine cases of pericarditis, three of aortic atheroma, and one aneurism.

In a study of thirty-nine patients with heart disease, D'Astros (*Ét. sur l'état mental des cardiaques*, 1881, Paris) concluded that they tend to exhibit a difficult character and mental abnormalities. Those with diseases of the aorta have nervous temperaments leading to outbursts of anger, while those with malfunctioning mitral valves display violent impulses. Heart disease, especially arrhythmia in contractions of the ventricle, can lead to cardiac insanity characterized by depression, melancholic delirium with hallucinations, and impulsiveness.

The results of D'Astros's study were predictable because the plethysmograph has already proven the close connection between psychological states and blood circulation.[24] Furthermore, autopsies frequently reveal cerebral lesions in criminals and the insane, including pigmentation of the cells, adherence and opacity of the membranes, sclerosis, and pachymeningitis. All the data of pathological anatomy point to abnormal distribution of the blood as a cause of mental affliction.

Liver. In 511 autopsies of criminals, Flesch found only six livers that were normal. Liver problems are common among criminals, partially the result of alcoholism. The offenders Milani, Agnoletti, and Passanante had livers that were as damaged as their brains.

Genitals. In nine out of twenty-four cases, examination of criminals' genitals revealed one case of parametritis, one of ophoritus, two of endometritis, one of hydrops of the tubes and follicles, one of cancer of the ovary, and one ovarian cyst.[25] In only one case were the genitals normal.

Stomach. Thirty-five autopsies on criminals' stomachs uncovered eight cases of phlegm, two of swollen mucous membranes, four of cancer, three of hyperaemia, one of distension, one of a polyp, and one of an ulcer. Only fifteen of the stomachs were healthy.

26

Photographs of Born Criminals

Serious and justified objections have been raised about my research, which is still in its initial phase. Of course, the number of honest people who have one or more anomalies is very high. Thus, before we attribute to anomalies a decisive significance in the understanding of crime, we need to find out what proportion of normal people display them.[26] A clue to criminal potential is found in the existence of not just one or two of these characteristics but many at once among individuals who have committed criminal or at least immoral acts. How often do we find the complete criminal type among offenders? How often do we encounter a cluster of anomalies among hardened repeat offenders?

To answer these questions without being accused of bias, I asked the illustrious Professor Liszt to send me a copy of his *Album of German Criminals*, which is the source of most of my photographs. I have reproduced others from local newspapers, as well as from the *Police Journal* of New York, which permits the study of the Anglo-American type of criminal.

In the 219 photographs of male criminals, 23 of the subjects are American, 1 English, 2 French and Belgian, 18 Italian, 164 German, 8 Jewish, and 4 Russian or Polish.[27] These criminals fall into the following categories:

Thieves and pickpockets	108
Murderers and assaulters	50
Swindlers, bankrupts, and forgers	54
Sex offenders	5
Bigamists	2
Total:	219

These photographs document the physiognomy of various types of criminals. Murderers are represented in photographs numbers 1 (who

28 Album of Criminal Photographs

Editors' note: Photography became a modern tool of criminal investigation in the late nineteenth century, allowing police to identify repeat offenders. Lombroso believed that he could identify born criminals solely from photographs sent to him from colleagues around the world.

Source: Lombroso, *L'uomo delinquente*, edition 4.

with his wife [no. 2] killed a poor elderly woman in order to rob her), 3, 4, 6, and 7. Swindlers can be seen in photographs nos. 45, 50, 51, 52, 54, 55, 56, 57, 58, 59, and 60. Pickpockets appear in nos. 38, 37, 28, 26, 31, 30, 29, and 36, a shoplifter in no. 42, burglars in nos. 8, 9, 10, 11, 12, 13, 14, 15, 16, 17, 18, 19, 20, 21, 22, 23, 24, and 25. No. 46 is a forger.

The anomalous physical characteristics encountered most frequently among these 219 criminals are:

—large jaws, found in eighty-one individuals or 37 percent, including nos. 7, 22, 25, 21, 19, 20, 16, 12, 9, 57, 55, 3, 5, 32, 33, 35, 29, 30, 28, 48, 47, 51, 50, 54, 53, I, and IV;

—scanty beard, found in seventy-three individuals or 32 percent, including nos. 19, 30, 42, 47, 20, 17, 16, 8, 57, 3, 4, and III;

—enlarged sinus cavities, found in 28 percent, including nos. 7, 18, 23, 24, 21, 15, 14, 9, 8, 58, 36, 31, 35, 29, 37, 26, 44, 47, 46, and 52;

—shifty gaze, found in 23 percent, including nos. 13, 22, 26, 28, 29, 31, 32, 24, 49, 42, 47, 45, 50, 55, 56, I, and IV;

—thick hair, found in forty-eight cases or 21 percent, including nos. 18, 47, 54, 19, 20, 15, 8, 3, and 4;

—jug ears, found in forty-one cases or 18 percent, including nos. 36, 28, 40, 54, 19, 21, 17, 12, 10, 9, 57, 55, 3, 4, and II;

—jutting cheekbones, found in twenty-four photographs or 10 percent, including nos. 20, 21, 17, 12, 14, 15, 53, 3, 5, 48, and 21;

—strabismus or wandering eye, found in twenty-two cases or 10 percent, including nos. III, IV, 10, 42, 37, 16;[1]

—sloping foreheads, found in nineteen cases or 8 percent, including nos. 8, 10, 14, 17, 23, 24, 45, and IV;

—prognathism, found in nine cases or 4 percent, including nos. 39 and IV;

—feminine physiognomy, found in 9 percent, including nos. 30, 6, 3, 4, and 42. Precisely the opposite occurs in women criminals, where the masculine type predominates.

Careful study of these photographs reveals that two, three, four, and even five physical anomalies are to be found in the same individual. Of 219 criminals, 52 or 23 percent reveal the physiognomy of the criminal

[1] I note only the very obvious cases of strabism documented in the *Album*, ignoring many examples that could be the result of the particular photographic pose. In some cases, such as photographs nos. 20 and 57, it is impossible to judge the eyes since the criminal closed them, being aware of the extreme importance of this feature.

type. Normal and even beautiful physiognomy is found in only a few very intelligent criminals, especially swindlers (nos. 11 and 14). Very few cases show a complete lack of abnormal characteristics (but see nos. 11, 14, 46, 59, 58, 60, 50, 51, 32, 54, 25, 24, and v). Even those who appear normal share a strange similarity, which tends to confirm the idea of their anthropological kinship (for example, nos. 50, 51, 55, 59, and 60).

An almost family resemblance marks born criminals, much as it does members of animal and vegetable species. The criminal type is so strong as to force one to wonder whether some of the portraits are no more than different shots of the same person (see especially, nos. 13, 31, 22, 9, 3, and 4). Rather than national types, we find a similarity among criminals from very distant regions. The reader will have certainly noticed a resemblance among the Italian, German, and American criminals.

Readers have thus been able to test our claims that the criminal type is to be found in about 25 percent of all lawbreakers. The highest proportions of the criminal type are found among murderers (36 percent) and thieves (25 percent); the lowest among occasional criminals (17 percent), bankrupts (12.5 percent), and swindlers and bigamists (6 percent each).

The abnormal characteristics that predominate among born criminals, especially murderers, are the absence of an ethnic type; a large jaw (37 percent); a scanty beard (32 percent); enlarged sinus cavities (28 percent); a shifty gaze (23 percent); thick hair (21 percent); and jug ears (18 percent). Secondarily, we find, in descending order, asymmetry, femininity, sloping foreheads, and prognathism.

27

Sensitivity and Blushing in Criminals

The frequency among criminals of tattooing, which is painful and dangerous, led me to suspect that criminals are less sensitive to pain than the average man.[m] This is also the case among the insane, especially those who are demented.

After long discussions with prison guards and doctors, I have been able to gather evidence of some cases of total analgesia or obliviousness to pain, but such cases usually involve insane criminals. For example, an old thief allowed a red-hot iron to be applied to his scrotum without crying out. He asked whether they had finished as if he were asking about something that did not involve him, although shortly after this he became delirious. Another completely apathetic man allowed one of his legs to be amputated and then started playing with it.

General Sensitivity. The question of sensitivity to pain among criminals is too important and complex for us to accept data that is incomplete or unverified by direct experience. I have therefore examined the sensitivity of sixty-six criminals, among whom fifty-six were certainly born or habitual criminals, four occasional criminals, one prostitute and thief, and two insane thieves.[28] They underwent tests for general sensitivity, sensitivity to pain, and sensory acuteness.[29] In terms of general sensitivity, simple finger contact revealed dullness of touch in thirty-eight out of these sixty-six criminals. Forty-six displayed different readings on the right and left sides of the body. Six out of eight epileptic thieves showed low levels of general sensitivity.

In another study, general sensitivity was measured on the back of the hand with an algometer (adapted from Du Bois-Reymond); the read-

---

[m] One criminal, in order to obtain a complex design on his back, lay supine on his stomach for three to four hours per day for three weeks in a row (Lacassagne). A Neapolitan criminal who washed himself with boiling lye after being tattooed, died of gangrene; he thought the gangrene was the result of a curse, though of course it was caused by imprudence (Curcio). At Nancy, tattooing caused syphilis among eight soldiers. Berchon (o. c.) noted that tattooing had led to seventeen cases of septic inflammation, eight of gangrene, one of aneurism, and seven deaths.

ings at which the subjects first felt the electric current differed notably between fifteen normal people and seventeen born criminals.[30] The first group felt the current at higher readings (averaging 64.2 millimeters) than the second group (averaging 49.6 mm).

Algometry.   More revealing is the study of sensitivity to pain that I executed by applying the algometer to the back of the hand (see *Algometria dell'uomo sano ed alienato*, 1874). The twenty-one normal individuals displayed greater sensitivity to pain (with readings averaging 49.1 mm) than the criminals, whose readings averaged 34.1. None of the twenty-one normal individuals exhibited sensitivity to pain as low as 0; only one measured at the level of 17; two measured at 62, and two others were in the range of 57–58. Among criminals, in contrast, four registered 0 (complete analgesia), and three fell into the 11–15 range. Their similarities to the normal sample were limited to the range of 40–49; and their highest figures were 50–55. Tests on the tongue and the forehead, although yielding fewer data on criminals' sensitivity, tend to confirm these figures.[n]

Sense of Touch.   Data on tactile sensitivity in thirty-seven individuals, as measured with an esthesiometer, appears in table 16.[31] This table demonstrates a remarkable dullness of touch in at least ten out of thirty-seven criminals, some dullness in thirty-two, and finer sensitivity in only two. We do not find a clear correspondence, however, between these figures and those for general sensitivity and sensitivity to pain in the same individuals. While unusual tactile dullness sometimes cor-

---

[n] The following table gives algometric readings for sensitivity to pain, as measured on the back of the hand. [The readings are grouped by ranges in the strength of electrical current, while the individual readings are indicated in parentheses. —Eds.]

STRENGTH OF CURRENT (mm)	CRIMINALS	NORMAL
0–9	4 (0)	0
10–19	3 (11, 13, 15)	1 (17)
20–29	3 (20, 23, 29)	0
30–39	2 (35, 35)	5 (31, 33, 32, 34, 35)
40–49	4 (40, 44, 44, 49)	9 (40, 43, 44, 45, 47, 47, 47, 48, 49)
50–59	5 (50, 51, 52, 52, 55)	4 (50, 54, 57, 58)
60–69	0	2 (60, 62)

Table 16: Tactile Sensitivity in Thirty-seven Criminals

SENSITIVITY (range in millimeters)	RIGHT SIDE (number of criminals)	LEFT SIDE (number of criminals)
0.8–1.4	2	4
1.5–1.8	13	16
2.0–2.8	12	9
3.0–3.5	5	8
4.0–4.8	4	–
16–30	1	–
32–40	1	1

Editors' note: Both columns add to 38 rather than 37. In tests for tactile sensitivity, lower readings indicate higher degrees of sensitivity. Readings of 4 and above thus indicate extreme insensitivity. Lombroso found criminals to have an imbalance between the two sides of their bodies, with tactile sensitivity generally more dull on the right side.

relates with low levels of general sensitivity and sensitivity to pain, in three cases the relationship was reversed.

Sight. Aside from sensitivity of touch, the other senses of criminals have not yet been studied systematically. Twelve experiments using quinine, bitter apple, and musk found no evidence of dullness of taste or even of smell. But everyone knows how difficult it is to draw conclusions about these senses, given the lack of precise measurement methods. Kraepelin and Buccola are only now starting to develop such tests (*Legge del tempo nei fenomeni del pensiero*, 1883, Dumolard).

As for sight, Dr. Bono conducted a diligent study in my laboratory of 227 criminals (most of them extremely young). He found that 15 offenders, or 6 percent, were color-blind. This was double the proportion for 800 students of the same age (3.09 percent) and for 590 workers (3.39 percent). This wonderful discovery becomes more important every day as we find that the ability to perceive color has more to do with the brain than the retina. Research by Schmitz shows that 55 percent of the color-blind and their families have major problems with their nervous systems, such as epilepsy, Huntington's Corea, and traumas to the head.[0]

Strength. Some criminals exhibit extraordinary agility, especially those who steal. The thieves Cecchini, Pietrotto, Rossignol, Villella, and Ros-

[0] *Archivio di psichiatria e scienze penali*, vol. iii, pag. 92.

Table 17: Strength of Offenders by Crime Type

TYPE OF CRIMINAL	TRACTIVE STRENGTH	COMPRESSIVE STRENGTH
Armed robbers	114	31.8
Murderers	114	31.9
Forgers	114	29.0
Rapists	109	33.0
Thieves	104	28.0
Brigands	103	33.0
Arsonists	84	32.0

Editors' note: Strength was measured with a dynamometer or an oval hoop of metal fitted with a scale that measured both the force of traction (pulling on the hoop) and compression (pushing on the hoop).

sotti all escaped from prison, and Rossotti organized the escape of his girlfriend the same day. Villella, already in his seventies, fled to the wilds of Calabria carrying a goat on his head as camouflage. And everyone remembers the famous thief of Pavia known as La Vecchia [The Old Woman], who eluded the guards by jumping over a very high wall. Occasionally, thieves' agility is almost simianlike. For example, Maria Perino evaded the law for several months by climbing trees, jumping onto rooftops, and breaking into houses (*Archivio di psichiatria*, 11). The agility of criminals seems to resemble that of children and primitives.

Despite this agility, 241 criminals measured only 30 for compressive strength and 110 for tractive strength on Broca's dynamometer, figures that are decidedly lower than those of healthy, or rather free, individuals, though higher than those of madmen.[32] Table 17 offers the results of dynamometer testing according to types of crime and shows clearly that results for strength of compression are not always equal to those for traction. Thieves are weak on both measures. If one considers only traction, murderers, robbers, and forgers show the greatest strength, while arsonists, rapists, and brigands show the least. On the other hand, tests of compression show rapists, brigands, and arsonists to be stronger than murderers and robbers, who are in turn stronger than forgers and thieves.

Blushing. Abnormalities of sensitivity among criminals are accompanied by weakening of the blood vessels. The simplest proof is failure to blush, a failure that for centuries has been considered a sign of dishonesty and immorality. We have focused our studies of blushing on the young because, as Darwin indicates, lack of color can be the result of advanced age.[p] With Darwin's remark in mind, we examined fifty-nine convicted criminals aged nineteen to twenty-six to see if they blushed in response to a reprimand or fixed stare. Only thirty-six blushed (61 percent); three became pale, and twenty displayed no facial changes whatsoever. Blushing was limited to the cheeks and forehead in eleven cases out of the thirty-six and reached the ears in two others; in twenty-four it was entirely limited to the cheeks and, in one case, only one cheek reddened.[33] Although these young criminals blushed when they argued, laughed, or were perturbed by the intrusion of someone into their cell, they did not redden in response to our reprimands, to reminders of their crimes, or to being fixed with a stare, in contrast with normal individuals.

Dr. Pasini and I (*Archivio di psich.*, vol. III, p. 281) observed a failure to blush in 81 percent of 122 criminal women or, more specifically, in 79 percent of murderesses, 80 percent of poisoners, 82 percent of women who committed infanticide, and 90 percent of thieves. Although these women did not blush when reminded of their crime or reprimanded, they reddened when asked about menstrual disorders. This finding is supported by an observation of Dr. Andronico about the prostitutes and young female offenders in his care at the Messina penitentiary. He writes: "When asked when they had begun this ugly profession, no prostitute blushed, but one did redden when asked if she had committed an unnatural sexual act."

Conclusions and Applications

These facts prove that all types of sensitivity are lower in criminals, including occasional criminals, than in normal individuals. This insensitivity to pain reminds one of those primitive peoples who tolerate puberty rites that would be torture for the white man.[q] Perhaps low levels of sensitivity help to explain why criminals, although ill from birth (and even earlier in the womb), display vitality during their lives. Of course, the life expectancy of criminals is less than that for average individu-

[p] *Fisionomia dell'espressione*, Turin, 1882.

[q] See *Rev. scientifique*, 1883, for the atrocious tortures that the young who want to become medicine men among the Redskins of Guyana have to undergo for several years. See also Lombroso, *Uomo bianco e uomo di colore*, Padua, 1872.

als, but this is explained by the noxious conditions of imprisonment. Criminals might outlive normal individuals if they enjoyed similar living conditions.

Left-Handedness. Compared to normal individuals, criminals show an almost twofold prevalence of left-handedness; in this they resemble children, primitives, and idiots, who are commonly ambidextrous (Le Bon, *Revue scientifique*, 1883). Everyone agrees that left-handedness is a result of the prevalence of the brain's right hemisphere over the left, as opposed to the normal prevalence of left over right, which results in right-handedness. While the honest person thinks with the left brain, the criminal thinks with the right (Ogle, *Med. Surgical Society*, 1871, London).

When people shy away from the left-handed person and refer to him as "sinister," they simply confirm Italian folk wisdom about left-handed people.[34] Lengthy research will be needed to confirm the popular belief, prevalent especially in Emilia and Lombardy, that swindlers tend to be left-handed. But my own findings provide preliminary proof that left-handedness is more prevalent among swindlers (33 percent) than among other types of criminals.

28

Moral Insanity and Born Criminality[1]

The cultivated reader will no doubt resist my identification of the morally insane with born criminals. For too many generations jurists have deemed the criminal's responsibility to be proportional to his crime and the public's need for revenge. Fearing to let the criminal go free, we saw no alternative but prison or death for evildoers. In short, the sentiments of revenge and fear, along with the tyranny of habit, closed off all other roads to expiation.

Earlier, I emphasized the differences rather than the similarities between the two wretched psychological pathologies of criminality and insanity. In many ways, born criminals seem to hark back more to sav-

[1] C. H. Hughes, *A case of moral insanity* (*The Alienist and Neurologist*, 1882, n. 4); Wright, *The phisical basis of moral insanity, viewed in relation to alcoholic impressions* (*The Alienist and Neurologist*, 1882, n. 4); A. Hollander, *Zur Lehre von der 'Moral Insanity'* (*Jarb. f. Psych.*, 1882, iv, 1, H. S. 1); Brancaleone Ribaudo, *Contributo sull'esistenza della follia morale*, Palermo, 1882; Salemi-Pace, *Un caso di follia morale*, Palermo, 1881; Tamburini e Seppilli, *Studio di psicopatologia criminale sopra un caso di imbecilità morale con idee fisse impulsive*, Reggio, 1883; G. B. Verga, *Caso tipico di follia morale*, Milano, 1881; Virgilio, *Delle malattie mentali*, 1882; Legrand de Saulle, *Les signes physiques des follies raisonnantes*, Paris, 1878; Mendel, *Die moralische Wahnsinne* (*Deutsch. Zeitschr. f. prakt. medicin.*, 1876, n. 52); Knap, *Ueber moral insanity* (*Allgemeine Zeitschrif. f. Pyschiatrie*, xxx, S.697); M. Gauster, *Ueber moralisches Irresein* (*Mittheilungen des Vereines der Aertze in Nieder Oesterreich.*, Bal. iii, 7, 1877, e *Wiener Klinik.*, Jahrg., iii, 4, 1877); Motet, *Cas de folie morale* (*Ann. méd.-psych.*, 1883); Reimer, *Moralisches Irresein nel Deutsche Wochenschrift*, 1878, 18, 19; H. Emminghaus, *Allgem. psyco-pathologie*, Leipzig, 1868; Savage, *Moral Insanity* (*Journal of medical sciences*, 1881); Todi, *I pazzi ragionanti*, Novara, 1879; Grohmann, *Nasse's Zeitschr.*, 1819, p. 162; Heinrich, *Allg. Zeitschrift. f. Pyschiatr.*, 1, p. 338; Prichard, *Treatise on insanity*; Id. *On the different forms of insanity*, 1842; Morel, *Traité des dégénérescences*, 1857; Brière de B., *Les fous criminals de l'Angleterre*, 1869; Solbrig, *Verbrechen und Wahnsinn*, 1867; Griesinger, *Vierteljahrschr. f. ger. u. öffentl. Med.*, N. F. iv n. 2; Krafft-Ebing, *Die Lehre v. moral. Wahnsinn*, 1871; Id. *Verbrechen u. Wahnsinn*, 1872; Stoltz, *Zeitschr. f. Psychiatrie*, 33 H. 5 u. 6; Livi, *Rivista sperimentale*, 1876, fascic. 5 and 6; Tamassia, *Ivi.*, 1877; Gauster, *Wien. med. Klinik*, iii, Jahrg. n. 4; Mendel, nel *Deutsche Zeitschr. f. prakt. med.*, 1876. n. 52; Maudsley, *Deutsche Klinik*, 1873, 2–3; Wahlberg, *Der Fall Hackler in Gesamwelte kleinere Schriften*, Wien, 1877; Bannister, *Chicago Journ.*, 1877, Oct.; Palmerini, Bonfigli, *Rivista sperim.*, 1877, fasc. 3 and 4.; Bonvecchiato, *Il senso morale e la follia morale*, Venezia, 1883; Dagonet, *Folie morale*, 1878; Lombroso, *Arch. di psichiatria e scienze penali*, vol. ii, p. 198; vol. iii, p. 365; vol. iv, p. 253; and Cantarano, nella *Psichiatria*, Napoli, 1883.

ages than do the insane. Unlike insanity, criminal behavior is congenital or begins at a young age, and its rates increase with the growth of civilization and cities. Born criminals—who are predominately tall, strong men with thick hair—are not subject to hereditary insanity or nervous diseases, and they harbor primitive instincts, like passion for orgies and vendettas, which are completely absent in madmen. Moreover, I instinctively feared that the two categories might be confused in terms of social dangerousness. And so, although everyone else—friend and foe alike—agreed on the similarities, I resisted making the connections.

But recent discoveries have changed my opinion completely. It is impossible to differentiate between insanity and crime now that researchers are uniting in support of criminal insane asylums and discovering cases, such as those of Verzeni, Guiteau, and Sbro . . . , that prove the similarity between the two conditions. In addition, authors like Krafft-Ebing, Holländer, Savage, and Mendel have recently outlined the characteristics of moral insanity.[35] I myself have found that both groups exhibit similar anomalies including insensitivity, analgesia, abnormal reflexes, left-handedness, and atypia of the cranium and brain.

One indirect proof of the similarity between moral insanity and criminality is the absence of the morally insane in mental hospitals and, conversely, their preponderance in prisons.[36] Of 16,856 patients in Italian public mental hospitals, Verga (*Annali di statistica*, 1883, vol. 8) found 0.56 percent to be morally insane (0.65 percent were men and 0.45 percent were women). The proportion of morally insane increases in private asylums serving the wealthy, where 3.9 percent of 585 patients were morally insane, but as Verga rightly pointed out, many of these rich people would probably have ended up in prison had they not had superior legal defense. Others had been admitted by their families early in the legal proceedings to preserve decorum. On the other hand, out of 960 insane in Italian prisons over ten years (*Stat. decenn. delle carceri*, 1882), 5.2 percent were officially classified as morally insane, a figure representing only a fraction of the true number.

Like criminality, moral insanity appears to be extremely rare among women. However, prostitution constitutes a sort of equivalent to both crime and moral insanity, at the same time serving as a safety valve for both.[37]

Classic cases of moral insanity reveal a cluster of characteristics resembling those of the born criminal.

Skulls. First Morel, then Legrand de Saulle (*Gaz. des hôpitaux*, Maggio, 1878), and now Krafft-Ebing have found among the morally insane skulls that are small and pointed, extremely large, elongated or abnormally round, or that exhibit bony crests. The faces of the morally insane display asymmetry between the two halves, thick lips, large mouths, malformed teeth with premature losses in the worst cases, and flattened, misshapen, or bifurcated roofs of the mouth. The ears of the morally insane are often large and unequal in size. We have already come across these abnormalities, particularly those of the skull, among criminals.

Physiognomy. The physiognomy of morally insane offenders reveals that they have all the characteristics of the criminal man: large jaws, facial asymmetry, unequal ears, scanty beards in men, and virile physiognomy in women. In the photographs from the *Album of German Criminals*, four out of the six morally insane individuals display the true criminal type.

Although the morally insane in general present fewer cranial and facial abnormalities than born criminals, this is because moral insanity is brought on by typhoid and other illnesses and tends to develop later in life. Thus the morally insane acquire their sinister physiognomy more slowly than born criminals. For criminals living in the midst of evil companions from infancy, environment shapes the face and gives them all a similar aspect, especially when communal life continues in reformatories and prisons. Fear of being caught and the anxiety of a life spent outside the law also mold their expression.

Analgesia. Moral insanity and criminality are even closer in their functional anomalies. According to Legrand de Saulle, Krafft-Ebing, and Bonvecchiato, these include astigmatism, nystagmus, convulsive tics of the face, light ataxia, club feet, temporary or periodic hypersensitivity, exaggerated sexual drive (or the complete lack of it), and intolerance of alcohol. Nearly all of these traits are also found among born criminals.

The latest scientific case studies prove that the inability to feel pain is not limited to criminals, as previously thought. Tamburini and Seppilli found analgesia in the case of Sbro . . . , who was not only a fratricide and parricide but a prime example of moral insanity (*Rivista sperimentale di freniatria*, 1882, p. 136). He showed not the slightest sign of pain when pricked on his flesh, tongue, and forehead with a sharp pin. Analgesia is therefore a characteristic of moral insanity as well as criminality.

Tattooing. According to De Paoli, not even the tattoo, a notable characteristic of criminal man, has failed to make an appearance among the morally insane. The only morally insane patient that I was able to find in the Turin mental hospital was tattooed. But the most astute criminals are now refusing to be tattooed, so that each year there are fewer of them.

Sexuality. Among the morally insane, Krafft-Ebing has observed early signs of sexual perversion and sexual overindulgence followed by impotence, a phenomenon I have seen in criminals. "The sexual impulses of the morally insane," Krafft-Ebing continues, "are often precocious or unnatural and preceded or accompanied by a ferocious bloodlust."

Moral Sense. In the realm of moral character, the analogy between criminals and the morally insane is incontestable. According to my fellow psychiatrist Battanoli (*Relazione statistica di San Servolo*, Venice, 1880), "The morally insane are unhappy about the madness in their blood, something they have had since conception and that was nourished at the maternal breast. They lack sentiments of affection and moral sense. They are born to savor evil and commit it. Always at war with society, they believe they are its victims. Easily influenced and therefore very dangerous, they often figure in political revolutions." He describes two morally insane patients as follows: "Both are bright and comprehending, with ready memories; they are both egoists, lacking feelings of affection. Concerned only with the present, they care nothing for the future."

Affection. The morally insane repay hatred with hatred. Even when the cause is slight, they react with anger, envy, and vengeance. Incapable of family life, they flee the paternal home, sleeping under bridges and devoting themselves to refined cruelties. A morally insane boy of ten years old, with black eyes, an insolent face, and a record of laziness at school, threw a companion into the water just to see him drown. He was the son of a thief. Callisto Grandi buried a boy alive because he took his tools and dirtied his overcoat (Morselli).[38] Sbro . . . developed a hatred of his brother and mother for no apparent reason. True criminals similarly seek revenge for the slightest of reasons.

Altruism. Although it is true that the morally insane sometimes display altruism rather than egotism, this altruism is a perversion that depletes more normal sentiments like love of family. In this sense many philanthropists and saints figure among the morally insane. Similarly, criminals who rob passersby or maltreat their wives and parents may try to please their friends. The Marchioness of Brinvilliers, although she was a criminal, sacrificed herself to save her lover's life; Trossarello passed her nights among the sick; and Rulfi, who starved her daughter to death, was generous to peasant women.

Excessive Vanity. The morally insane and born criminals share a tendency to excessive vanity and megalomania. Agnoletti repeated continually, "It is God who permits me to survive and punish those who slander me. It is God who made my enemy, a judge, die. God, or his mother, made me eloquent at my trial."[s] He told me very seriously that a Milanese artist was sculpting his bust, as if he were a great man. He once asked me if the *Revue des Deux Mondes*, which I had in my hand, mentioned him. Finally, after having rambled on about Italy and its government, he told me that as soon as he was free, he would personally see to the triumph of a Garibaldino government, the only one that suited Italy.[39] The morally insane, notes Hollander, make no effort to hide their crimes, believing they have "the right to do it." He explains this as a sort of delusion of grandeur that makes them believe they are superior to everyone else and need not worry about their crimes.

Intelligence. The intelligence of the morally insane is not as deficient as their emotions and affections; and yet, because all psychic functions are linked, their intelligence cannot be completely healthy. Some authorities, including Prichard, Pinel, Nicolson, Maudsley, and Tamassia, hold that the morally insane show complete intellectual integrity,

[s] It is important for the history of religion to see how the morally insane attribute their impulses to God, possibly because these impulses seem irresistible. Thus Guiteau said, "Without the pressure of God on my free will, Garfield would not have been killed. God supported my actions just as he did those of Abraham. I cannot be insane. God does not choose his servants from among madmen." And Sbro . . . said, "It was destined by God that my brother should die." Born criminals, like the one who affirmed that the Madonna was his accomplice in parricide, say similar things.

with neither hallucinations nor illusions, neither defects nor disorders.[40] Others have identified cases of weak and inconsistent reasoning among the morally insane. While he found no abnormalities in the intelligence of the morally insane, Krafft-Ebing admits that some have a simplicity of spirit bordering on the absurd, with no thought of the consequences of their crimes. Battanoli writes of two morally insane children that "they have a great breadth of understanding but are not always wise; they write and speak gracefully, but like well-trained and clever parrots."

Such contradictions are also to be found in criminals, although there are many different combinations of moral insanity and criminality. As animal species become more numerous and differentiated, they generate subspecies. The same proliferation of subspecies occurs among the morally insane and criminals, although shallowness and cunning remain their principal intellectual characteristics.

All of the morally insane, even those who appear to be perfectly sound of mind, exhibit errors of judgment that derive from vanity and lead them to absurd contradictions. For example, Agnoletti recited the following nonsensical aphorisms:

> "A false name that has already been used is no longer a false name."
> "Obscene books are more moral than books on French philosophy."
> "When there is no remorse there is no guilt."
> "Killing one's own son is not a crime if you kill yourself at the same time."

Moral insanity is a genus of which crime is a species. Thus criminals with seemingly normal intelligence may in fact be morally insane (2.5 percent) and epileptic. We have seen traces of bizarreness in criminals' songs and jargon. Nicolson (*Journal of Mental Science*, 1877) found what he called "perversion of ideas" among prisoners, who tend to explain the simplest facts in the most complicated and misleading way possible. They believe, for example, that there is a pact among all prison employees to torment them, and they interpret even the simplest of disciplinary measures in this light.

Vanity in Crime—Autobiography. The vanity of criminals—their strange desire to eternalize their misdeeds in writing—has also been noted in cases of moral insanity, where it frequently provides a clue to or an explanation of their crimes. Maudsley describes a madman who washed his hands immediately after a murder and then wrote in his diary: "I killed a little girl, she was nice and warm." And vanity explains the strange poem of the rapist and child murderer Menesclou:

> I saw her, I took her
> I am angry with myself now
> But furor made me drunk
> And the pleasure lasted but a moment
> In my blind fury
> I did not see what I was doing.

Even though Menesclou denied the crime, this poem helped to convict him. It is their disordered passions that drive the morally insane, like other types of madmen and savages, to write doggerel (*Genio e folia*, p. 124).

Heredity. The most solid proof of the similarity between moral insanity and crime lies in the etiology of these disorders. Both born criminals and the morally insane manifest their tendencies from infancy or puberty. Savage, Mendel, and Krafft-Ebing have identified an early form of moral insanity that appears between the ages of five and eleven years in the form of thefts, an eccentric aversion to family life, disinterest in education, cruelty toward animals and fellow students, lying, cunning, cynicism in concealing misdeeds, and sexual precocity, especially masturbation.

Many of the morally insane have mad parents. This is also true of the insane, although the proportions are smaller. In addition, the morally insane have a greater proportion of egotistic, vice-ridden, and criminal relatives than do common madmen. The hereditary nature of moral insanity fits with our findings on the criminal tendencies in children. The physiological state of many children resembles moral insanity and will persist into adulthood if not reined in by environmental factors. Even if a child has no specific criminal tendencies, his pathological state may become habitual. This explains the frequency of moral insanity among not only kings, including many of the Caesars, but also petty tyrants such as Masaniello, Cola di Rienzo, Marat, and the dictators of many Spanish American countries.[41]

Irresistible Force

The irresistible nature of the crimes committed by the morally insane derives from the factors reviewed above: perverted emotions, excessive and unreasoned hatred, lack of restraint, and heredity. Pinel tells of a morally insane man who, having been badly brought up, committed the most absurd excesses. He killed horses that were difficult to manage; thrashed political opponents; and threw a woman who had contradicted him into a well. Although impulsivity is not limited to the morally insane, it is part of their nature because their brains suffer arrested development due to poor nourishment. While in the normal course of development, good upbringing tends to diminish the criminal impulses of childhood, these persist when they are favored by heredity and by absence of parental discipline. They can suddenly flare up among individuals whose egotism is stronger than their altruistic sentiments; with no force to resist egotism, all motives encourage wickedness and none works toward good. After a repeated series of evil acts, immorality becomes a habit.

Thus the development of moral insanity is a question of degree. How can we make a distinction between the true criminal and the morally insane individual who is afflicted with irresistible instinctive tendencies? For example, P. fancied gravestones and stole those that were not too heavy to carry. By giving the gravestones as gifts to his friends, he revealed the evidence of his crimes. Yet no one considered him mad. Similarly, Patetot was so miserly that he almost starved his wife and children. He tried to drown his wife in a river, and he cut the throat of a son who had spent eighty cents. When condemned to death, Patetot refused to appeal the sentence because he was too stingy to pay a lawyer. He had an uncle and a great-great-grandfather who were wife killers. Another example is provided by the shepherd Legier, who led an isolated life in the mountain cliffs. After a long period of celibacy, he suddenly felt an urge to rape a boy passing in the woods, eviscerate him, and drink his blood.

All of these men were sentenced as criminals, despite the obvious mixture of criminality and the impulsivity of moral insanity in their behavior. The complete similarity between the morally insane and the born criminal puts to rest the endless debates over criminal responsibility among moralists, lawyers, and psychiatrists and, indeed, among different schools of psychiatry. Although it is not true, as metaphysicians think, that healthy individuals exercise true free will, their actions are nevertheless determined by motives and desires that do not clash with the collective good. When they rebel, they are more or less restrained by the pleasure of praise; fear of punishment, infamy, and the Church; and heredity—or good habits developed through the continual exercise of the moral faculties. These restraints have no effect on either the morally insane or born criminals, who therefore have high rates of recidivism.

29

Summary of Edition 3

The research reported in this third edition demonstrates that disease and atavism are the two main causes of criminality.

Disease and Crime

This volume corrects my theory of atavism by adding brain malnutrition and poor nerve conductivity to the causes of crime. In other words, following the lead of Sergi (*Rivista di filosofia scientifica*, 1883) and Bonvecchiato (op. cit), I have synthesized disease with atavism to explain the monstrosities of born criminals. Disease explains many anomalies in the born criminal: plagiocephaly, cranial sclerosis, adhesions of the brain lining, cerebral softening and sclerosis, weak heart valves, cancerous and tubercular livers, cancer of the stomach, cellular hyperplasia of the nerves, and temporal atheroma. In turn, these conditions explain unequal dilation of the pupils, abnormal reflexes, muscular contractions, insensitivity to pain, incoherent and bizarre behavior, cruelty, pleasure in harm for harm's sake, and loss of affections.[42]

Arrested Development. It would be easy for me to explain the genesis of these diseases by aligning myself with the overwhelming number of psychiatrists who endorse the concept of degeneration. According to this theory, physical and psychological disorders are passed down through inheritance and, because they become increasingly more serious, eventually result in sterility. This school of thought, however, exaggerates the importance of degeneration by claiming that even the most insignificant symptoms of illness prove their theory.

In an era in which the goal of science is careful analysis, the concept of degeneration has become too broad, being used to explain pathologies from cretinism to genius, from deaf-mutism to cancer. More acceptable in my view is the theory of arrested development, which has an anatomical basis. Arrested development, the cause of physical and psychological pathology, explains the infinite variety in the combinations of criminality and moral insanity.

Atavism and Crime

Thus the concept of arrested development forms an important addition to the more predominant factor of atavism in the etiology of crime. Atavism remains one of the most constant characteristics of the born criminal, in spite of, or rather together with, pathology. This book has provided convincing evidence that many of the characteristics of primitive man are also commonly found in the born criminal, including low, sloping foreheads, overdeveloped sinuses, frequent occurrence of the medium occipital fossetta, overdevelopment of the jaw and cheekbones, prognathism, oblique and large eye sockets, dark skin, thick and curly head hair, large or protuberant ears, long arms, similarity between the sexes, left-handedness, waywardness among women, low sensitivity to pain, complete absence of moral and affective sensibility, laziness, absence of remorse and foresight, great vanity, and fleeting, violent passions.[43]

The concept of atavism is particularly useful in explaining the nature and recurrence of certain crimes. It explains pederasty and infanticide, which are holdovers from past epochs and peoples—such as the Romans, Greeks, Chinese, and Tahitians—who regarded these acts as national customs rather than crimes. Atavism also accounts for the aestheticism of contemporary pederasts, who in this respect resemble the ancient Greeks. According to Sergi, heredity, especially in criminals, is stratified and tends to reproduce the instincts of not only prehistoric but also medieval man.[t] This reappearance of medieval passions helps us understand the recent upsurge of anti-Semitism and the irrepressibility of dueling.

Knowing that the difference between the criminal, the uneducated normal man, and the primitive is not great, we understand why ordinary men who are not immoral often admire the criminal,[u] turning him

---

[t] *Della stratificazione del carattere nei delinquenti*, Turin, 1883.

[u] Neri Tanfucio, *Cento sonetti*, Florence, 1873, p. 39. "Look at the poor criminal. What has he done? Oh! Almost nothing. He's strangled his boss."

29 Thief from Milan
Editors' note: Lombroso found numerous anomalies in the face of this Milanese thief: a drooping nose, big ears, a broad forehead, and a large space between the nose and mouth. Aged thirty-four, the thief had already been arrested thirteen times.
Source: Lombroso, *L'uomo delinquente*, edition 1. Photo courtesy of the National Library of Medicine.

into a sort of hero who is adored after his death.[v] We can also see why convicts mix so easily with primitive peoples in the penal colonies of Australia and French Guyana, adopting their customs, including cannibalism (Bouvier, *Voyage à la Guyane*, 1866).

Atavism also helps us to understand the limited efficacy of punishment and the consistency in the yearly aggregate number of crimes. Both statistics and anthropology show crime to be a natural phenomenon or, to use the language of philosophy, a phenomenon as necessary as birth, death, and conception, and one that is so similar to mental illnesses to be simply a variant. From the perspective of atavism, the difference between the instinctively cruel acts of animals, plants, and criminals is very small.

Everything we have said about the criminal type relates to only a small proportion of offenders. Physiognomical studies suggest that the criminal type constitutes 23 percent of all offenders. Among children, the proportion is significantly larger (59 percent) if we count all physical and cranial anomalies. Abnormal characteristics tend to appear in clusters, resulting in monstrous criminals. Yet previous studies have also

---

[v] The ancients gave the name "Hercules" to great wrongdoers after they died (Varone o. c. 44) and worshiped them (Smith, *Biog. and Mith.*, ii).

shown that even isolated anomalies do not lack significance. Therefore, I can confidently estimate the actual proportion of born criminals to be close to 40 percent of all offenders.[w]

[w] It gives me pleasure to conclude this volume with data from a comparative study of physical anomalies among criminals that confirms my own conclusions. Knetch has established that out of 1,214 male convicts at Waldheim prison, 579 (46 percent) deviated physically from the normal type. Ten percent, or 130, of these inmates had one anomaly, and 36 percent showed multiple abnormal characteristics. He found that 7 percent had psychic disorders, 5 percent were epileptic, 11 had other nervous problems, 72 had scars from fights, 212 were drinkers (17.5 percent; compare Baer's rate of 19.6 percent). These signs of degeneration usually denote neuropathic dispositions. But even those who lack anomalies continue to have hereditary tendencies from illness. Descendants of epileptics and alcoholics are at highest risk for criminality (Knecht, *Allg. Zeitschrift. für Psychiatrie*, Bd. 40, H. 4). [Lombroso seems to use degeneration here as a substitute for atavism.—Eds.]

EDITION FOUR

1889

Editors' Foreword

By the time of the publication of the fourth edition (1889), only five years after the third, *Criminal Man* had grown to two volumes.[1] The first volume closely follows the organization of edition 3. Lombroso expands the section on prisoner speech, writing, and art, adding a new chapter on criminal communication in which he argues that criminals can be identified by their preference for primitive drawing over cursive script and by their use of gestures as secret speech. He closes the first volume with an admiring overview of the vast array of artistic and mechanical objects fashioned by prisoners in their spare time. Using the United States as a model, he proposes the expansion of prison industries to harness the energy and creativity of offenders.

The second volume, entirely new and surprising in its content, adds epilepsy to atavism and moral insanity as a primary cause of offending. As he did with moral insanity in the third edition, Lombroso here exhaustively analyzes epilepsy, cataloguing the anatomical, physiological, and psychological similarities of the epileptic and the born criminal. After recounting the famous case of the soldier Misdea, who slaughtered a number of his military companions, Lombroso warns that epilepsy is often not recognized in criminals like Misdea who do not experience convulsions. Yet he argues that such hidden epilepsy underlies the moral insanity and criminal behavior of many lawbreakers.

Volume 2 moves on to discuss the criminally insane, detailing their biological and psychological characteristics and defining new subcategories of mental illness. He paints memorable portraits of specific types of insane criminals—the alcoholic, the hysteric, and the mattoid—that have long endured in the criminological imagination. Emphasizing the strong links between alcohol consumption and crime, Lombroso presents a harrowing account of the physical and psychological deterioration caused by excessive drinking. He turns next to hysterical offenders, who are most often women and exhibit heightened eroticism during fits that resemble epileptic convulsions. Finally, in some of his most memorable pages, Lombroso creates a new criminal subtype of the insane criminal, the intelligent and affectionate mattoid who espouses grandiose political and religious causes. In his discussion of both epilepsy and criminal insanity, Lombroso gives increasing prominence to degeneration theory as an explanation for physical and psychological abnormalities.

Lombroso concludes the second volume with an extended analysis of occasional criminals, a group absent from earlier editions of *Criminal Man*. Occasional criminals are normal individuals who are pushed by social forces or bad companions to break the law. The long, detailed section on occasional criminals shows that Lombroso was listening to his critics, who had complained that he slighted environmental factors in his analysis of the etiology of crime. He defines four subcategories of the occasional criminal: pseudocriminals, who commit crimes by chance or break laws that lack popular support; habitual criminals, who become dangerous to society through a life of recidivism; latent criminals, who never encounter an opportunity to commit crime; and criminaloids, who display too few anomalies to constitute the full criminal type. Yet in his inability to define precisely the occasional criminal, Lombroso demonstrates his loyalty to the born criminal, the enduring central figure in his positivist theory of crime.

Author's Preface

I am proud to present the fourth edition of *Criminal Man*, which could be considered the eighth because four translations of earlier editions have appeared in German, Russian, and French.[2] With this edition, I have come close to my final goal of analyzing criminal man from an anthropological perspective. Although I hesitated many times on this new path of criminological inquiry, I received valuable aid from illustrious colleagues such as Marro, Knecht, Drago, Ferri, Garofalo, Drill, Frigerio, Pitrè, Pinero, Senna, Rossi, and Ottolenghi.[3] By offering extensive data to fill the lacunae in my research, they removed difficulties from my path.

Thanks to their help, I have been able to take daring steps on behalf of the new positivist school: the fusion of the born criminal and the morally insane with the epileptic; the addition of suicide to the category of crimes of passion and the linking of both to epilepsy; and the amplification of research on the criminally insane to show similarities and differences between them and common criminals. Thanks especially to Ferri, Marro, and Rossi, I have been able to draw the contours of the occasional criminal. Like a mirage, the figure of the occasional criminal at first appears clear and obvious, but vanishes as you approach. Nevertheless, I was able to overcome most, if not all, of the problems in defining this category of criminal.

That I have almost reached my goal is shown by the ease with which my colleagues and I have settled questions raised by my adversaries. For example, some critics complained that the rates of criminal anomalies vary, being 10 percent in one study, 20 percent in a second, and 50 percent in a third. Ferri has provided a more than adequate response to this objection: "Pure logic does require that the numerical results of different studies agree and fall into symmetrical categories; this is required by every a priori system. Real life, however, produces data that is complex and multiform, resulting in a range of percentages. Thus what for the syllogist is a defect, for the naturalist is a reconfirmation that these data do not derive from preconceptions of criminal anthropologists, but reproduce the multiformity of nature."[a]

Other critics, employing one of those ready-made phrases dear to the mediocre, claim that I construct laws from a pile of exceptions. These critics fail to understand that no group of facts exists without a law, all the more so when the facts are so numerous and consistent!

Some adversaries, particularly foreigners, misread or misunderstand me and accuse me of being exclusively atavistophile or epileptophile in my etiology of crime. Others cannot accept that I have added pathology and epilepsy to atavism as causes of crime, as if the latter should exclude the former. They do not understand that atavism may have a pathological cause. Moreover, in conditions such as microcephaly and cretinism, atavism and pathology together explain arrested development.

Critics also object that no criminal is completely atavistic and that many are not cannibalistic (Biswanger) or tattooed. But who would argue for the existence of complete atavism in contemporary races or individuals? We see only traces of atavism in individuals; otherwise we would be looking at a mammal, not a man. Even cretins and microcephalics may have normal faces, craniums, or torsos. According to Étienne Geoffroy Saint-Hilaire's law of correlation or correspondence between organs, and to Darwin's law of adaptation, it is rare to find an anomaly that is completely isolated.[4] Any anomaly may be associated with others, but total atavistic regression is impossible.[5]

Topinard denies the existence of atavism.[b] Yet the study of craniometric anthropology, which is his specialty, must convince even the most myopic observer that atavism exists. It is curious to hear him ask, "Why should I be concerned with the color of the eyes, the cephalic index, the shape of the jaws, and the height of criminals? These are characteristics of race." He does not understand that we find differences when comparing these characteristics in criminal and normal individuals of the same race. These anthropological and pathological features distinguish a criminal type within each race.[6]

Some phenomena such as the median occipital fossetta, the olecranial foramen, the hypertrophied cerebellar vermis, or left-handedness find their only explanation in atavism. Others that have no connec-

[a] Ferri, *Uno spiritista del diritto penale*, 1887.
[b] *L'anthropologie criminelle* (*Revue d'Anthropologie*, 1888, n. 6).

tion whatever with atavism, such as facial asymmetry and insensitivity of smell, are matters of pathology.

According to some ingenious but superficial critiques, Marro's marvelous discovery of the distinct characteristics of each species of criminal works against the idea of a criminal type. But this assertion is false because all criminals share the important traits of impulsiveness, cortical irritation, insensitivity, and immorality. Furthermore, the existence of various species of genius has never undermined the idea of genius per se, but instead confirmed it. Who believes that admitting the difference between mathematical and poetic geniuses undermines the existence of genius itself?

Certain lawyers have deliberately misinterpreted my theories, turning them to the advantage of their least deserving clients. Not only can I not be held guilty for false applications by others of my discoveries but the problem would not exist if my recommendations for practical policies were enacted. I await the day when the opinion of technical experts replaces the empty rhetoric of defense attorneys in courtrooms. New laws regulating alcohol use and divorce would prevent many violent and sexual crimes, while institutions for incorrigibles and the application of the death penalty would eliminate the eternal clients of the criminal justice system who pose a danger to society. But until the measures I have recommended are realized, accusations against me are unjust, as would be the condemnation of gas for lighting on the grounds that it can explode and cause fires.

How can authoritative people in the field of anthropology, much less anthropometrists such as Topinard, deny the existence of a criminal type? I have replied to them with a completely impartial type of proof, that of the composite photograph.[7] But I can also easily defend myself using their own weapons and definitions. For example, Broca writes that "human types are not real but abstract concepts drawn from the comparison of ethnic groups and identification of common characteristics within each group." We agree and would simply point out that the most salient and numerous of these traits constitute a "type," whether that type be criminal or ethnic.

I can also respond to Tarde's claim that professional specialization, rather than degree of atavism, explains differences among criminal types. It is true that facial features and gestures are acquired through mutual contact, and this may also apply to the voice, jargon, tattoos,

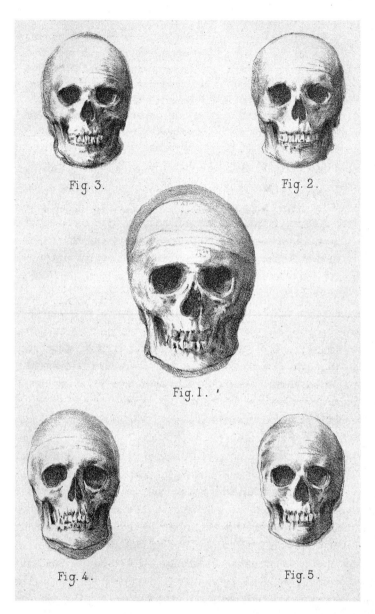

Fig. 3.

Fig. 2.

Fig. I. '

Fig. 4.

Fig. 5.

30 Composite Photographs, Galtonian Method
Editors' note: Lombroso used Galton's method of composite photography
to try to define criminal types. By superimposing photographs of criminal
skulls, he claimed to have identified the typical cranial anomalies of murders (no. 1), highwaymen (no. 2), swindlers and thieves (no. 4),
and criminals in general (nos. 3 and 5).
Source: Lombroso, *L'uomo delinquente*, edition 4.

and even the lengthening of the fingers. But it certainly does not apply to facial asymmetry or enlargements of the jaws, nose, and ears, as Frigerio and Amadei have recently shown. How can anyone say some anomalies are acquired professionally when observation demonstrates that they have existed from early childhood?

Maudsley, Meynert, and Biswanger chant in unison that the question of the criminal type can only be resolved through individual examination. My method is precisely the examination of criminal, insane, and normal individuals, the results of which appear in these volumes in the form of photographs and statistics. As shown in table 18, this edition of *Criminal Man* draws on 52,313 individual cases taken from both my own research and that of Marro, Ferri, and Rossi (*Centuria*). This table also answers another criticism, that I do not draw conclusions from a large enough numbers of cases. These contradictory accusations—that I do not study individual criminals or a large enough number of cases—prove nothing except that critics have not looked at or even skimmed my writings.

The ability to ascertain moral temperament from physiognomy and the cranium is not equivalent to solving a riddle or telling fortunes, as ordinary people believe, and with them, undiscerning critics. Instead, it is a scientific method of discerning character and is made all the easier because we are not limited to the face but can also take account of handwriting, gestures, and sensitivity. We recommend this method of reading moral temperament only for individuals already convicted of crime.[8]

We do not claim that every infraction of the law correlates with specific anomalies. Fewer than 60 percent of all criminals—usually those convicted of very serious crimes like murder, arson, rape, and robbery—have anomalies. Occasional criminals, who commit minor crimes like libel, political agitation, abortion, infanticide, duels, and adultery, have no physical abnormalities. Anomalies are also rare in criminals of passion.

Works by Baer and Meynert (*Revue scientifique*, 1888), based on profound knowledge of other people's studies but no original research, attempt to destroy the most important concept of my studies, that of the born criminal.[c] They argue that the degenerative characteristics I at-

---

[c] Baer, *Il delinquente dal punto di vista antropologico e sociologico*, which won a prize from the *Rivista di discipline carcerarie* and was reprinted in issues 12–15 (1885–1888).

Table 18: Quantitative Studies by Criminal Anthropologists

VOLUME I:

SUBJECT	CRIMINOLOGIST	CRIMINALS	NORMAL INDIVIDUALS	INSANE
Cadavers	Lombroso	742	551	180
	Giacomini	56	164	—
Children	Lombroso	265	697	—
Adults	Ferri	699	711	301
	Marro	500	105	—
	Rossi	102	—	—
	Lombroso	788	2,549	165
	Lombroso (photographs)	302	300	—
	Lombroso (women)	258	—	253
	Tarnowski (women)	250	150	—
	Andronico (women)	485	—	—
	Troiski	358	—	—
	Baroffio and Riva	—	14,000	262
	Franchini	—	1,331	—
	Corre	121	—	—
	Knecht	1,211	—	—
	Thomson	326	—	—
	Ottolenghi	2,200	900	—
	Biliakow	100	—	—
	Lacassagne	800	—	—
	Ottolenghi (metabolism)	47	5	—
	Ottolenghi (sensitivity)	146	21	—
	Ottolenghi (sense of smell)	80	50	—
	Lombroso (strength)	241	—	—
	Lombroso (psychometry)	10	7	—
	Lombroso et al. (tattoos)	6,348	3,886	1,938
Total		16,435	25,427	3,099

VOLUME 2:

SUBJECT	CRIMINALS	NORMAL INDIVIDUALS	MURDERERS
Epileptics	492	—	—
Criminals of passion	71	—	4,595
Insane criminals	—	—	1,842
Insane criminals (studied by Knecht, Tarde, and Richter)	—	—	321
Occasional Criminals	31	—	—
Total	17,029	25,427	9,857

Grand Total for two volumes: 52,313

Table 18: continued

Editors' note: The top section of this table lists the data sets used in the first volume of the fourth edition, and the lower section lists the data sets used in the second volume. As the top section shows, Lombroso mixes together data from autopsies, examinations of living individuals, and photographs. Confusion also arises from Lombroso's shift of categories in the lower section of the table: in column 1, he replaces general categories of subjects with types of criminals. In addition, he labels the last column "murderers" instead of "insane" as in the corresponding column in the top section. Because it seems unlikely that Lombroso found such large numbers of insane murderers, we assume that the label was a mistake, with his numbers actually referring to the insane.

tribute to born criminals are actually general traits of the lower classes from which criminals come. They forget that no single class produces criminals. Statistics prove that the poor take a lesser part than the rich in some types of serious crime. On the other hand, are all members of the lower classes left-handed, color-blind, and insensitive to pain? Baer and Meynert would answer that alcoholism causes these abnormalities, and in some cases I agree; but we must also note that many women and children who have not touched alcohol exhibit these anomalies.

Adversaries claim that my new methods, relying on clues from physiognomy and craniometry, threaten individual safety by encouraging arrests of individuals having jug ears or insensitive touch! How can they say this, when I am suggesting the use of these methods only on individuals already suspected of crime? I would not dream of detaining for life anyone with abnormal features until he is accused and convicted by the courts. On the other hand, absence of these features can save an innocent person from a libelous charge, as in a recent case.[d] My methods simply add evidence to that gained from witnesses and confessions. To claim that criminal anthropology threatens individual liberty is as absurd as concluding that when you add two numbers, the result is a lesser rather than greater sum.

Vaccaro and Grassi believe they need to attack the new school for its supposed foundation in Darwinism.[e] They want to fight Darwinism and make it disappear. This is typical of the academic world, where professors combat any new theory. But the positivist school is not founded on a theoretical system. As a psychiatrist rather than a natural scientist, I simply replaced the abstract approach of the past with clinical and anthropological methods in the individual study of the madman

[d] *Archivio di psichiatria*, 1886, vii, 2.
[e] *Rivista di discipline carcerarie*, n. 2, 1888; Vaccaro, op. cit.

and the criminal.[f] If, after applying these new methods, I became aware
that they smacked of Darwinism, I had no regrets. Instead, I made use
of Darwinian theory in studying the median occipital fossetta, as well
as crimes among animals, children, and savages. But far from being
one of Darwin's acolytes, I never mentioned him in the first and second editions of *Criminal Man*.[9] Even in the last edition, I added *disease* to atavism as an explanation of crime—and disease has no place
in Darwinian theory. Similarly, Sergi, Garofalo, and Ferri incorporated
into our theory the notion of occasional crime, which is not at all Darwinian.

Some have accused the positivist school of denying free will to offenders, thereby weakening morals and lessening contempt for crime.
Tammeo (op. cit.) has replied that the criteria of merit do not change
simply because virtues and vices are found to be the effects of molecular
mutation. No criminal anthropologist would shake the hand of a criminal or value a cretin as much as a genius simply because he believed that
biological constitution determined the perversity of the former and the
low intelligence of the latter. As Tammeo states, "anyone who claims
that denying certain ethical principles will destroy human liberty resembles those who claimed that the argument of Galileo and Coperni-
cus—that the sun is fixed and the earth moves—would ruin the solar
system."

Barine writes that "the conclusions of the new positivist school leap
out straight away; the principles of penal law can never be the same,
nor can the procedures of the courts or the aims of the penitentiary system.[9] We are witnessing a complete cataclysm in the heart of our social
organization. Modeled on nature, the new system will function according to logic rather than emotion. It will be harsh but not cruel, because
the guilty individual will no longer be disdained. He will be arrested
and interned, but without anger. The right of social defense will replace
revenge, a vestige of the old theological concept of sin, as the basis of
punishment."

I have often defended myself through the mouths of others because
the approving words of authorities, many of them from abroad, prove
the headway the new doctrines have made in the world.

[f] *Klinische Beitrage zur Psychiatrie*, 1876.
[9] *Revue Littéraire Bleu*, 15 agosto, 1887.

30

Metabolism, Menstruation, and Fertility

Armpit Temperature

In a study published in 1888, Ottolenghi and I found that the armpit temperatures of fifteen criminals examined in our laboratory (at 3 PM) were:

97.88°	1 insane rapist
98.06°	2 epileptic thieves
98.96°	3 revolutionaries (1 was epileptic)
99.50°	6 who committed assault (1 was insane and 1 epileptic)
99.86°	2 murderers (1 was epileptic)
101.84°	1 swindler

The average temperature was 99.32°. Overall, these temperatures are slightly above normal.

Nitrogen, Chlorine, and Phosphoric Acid in Urine

In my laboratory Doctor Ottolenghi carried out tests on the content of nitrogen, chlorine, and phosphoric acid over twenty-four hours in the urine of fifteen typically robust born criminals, three alcoholics, two epileptics, and five normal individuals charged with military insubordination. All men had the same diet.

The results show that born criminals eliminated the least amount of nitrogen over the twenty-four-hour period. In fact, they eliminated .38 grams per 1,000 grams of body weight, whereas the occasional criminals eliminated .52 grams. Nitrogen is the most important waste product of the organism, and there are three principal elements that influence the rate of elimination: physical constitution, diet, and metabolic rate. Which of these can we hypothesize played a role in the cases we examined? Not physical constitution, since we chose robust examples; not diet, since all cases had an identical diet. We can therefore safely say that the decreased elimination of nitrogen is due to a diminished activity of protein exchange. The rates of nitrogen elimination in born criminals accord with those found by Rivano in individuals with overexcited cerebral cortexes and in epileptics when not undergoing seizures.

Menstruation

Menstruation begins at the following ages in criminal and normal women:

Age	Criminal Women	Normal Women
12	2	2
13	10	1
14	12	1
15	7	6
16	7	4
17	3	3
18	—	3

The average age of onset of menstruation was fourteen years among criminals and between fifteen and sixteen years in honest and insane women.[10] In another study, by Salsotto, menstruation began at the average age of 14.3 years for twenty poisoners.[11]

Childbirth

Criminal women bear on the average 4.09 children (poisoners 4.1), a figure little different from that of normal women but less than that for Sicilian and Calabrese women.[12] Tarnowski found that 25 percent of female thieves had experienced childbirth, compared to 52 percent of peasant women.[13]

31

Criminal Communication

Pictography

Criminals tend to express their thoughts through drawings, even when they could express them in words, a tendency ethnologists call pictography. I have already mentioned the strange drawing by the assassin Troppman, who painted the scene of his crime to make people believe that the murderer of the Kinke family was the father, not him.

Another offender, Caviglià, was well educated but felt the need to paint the story of his crime, his imprisonment, and his suicide on his water jug.[14] In yet another example of pictography, a thief painted himself dining at a restaurant with a gentleman, robbing this gentleman, being arrested by police, and being sentenced in court. A hunchback thief illustrated the story of his contemporaneous love affairs in which both women got pregnant, became angry, and brought charges against him in court.

The example I find most eloquent is the design that a cobbler, a completely illiterate thief, embroidered on his waistcoat. Next to his own portrait, he formed the phrase *Giuseppino innocente* [little Giuseppe is innocent] by copying from an alphabet. He claimed this design should serve as proof of his innocence and had me send it to the supreme court during the appeal of his case. When it was sent back to him with no change to his sentence, he became furious, threatened me, and destroyed the waistcoat, refusing to reproduce it at any price even though he was poor and without support. This proves the light-mindedness of criminals, as well as the fact that, as an illiterate, he imbued the design on the waistcoat with more importance than a written appeal.

Tattoos function as pictographs for criminals as they do for savages. Apart from atavism, it is impossible to find another explanation for the custom of tattooing. Even literate criminals feel a need to express themselves in the primitive form of a picture and use writing only as a second

31 Troppman's Drawing of the Scene of His Crime
Editors' note: Lombroso interpreted this drawing by Troppman
as a confession of his crime, despite the inscription blaming "Kinke"
for the slaughter of the family.
Source: Lombroso, *L'uomo delinquente*, edition 4.

choice, as if it were less capable of expressing their ideas. Criminals use
pictographs, like jargon, to pour out their thoughts rather than to hide
them.

Hieroglyphics

Jargon is related to hieroglyphics, which are the expression of words in
pictures. In hieroglyphics, poison is signified by a snake; prison by a
cage; a chief *camorrista* by a hand with a ring; and a brigand by a belt
with a fist. A cat hanging on the gallows signifies a successful theft. A
tricolor flag means the royal prosecutor. A horseshoe means a doctor
(a rather dishonorable allusion to a veterinarian). A head prison guard
is represented by an entire face with a beard, a middle-level guard by
the lower half of the face, and a subordinate guard by the upper half of
the face. A robbery in the country is shown with a bunch of grapes, a

very successful robbery with a star or a rose, and a partially successful robbery with a chisel or scissors.

Handwriting under Hypnosis

I conducted an experiment that stupendously confirmed the atavistic nature of the handwriting of criminals. Under hypnosis, I suggested to a young person of honest habits that he was in fact the brigand La Gala.[15] His handwriting—normally civilized, cultivated, and almost feminine—became rough and malformed, resembling that of the criminals Boggia, Francesconi, and Gribaldo, who cross their *t*s with flourishes. When told he was a little boy, he conserved some of the brigand's energy in his infantile script; when told he was again the brigand La Gala, he returned to a rough script that conserved, however, a certain roundness from his previous identity as a child. This experiment confirms the wonderful discovery by Sergi that each individual's character has many layers.

Gesture

Criminals have long had a special way of communicating with gestures. Avé-Lallemant (o. c., 11) has brought to light the gestures of German thieves—a veritable language using just one finger. According to Vidocq, when *flouers* (thieves who lure victims with gambling, wine, and lotteries) have found their victim, they give the sign of Saint Joan, which is to bring the hand up to the tie or touch their cap (pag. 335). He describes (pag. 485) the sign of recognition among thieves, the *arçon*, which consists of rubbing the nose with the thumb and then spitting.

Pitrè has gathered the most important data on gestures and published them in his book, *Usi e costumi* [*Practices and Customs*]. His forty-eight examples come from Sicily, where specialized gestures have been common among honest people from ancient times and are therefore rampant among criminals. Robbers recognize each other by opening the right eye with the thumb, so as to show the red of the eye and reveal that they are ready for blood. To put one's finger under the left eye means "beware"; to touch the lips with the finger means "be quiet";

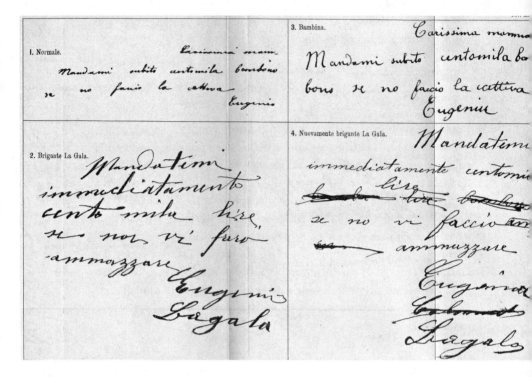

32 Handwriting under Hypnosis
Editors' note: To prove that handwriting reveals criminal character, Lombroso
subjected Eugenio, an honest student, to hypnosis. Eugenio's normal script
(no. 1) became erratic under the suggestion of being a brigand (nos. 2 and 4)
and childish under the suggestion of being a boy (no. 3).
Source: Lombroso, *L'uomo delinquente*, edition 4.

and to take out a handkerchief and wave it means "arm yourself." Extending the index finger of the right hand and then lowering it means "he has talked, he has confessed."

Atavism explains the use of hieroglyphics and pictographs since there was an epoch in which man was completely ignorant of writing and made up for it with drawings, like those of the Iroquois on rocks. With the progress of writing, letters became simplified and hieroglyphics gradually disappeared. The use of specialized gestures also originates in atavism or a reversion to a preliterate epoch. Ancient rituals and legal acts, like marriage and the emancipation of slaves, continued to be expressed in gestures even after the invention of writing. Wild gesticulation characterizes idiots, children, and demented individuals. It is perhaps not too far-fetched to recall that continuous movement is a dominant trait of turtles (studied by Fano), fish, carnivores, and rodents. The great agility and the numerous muscular tics of born criminals demonstrate—as they do in children and microcephalic individuals—a dominance of the body over the mind and the absence of psychological inhibitions over motor reflexes.

32

Art and Industry among Criminals[h]

While criminals in prison shy away from the occupations imposed on them, often simulating illness, they apply themselves energetically to other types of work that may bring punishment. The motives for these informal occupations include escape, aesthetics, gambling, sexual stimulation, communication, money, crime, suicide, and love of crafts.

Escape. Since freedom is the dream and continual preoccupation of all prisoners, they often expend a great deal of time and patience constructing tools for escape. A piece of wood, a nail, almost any object can be used for this purpose. A Lombard thief, trained as a prison tailor, made a three-meter cord from snippets of cloth and thread. "This cord," he told me, "took six months of work; with patience I will make another." Asked the purpose of the cord, he replied, "I would have used it to flee, had the Madonna helped me."

Aesthetics. Lattes writes that "vanity, always strong in criminals, inspires them secretly to construct objects that are useful for their *toilette* or as simple pastimes, even though this leads to punishment." The inmate S. V. used bread crumbs to make a bust of Garibaldi that resembled his hero exactly. A Piedmontese thief used bread to make a flute that played perfectly. Another thief, a recidivist who died of a cardiac aneurysm, constructed curious mechanical games. Using bread and clay, he also made a sculpture of a cell with an inmate, a court scene, and someone who had been decapitated. A third thief, who was insane, constructed in minute detail a sculpture of a madman who was gagged and bound, as well as the scene of a robbery in which he had probably taken part. These artistic works show the tendency of criminals to return mentally to the scene of the crime and to mix together—in the manner of mattoids and primitives—writings and epigraphs with human figures, exaggerating the details.[16]

[h] Lattes, *L'arte nei criminali* (*Archivio di psichiatria*, 1886, vol. vii; *Actes du Congrès d'anthropol. crim.*, 1886); Id., *Rivista di discipline carcerarie*, 1880; Id., 1888; Claude, *Le monde des coquins*, Paris, 1883.

33 Art of an Insane Criminal
Editors' note: Lombroso collected objects made by inmates out of bread or clay, like this scene of an insane thief being strapped to his bed.
Source: Lombroso, *L'uomo delinquente*, edition 4.

Gambling. The thief B. C. laboriously molded a complete set of dominoes with the soft part of bread. Using pieces of paper, E. Z. fashioned a pack of playing cards, coloring the black ones with a pencil and the red ones with his own blood. Instead of the government imprint, he wrote "Made in the factory of the thieves of S." The drawings on the cards were strange and childish.

Sexual Stimulation. The obscenity of certain bread sculptures confiscated in prison is extraordinary and seems to provide a safety valve for repressed sexual desire. One thief, although a waiter rather than a mechanic, made a sculpture of cork and bread whose moving parts simulated a couple in the act of coitus. Another thief who also lacked technical training constructed a little mechanical theater in which a man, using gestures, began to make love to a woman, and after he was accepted as her betrothed, married and copulated with her. The entire scene, activated by a small chain, lasted more than a minute.

Communication. The need to express ideas, coordinate escape plans, and plot crimes stimulates inmates to invent incredible means of communication. For example, they hide notes in loaves of bread or containers of tobacco, and they write directly on the inside of tobacco papers which are then passed from one prisoner to the next.

Money. Inmates have made an industry of hiding money. Gauthner writes that "gold is hidden everywhere in prisons: in hair, in beards, in ears, and between the gums. I knew one prisoner who grafted (no other word comes to my pen) gold coins under his skin, like a sort of hypodermic injection; others concealed money or compromising notes in sores and ulcers."

Crime. As a consequence of their limitless pride and overdeveloped egos, criminals are inclined to revenge themselves even for the slightest reason. They continuously seek ways to carry out their nefarious plans, particularly in the solitude of prison. A Piedmontese thief fashioned a piece of tin he found in the courtyard into a small knife, using it to wound a fellow inmate who had refused to give him a piece of bread.

Suicide. When confined to their cells, where it is difficult to harm others, criminals find ingenious ways to commit—or more often feign—suicide. Many inmates break glass and cut themselves with the pieces to simulate serious wounds. More frequently, they make cords by ripping up their clothes or blankets.

Love of Crafts. I have often been struck by the large number of serious criminals who are also such clever mechanics that they invent fascinating machines while in prison. One inmate used fish bones to make a clock that worked perfectly; another did the same thing with bread. At the Nisida prison, a prisoner made a braking mechanism for trains.

These examples demonstrate how useful criminals can be to mechanical industries. At the end of 1879, the number of inmates in Italian prisons engaged in industrial labor came to 16,832 out of a total of 29,910 or about 56 percent. If this figure seems low, it nevertheless demonstrates how society profits from men who would be a scourge outside prison. For a higher figure we can look to the United States, where prisoners are engaged in the production of agricultural machines, barrels, packing cases, wooden and iron furniture, carts, vehicles, wagons, shoes, saddlery, clothes, underwear, bed linens, brushes, baskets, shopping bags, and cigars.[i]

[i] *Rivista di discipline carcerarie*, issue 7–8, 1888.

33

The Epileptic Criminal[j]

After reading the third edition of *Criminal Man*, many objected to my synthesis of born criminals with the morally insane, complaining that I had too few cases. This was true but inevitable, since very few morally insane born criminals are found in insane asylums. Nor is it actually possible to compare born criminals with the morally insane because identical objects are better added than compared. On the other hand, epilepsy provides an obvious and important point of contact between born criminality and moral insanity, suggesting a larger framework for bringing the two phenomena together into one great natural family.[17]

The identification of epilepsy with born criminality and moral insanity will seem absurd to those who define epilepsy in terms of convulsions (or their psychological equivalents) or lapses of consciousness and vertigo. But what I call the epileptic type includes not only obvious epiphenomena but also secondary characteristics, bringing together all the traits of the morally insane and the born criminal in a pronounced way.

  j I would have been unable to complete this work without the help of my colleagues Bonvecchiato, Frigerio, Tamburini, Raggi, Bergonzoli, Albertotti, Marro, Morselli, Adriani, Bianchi, Cividalli, Amati, G. B. Verga, and Gonzales, who provided me with 260 photographs of epileptics and their histories. Frigerio gave me images made with his own hand and four special monographs. I owe the notes on the weights and tactile sensitivity of epileptics to Albertotti. Some of the data from Cividalli and Frigerio were published in *Archivio di psichiatria*, vii, 1886 and in the *Actes du Congrès d'anthropologie criminelle*, Rome, 1887; Tonnini's data were published in a separate volume, *Le epilessie*, Bocca, 1886; and G. B. Verga's data in the *Arch. di psichiatria*, viii, 1887 and in the acts of the *Congresso Freniatrico*, 1887. See also Devergie and Chaudé, *Responsabilité des acts commis par les épileptiques* (*Ann. d'hyg. et méd. légale*, 1875, p. 401); Samt, *Epileptische Irresein formen*. (*Arch. für Psych. und Nervenkr.*, Band. v, Heft ii, 1875, Band. vi, Heft i, 1876); Krafft-Ebing, *Beiträge zur klinisch-forensischen Diagnostik epileptischer Traumund Dämmerzustände* (*Friedrich's Blätter für gerichtl. Med.*, 1876); Idem, *Ueber epileptoide Dämmerund-Traumenzustände* (*Allgemeine Zeitschrift für Psych.*, Band 33, Heft. ii, 1876); Tamassia, *Riv. di freniatria*, 1878; Bonfigli, idem.; Tamburini, idem.; Mendel (*Deut. Zeits.*, 1884); Liman, *Zweifelhafte Geisteszustände*, 1869; Gowers, *Epilepsy*, London, 1883; and Brunati, G.B. Verga, Gonzales, *Arch. delle mal. nervose*, 1887, 2.

Cranium

Cranial asymmetry occurs in 12 to 37 percent of all criminals; similarly, it is characteristic of epileptics, according to authors like Lasegue. Other studies have found the anomalies typical of born criminals among epileptics as well, including voluminous jaws, jutting cheekbones, and the median occipital fossetta. This latter trait is also found among the morally insane.

Physiognomy

Epileptics further resemble born criminals and the morally insane in physiognomy. On the basis of photographs supplied by Bonvecchiato, Tamburini, Bergonzoli, Testi, and Adriani, drawings made by the illustrious Doctor Frigerio, and the examination of 278 of my own patients, I have studied the physiognomy of 410 epileptics (110 female and 300 male). The results show that all the anomalies of the born criminal, except microcephaly in the brain's frontal lobes, appear in similar proportions in epileptics. In 26.9 percent of the epileptic men and 25.8 percent of the epileptic women, I found clusters of five to seven degenerative anomalies, that is, the sign of the full criminal type. The half type, marked by four to five anomalies, characterized 9.5 percent of the epileptic men and 10.3 percent of the epileptic women. Only 63.4 percent of the epileptic males and 63.7 percent of the epileptic females completely lacked physical anomalies, a proportion that corresponds almost exactly to the figure I noted among criminal men (75 percent) and that is only slightly smaller than the figure for criminal women (72 percent).[18]

Sensitivity

Like born criminals, epileptics display tactile insensitivity. Dr. Alberttotti and I tested thirty-five individuals with epilepsy of whom: 6 showed normal sensitivity of touch; 8 showed insensitivity of touch (3 millimeters); 8 showed extreme insensitivity of touch (4–5 mm). In one case, the results (12.1 mm on the left hand and 6.8 mm on the

34 Portraits of Epileptics
Editors' note: In the fourth edition of *Criminal Man*, Lombroso added epilepsy to atavism and moral insanity as a cause of crime. Among these photographs of epileptics, he identifies nos. 1, 2, 6, 10, and 12 as born criminals.
Source: Lombroso, *L'uomo delinquente*, edition 4.

right) indicated extraordinary dullness of touch.[19] Thomsen (*Central-blatt*, 1884) has found dullness of the other four senses in epileptics, as have Cividalli and Tonnini (in 35 percent when not having seizures).

Left-Handedness

Out of 176 epileptics, I found 18 to be left-handed and 9 to be ambidextrous. These rates are lower than those for criminals, but certainly higher than those for normal individuals.

Agility

Nine epileptics out of fifty-eight demonstrated extraordinary agility, a characteristic of the morally insane. One was an acrobat, one an extremely able charioteer, and a third was able to slide through barred windows to escape.

Psychology

The completely overlapping identity of epileptics, criminals, and the morally insane is revealed most clearly by psychological studies. For example, epileptics show the same vast intellectual range, from genius to complete imbecility, that we find among the morally insane and criminals. Liman (*Zweifelhafte Geisteszustände vor Gericht.*, p. 69) reminds us that Julius Caesar, Petrarch, Newton, Mohammed, Peter the Great, Molière, and Napoleon were epileptic, to which I would add that they had many criminal or insane descendants and frequent hallucinations. Furthermore, as I demonstrated in my book, *Genio e folia* [*Genius and Insanity*], genius resembles epileptic fits in the spontaneous and intermittent nature of its eruptions, which are followed by periods of unconsciousness and sometimes even amnesia.

Krafft-Ebing writes of epileptics that "at times their expansive nature and inspired fantasy make them dream up romantic stories, which they end up believing; at the same time they have deliria, which bring on great seizures. When they come into conflict with the law, their apparent lucidity makes them seem like feigned rather than real epileptics, a state that can last for hours, days, or weeks." One epileptic dreamed of conquering India with sixty peasants whom he intended to hire with stolen money; he thought himself a count or a member of parliament (see *Archivio di psichiatria*, VIII, 3). Another boasted that his powerful friends would protect him. Such fantasies bring to mind the excessive vanity of criminals.

According to Schüle (*Handb. Der Geisteskr.*, p. 408), "The epileptic character shows an extraordinary morbid irritability that rapidly transforms itself into impulsive acts. While epileptics can be punctual in commerce, conscientious, and courteous, in a flash they can become rude, cruel, and dishonest to the point of theft. No madman has such a strong tendency to kleptomania as those in a permanent epileptic state. At the beginning of their epileptic fits, these sick individuals tranquilly steal anything they find, either carrying out the most sophisticated thefts or stealing randomly; immediately after the convulsion, however, they reveal their crimes by throwing the stolen objects away."

The anthropological character of epileptics is marked by moral degeneration and a tendency to evil. While epileptics blame their crimes on their physical condition, we must note other causational factors that form a sort of clinical trinity. These are a blurring of the conscience that facilitates impulsive behavior and flightiness of character and thought (Schüle). The epileptic's impulsivity, fleeting sentiments, and tendency to inflict harm for harm's sake are also characteristics of the born criminal and the morally insane.

As Fischer (*Zur Lehre von Epilept. Irres.*, 1884) and Pick (*Encycl.*, v. *Epilept.*) write, "In sum, contradictory behavior and immorality are the dominant characteristics of epileptics. Those who are cynical may at times become religious; those who throw themselves at their wives' feet may become wife-murderers. They always oscillate between two extremes."

Moral Statistics

To complete this psychological portrait with my usual statistics, I provide in table 19 the results of studies by Cividalli, Bianchi, and Tonnini. As this table shows, epileptics display the same vices as criminals, above all the impulsiveness that so frequently leads to crimes against persons. Even those few who possess a moral sense and lead virtuous lives may

Table 19: Psychological Anomalies of Epileptics

ANOMALIES	PERCENTAGE OF MEN		PERCENTAGE OF WOMEN
	65 cases observed by Cividalli	42 cases observed by Tonnini/Bianchi	52 cases observed by Cividalli
Limited intelligence	61	30	69
Weak memory	91	14	78
Hallucinations	41	20	36
Impulsivity	50	2.3	49
Delusions of grandeur	1	2.3	—
Irascibility	100	30	61
Lying	100	7	100
Theft	63	4.6	75
Religious delusions	86	14	100
Pederasty	39	2.3	38
Perversity	57	30	15
Masturbation	67	—	21
Intact moral sense	—	16	—

experience exaggerated emotions culminating in violence. This type of epileptic corresponds to the so-called criminal of passion. Now we understand why prison doctors claim that epileptics commit more crimes than other inmates.

Religiosity

Religiosity, a characteristic of criminals, is also found in epileptics, where it alternates with cynicism and serves as a pretext for impulsive acts. I knew one epileptic who killed his wife and mother-in-law, believing himself to be carrying out the wishes of a saint-protector who incited the crime with signs and words. Doctor Albertotti found religiosity in seventeen out of his thirty cases of epilepsy, and it was always mixed with contrary tendencies like the impulse to rape or murder. One patient, showing a truly atavistic character that recalled primitive religiosity, offered gifts to the sun god and went around placing them on trees. Some epileptics become bigots immediately before and after their fits and then return to being cynics. A female epileptic alternated prayer with cursing and even nymphomania.

34

Epileptics and Born Criminals

Other characteristics of epileptics enable us to complete the moral portrait of members of this group and reaffirm the links between epilepsy and born criminality. These psychological traits do not appear frequently enough to be studied statistically, but are obvious enough to give what artists call local color.

Tendency to Vagabondage. Epileptics share with born criminals a tendency to vagabondage. Sometimes this is the effect of temporary loss of consciousness, which makes them wander like sleepwalkers far from home. More often vagabondage results from the inner disquiet of epileptics; projecting their internal disturbance onto the external world, they feel a need to keep in motion. They hope that change will ease their difficulties, which are all the worse for the lack of any strong bonds to family or fatherland. Tissié (*Les alienés voyageurs*, 1887) describes one epileptic who moved involuntarily from Paris to Bombay, a second who walked seventy-one kilometers unconsciously, and a third who wandered aimlessly for thirty-one months!

Love of animals. Some epileptics feel extreme love for animals, especially domestic ones. Two epileptics, young and rich, were able to think of nothing but their horse, which they loved more than their family. An epileptic prisoner rounded up common rats and tried to educate them. An epileptic student collected fleas and attempted to drill them in military exercises, while another tried to train a goose to do the same thing. An epileptic mountain shepherd took his love for his goats to the point of carnal relations.

Somnambulism. Like the morally insane, epileptics are frequently somnambulists. Krafft-Ebing writes, "After an epileptic seizure, often the ill person enters a state similar to somnambulism, in which he seems to have regained consciousness, talking logically, acting rationally, and continuing his daily life, but later he remembers nothing, showing that

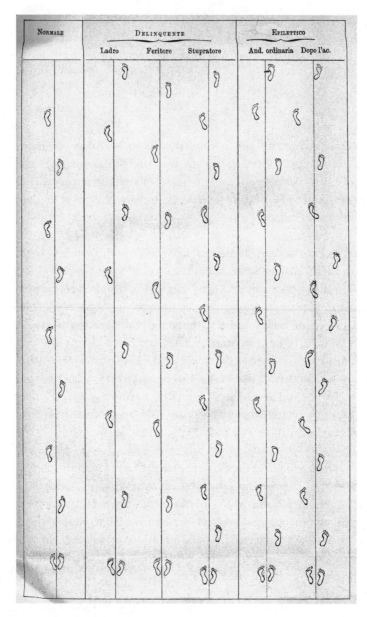

35 Gaits of Normal, Criminal, and Epileptic Men

Editors' note: Lombroso expected criminals and epileptics to walk differently from normal men. Here he distinguishes between the gaits of normal men (left column); thieves, assaulters, and rapists (middle columns); and epileptics (two right columns).

Source: Lombroso, *L'uomo delinquente*, edition 4.

he was not conscious after all. This state of psychological blindness can last a long time, sometimes for the entire period between seizures." According to Weiss and Garimond, the somnambulistic state of epileptics can last for months and up to ten years—a fact that will not seem strange to those who have studied serious fits of hysteria (Weiss, *Med. Wien. Wochens.*, 1885). Dostoevsky notes that it is very common for criminals to gesticulate and talk in their sleep.[20]

Obscenity. Epileptics often indulge in obscene behavior. Kowalewski (*Archiv. psichiatrii*, 1885) has noted that coitus resembles an epileptic fit in the tensing of muscles, dilation of the pupils, and loss of consciousness. Not only are epileptic fits frequently accompanied by a desire for sexual intercourse, but the first seizure often coincides with sexual initiation and may be linked to forms of sexual perversion.

A very intelligent epileptic observed by Da Costa (*The Journ. of nervous diseases*, 1887) ate excrement during his fits, attempted sodomy, and, with a maneuver that would be difficult for anyone else, orally masturbated his own penis. A man of fifty-two, an excellent accountant, was arrested for trying to masturbate his office companions. The son of a drunkard, he had an insane grandmother, epileptic uncle, and a suicidal brother; he had tried to drown his wife and still wet his bed at age twenty-one. Discovered to be an epileptic, he was absolved from the initial charges but arrested months later for further obscene acts.

Recuperative Power. Tonnini brought to my attention a characteristic that is also common in criminals, "the great ease with which wounds heal over and traumas are repaired in the epileptic." This recuperative power, in his view, represents an atavistic return to the animalian stage of evolution, in which creatures like lizards and salamanders can reproduce entire limbs. All degenerates, epileptics, imbeciles, and moral madmen possess this ability to heal quickly. Tonnini continues, "One of my morally insane patients tore off his moustache, along with a large chunk of skin; but after a few days, his lip was completely healed."

Destruction and Cannibalism. Like children, epileptics have an automatic need to destroy inanimate objects, especially ones associated with wounds, suicide, and homicide. Misdea, a regimental barber who became an assassin, chewed up four razors after he was relieved from office.[21] Piz . . . regularly broke all the crockery in his cell, saying that he was "letting off steam." Epileptics' tendency to destroy things can reach the point of cannibalism, even in circumstances unrelated to any desire for revenge. After slaughtering his companions, Misdea shouted that he wanted to devour their livers.

Special Words. Like monomaniacs, epileptics give special names to the automatic impulses that govern them. Every time he had epileptic suicidal impulses, Misdea said, "I'm getting capricious" or "my head is spinning." Legrand du Saulle observed that epileptics use set phrases for their murderous fits like, "The heat is mounting. I'm burning. I feel pushed. My head is spinning and exploding." With such phrases epileptics interpret behavior that seems to be voluntary but in fact results from their illness.

Suicide. Out of 128 epileptics, Leidesdorf found 13 who were suicidal; I found 11 out of 306. Thus suicidal tendencies occur frequently in epileptics. They are sometimes genuine, often simulated, and even more often automatic and motiveless. Like criminals, epileptics sometimes commit suicide to escape punishment or to prevent themselves from committing a crime. Morel describes an epileptic woman who, when he forced her to take a cold shower for having struck her companions, took a piece of glass and cut her jugular vein.[22]

Tattoos. Severi studied forty-six madmen with tattoos, two of whom were epileptic. One had tattoos covering his whole body, just as one sees among prisoners. In the prison where I am the doctor, at one point epileptics were seized by such a mania for tattooing that after a few days, seven out of thirteen were covered with designs.

Fraternization. Epileptics are the only inmates in insane asylums who seek each other out and associate, as do criminals in prisons. They conspire not only with other epileptics but also with the morally insane. In Schonberg's hospital for the mentally ill (*Allgem. Zeit. f. Psich.*, 1884), five madmen planned an escape, burning down their own building. Of these, three were morally insane and one epileptic. Frigerio told me about a certain L. I., an epileptic who stole with great skill and trained his insane asylum companions to do likewise. Overall, epileptics have the characteristics of the morally insane writ large.

Statistics on Criminal Epilepsy

The inexorable weight of statistics confirms the family relationship—indeed the unity—of criminality, moral insanity, and epilepsy. Recent studies by Sommer and Knecht (*Archivio di psichiatria e scienze penali*, vol. v), Marro, and Virgilio show the proportion of epileptics among prison inmates to be 5 percent (it goes up to 6.10 percent among thieves, according to Virgilio). In the noncriminal population, the rate of epilepsy is 6 per 1,000 according to Rayer, 5 per 1,000 according to Villeneuve (*Statistique des Bouches du Rhône*, 1826), 1 per 1,000 according to Hirsch, 1.13 per 1,000 according to Morselli, and 2.4 per 1,000 according to Sormani. Thus the rate of epilepsy among prisoners is five to nine times that of the general population. Clark claims that 11 percent of epileptics commit crimes (*Heredity and crime in epilepsy*, 1880).

Hidden Epilepsy

The sharp, sudden outbursts that characterize hidden epilepsy demonstrate that this affliction is similar to criminality and moral insanity.[23] These psychological equivalents of physical seizures, marked by unpredictability and ferocity, concentrate the usual epileptic behavior into a brief caricature of crime. The low levels of sensory perception and the momentary stupidity that follow or accompany fits of hidden epilepsy are equivalent to the habitual and often congenital states of common epileptics, conditions often found in criminals.

The classic example of hidden epilepsy is the soldier Misdea, whose role in the tragedy of Pizzofalcone is well known. On the thirteenth of April 1884, the first day of Easter, the soldiers of the nineteenth Italian regiment were talking in their barracks after having drunk many toasts. Several soldiers from northern Italy began insulting two companions from Calabria in the south by remarking on the area's aridity.

The soldier Misdea, from Girifalco in the south, then returned to the barracks after having consumed several drinks. Twenty-two years old, he had been charged with bodily harm, carrying weapons, and suspicion of theft before the age of eighteen. He was so well known in his regiment for violent and threatening behavior that his captain—a mild fellow—had relieved him of his duties as the regiment's barber.

When the northern soldier Codara saw him, Misdea warned: "Leave me alone. My head is feeling very odd and I'm not sure how things will end up!"

"But you've always got it in for us northerners from Piedmont and Lombardy; what have we ever done to you?"

Misdea answered: "Yes, I do have a thing against the Piedmontese" and punched him in the chest, shouting, "And look, I'm capable of doing this to all of you, one by one, while I laugh at my victims!"

Going to his bed, he fetched his cartridges and those of his companions.

There was silence. Some soldiers returned to chatting. Suddenly there was an explosion, and three soldiers were severely wounded, while another three sought refuge in the latrines. Misdea followed them, firing against the latrine door and wounding several companions. But the massacre was not yet over. He chased those who had gotten away, shooting them one by one, firing a total of fifty-two shots, wounding thirteen and killing seven.

Once imprisoned in a cell, he continued to call for revenge, saying that he wanted to kill people, burn them alive, and eat their livers. He then slept so soundly that it was difficult to wake him, and thereafter he ate little for three days. Subsequently he felt better, complaining only of dizziness, but after six days he experienced such pain that he feared death at any moment. The doctor believed him to be simulating illness and refused treatment. During his long epileptic and homicidal attack, he experienced periods of complete lucidity in which he could name each of his victims.

Descended from a family of madmen, epileptics, sexual deviants, and criminals, Misdea was 1.63 meters tall and weighed 56.2 kilograms.[24] He had thick hair on his head and limbs; scars from fights on his arms, face, and head; protuberances on his skull, which was flattened on the upper forehead; indentations like those of microcephalics on his lower forehead, above projecting eyebrows; enormous cheekbones; and mild strabismus.

Misdea was limited in intelligence, weak in memory, nervous, illogical, and incapable of understanding abstract concepts, although he simulated sanity at his trial. His insensitivity, laziness, vanity, violence, and desire for revenge to the point of cannibalism likened him to the born criminal and the madman. That these characteristics were aggravated by epilepsy was clear even to the medical experts for the prosecution. Additional facts confirmed the diagnosis of epilepsy: his indiscriminate slaughter of both friend and foe; his extraordinary muscular strength at the time of his arrest (despite a dynamometer reading of merely 34.37 kg. for compressive strength); his ability to act in cold blood and stay calm after his crime; his extraordinary courage alternating with habitual cowardice; his capricious and irascible character; his abuse of wine, dizziness, and suicidal impulses; his previous history of epileptic fits; his use of stock phrases before his seizures such as *I have my caprices*, *my head is spinning*; his headaches and profound sleep after the slaughter; and above all his family background, which included epileptic, alcoholic, insane, and criminal relatives.

In such cases, hidden epilepsy allows malicious individuals to carry out violence and recall their actions afterwards. These psychological seizures, lasting days or even months, cannot be distinguished from criminal behavior. We only have to stretch the definition of epilepsy a bit to draw a comparison between the psychological state of an epileptic during a fit and of the born criminal during his entire life.

35

Physiology and Etiology of Epilepsy[k]

Physiology

Epilepsy often lacks physical symptoms because it involves an irritation of the cortical centers of the brain that may produce psychological rather than motor reactions. Recent studies have proven what previously were only hypotheses: epileptic convulsions result from irritation of the motor zones of the brain's cerebral cortex; epileptic hallucination is the consequence of excitement of its sensory zones; and loss of consciousness during epileptic seizures, which leads to criminal impulses, involves irritation of even higher psychological centers. Although I am emphasizing irritation in the causation of epilepsy, I do not want to slight the importance of degeneration. Indeed, brain irritation can result from degeneration, traumas, or alcohol, all of which weaken the cortex and thus predispose it to epilepsy.[25]

While crime and epilepsy are similar, there is an important anatomical difference. Criminals often exhibit frontal microcephaly, leading to cranial anomalies not found in normal men such as small, low foreheads and flattening of the upper face and sinus cavities.[l] These anoma-

---

[k] Luciani, *Sulla patogenesi dell'epilessia da traumi*, 1880; Raggi e Seppelli, *Studi intorno all'epilessia*, 1886; Luciani e Seppilli, *Sulle localizzazioni funzionali*, Naples, 1885; Zehen, *Ueber die Krampfe in Folge elektriz. Reiznung der Grosshirn.*, 1885 (*Archiv. f. Psych.*, xiii); Noel-Paton, nel *Brain*, 1886; Seppilli, *L'epilessia corticale*, 1884; Idem., *Studio anatomico intorno all'epilessia corticale*, 1886; Maragliano, *Sulla sintomologia delle lesioni corticali*, 1878; Silvestri, nella *Riv. di freniatria*, 1880, i and ii; and Unverricht, nell' *Arch. f. Psych. und Nerv.*, 1883, ii.

[l] In *I caratteri dei criminali* [*Characteristics of Criminals*], Marro compared foreheads of criminals and healthy individuals, as follows:

	PERCENT OF CRIMINALS	PERCENT OF NORMAL MEN
Narrow forehead	86	59
Low forehead	41	15
Wide forehead	13	41
High forehead	58	84

lies are found rarely in convulsive epileptics, who instead display abnormal convolutions of the parietal lobe of the upper brain. Epileptics are therefore less likely to experience criminalistic outbursts during which they lose conscience, foresight, and inhibitions against base impulses.[26] Everyone agrees that the psychological centers responsible for resisting primitive instincts are situated in the lobes that in criminals are constricted by frontal microcephaly.

Recent experimental and clinical studies have shown that dizziness, epigastric blockage, headaches, and excessive saliva flow—when preceded by an aura—are signs of hidden epileptic episodes, and that hidden epilepsy may manifest itself in psychological rather than physical disturbances.[27] Then why should it be a problem to categorize moral insanity as a chronic state of hidden epilepsy?

Etiology

Geographical Distribution. The geographical distribution of epilepsy confirms that it is closely related to crime and moral insanity. To demonstrate this, we can compare statistics on Italian criminality from the study of Doctor Rossi (for 1879–83) with those on epilepsy in military draftees provided by Sormani (for 1863–76).[m] Thirty-five of the sixty-nine Italian provinces had below-average rates of epilepsy, and of these, twenty-five were below average for crimes of rebellion, twenty-five for offenses against morality, and twenty-three for violent crime.[n] Conversely, of thirty-two provinces with above-average rates of epilepsy, eleven were also above average for crimes of rebellion, thirteen for offenses against morality, and thirteen for crimes of violence. Thus there is a correlation in the geographical distribution of epilepsy and crime.

Age. That the onset of epilepsy occurs at a young age demonstrates its congenital nature and similarity to moral insanity. Cividalli found that epilepsy with convulsions appeared before the age of fourteen in 78 out

[m] Rossi's figures are based on Bodio, *Movimento della criminalità in Italia nel quinquennio 1879–1883*; Sormani, *Geografia nosologica d'Italia.*

[n] The category of crimes of rebellion includes "rebellion, violence, attacks on government agents, the army, and police"; offenses against morality include "crimes against public decency and against the family"; crimes of violence include "simple and aggravated homicide, assaults causing death, animal rustling, blackmail, extortion, and armed robbery with homicide."

Table 20: Causes of Epilepsy

CAUSES	STUDY BY HAMMOND (206 cases)	STUDY BY REYNOLDS (60 cases)	STUDY BY LEIDERSDORF (128 cases)	STUDY BY GOWERS (428 cases)
Fear, anxiety	15	29	24	186
Scarlet fever, typhoid	11	9	4	35
Sun exposure	–	–	–	27
Head injuries	10	9	13	65
Intellectual excesses	17	–	–	–
Sexual excesses	15	–	–	–
Childhood teething, indigestion	11	16	–	72(*)
Menstrual problems	10	–	–	–
Pregnancy	3	–	–	6
Syphilis	3	–	–	–
Infantile meningitis	–	–	7	–
Alcoholism	–	–	4	13
Post-partum eclampsia	–	–	3	–
Cold water on the head	–	–	2	–
First coitus in hysterical women	–	–	2	–
No cause	104	–	67	–

(*) This number includes 6 cases of worms, 9 of asphyxia, 6 of lead poisoning, 1 of tobacco poisoning, 2 of renal infection, and 1 of loss of consciousness.

Editors' note: In every column, the number of causes is either higher or lower than the number of cases.

of 120 epileptic madmen. This precocity parallels delinquency's early age of onset. Hidden epilepsy often manifests itself at a later age, according to Griesinger, which explains why honest men suddenly commit violent crime after experiencing an attack of dizziness.[28]

Causes. Five causes of epilepsy are identical to those for criminality: alcoholism, head trauma, meningitis, skin eruptions, and cranial tumors. Table 20 gives the full list of causes of epilepsy.

Parental Disease. Many criminals and epileptics have tubercular parents, as shown by Marro for the former and Ball for the latter. Moreover, hysteria, neurosis, and alcoholism characterize the parents of not only criminals and epileptics but also of the morally insane. When one constructs a genealogical tree of a criminal or an epileptic, one finds a mixture of criminality and epilepsy with tuberculosis (as in the wife killer Ratti), with alcoholism (as in the case of Misdea), or with madness. The effects of parental diseases are documented in tables 21 and 22.

Table 21: Genealogy of Ratti

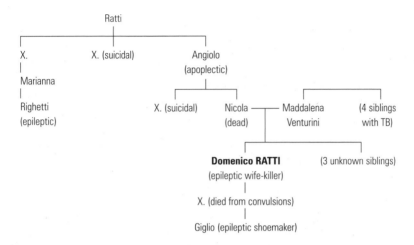

Even criminals and epileptics with healthy parents do not contradict this point because when one studies in detail the various branches of the same family, one discovers that a complete absence of degenerative phenomena in one branch of the family is balanced by an excess of examples in another branch. This genealogical type of study confirms that moral insanity, criminality, and epilepsy are analogous degenerative diseases.

Epilepsy and Moral Insanity

I am not arguing that moral insanity is the same thing as epilepsy or that all epileptics are morally insane. Rather, I am interested in a type of epilepsy that is becoming more common and has been little studied. It takes many forms including epilepsy from absinthe, alcoholic epilepsy, toxic epilepsy, epilepsy with vertigo, and hidden epilepsy, all of which also constitute acute forms of moral insanity and congenital criminality.

Essentially, the difference among epilepsy, moral insanity, and born criminality is only a matter of degree. The most serious cases of moral insanity overlap with those of congenital criminality, while epileptic criminals who experience fits of violence resemble the morally insane. Overall, the three phenomena are similar. And since two things that resemble a third thing are therefore identical to each other, it is clear

Table 22: Genealogy of Misdea

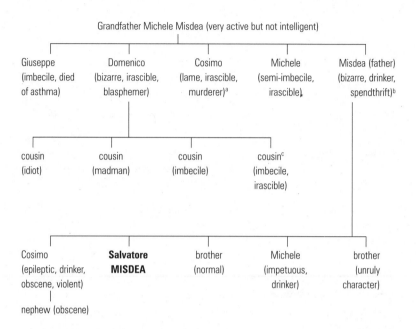

Grandfather Michele Misdea (very active but not intelligent)

Giuseppe (imbecile, died of asthma)

Domenico (bizarre, irascible, blasphemer)

Cosimo (lame, irascible, murderer)[a]

Michele (semi-imbecile, irascible)

Misdea (father) (bizarre, drinker, spendthrift)[b]

cousin (idiot)

cousin (madman)

cousin (imbecile)

cousin[c] (imbecile, irascible)

Cosimo (epileptic, drinker, obscene, violent)

Salvatore MISDEA

brother (normal)

Michele (impetuous, drinker)

brother (unruly character)

nephew (obscene)

[a] Uncle Cosimo killed a friend for a minor cause and died in prison of pneumonia.

[b] Misdea's father wasted all his money on gambling, women, and drink. He married a woman who was honest but hysterical and whose brothers included a brigand and a thief.

[c] Cousin Michele, a priest, publicly struck the Archbishop during a religious procession because the Archbishop had given him little notice of the event. While Michele was at seminary, his companions put a turtle in his bed and convinced him that he had given birth to it; after that he referred to the turtle as his daughter and considered her a miracle.

that congenital criminality and moral insanity are nothing but special forms of epilepsy. They are, as Griesinger might say, epileptoid states. For greater clarity here is a summary of my ideas:

	Epileptoids	
Grade 1	Hidden epileptic	Criminal of passion
Grade 2	Chronic epileptic	Occasional criminal
Grade 3	Morally insane	
Grade 4	Born criminal	

This diagram illustrates how different degrees of epilepsy form the substratum for both mildly pathological behavior (crimes of passion and occasional crime) and, when combined with atavism, for moral insanity and born criminality

Many critics object to my fusion of moral insanity with criminality and epilepsy because they recognize so many types of moral insanity and fail to realize that great variety also characterizes criminality and epilepsy. Variations exist not only among species in the same genus but also among individuals in the same species. For example, the male bird of paradise differs so much from the female as to seem to belong to a different genus. Similarly, while the morally insane, criminals, and epileptics may seem to constitute disparate categories, they are, nevertheless, united by strange habits and strong impulses that are absent in honest men. Despite the gradations among them, however marked or slight these may be, these groups do not constitute species, but rather subgroups of the same species. Statistical law teaches that all phenomena are graduated, with many intermediate steps between the minimum and maximum forms. Who could deny that the malarial fever is the same thing as cephalic fever and as pneumonia, even though these diseases appear to differ radically from one another?

My assertion of the identity of epilepsy, moral insanity, and criminality is nothing new, for many others have also assumed it to be the case. Maudsley, for instance, writes that those who lack a moral sense are often epileptics or imbeciles (*Mental science*, 1882). Krafft-Ebing (*Lehrb. der Gericht. Psych.*, 1882, p. 248) and Bonvecchiato argue that moral insanity characterizes epileptics, drunkards, and the mad (who often display epileptic symptoms). Krafft-Ebing concludes that "the fleetingness and frequency of psychopathic phenomena, and the ever increased probability that a criminal act may be committed during a fit of vertiginous epilepsy or in its crepuscular stage, lead to the belief that many crimes are no more than misinterpreted epileptic phenomena" (p. 192). Furthermore, forensic medicine assumed a fusion of the three phenomena for many years before it could be proven physiologically.[o]

---

[o] There are even traces in literature of the interrelation of criminality, epilepsy, and moral insanity. According to Shakespeare, Macbeth was epileptic from infancy (Act ii). Prof. Maclokoff has pointed out to me how Shakespeare underlined Macbeth's epilepsy, characterized by hallucinations, physical convulsions, and other psychological abnormalities: "There comes my fit again" (Macbeth, act ii, scene iii). Similarly, in *Crime and Punishment* Dostoevsky portrayed a criminal with loss of consciousness and amnesia. Furthermore, in *The House of the Dead* he included this curious sentence: "An inmate was calm

Atavism. The fusion of moral insanity and epilepsy does not exclude atavism as a cause of crime. All mental illnesses result in intermittent moral insanity, but epilepsy does so more continuously by affecting the motor and the psychological centers of the brain. As a result, in epilepsy the mental capacities that appeared late in human development are arrested or lost. If a brain lesion removes the ability to recognize colors, the first color to disappear is the last one to have appeared in the process of differentiation (violet). Similarly, the moral sense—the highest point of evolution of the human brain—is the first to disappear when the brain becomes infirm.[29]

Epilepsy, like a complete type of atavism, is characterized by primordial religiosity, ferocity, instability, impetuosity, agility, cannibalism, irascibility, precocity, and animal instincts. As Gowers notes, epileptics frequently bark, meow, drink blood, and devour live animals, including their fur, as in a case where a child bit the neck of a cat. He concludes that "these are manifestations of that instinctive animality that we all possess in a latent state" (*Epilepsy*, London 1880). I particularly value this assessment because it comes from a practicing doctor with no knowledge of my theories.[30]

---

for many years until he became the head of his work team. Then, to the surprise of the prison guards, he mutinied and committed capital crimes like murder. The cause was a restless desire to display his personality, a melancholy instinct to affirm his own ego even under impossible circumstances. It resembled an epileptic fit."

36

The Insane Criminal

Statistics[p]

That insanity occurs frequently among criminals becomes clearer every day. Sommer estimates that while the rate of insanity in Prussia is only 1 for every 250 to 400 people in the general population, it is 1 for every 20 to 40 Prussian inmates (based on a study of 111 insane criminals in Allenbenger prison from 1852–82). Thirty-five percent of inmates were insane in the Gand penitentiary (1831–60), 23 percent in that of Lovanio (1861 and 1869).

In his valuable book, *Statistics of Prisoners, Their Mental Condition and Diseases* (1854), Thomson notes that 673—or 12 percent—of 5,432 Scottish prisoners were insane, including 58 imbeciles and 57 epileptics. Yet at their trials a mere 53 had been recognized as mentally ill! According to official Italian statistics, only 4.9 percent of Italian inmates are insane, a statistic so low that it must be inexact.[q] One specialist has estimated tenfold that number, while Dr. Grilli has found 44 out of 351 inmates at the Volterra prison to be insane. Many of them were monomaniacal or demented while 5 were so violent that they had to be put in straitjackets and left in their cells so they could not hurt themselves.

---

[p] Rossi, *Pazzi criminali in Italia*, Rome, 1887; Sommer, *Beitrage zur Kenntniss der Criminal Irren.*, Berlin, 1883; Beltrani-Scalia, *Statistica decennale delle carceri*, 1880; Knecht, *Ueber die Vebreitung physicher Degeneration bei Verbrechern und die Beziehungen zwischen Degenerationszeichen und Neuropatien* (*Allgemeine Zeitschrift für Psychiatrie*), Berlin, 1883; Piper, *Geistesstörungen im Gefängnisse*, 1877 (*Allg. Zeit. f. Psych.*), 1883; Grilli, *Visita al Penitenziario*, Milano, 1879; Duffield Robinson, *Simulated insanity in the crime classe* (*Journal of nervous and mental disease*, mars 1887); P. Max-Simon, *Crimes et délits dans la folie*, Paris, 1886; A. Maria de Senna, *Relatorio do serviço medico e administrativo do Hospital do conde de Ferreira*, Porto, 1887; Sander und Richter, *Die Beziehungen Zwischen Geistesstörungen und Verbrechen*, Berlin, 1886; Langreuter, *Uber der Geistesskr. Verbrechen*, 1887; Delbruck, *Viertel-jahr. f. Gericht. Mediz.*, aprile, 1886; Bar, *Die Gefängnisse*, 1871; and Tamburini, negli *Actes du Congrès d'Anthropologie criminelle*, 1887.

[q] In Italy, the rate of insanity oscillates between 21 percent and 49 percent in the long-term prisons (1866–71) and between 16 percent and 23 percent in short-term jails (1872). (See the *Rivista di discipline carcerarie*, 1880, issues 5–6. Beltrani-Scalia, *Statistica decennale delle carceri*.)

The reason for the gap between official and actual Italian statistics for criminal insanity is the fear that madness may serve as an excuse for crime and impede punishment. Some experts warn that diagnoses of criminal insanity might open the gates of prisons and return dangerous lawbreakers to society. Prison directors hesitate to acknowledge insanity in their inmates, and they punish bizarre behavior as rule breaking. Moreover, judges, having little knowledge of psychiatry, tend to accept the recommendations of prison directors rather than those of doctors. In addition, prison doctors, even if they are psychiatrists, spend little time studying insanity among their patients, or study it simply to satisfy their noble but sterile scientific curiosity. To sum up, the rate of insanity among Italian offenders is not 4.9 percent, as official statistics proclaim, but in fact 30 percent—thirty times the rate (1 percent) among normal individuals.

In a goodly proportion of insane prisoners—39 out of 168 cases (23 percent) in Germany (according to Knecht) and 350 out of 1,742 cases (19 percent) in Italy—the delirium was in its initial stages before imprisonment and thus probably set in even before the crime. Table 23 details types of insanity among Italian prisoners for a period of seventeen years; the total number of cases, 1,742, is impressive. According to this table, the predominant forms of insanity among prisoners are persecution monomania and melancholy, both of which are exacerbated by the agony of conviction and rigors of incarceration.[31] Although the table lists only one case of simulated insanity, we know that criminals frequently pretend to be mad.

Table 23 further shows large numbers of criminals with suicidal monomania and epileptic insanity, as well as 72 with imbecility, 47 with weak intelligence, 11 with cretinism, 19 with insanity from pellagra, 113 with dementia, and 88 with moral insanity. Probably these abnormal mental conditions developed before the crimes. Therefore, out of 1,742 insane criminals, 350 were mad well before incarceration and of these, 218 from birth (!!). If we add the feebleminded (who are usually left out of statistics on mental illness), the proportion of inmates with insanity that is congenital or that at least preceded the crime would be even greater.

The high figures for delirium, violent monomania, and mania—429 cases, or 25 percent in all—would seem to contradict my contention that insanity tends to precede the commission of crimes. Ignorant

Table 23: Types of Insanity among Italian Criminals

TYPES OF INSANITY	NUMBER OF CASES	TYPES OF INSANITY	NUMBER OF CASES
Mania	286	Multiple phobias	8
Melancholy	217	Paralytic insanity	17
Acute delirium	126	Epileptic insanity	37
Imbecility	72	Alcoholic insanity	22
Dementia	113	Insanity from pellagra	19
Moral insanity	88	Cretinism	11
Weak intelligence	47	Simulated insanity	1
Monomania: persecution	236		
hypochondria	116	Total	1,742
sensory	106		
suicidal	86		
violent[a]	17		
nostalgic	37		
ostentatious	33		
erotic	24		
religious	3		
homicidal	20		

[a]There is no such disease as violent monomania; therefore, this category must refer to mania.
Editors' note: These data are drawn from official Italian statistics on the number of insane criminals in Italian short-term jails and long-term prisons over a period of seventeen years (dates unspecified).

prison directors and doctors misinterpret these forms of insanity as rebellion and insubordination and thus punish them. Often these illnesses explode under prison discipline designed to control them. We now understand that these explosions are identical to the violent and angry outbreaks of the morally insane, the epileptic, and the born criminal.[32]

The congenital nature of criminal insanity is demonstrated by the fact that most inmates show the first symptoms of mental illness shortly after admission to prison. In Italy between 1866 and 1876 (Beltrani-Scalia, o.c.), inmates were diagnosed as insane after the following periods of incarceration:

1–6 months	140	7–10 years	10
6 months to 1 year	103	11–25 years	1
1–3 years	196	25 years +	2
3–5 years	76		
5–7 years	18		

Thus the principal cause of insanity among criminals is not lengthy prison sentences, but an innate condition.

Without doubt, prisons themselves call forth violent outbursts of mania, the highest proportion of which is found in cellular prisons. The declining number of such eruptions in successive years can be explained, at least in nonrecidivist cases, by the calming influence of acclimatization. The highest rates of insanity are found in prisons where silence is obligatory, where inmates live in solitary confinement doing nothing, or where punishment calls for little physical effort. The proportion of madmen in our short-term jails is 31 percent and in long-term prisons 21 percent, but the rate falls to 14 percent among those doing forced labor for a fixed period and to 6 percent for those doing it for life.

37

Biology and Psychology of Insane Criminals

Biology

I examined one hundred photographs of insane criminals, who were mad before committing their crimes and not epileptic. These photographs reveal that 44 percent of these insane criminals embody the full criminal type, which is marked by five or six degenerative characteristics, particularly jug ears, enlarged sinuses, large jaws and cheekbones, sullen or crossed eyes, and thin upper lips. This is a higher proportion than for criminals in general.

Etiological and somatic similarities demonstrate that insanity and criminality are so closely linked as to be nearly identical. The same factors predispose individuals to either insanity or criminality: civilization, celibacy, hot climate, being male, urban residence, and membership in certain professions (such as cobbler, cook, domestic, and, perhaps, soldier). Moreover, many criminals have insane relatives. Crime and insanity are both provoked by trauma, cranial malformations, and alcoholism. Among the insane as among murderers, meteorological conditions—especially hot temperatures—bring on abnormal behavior and fits. According to Thomson, both madmen and criminals are prone to such illnesses as meningitis, softening of the brain, and somnambulism.

Psychology[r]

The diversity in types of mental illness makes it impossible to construct a single profile of the insane criminal. The best we can do is to

[r] *Archivio di psichiatria, scienze penalii ed antropologia criminale*, Turin, 1880–1888; *Annales medico-psychologiques*, Paris, 1843–1887; Le Grand du Saulle, *La folie devant les tribunaux*, Paris, 1864; Marc, *De la folie considérée dans ses rapports avec les questions medico-judiciares*, Paris, 1840; Liman, *Zweifelhafte Geisteszustande*, Berlin, 1869; Krafft-Ebing, *Responsabilità criminale*, Naples, 1886; Esquirol, *Delle malattie mentali*, 1846; P. Max Simon, *Crimes et délits dans la folie*, Paris, 1886; A. Maria de Senna, *Relatorio do serviço medico ed administrativo do Hospital do conde de Ferreira*, Porto, 1887;

identify the similarities and differences between criminals and the insane, especially at that most interesting moment when they are about to commit a crime or have just committed one. From this point of view, the analogies between the insane and born criminals are numerous.

Like criminals, the insane often begin to commit crimes when they are very young and quickly become recidivists. Many commit an extraordinary number of crimes over a brief period. Out of thirty insane rapists, one committed eleven crimes, one eight, one five, and one three; a cretinous youth of nineteen committed or tried to commit fifteen rapes in a single day after he was released from prison.

It is natural to find such strong resemblances. For criminals and especially the insane, it is difficult to do good and easy to do harm. Mental illness causes the loss or at least diminution of the moral sense and thus erodes that distaste for crime, that sense of compassion, justice, and scruple which comes naturally to well-organized and healthy men. The major incentive for recidivism among insane criminals is the knowledge that they will be sent to an insane asylum rather than prison. For many, the asylum is a gentle, temporary refuge.

Certain types of insanity lie at the root of specific subcategories of criminality. For example, the mental aberrations of *pyromania* and *homicidal monomania* lead to the crimes of arson and murder, respectively. Women often steal impulsively due to *kleptomania*, a tendency to appropriate things that are of little use or value and that are usually returned. Degeneration causes these psychological disorders, which are symptoms of defective sentiments and instincts that obstruct the development of a resolute character and weaken the subject's resistance to impulse.

Homicidal Monomania. According to Esquirol, some homicidal monomaniacs have a quiet, melancholy, inconstant, and impetuous charac-

---

Willers Jessen, *Die Brandstiftungen in affectens und Geistesstorungen*, Kiel, 1860; Casper-Liman, *Handbuch der Gerichtlichen Medicin*, Berlin, 1881; Krauss, *Die Psychologie des Verbrechens*, Tübingen, 1884; Sander und Richter, *Die Beziehungen Zwischen Geistesstorungen und Verbrechen*, Berlin, 1886; Lombroso, *Memorie del laboratorio di medicina legale*, Turin, 1881; Tamburini, *Rivista sperimentale di freniatria*, 1870–1887; Gudder, *Geistesstörung nach Verletzungen*, Jena, 1886; Idem., *Centralblatt fur Nervenheilkunde, Psychiatrie und gerichtliche Psychopatologie*, Leipzig, 1887; Maudsley, *La responsabilità criminale*, 1874; Idem., *Archivio italiano per le malattie mentali*, Milan, 1863–1872; Ferri, *Actes du Congrès d'anthropologie criminelle*, Rome, 1887; Moeli, *Ueber Irren-Verbrecher*, Berlin, 1888; and Berti, *Pazzia ed omicidio*, Venice, 1881.

ter, while others are known for their kindness.[s] When they are violent, the catalysts include the weather, abnormal digestion, overexcitement of the nerves, religious exaltation, imitation, misfortune, and extreme poverty.

Ten days after giving birth, a woman felt a sudden urge to kill her small son. During menstruation, another woman wanted to kill her husband and children while they were sleeping. It was not faulty reasoning that persuaded these wretches to kill; no cause or moral passion motivated their actions. Rather, they followed their instincts. How else can we explain why a husband kills his bride, a father his dear son, a mother her nursing baby or favorite child? Only a suspension of the intellectual and moral powers can explain such extraordinary events.

Kleptomania. The legal category of theft corresponds to the psychiatric diagnoses of kleptomania. Although many experts deny the reality of kleptomania, it occurs so frequently that it must exist. Krafft-Ebing (*La responsabilità*, pag. 73) writes that "kleptomania, a symptom of mania or a similar state, is often observed in pregnant women, who suffer from so-called needs; the things they desire can be food, precious objects, or anything at all. Kleptomania also occurs frequently in women with nervous illnesses, especially hysteria, which can inspire them to swallow inedible or even repugnant substances such as straw, wood, sand, and human flesh. It is common in individuals who suffer psychological depression linked to fixed ideas. Then again, theft of valuable objects may be rooted in maniacal excitement."

Sexual Inversion. The crimes of rape and pederasty may be caused by sexual inversion (*Conträre Sexualempfindung*, to use Krafft-Ebing's term). When the erotic impulses of an individual do not correspond to his physical constitution, he seeks sexual satisfaction among his own kind. Sexual inversion leads not only to perverted lust (pederasty and lesbianism) but also to a morbid propensity for platonic love and idealization of individuals of the same sex. This strange anomaly often shapes the person's entire psychology.

Tamassia describes a certain P. C., a peasant who had one idiot uncle, another eccentric uncle, and a hysterical mother. He did poorly in school and at the age of twelve became timid with men and ostenta-

---

[s] Esquirol, *Delle malattie mentali*, Florence, 1846.

tiously modest with women. Between the ages of fifteen and seventeen, he grew his hair long, dressed in such a way as to show off the curves of his body, used the pronoun *we* when referring to women, and feminized his own name. Arranging his hair as if he were a woman, he attracted much public ridicule. He went to church and frequented female circles, claimed to have many male lovers, and said he had borne a child to the man for whom he worked as a servant. He served in this capacity for some years, preferring female work and gaining great satisfaction if men mistook him for a woman. He had no close emotional ties. He was expelled from one household for theft, but the nature of the theft (he stole only a few beans) showed his mental incapacity. When P. C. was eventually sent to prison for stealing a woman's ring, he resisted examination. He had no physical peculiarities except a slightly cylindrical chest and rounded thighs. His genitals were normal, his voice weak and high pitched. He put small cushions under his waistcoat to simulate breasts, and lined his trousers with stuffing to affect a feminine shape.

At Castelnovo prison, I observed a sexual invert who tied his thin hair in a female fashion, wore a woman's scarf and slippers, and affected feminine tones and gestures. He was an old sodomite who for many years thought he was a woman and spent all his money on young male prostitutes. Nothing irritated him more than to be called Louis rather than Louise.

Satyriasis and Nymphomania. Sex crimes can originate in satyriasis and nymphomania, psychological illnesses that themselves can be symptoms of creeping paralysis, senile dementia, epilepsy, spinal sclerosis, tuberculosis, hydrophobia, or juvenile insanity.[33] Other causes include excessive heat, heavy clothing, obscene books, heavy menstruation, and, above all, masturbation.

One of my patients was an onanistic boy with a hysterical mother, whom he tried to rape when he was eight. He had the habit of masturbating into the hollows of trees. Gall studied two boys with satyriasis, one aged three and another five (though the latter became sexually inverted only as an adult). In general, men with satyriasis are hypersensitive to light, sound, and touch. The lightest brush of the genitals triggers emission; they throw themselves at women without regard for their age or ugliness; and when impeded, they become aggressive (Moreau).

Insane women far exceed insane men in sexual aberrations and erotic

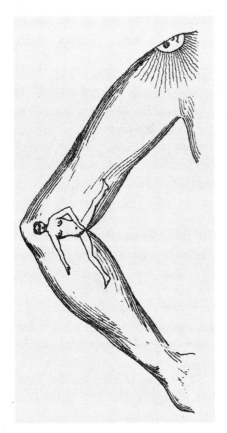

36 Sexual Tattoo
Editors' note: For Lombroso, tattoos signaled the sexual abnormality—but also the ingenuity—of many criminals. A prisoner placed this tattoo in the crook of his arm so that the naked woman seemed to masturbate as he moved.
Source: Lombroso, *L'uomo delinquente*, edition 4.

impulses. After long years of observation, I agree with Hergt (*Alleg. Zeits. Psych.*, XXVII) that two-thirds of insane women suffer from genital problems including hypertrophy of the cervix, ulcers of the vaginal canal, utero-vaginal adhesions, vaginal discharge, and ovaritis.

Types of Crime by the Mentally Ill

Every mental abnormality makes its own contribution to criminality, causing a specific type of crime.

The *idiot* is given to explosions of rage, assaults, murder, rape, and arson for the mere pleasure of seeing the flames. The *imbecile* and *feeble-minded*, succumbing easily to their first impulses or the suggestions of others, become accomplices to crime at the slightest prospect of gain.

The *melancholic* is driven by his overwhelming misery or by hallucinatory impulses to commit suicide. He often kills to provoke punishment and will even kill his own children to save them from a destiny like his.

The *demented* do not keep their word because they lack memory. In a state of cerebral irritability, they will commit violent acts or even kill.

Madmen with *pellagra*, *epilepsy*, and *alcoholism* often manifest homicidal and suicidal tendencies at the faintest provocation. During puberty, amenorrhea, and pregnancy women experience a tendency to arson and sometimes to sexual violence. The pregnant are inclined to theft.

Maniacs tend to satyriasis or sexual excess. They masturbate in public and throw themselves on the first women they find. They steal valuable objects to give gifts to someone they love or to finance new vices. Because they have no consciousness of the harm they do or because they are megalomaniacs, they believe their gains through theft belong to them. At other times they steal because they are hyperactive.

Monomaniacs, particularly when they are hallucinating, have a special tendency to murder both loved ones and strangers to escape illusory persecution or to obey imaginary orders. The same motives drive them to theft or arson.

Hysterics have a tendency to steal, swindle, commit fraud and calumny, dissimulate, or poison others.

38

The Alcoholic Criminal[t]

One type of insane criminal deserves special attention: the alcoholic criminal. It is well known that drunkenness causes crime.[34]

In Belgium, alcoholism lies behind 25 to 27 percent of all crimes. In New York, 30,509 of 49,423 persons accused of crime were professional drunks. In Holland, four-fifths of all crimes are attributed to drink: specifically, seven-eighths of brawls, three-fourths of violent assault, and one-fourth of property crimes (Bertrand, *Essai sur l'intemp.*, Paris, 1871). Ferri's eighteen-year study of crime in France offers decisive proof of the close relationship between crime and drink. Rates of assault and murder perfectly paralleled changes in the consumption of wine and alcohol, at least when the latter rose sharply (1850, 1858, 1865, 1869, and 1875) or declined sharply (1851, 1853, 1856, 1866, 1867, and 1873).

All stimulants have the capacity to drive us to crime, suicide, or insanity, phenomena that are inextricably intertwined. Alcohol and drugs irritate the nervous centers, causing acute arachnitis and congestive hyperaemia, or at least degeneration of brain tissue (which becomes fatty, sclerotic, and pigmented) and atrophy of the nerve cells. Cerebral degeneration leads irrevocably to the loss of physiological functions. All this happens independently of the chemical nature of the ingested substance.

In Africa, the explorer Stanley found a species of bandit called Ruga-Ruga, an indigenous people who made use of cannabis. He also recorded a Ugandan legend according to which crime appeared only after the introduction of beer (Stanley).

[t] Vétault, *Etude médico-légale sur l'alcoolisme*, 1887; Peeters, *Alcohol, his place and power*, 1839; Motet, *Considérations générales sur l'alcoolisme*, 1859; Brière de Boismont, *De quelques observations sur la folie des ivrognes*, 1850; Dujardin-Beaumetz, *Recherches expérimentales sur la puissance toxique des alcools*, 1879; Grasset, *Etudes sur les troubles de la sensibilité dans les alcoolistes*, 1888; Lentz, F., *De l'alcoolisme et de ses diverses manifestations considérées au point de vue physiologique, pathologique, clinique et médico-légale*, 1884; Morfaing, *De l'alcoolisme considéré dans ses rapports avec l'aliénation mentale*, 1875; Baer, *Der Alkoholismus*, 1878; Bertrand, *Sur l'intempérance*, 1871; Magnan, *De l'alcoolisme*, 1874; and Fazio, *Dell'ubbriachezza in Italia*, 1871.

While most offenders regard prison as an unmitigated evil, alcoholic criminals may come out purified in both body and soul. In cases of intoxication, taking away the source of the poison is often enough to cure the illness. I knew six drunkards who were returned to a state of honesty after two months of incarceration and recalled their criminal acts with horror and surprise. However, they returned to crime not long after release.

Hereditary Alcoholism. Marro has observed that the offspring of alcoholics may be resistant to great quantities of alcohol at one moment yet become drunk on tiny amounts the next; moreover, like epileptics and the morally insane, they have a propensity for cruelty. He further reports (*Caratteri dei delinquenti*, Turin, Bocca, 1887) that criminals with two alcoholic parents have the greatest deficit of moral sense. R., the son of alcoholic parents, told Marro that "it's a myth that companions teach one to steal; I taught myself." At the age of twenty-three he had already been convicted six times for theft, three for assault, and one for escaping from prison.

Chronic Alcoholism. Chronic abuse of alcohol leads to either simple dementia or general paralysis. At first the body gains weight (because of the greater amount of fat in the blood), but then it grows thin. The skin, initially oily and damp as a result of hyperactivity of the sweat glands, becomes dry (sometimes with eczema) and finally yellowish. The mucous membranes become violet and dry, and the hair grows thin. Memory weakens, speech falters, the association of ideas slows down, sensitivity decreases, perception clouds, nights become sleepless, and errors of judgment make the continuation of work impossible. Old hallucinations reappear, though less vividly and at greater intervals, and they change continuously as if they were being seen through a kaleidoscope. The drinker experiences a constant feeling of persecution. As the senses weaken, the strongest odors go unnoticed, until finally the mucous membranes do not react at all, even if stimulated. Chronic alcoholics seem to be automatons except for that strange smile when they behold their fatal drink. They speak of themselves in the third person: "Carlo has drunk, has eaten, is hungry." Because of brain damage, they have difficulty speaking, but when they do manage to formulate a word, they repeat it or at least its last syllable with desperate intensity for hours on

37 Pietro Belm,
a Chronic Alcoholic
Editors' note: This portrait
is meant to convey the
ill effects of alcoholism.
Source: Lombroso, *L'uomo
delinquente*, edition 4.

end. Finally even the pulse changes: there is a quick increase, a flattened peak, and finally a sudden decrease (Magnan).

Pietro Belm . . . , forty-one years old, had been charged with vagabondage on several occasions. Born in Sassari to parents from Nice, he wore greasy clothes, and his hair and breath smelled of alcohol. He was 5 feet 1 inch tall and weighed 128 lbs. His hands and nose were redder than normal, his eyes bulbous, and the left eye less sensitive to touch than the right. Although his pupils reacted properly, there was a blurring at the back of the eyes. His tongue trembled and his lips formed a constant smile that sometimes shifted to lament for no reason. His cephalic index was eighty-three, his cranial capacity slightly above average (1,545 cc), and his forehead sloping.

At first Belm talked calmly about persecution by his uncle Bla. . . . He filled a notebook with minute facts about his life, often repeated. His many complaints included lack of breath and a sensation of being strangled, a continuous murmur in his ears (especially on the left), and congestion of the head. Finally he exhausted his impulse to write; his spelling became awful; he left out the most important words, repeated first syllables, and omitted the *p*s and the *s*s. After fits of delirium tremens, he died a paralytic.

Initially, heavy drinkers of wine and spirits (and one always leads to the other because of the search for stronger effects) suffer pains in their bones and fleeting neuralgia, like electrical shivers, or a profound sense of weakness that seems to be reduced by wine. Then their vision becomes blurred. Later on their hands and arms start to tremble, particularly in the morning, and this will extend to the tongue and the torso; involuntary muscular contractions also affect the feet and the calves. Soon after, illusions and hallucinations begin to appear, particularly in those weakened by incipient paralysis, a previous bout of typhoid, or a head trauma (Emminghaus, *Pathol. der Irrenkr.*, 1879). Rarely pleasant, these hallucinations are always changing and, like nightmares, leave lasting terrible impressions.[u] In 1859, Italians hallucinated about the Austrians; today they have nightmares about police, spies, and political assassins.[35]

Statistics show that convulsions and epilepsy are common among alcoholics. Drouet found 54 epileptics out of 524 alcoholics. From the perspective of criminal anthropology, I have no doubt that the criminal alcoholic is a special variant of the epileptic even though he often lacks physical degenerative anomalies. However, there is one important difference between the two groups: if alcoholics give up drinking entirely, they have a greater possibility of cure than epileptics.

---

[u] Rose classifies the objects of hallucinations into five categories: (1) small, disgusting objects; (2) large, numerous animals; (3) corpses; (4) guards, soldiers, and spies; and (5) objects pertaining to the sufferer's profession. However, a sixth category should be added: tactile hallucinations produced by cutaneous hypersensitivity, including the sensation of burning under the skin or snakebites, and other tactile hallucinations produced by psychological conditions such as partial analgesia, partial paralysis, and neuralgia. In truth these sensations are too numerous to be confined within traditional classifications of hallucinatory experiences.

39

The Hysterical Criminal[v]

Hysterical criminals, too, need to be considered separately, partly because they form a numerous subtype of insane criminals and partly because they are distinctive in terms of sex, crime types, and modus operandi.[36] Hysteria is twenty times more frequent in women than in men (Briquet). It arises from problems of the sexual organs in one-sixth of all cases and is related to the onset of puberty in one-half of all cases. Hysteria appears most frequently in those fifteen to twenty years old, followed by the age group of twenty to twenty-five, and it disappears completely after the age of forty.[w] Thus the hysterical criminal is nearly always a young woman. Cases among men, though much more serious, are rare, as are cases in children.

Heredity influences hysteria just as it does epilepsy. Twenty-five percent of hysterics have neuropathic relatives (usually epileptic), in contrast to 2.8 percent of normal women (Legrand du Saulle).

So-called hysterical fits pass through the following stages: a premonitory symptom; an epileptic attack; gross contortions like those of clowns; hallucinations accompanied by comic and exaggerated movements; and angry or melancholic delirium. Sometimes hysterics, like alcoholics, see small animals; at other times the attack becomes a permanent contraction; and in eleven out of four hundred cases, according to Briquet, the sufferer appeared dead or had spasms. Sometimes hysterics simply experience a real epileptic attack.

[v] Legrand du Saulle, Les *hystériques*, 1883; Briquet, *Traité clinique . . . de l'hystérie*, 1884; Marcé, *Traité de la folie des femmes eincentes, des nouvelles accouchées et des nourrices, et considérations médico-légales qui se rattachent à ce sujet*, Paris, 1858; Girard, *Considérations physiologiques et pathologiques sur les affections nerveuses, dites hystériques*, Paris, 1841; Motet, *Les aliénés devant la loi*, Paris, 1866; Idem., *Accès de sonnambulisme spontané et provoqué*, Paris, 1881; Richet, *Études cliniques sur l'hystéro-épilepsie*, 1881; Bérautz, *Art. Hyst., Nouv. Dict.*, 1871; Bulard, *Étude sur la folie hystérique*, 1888; Huchard, *Archives de névrologie*, 1882; Wittack, *Die Hystérie*, Leipzig, 1857; Charcot, *Leçons sur les maladies du système nerveux*, 1886; L. Bianchi, nell' *Archivio di psichiatria e scienze penali*, Torino, 1876; Schüle, *Handb. der Geisteskrankheiten*, 1882; and Jolly, Hyst., *Ziemssen's Handbuch*, xii, 2.

[w] Out of 139 cases of hysteria, 67 occurred between the ages of twenty-five and thirty, 47 between the ages of thirty and thirty-five, and 25 between the ages of thirty-five and forty (Bérautz, op. cit.).

Psychology

In more than half of all cases of hysteria, the intelligence remains normal although there is a shortening of the attention span. But the character is profoundly affected by egoism and a self-preoccupation, which leads to a desire for scandal and public attention. Excessively impressionable, hysterics become angry and aggressive for the slightest reason, suddenly shifting from charm to nastiness and unreasonableness. They get satisfaction out of gossip, and if they do not succeed in attracting public attention through scandalous reprisals and irrational legal trials, they give vent to their needs in private, making life a misery for those around them with continual arguments and struggles.

Other psychological characteristics of hysterics include:

- Emotional lability. Hysterics quickly switch from laughter to sobs "like children, whom one sees guffawing when they still have tears in their eyes" (Richet).
- A need to lie. Charcot writes that "the motto *Homines mendaces* [Men are liars] seems to be made for hysterics; they simulate suicide and illness and send anonymous letters."[37]
- Eroticism. Among eighty-three hysterics, Legrand found 12 percent who prostituted themselves even though they had no need. Two others committed acts against public decency, and a mother tried to force her daughter to masturbate her. It strikes me that all hysterical criminality centers on sexual functions. Of twenty-one hysterics who committed calumny, nine reported imaginary rapes, four violent abuse by their husbands, and one a sexual act against nature. False accusations of rape made by minors nearly always include erotic details repugnant to adults.[x] Hysterics who commit theft and arson are usually menstruating. Their sexual instincts are so overdeveloped that they have hallucinations of sexual intercourse in which demons pursue and rape them. After exhausting their sexual passion, they envision

---

[x] A girl went to a doctor and said, "I am a virgin, take me," and then claimed that the doctor had abused her. In another case, a rich girl met a worker on the street, gave herself to him, and then went home laughing to tell everyone. A third girl wandered in the streets hoping to find a syphilitic who would infect her, so she could infect her husband. A fourth sent an erotic letter to a horseman; she showed the reply to her husband, urging him to fight the horseman.

themselves transformed into saints with a direct relationship—
even a mystical marriage—to God.

—A passion for theft. Out of eighty-three hysteric criminals in one
study, seventeen were thieves. C. H. went from one village to the
next to keep an eye on her husband. When she did not find him,
she decided to steal some chickens. She took twenty-one and
sold them so cheaply that the merchant who bought them
accused her of theft. She confessed, at the same time eating
greedily and telling everyone about her crime. When arrested,
she threatened to kill herself.

Hysteria and moral insensitivity make women, like children, tenacious in false accusations and lies. They perceive truth much less clearly
than men and thus can more easily deny it, above all when they are
hysterical. Hysterics provide the most singular and lugubrious cases of
calumny, swindling, and lying, not only in the marketplace but even in
law courts. Because hysteria increases muscular force, even while per-
verting the moral sense, it leads to atrocious murders. Naturally, there
is no lack of poisoners among hysterics.

Similarities between Hysteria and Epilepsy

The links between hysteria and epilepsy are obvious. Hysterical convulsions are almost always indistinguishable from epileptic seizures except
that the former can sometimes be alleviated by such measures as pressure on the ovaries, an alternating electric current, and hydrotherapy.
Aside from this minor difference, however, the hysteric offers many parallels with epileptics—and with children, born criminals, and the morally insane as well. Characteristics that hysterics share with epileptics include lability of symptoms, restlessness, the desire to do harm for harm's
sake, gratuitous lying, and unprovoked irascibility. I now realize that
my previous discussion of the born criminal underestimated the importance of one pathological abnormality, the tendency to lie gratuitously,
which is the most noteworthy characteristic of hysterics.

40

The Mattoid

Another variety of insanity that merits special attention, not for its frequency but for its unusual character and the crimes to which it gives rise, is mattoidism. Few mattoids are women (only one female mattoid, Madame Michel, has been found in France, and I have come across only one in Italy in twenty years). Neither are they young, for I have encountered only two youthful mattoids. Mattoids are rarely soldiers or peasants, but are found frequently among bureaucrats, doctors, and theologians.

In general, mattoids display few signs of physical degeneration. Only twenty-one mattoids in a group of thirty had more than one anomaly: twelve had two, two had three, two had four, and one had six.[38] Nearly all these cases had a mania for writing. Several even had an intelligent and harmonious physiognomy. A careful study of ten of them revealed no abnormalities of weight, strength (measured with the dynamometer), touch, or sensitivity to pain.

Unlike born criminals, mattoids show affection for their families—even, among men, to the point of excess. But such extreme displays of altruism simply mask their great vanity. Other positive characteristics, which again they can exaggerate, include an ethical sense, belief in order, and sobriety. Their abstemiousness can be seen in the cases of criminals such as Bosisio, who ate polenta without salt; Passanante, who ate only bread; and Mangione, who ate only chickpeas and beans.

Lacking anomalies of intelligence, mattoids can be crafty and capable in daily life, succeeding as doctors, politicians, soldiers, professors, and counselors of state. But they are distinguished by a morbidly exaggerated energy for work that lies outside their own field and beyond their own modest capabilities. This energy resembles that of the genius but does not produce the same results. For example, Passanante went from being a cook to a legislator; Lazzaretti transformed himself from a carter to a prophet and theologian; and two middle-aged finance clerks became, respectively, an amateur philologist and a forensic scientist.

The most distinctive feature of mattoids is the abundance of their writings. Bluet, a shepherd, left no fewer than 180 notebooks, each more inane than the other. Passanante, who cared more about the publication of his letters than for his life, filled reams of paper. When I asked Bosisio why he paraded around seminude in the middle of June, wearing sandals but no shirt, he replied: "To imitate the ancient Romans, for my health, and finally to draw public attention to my theories. Would you have stopped me had I not been decked out in this manner?"

Although their writings are more demented than those of insane asylum inmates, mattoids demonstrate good sense, craftiness, and orderliness in their personal lives. Their exaggerated sense of their own worth comes out more in their writings than in their everyday words and behavior. Like monomaniacs and geniuses, mattoids seem to espouse serious ideas, yet their writings are also marked by absurdity, contradictions, prolixity, mad trivialities, and, above all, vanity. For example, Passanante initially preached that we "must not destroy human life or property" and should "respect the Government." He then contradicted himself by calling for the death of members of parliament, insulting the monarchy, and attempting regicide.

The main sign of madness in mattoids is not so much the grandiosity of their ideas but the disproportion among these ideas themselves. After formulating a well-expressed and even sublime concept, they add a mediocre, ignoble, and paradoxical one that contradicts their main theory. Like the insane, they tend to repeat certain words and phrases hundreds of times, even on the same page. Thus in one of Passanante's chapters the word *retry* was repeated 143 times.

Criminal law takes interest in mattoids only when their egoism gains the upper hand. Then their calm vanishes in a flash, giving way to delirious behavior, especially when their reputation is besmirched or their neuroses become acute. Their crimes are nearly always committed in public under the pretext of contributing to the general good and with the irresistible impulsiveness common to epileptics and the morally insane.

The assassin Guiteau wrote that "when the mind is seized by inspiration, it is truly out of itself. At first I found the idea of murder horrifying, but then I saw that it was a true inspiration. . . . For fifteen days I

1. Cola da Rienzi. 2. Marat. 3. Louis Riel. 4. Allix.
5. Cavalier. 6. Louise Michel. 7. Passanante. 8. Lazzaretti.
9. Carrier. 10. Jourdain. 11. Fieschi 12. Dard.
13 Gargotte. 14. Stellmacher. 15. Kammerer. 16. Reinsdorf.
17. Hoedel. 18. Brady. 19. Hanlon. 20. Fitzharris.

38 Mattoids and Morally Insane Revolutionaries

Editors' note: Lombroso created the label of *mattoid* for political criminals who were mentally unbalanced but not atavistic. Among this gallery of political agitators, he identifies Passanante, Lazzaretti, Allix, and Luisa Michel as mattoids, noting that the last—a French female revolutionary—had a particularly virile physiognomy.

Source: Lombroso, *Der Verbrecher* (*Atlas*). Photo courtesy of the Lloyd Sealy Library, John Jay College of Criminal Justice.

felt inspired; I did not eat or sleep until I had done my work; and then I slept very well indeed." What he describes is epileptic impulsiveness.[y]

Mattoids excuse themselves by claiming altruistic motives, but the claim is merely a cover-up for their self-importance. They lead revolutions, commit regicides, and organize revolts to disguise personal vendettas as justifiable public causes. In short, their feigned generosity conceals their crimes from themselves and others. Mattoidism forms a branch on the degenerate tree of moral insanity, just as do persecution mania, alcoholism, and hysteria. The mattoid Sbarbaro combined alcoholism with a persecution complex and erotic delirium. Guiteau suffered from religiosity, fantasies of persecution, and overblown ambition.

Another variety of mattoid, already much studied by others, consists of perpetual plaintiffs, also known as litigious maniacs. With normal craniums and faces but enlarged livers, they continuously hound others by bringing suits. Exemplifying this type is Guiteau, the swindler, adulterer, moral madman, and political assassin who constantly pestered high administrators in order to be nominated ambassador or cabinet secretary; he also wrote strange theological books and articles. Litigious maniacs unite aspects of monomania, mattoidism, and criminality.

[y] For further details on Guiteau, see my *Tre Tribune*. See also Bonvecchiato, *Un processo scandaloso*, Venice, 1886.

41

The Occasional Criminal

Production of this book has been delayed for years because of my difficulties in completing this part on occasional criminals, those who are driven to crime through external circumstances. Despite an abundance of secondary research on the subject, I wanted to become directly familiar with the facts. The wealth and variety of secondary sources actually increased my uncertainty by making it difficult to reach firm conclusions.

Legal scholars agree that the number of occasional criminals is large. Moreover, since antiquity proverbs have suggested that circumstances influence crime:

> *Necessity makes hands wander.*
> *Need causes fisticuffs with the law.*
> *Necessity turns man into a thief.*
> *Hunger provokes crime.* (from Tuscany)

In addition, statistics confirm the influence of environment on crime. For example, Lacomte (*Relazione sui carcerati di Filadelfia*, Philadelphia, 1840) studied 368 offenders and found that 116 had become criminals through impulsiveness, 115 by breakdown of traditions, and 137 by circumstance. Without great statistical rigor, he categorized the circumstantial or environmental causes as evil companions (70), gambling (9), love of carousing (2), domestic quarrels (1), financial difficulties (4), desire for revenge (17), bets (3), love affairs (2), and so on.

Yet the general consensus about occasional criminals should give us pause because in science nothing is more suspect than that which seems obvious. This is precisely what has happened in this case. Many of the facts that seem to prove the existence of an occasional criminal type collapse in the face of more rigorous reasoning and individual observation.

As Garofalo points out,[39] "at this point we are facing a grave psychological question: might there be a purely occasional thief? I believe that notwithstanding its venerably ancient origins, the adage 'Opportunity makes the thief' is wrong, or rather, incomplete, and would be better formulated as 'Opportunity allows the thief to rob.' A deficiency in the innate sense of justice, or what I call the sense of probity, is a *sine qua non* of every crime against the property of others."[2]

In fact, every human action, even those of the insane and of criminals, is accompanied by greater or lesser opportunity, but opportunity is not the straw that breaks the camel's back. Today crimes rooted in biology are easily passed off as crimes of opportunity because of ignorance about the importance of heredity and criminals' great ability to lie. The public, understanding little about the human heart, longs for easy answers. Only a small number of specialists can discern the organic and congenital causes of crime, while anyone can identify environmental causes; indeed, they find them even when they do not exist. Out of two thousand prison inmates, I identified only forty-three occasional criminals, and of these nineteen had degenerative anomalies and eighteen hereditary illnesses.

Notwithstanding these caveats, we should not deny the existence of the occasional criminal type, characterized by minimal criminality, maximum environmental influence, and few abnormalities. The occasional criminal does not offer a homogenous type in the same way as born criminals or criminals of passion. Rather, the category is composed of disparate groups including pseudocriminals and criminaloids.

Pseudocriminals

Pseudocriminals fall into two subgroups:

—individuals who commit crimes involuntarily (as in the case of manslaughter, when a gun goes off accidentally) and therefore are criminals in the eyes of neither society nor criminal anthropology. Nevertheless, they are liable to punishment;
—individuals who commit crimes voluntarily but lack anomalies and pose no danger to society. Considered criminals by the legal system and popular opinion, they will continue to be so as long as public prejudice, which gives force to the law, regards them as such. For example, certain countries punish blasphemy, abortion, and journalistic slander. As Garofalo says, "These acts are not in

[2] *Riparazione del danno,* Torino 1887.

and of themselves incompatible with public morality, but are nevertheless forbidden by law."[aa]

Moreover, members of the general public do not view certain crimes as immoral, either because they do not understand the relevant legal issues or because they themselves commit these offenses out of habit or necessity. In countries dominated by the Camorra and Mafia, it is dangerous for honest but weak men to resist complicity in organized crime. During former eras of widespread brigandage and frequent poisonings of heirs to aristocratic titles, offenders often considered themselves honest. In many instances crime is extremely common and honesty an exception. Think about how many vendors cheat on price and weight; how many professionals swindle clients; how many professors knowingly lie; how many clerks turn a blind eye because of favoritism; and how many politicians abuse their power and the legal system. The number of such offenses far exceeds the official figures.

Since morality differs according to place and time, few crimes committed in barbarous epochs were considered immoral. In seventeenth-century Italy, gallant brigands abounded and became part of history; Mancini, a common thief, occupied the Gargano and then became a colonel under the king of Sardinia. Gazzola, who skinned priests alive, was given an almost royal welcome in Rome and was honored in Spain and the Grand Duchy of Tuscany (Gozzadini, *Pepoli e Sisto V*, 1878). A century ago university students—exemplified by Casanova—believed they had the right to do things that were truly criminal: stealing local banners, assaulting guards, betraying girls, and cheating at cards.[40] Social conditions, including the protection offered by large groups of young people and the immunity offered by university privileges, created criminals out of those who were not truly immoral.

Occasional crimes can also include theft, arson, assault, or duels when these are motivated by unusual circumstances such as defense of honor, self-defense, or the need to support a family. Like crimes of passion, these are offenses in which the cause has maximum importance and the personality of the criminal virtually none.

Captain Thomas Dudley, Edward Stephens, Edward Brooks, and a seventeen-year-old ship's boy, Richard Parker, undertook to sail the

---

[aa] R. Garofalo, *Riparazione alle vittime del delitto*, Turin, Bocca, 1882; Idem., *Criminologie*, Paris, 1888.

yacht *Mignonette* to Sydney, Australia. Shortly after crossing the equator, they encountered a terrible storm, and the vessel sank. The unfortunate foursome just had time to launch the life raft, in which they floated over the ocean with no food or water except for a container of turnips. Once they had finished this, they managed to catch a seagull; but for another fifteen days they lacked food and were tormented by thirst.[41]

Occasionally Parker was seized with delirium. He slept badly and afterwards tried to throw himself into the sea. Captain Stephens, indicating to Brooks that he was about to kill the boy, knelt in the bottom of the boat and recited this brief prayer: "Lord God of heaven and earth, permit this dreadful deed and have pity on us who are reduced to desperation. Pardon us for the inhuman act we are about to commit." He grabbed Parker by the head and while Brooks held him by the legs, plunged a knife into his jugular. The survivors avidly drank the warm blood as it spurted from the wound. After they were rescued, they were condemned to death but later pardoned.

This was a crime of pure opportunity in which perversity was minimal, particularly for Brooks, who visibly suffered at the idea of the murder that saved him. Neither man represented a future threat to society. Their act was neither a crime nor even a semicrime, but falls into the category that Garofalo labels legal crimes—offenses that result from imperfections of the law rather than of men. Because such offenses breed no fear of recidivism and do not disturb moral values, I call them pseudocrimes.

Criminaloids

Another subgroup of occasional criminals, which I call criminaloids, is completely different from pseudocriminals. Although criminaloids break the law only when circumstances push them to it, they are predisposed to crime. One example can be found in the honest merchant named Salvador, who had a normal skull and physiognomy. Returning from a business trip, he found that his wife had stripped the house clean and taken off. He then became a thief and gang leader, escaping from the authorities thirty times. Here is one of those rare cases that confirms the proverb, "Opportunity makes the thief."[42]

In civilized countries, men turn to crime to imitate those whom they consider heroes, such as brigands, *mafiosi*, and bandits. Imitation explains the lack of shame they feel in taking up such crimes; few have distorted physiognomies.[bb] (In my photographic collection, 41 percent of the brigands have normal faces.) Through imitation, normal men (or almost normal, I should say) may begin to present symptoms of sexual inversion or even become pederasts and sodomites after entering religious seminaries, undergoing treatment in single-sex syphilis clinics, having extended contact with pederasts, or being forced to remain chaste.[cc] Prisons, as currently organized, actively promote crime by throwing criminaloids together with born criminals. In his book of 1844, *Les moyens de diminuer les crimes* [methods to decrease crime], Vidocq declares that receivers of stolen goods are nearly always honest men who, out of shame and resentment, become immoral after release from prison. He gives an example of an honest worker named Leudet who was framed and sent to prison. Befriended by inmate thieves, he became a receiver of stolen property. Had he not gone to prison, Leudet would have remained honest.

While the protagonists in these cases are not born criminals, neither are they completely honest men who have been treated unfairly by the law. Unlike born criminals, they commit crimes only when they have motives. They are, however, more prone than other men to crime due to background conditions such as insanity, meningitis, alcoholism, bad heredity, or sexual abuse.

Moro . . . , who at age twenty-six killed his brother in a fight, had no degenerative anomalies. However, he had an alcoholic father and brother, and he himself drank up to six liters per day. Provoked by his brother's insults about the division of their estate, he killed him. When he was arrested, he revealed his degeneracy by declaring nonsensically that *he did not know whether his brother had gone to heaven or hell*.

Cog . . . Pietro, to give another example, had a regular physiognomy and relatives who were honest but drunks. His only anomalies were a very large jaw, low levels of tactile sensitivity, and slight left-handedness. His cranial capacity was 1,549 cc, and his cephalic index was 85; he suffered vertigo and had an underdeveloped moral sense.

[bb] Tarde, *Revue philosoph.*, 1886–87.

[cc] See Krafft-Ebing, *La psicopatia sessuale*, Torino, Bocca, 189. Lerdeun, *Recherches cliniques sur les anomalies de l'instinct sexuel*, Paris, 1888.

After he attacked another man over a woman, I asked him whether he was upset to hear that his victim was dead, and he revealed atavistic cruelty by replying: *there are too many people in this world; if I killed him it's a good thing.*

Criminaloids illustrate the gradations between the criminal and the honest individual. Because they are only slightly abnormal physiologically, with mere hints of degeneration, I call them *criminaloids*. For them the opportunity that gives rise to the crime is decisive. For born criminals, in contrast, an opportunity is just a pretext, and they will commit crime of savage brutality even without it.

In the criminaloid, the gradations of the psyche are echoed in physical characteristics. For two years I studied inmates whom I initially believed to be occasional criminals on the basis of information from their companions, trial testimony, and their lack of degenerative characteristics. In the end, out of more than two thousand inmates in this prison, I identified only forty-three occasional criminals (all but one of whom was male). Their crimes were assault (14), military infractions (7), rebellion (1), swindling (10), theft (7), murder (3), and vagabondage (1). As these figures show, assault, theft, and swindling predominate among occasional crimes. The anomalies in the group included degenerative characteristics (9), large jaws (8), swollen sinuses (6), jug ears (4), microcephaly (2), crooked noses (2), prognathism (3), head trauma (1), epilepsy (4), and alcoholism (3). In addition, twenty were left-handed, and nine showed tactile insensitivity. Only twenty-four were entirely free of anomalies. Thus we see the same abnormalities in the criminaloid as in the born criminal, but at lower rates.

The need to do harm for harm's sake is less intense in criminaloids than in the morally insane and born criminals. For example, among criminaloids, including those with degenerative anomalies, the impulse to swindle is semi-inhibited because it passes through an active intellect. Similarly, the emotions of criminaloids are close to normal levels. In contrast to born criminals, criminaloids are repelled by other offenders and prefer to be isolated from them in prison. Nearly all remain fond of their families. Once released from prison, criminaloids make excellent fathers.

My one study of forty-three criminaloids identified four men who, even though they showed no degenerative characteristics, later turned out to be hereditary epileptics. Epilepsy, according to Marro, afflicts

10 percent of pickpockets. It explains why criminaloids are frequently as impulsive as born criminals. Many pickpockets have told me that "when the moment of inspiration comes, we are unable to stop ourselves; we have to rob."

That the occasional criminal is a weak version of the born criminal is a point underscored by Ferri: "The fundamental difference between the occasional criminal and the born criminal," he writes (op. cit.), "is that the former simply has weak resistance to external incentives to commit crime, while the latter is driven by an internal compulsion to find a crime and commit it." In *Crime and Punishment*, Dostoevsky provides in the figure of Raskolnikov a marvelous portrait of an occasional criminal as a variant of the born criminal.

Habitual Criminals

Most occasional criminals are born without any particular tendencies to crime over and above those inherent in all children. However, if children lack good upbringing and education, they will never mature into honest adults. Instead, their potential criminality grows stronger and worsens. Good upbringing and education can never transform the born criminal into a gallant fellow, but they can prevent normal children from developing into habitual criminals.

Occasional criminals have low crime rates early in life. Moreover, their crimes are minor, like petty theft, swindling, and assault. But once their latent tendency to crime begins to thrive, it becomes habitual, ingrained, and ever more serious. This criminal habit is aggravated by the anaesthetizing abuse of alcohol and by anger against society (which blindly punishes those who least deserve it, and vice versa). It is also aggravated by that vanity that is found in every occupation and every profession.

What does one of these wretched minor offenders do when, arrested initially for having attacked an adversary in a fit of rage or for roaming like a vagabond, he is thrown into prison? Baptized into the confraternity of inmates and welcomed into their ranks, he loses all sense of morality. What choice does he have but to join those who offer him a sort of family, a society in the midst of which crime brings not shame but fame? Is it not inevitable, given that human nature is inclined to crime, for him to persevere and perfect his abilities until he becomes indistinguishable from the born criminal?[dd]

Habitual criminals resemble born criminals in both recidivism and the early onset of their offending. Never having lost their infantile immorality, for them crime becomes an organic phenomenon, flesh of their own flesh. In an environment that encourages struggle against all, mutual defense, and seditious impulses, habitual criminals develop pride in their abilities. And then repetition reinforces their tendencies toward recidivism.

Latent Criminals[ee]

Latent criminals are those offenders who do not reveal their criminalistic tendencies, either because they lack an opportunity or because wealth or power gives them means to satisfy their depraved instincts without breaking the law. I know three men with all the physical and psychological anomalies of the born criminal but whose high social position protects them from imprisonment. One confessed that "if I had not been rich, I would have been a thief." Other latent criminals take up a marginal but tolerated occupation—like usury or prostitution—to give vent to instincts that in different circumstances would become fully criminal.

Today, political and social struggles serve as a safety valve or a mask for criminal tendencies just as religion once did.[ff] Criminal types with obvious neuropathic disorders may dedicate themselves with seeming self-abnegation to political life. When they dominate despotic governments, their lack of moral sense expresses itself through savage persecutions; when they lead parliamentary governments like ours, it expresses itself through violent words and deeds.

During the revolutions of 1848, political fervor gradually degenerated into openly criminal behavior, as Chenu shows.[gg] One revolu-

[dd] Prins has written sublime pages on this in *La loi sur la liberation conditionelle* (*Revue de Belgique*, 1888, p. 357, and *Arch. di psich.*, x, 3).

[ee] See Joly, *Le crime*, 1888. Corre, *Les criminals*, 1888. Rizzone-Navarra, *Delinquente e punibilità*, 1888. Garofalo, *La criminologie*, 1888.

[ff] See Lombroso and Laschi, *Il delitto politico*, 1889.

[gg] *Les conspirateurs*, 1845–1846.

tionary leader, Coffineau, used communist theory to raise theft to a political principle. His followers sacked the commercial warehouses of merchants whom they denounced as thieves. They claimed they were taking back stolen goods and hoped to inspire other malcontents to join them in the revolution. Felice, an epileptic and the most fanatical member of a group of fifteen Neapolitan anarchists, was indicted twelve times for defamation, staging strikes, and murder.

True, among political geniuses like Napoleon criminality is usually disguised by the prestige of success. Some argue that in another period Napoleon would have made a fine little colonel, while others maintain that he would have made a better brigand chief.

Epileptoids

As this book demonstrates, an epileptoid condition—along with atavism—underlies the behavior of not only the morally insane but almost every figure in the world of crime: the latent criminal, occasional criminal, criminaloid, criminal of passion, suicidal criminal, hysteric, the alcoholic, mattoid, and monomaniac. Now that we know that congenital deformities are but reflections of a substratum of epilepsy, we can better understand the fusion of illness and physical anomalies in the born criminal. We can also grasp more clearly why successive gradations lead from the born criminal to the criminal of passion, and from the occasional criminal to normal man.

EDITION FIVE

1896–97

Editors' Foreword

The final edition of *Criminal Man* (1896–97) marks the culmination of Lombroso's project. It is twice as long as the preceding edition, numbering four volumes instead of two. These four volumes revisit all topics from the fourth edition, as well as earlier material: the discussion of moral insanity from edition 3 and long sections on the etiology, prevention, and punishment of crime from edition 2. Lombroso's purpose—to synthesize the previous volumes in a final edition—even extends to his treatment of the illustrations and tables that had become increasingly numerous with each edition. Most of these are collected in the *Atlas*, the last volume of edition 5.

Because of the repetition of large blocks of material from previous editions, edition 5 is notable mainly for Lombroso's expansion and updating of familiar material. For example, this final edition retains the two chapters on criminal craniums and on criminal anthropometry and physiognomy that opened the first edition in 1876, but he has notably increased the amount of data in each chapter. While he has not revised his argument that physical anomalies constitute signs of born criminality, his analysis of criminal craniums now rests on 689 skulls rather than the sixty-six of the first edition; and his discussion of criminal anthropometry and physiognomy draws on 6,608 live subjects rather than 832.

Lombroso also expands his discussions of the etiology, prevention, and punishment of crime, topics that have not appeared since the second edition. He emphasizes the difficulty of measuring the effects of factors like population density and immigration/emigration on crime rates. Urbanization, for example, correlates with rising rates of theft but with falling rates of homicide. He also warns against simplistic arguments that blame crime on poverty, since consumption of alcohol, tobacco, and drugs do more harm to the lower classes than indigence. Thus, despite his disdain for primitive societies, Lombroso expresses ambivalence about civilization, which gives people new appetites and new techniques for committing crime.

In the sections on the prevention and punishment of crime, Lombroso reveals his socialist sympathies by recommending that the state tax the rich and aid the poor. He takes progressive stances on divorce, which he favors to reduce adultery and domestic homicide, and on infanticide and abortion, whose perpetrators deserve leniency as occasional criminals. Eager to promote alternatives to incarceration, Lombroso applauds the United States for its probation system that allows judges to individualize sentences for nonrecidivist offenders. On the other hand, Lombroso advocates the death penalty for born criminals more forthrightly than in the second edition, especially when they are involved in organized crime.

Edition 4 highlighted political criminals who, as liberals, socialists, anarchists, and workers, called for reform or even the overthrow of the nineteenth-century state. In edition 5, political criminals receive for the first time their own chapter, rather than being subsumed under the category of criminals by passion. As in earlier editions, they are identified as mostly honest and altruistic individuals who lack the stigmata of born criminality. Returning to the political criminal in his sections on the etiology and prevention of crime, Lombroso promotes race mixing, governmental reform, and the reduction of class inequality to prevent social unrest and revolution. He opposes severe punishment of political criminals who, he believes, will either grow out of their youthful fanaticism or, if mentally unbalanced, receive appropriate care in criminal insane asylums.

Lombroso concludes the last volume of his life's work with the startling declaration that crime serves a useful purpose. He argues that all criminals—including born criminals—promote not only destruction but also renovation of the social order. Unlike normal individuals, who are crippled by misoneism or fear of change, criminals possess the violent emotions, energy, and sometimes intelligence necessary to promote political and economic progress. Lombroso suggests that society harness the innovative energies of criminals for its own good, a process he labels "symbiosis." Lombroso thus closes his monumental work on a more optimistic note than might be expected from the dark prophet of a future society infected by the atavistic born criminal.

42

Criminal Craniums (689 Skulls)

An anthropological study of criminal man must begin with a statistical overview of fundamental physical characteristics. My conclusions are based on the examination of 689 criminal skulls, a number that has grown from fifty-five in the first edition of *Criminal Man*.[1]

Cranial Capacity[a]

My comparative study of the cranial capacity of 121 Italian male criminals and 328 normal Italians revealed that the former exceeded the latter

[a] Cougnet e De Paoli, *Su 26 crani di animali* (*Archivio di psichiatria, scienze penali*, 1882, p. 107); Bordier, *Études anthropologiques sur une série de crânes d'assassins* (*Revue d'anthropologie*, ii série, fasc. ii); Amadei, *Crani di assassini e considerazioni di craniologia psichiatrico-criminale* (*Archivio di psichiatria, scienze penali*, 1883, p. 98); Ferri, *Studi di antropometria su criminali, pazzi e sani* (*Arch. di psichiatria, scienze penali*, 1881, p. 475); Lombroso e Manuelli, *Craniometria di 39 delinquenti e 64 normali del Piemonte* (*Archivio di psichiatria, scienze penali*, 1881, p. 93); Boggio e Collino, *Tipi di delinquenti mattoidi* (*Archivio di psichiatria, scienze penali*, 1881, p. 95); Lenhossek, *Crani di delinquenti rumeni, ungheresi e croati* (*Archivio di psichiatria, scienze penali*, 1880, p. 331); De Paoli, *Quattro crani di delinquenti* (*Archivio di psichiatria, scienze penali*, 1880, p. 337); Ten-Kate e Pawloski, *Sur quelques crânes de criminals* (*Revue d'anthr.*, 1881, p. 116); M. Flesch, *Untersuchungen über Verbrecher Gehirne*, Würzburg, 1881); Corre, *Crânes de criminels* (*Bulletin de la Soc. d'anthr.*, 1881); Ardouin, *Craniologie des assassins* (*Bulletin de la Soc. d'anthr.*, 1879); Heger e Dallemagne, *Études sur les caractères craniologiques d'assassins exécutés en Belgique*, 1881; Giacomini, *Varietà delle circonvoluzioni cerebrali dell'uomo*, 1881; Peli, *Intorno alla craniologia degli alienati*, 1882; Schwekendiek, *Untersuchungen an zehn Gehirnen von Verbrechern und Selbstmörden*, Würzburg, 1881; D. M. Benedikt, *Anatomische Studien an Verbrecher Gehirnen*, Wien, 1879; Idem., *Schädelmessung Kranio und Cephalometrie*, Wien, 1883; D. A. Weisbach, *Beiträge zur Kentniss der Schädel formen österreichischer Völker* (*Wiener med. Jahrbücher*, 1864, n. 1867); D. Hermann Welcker, *Untersuchungen über Wachstum und Bau des menschlichen Shädels*, 1882; Emil Huschke, *Schädel, Hirn und Seele nach Alter, Geschlecht und Race*, 1854; D. E. Zuckerkandl, *Morphol. Des Gesichtsschädels*, 1877; *Messungen der Schädel von Irren* (*Wien Jahrbücher für Psychiatrie*, 1879, 2 Heft); E. Morselli, *Critica e riforma del metodo in antropologia*, Rome, 1880; Orchanski, *Crânes d'assassins* (*Bulletin de la Soc. d'anthrop.*, 1882); Roncoroni e Ardù, *Emicenturia di cranii di criminali* (*Giornale della R. Acc. di Med.*, Torino, 1892); and M. Baca y Vargara, *Estudios de Antropolog. Cremenal*, 1893, Puebla.

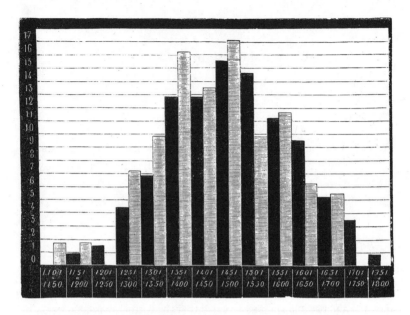

39 Cranial Capacity of 121 Male Criminals
Editors' note: Lombroso uses this bar graph to argue that male criminals (in gray) have smaller cranial capacities than normal men (in black). The measurements at the bottom are in cubic centimeters.
Source: Lombroso, *L'uomo delinquente*, edition 4.

in the category of small skulls (those from 1,101 cc to 1,300 cc). The two groups had almost an identical number of members with cranial capacities in the range of 1,401 to 1,450 cc, and criminals slightly exceeded normal Italians in the range of 1,451 cc to 1,500 cc. Normal men generally outpaced criminals in the capacities above 1,501 cc, and criminals did not figure at all in the range over 1,700 cc. Overall in criminals, low capacities prevailed (except for the 1,451 cc to 1,500 cc range), and large capacities were scarce. If we break down the numbers according to categories of crime, the cranial capacities of thieves are particularly small compared to those of healthy and insane individuals.

Cephalic Index

The cephalic indices of criminals generally correlate with regional types, according to our statistics.[2] Therefore, criminals from Piedmont in northern Italy tend to be brachycephalic, or flat-headed, while those from Sicily and Sardinia in the south are predominantly dolichocephalic, or long-headed. Sergi compared the cephalic indices of a group of forty-nine offenders with those of eighty-three students, both from Piedmont, with the following results:

	Criminals	Students
Dolichocephalic	8%	10%
Mesaticephalic	12%	19%
Brachycephalic	80%	69%[3]

As this table shows, the majority of both Piedmontese criminals and students were flat-headed, although the rate of brachycephaly among criminals was abnormally high.

Flat-headedness is characteristic of murderers, especially those from Piedmont, who exhibit cephalic indices as high as eighty-eight or ninety. Phrenologists have exaggerated the importance of this curious fact, finding in it a confirmation that the "organ of cruelty" resides in the lobe of the brain near the temples. On the other hand, several ferocious murderers have had low cephalic indices, such as Gasparone (72), Lacenaire (76), and Avril (72). Dolichocephaly predominates in thieves; one thief, Amadei, was also scaphocephalic, having a skull shaped like the keel of a boat. In sum, the contradictory nature of our data leads to the conclusion that shapes of criminal skulls conform less to categories of offense than to ethnic types, often in their extreme forms.

Jaws

Among criminals the jaw is more developed than in normal men. The average weight of the jaw is 84 grams in criminals, 80 g among normal men, and 78 g among the insane. A similar pattern emerges when we measure the diameter of the jaw, which on average is 103.9 mm in criminals, 98.2 mm in normal men, and 97.8 mm in the insane. In his study of twenty-four French murderers, Orchanski (*Bull. Soc. anthrop.*, 1882) confirmed that offenders exhibit large jaws similar to those of savage men.

Cranial Anomalies

In a study of 452 craniums, we found the most frequent abnormalities to be protuberant brows (46.7 percent); anomalous wisdom teeth (44.6 percent); small cranial capacities (32.5 percent); plagiocephaly, or lateral protuberances on the skull (25.8 percent); sloping foreheads (19.1 percent); simplicity of the sutures (18.4 percent); and the median occipital fossetta (16.7 percent). Less frequent were small, narrow, or flat foreheads (10 percent); trochocephaly, or abnormally round heads (9 percent); thin cranial bones (8.4 percent); and overdevelopment of the canines (6.2 percent).[4] Most important, we found that only 21 percent of the skulls exhibited a single anomaly, while 43 percent were monstrous in their multiplicity of anomalies.

The scarcity of data makes it impossible to answer the question of whether thieves, for example, exhibit more cranial anomalies than murderers. It does appear, however, that craniums of thieves are frequently marred by extreme microcephaly, ossification of connective tissue, sloping foreheads, oxicephaly, or extremely high heads, and thick bone, while those of murderers exhibit large jaws and median frontal sutures. Sloping foreheads predominate among homicidal women and prostitutes.

The study of cranial anomalies suggests that the criminal is closer to the savage than to the madman, particularly in the frequency of large jaws, jutting brows, and the median occipital fossetta.[b] In a study of 1,320 healthy European skulls, I found a median occipital fossetta in only 4.1 percent—a frequency much lower than its occurrence in primitive peoples:

	Number of Skulls	Percent with Median Occipital Fossetta
Ancient Egyptians and Etruscans	126	19
Modern Negroes	16	6
American Indians	46[c]	26
Semites	9	22
Prehistoric peoples	11	18
Papuans	222	22
Ancient Ostians	(unknown)	25
New Zealanders	22	50

According to research by Maccabruni and Morselli, the median occipital fossetta characterizes most of the lower branches of the monkey family, although only a small number (one out of thirty) of more evolved
apes like orangutans and gibbons retain this atavistic feature (*Archivio
di Psichiatria*, XI). This cranial anomaly also characterizes several savage
peoples, particularly the New Zealanders and the Aymaras.

We can conclude that each professional category of criminal is
marked by specific anomalies that give the group a family resemblance.
Like subspecies of a common race, all these categories of offenders
nevertheless exhibit some features of the born criminal. Thus we can say
that even incomplete examples of the criminal type provide impartial
proof of its reality. The results of our studies of criminal craniums show
that large statistical studies often give very generic and insignificant results, while research on smaller, homogeneous groups leads to more
meaningful outcomes. The study of subgroups offers a new road for
statistical research,[d] one that will temper traditional skepticism about
numerical data and guarantee that such studies no longer waste paper
and time.[5]

[b] See Lombroso, *De la fossette occipitale moyenne dans les criminels et dans les races humaines* (*Revue scientifique*, 1883); Anutchine, *Ueber eine Anomalien des Mensch, Schädel.*, 1880; Idem., *De l'os des Incas, Bull. Des Amis des sciences nat. de Moscou*, 1881–82; Marimò, *Contribuzione allo studio della fossetta occipitale mediana*, Firenze, 1887.

[c] Forty-six percent of the Aymaras have a median occipital fossetta; Marimò's study of 184 ancient Peruvian skulls found a rate of 45.7 percent. [The Aymaras are an indigenous people of Bolivia.—Eds.]

[d] Rossi and Lombroso, *Centuria di criminali* (Introd.), Torino, 1888.

43

Anthropometry and Physiognomy
of 6,608 Criminals

I have been able to compare my conclusions about the cranial forma-
tions of the criminal, which I based initially on measurements taken
from corpses, with another group of 6,608 live cases. Data on the anthropometry and physiognomy of live criminals came from new studies
by Bischoff (o.c., on 134 criminals from Bonn), Corre (*Arch. d'Anthropol.*, 1883), Lacassagne (*Arch. di psichiatria*, vol. IV, fasc. II, on 1,000
French criminals), B. Ribaudo (*Studio antropologico del militare delinquente*, 1894, 2nd ed., on 100 normal soldiers and 559 criminals), Ferri
(*Arch. di psichiatria e scienze penali*, vol. IV, fasc. I, on 699 Italian criminals, 301 madmen, and 711 soldiers), Marro (*Caratteri dei delinquenti*,
1886, on 500 criminals and 105 normal men), Virgilio (*Centuria di delinquenti*, 1889), and Baer (*Der Verbrecher*, 1893, on 968 criminals). I also
relied on photographs and biographies of 300 criminals taken from the
pages of the *Album of German Criminals*, the *National Police Gazette*
(New York), and the *Illustrated Police News* (Boston) supplied to me by
professors von Liszt and von Holtzendorf and by Dr. Kornfeld.

Aperture of the Arm. In his study of 800 French criminals, Lacassagne
found that 623 had an arm span greater than their height, 86 an arm
span roughly equal to their height, and 91 an arm span shorter than
their height (*Arch. di psich.*, v. IV, fasc. II).[6]

On the other hand, Marro found that the arm span of most criminals equaled their height. In his study, differences correlated with type
of crime: arm span was greater than height in murderers (by 5.1 cm),
thieves (by 5.3 cm), arsonists (by 5.8 cm), and those convicted of assault (by 6.20 cm); it was less in rapists and pickpockets (by 4.4 cm),
perhaps because they were younger.

M. Du Camp noted strangely long arms in the violent communard
Verïg (Du Camp, *Sur les prisons de la Commune*, 1877). The criminal
Thiebert was known for his very long, chimpanzee-like arms, as well as
for his enormous jaw.

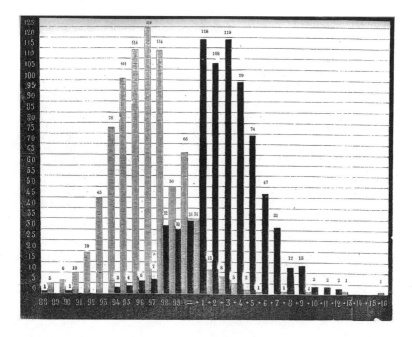

40 Height and Arm Span of 800 Criminals
Editors' note: Based on data from Lacassagne, this graph purports to prove
that the arm spans of most criminals measure more than their height. The arm
spans (in black) tend to exceed the heights (in gray) by several millimeters.
Source: Lombroso, *L'uomo delinquente*, edition 4.

Hands. Marro compared different categories of criminals and found
that the ratio of hand size to height was very low among assassins and
rapists. Offenders had fingers that were equal in length or longer than
the width of the hand, with property offenders having the longest fingers. Penta found that 4.1 percent of criminals have serious malformations of the hand including webbed skin between the fingers, which is
often accompanied by prehensile feet.

Prehensile Feet. The anomaly of prehensile feet, where the first two toes
have a monkeylike ability to grasp objects, was the focus of a recent
study by doctors Ottolenghi and Carrara, who compared one hundred
normal men, two hundred criminal men, thirty-one epileptics, sixty-
two normal women, fifty prostitutes, sixty-four criminal women, and
fifty-six idiots (*Giornale della R. Accad. Di Medicina*, 1892 and *Archivio di psich.*, XIII, fasc. IV). On sheets of paper, they outlined the foot

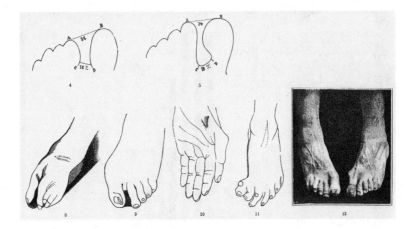

41 Criminal Feet
Editors' note: Lombroso believed that even the feet of criminals could exhibit
anomalies. Feet with a wide separation between the first and second toes
(no. 5) reminded him of the prehensile feet of apes and monkeys.
Source: Lombroso, *Der Verbrecher* (*Atlas*). Photo courtesy of the Lloyd Sealy
Library, John Jay College of Criminal Justice.

of each individual and the space between the first two toes. This space
measured more than 3 mm in 33 percent of criminals, but in only 11 percent of normal men; more important, it measured more than 8 mm in
27 percent of criminals, but in only 5 percent of normal men.

I observed two cases of truly prehensile feet among criminals endowed with wide gaps between their toes. The baker M., convicted of
assault, had such a large space between the first two toes that he could
grasp a bottle of water (weighing 3,181 grams) with his right foot and
shake it without spilling a drop. The traveling salesman V., a criminaloid epileptic, had a space between his first two toes of 30 mm on the
right foot and 35 mm on the left foot. Since childhood he had used his
feet like hands to dress, to pick up even very small objects, and to carry
out minor tasks. Everyone in his family had the same agility.

Particular professions can increase mobility of the toes but cannot
produce a separation between the first and second toe. Many honest
laborers work with their feet but show no signs of prehensility. Thus
prehensile feet are an atavistic anomaly that in superior races is found
more often in women than men and more often in congenital idiots,
criminals, epileptics, and prostitutes than in normal individuals.

Gray Hair and Baldness. Premature grayness is common among normal people, particularly in the professional classes. It is rare among criminals and epileptics and unheard of among cretins.

Many studies have shown that baldness is extremely rare among criminals. Even between the ages of fifty to seventy, when grayness occurs with more or less the same frequency in criminals and normal men, baldness remains rare among criminals, cretins, and epileptics. Proverbs confirm the correlation of gray hair and baldness with healthy individuals:

> *Madmen never go gray.* (Italian)
> *The wise go gray early.* (Italian)
> *He who seeks wisdom goes gray on the head, and he who works for food goes*
>   *gray in the beard.* (German; Eiselein, *Sprüchwörten*, 1840)

Wrinkles. I studied wrinkles in the faces of two hundred criminals and two hundred normal workers and peasants, including wrinkles on the forehead, around the nose, and on the cheeks. Table 24 compares seven types of wrinkles in normal and criminal men by age. Overall, the results in this table confirm that wrinkles are more frequent and more marked in criminals than normal individuals. Because of the precocity of their wrinkles, some juvenile delinquents show deep lines in their faces by the age of fourteen, a feature that accentuates their virile appearance.

Anatomy is the most important explanation for the precocity of wrinkles in criminals. The deep lines in the faces of some juvenile delinquents are comparable to those normally found in cretins and fetuses (Virchow), where hypertrophy of the connective tissue has diminished skin elasticity and accentuated creases and furrows on the face. In addition to this anatomical predisposition to wrinkles, criminals also acquire wrinkles because of their habit of mimicry. Dostoyevsky has noted the cynical and bitter smile of criminals, as well as the rhythmical movements of their face muscles, both of which resemble the grimaces of epileptics and hysterics.

The faces of certain elderly criminals present such an extraordinary mass of lines that they resemble iron gratings. Such was the case with the female poisoner from Palermo, the so-called Old Woman of the

Table 24: Wrinkles in Normal and Criminal Men

TYPE OF WRINKLE	14–24 YEARS OLD		25–49 YEARS OLD		OVER 50 YEARS OLD	
	54 norm. (percents)	55 crim.	80 norm. (percents)	100 crim.	66 norm. (percents)	18 crim.
Forehead (horizontal)	3	16	12.2	32	91	98.4
Forehead (vertical)	6.8	18	50	54	65.7	86.6
Crows feet	11	20	35	45	80	83
Under eyes	1.9	7.2	6.3	20	21.2	30
Under nose	22.2	69	62.5	78	87.8	94.4
Cheek	0	16.8	18.7	33	19.7	33.3
Chin	1.9	10.8	2.5	22	12.1	22.2

Editors' note: The number of criminals adds up to 173 rather than the 200 stated in the text.

Vinegar, whose face, preserved on a bust in the Museum of Palermo, presents a true tangle of lines.[7]

The most active and therefore most wrinkled part of the criminal's face (as in the case of other degenerates) is the nose and mouth, which constitute its least contemplative and therefore most material features. Indeed, with the exception of a few murderers who have a menacing look and a lined forehead, the common criminal typically shows few wrinkles on the forehead. This absence of wrinkles on the most contemplative part of the face indicates low levels of mental activity.

Statistical Proof

Anthropology requires numbers rather than isolated and generic descriptions to prove its theories. The following conclusions are based on a study of more than 2,500 criminals and 1,200 honest individuals conducted by me, Ferri, Ribaudo, Ottolenghi, Baer, and Hansen.

Ears. Jug ears were found in 28 percent of the criminals in our study, and extremely long ears in 9 percent. Jug ears correspond to the embryonic stage of humans and mammals in which the ear flaps are folded over the auditory canal.

Noses. In 10 out of 379 criminals, I found the nose bent either to the left or right (a proportion similar to that found in the insane) and an even higher rate of curved noses. In another study, Virgilio found crooked noses in 5 percent of his cases.

In general, criminals have straight (40.31 percent) or bumpy noses (27.81 percent) with horizontal lower edges (60.97 percent). These noses are of average length (48.73 percent), rather wide (54.14 percent), usually quite prominent, and often slightly crooked (48.13 percent).

Teeth. Four percent of criminals, mainly murderers, have overdeveloped canine teeth. Seven percent of offenders exhibit other dental irregularities such as lack of incisors, crookedness or extraordinary smallness of the canines, or overlapping of teeth.[8]

Proverbs. Critics have claimed that our assertions about criminal physiognomy are out of step with public opinion.[e] Although common sense is not the best guide in science, many of our conclusions in fact accord with popular perceptions, as shown by proverbs, popular songs, and verse, all of which reflect the ideas of the common people like a well-polished mirror. For example, the following proverbs attest to the particular physiognomy of the born criminal:

> *Poca barba e niun colore, sotto il ciel non vi ha peggiore* [Thin beard and little color, there's nothing worse under the sun].
> *Omo rosso o femina barbuta da lontan xe mejo (meglio) la saluta* [Red men or bearded women are best greeted from afar].
> *Vardete de la dona che gha ose de omo (voce virile)* [Be careful about women with deep voices].
> *Guardati da chi ride e guarda in là e dagli occhi piccoli e molto mobili* [Watch out for the man who laughs and looks ahead with small mobile eyes].
> *Naso che guarda in testa è peggior della tempesta* [A turned-up nose is worse than a storm].

Some people, particularly women, have an instinctive understanding of criminal physiognomy. Although they have no knowledge of criminal anthropology, they feel an innate repugnance for a face with irregular characteristics, which they identify as the face of a malefactor. My mother, who lived, as they say, out of the real world and had little

---

[e] Orano, *Archivio di psichiatria*, vol. iii, fasc. iv, pag. 451.

practical experience with society, suspected that two youths had criminal characters. Ignored by everyone else, the youths were unmasked as criminals several years later.

Great artists depicted criminal physiognomy in their painting long before criminal anthropologists demonstrated scientifically the existence of a criminal type. In a painting by Andrea Mantegna, the executioner about to strike a Christian martyr has a receding forehead, squashed nose, wide mouth, full lips with protuberant lower lip, and a square chin. The artist Titian, in his painting *The Martyrdom of San Lorenzo*, shows an executioner with an oversized skull, broad face, and abundant hair growing low on his forehead. Rubens depicts Judith, who cut off the head of Holofernes, as a young muscular girl with attractive physiognomy marred by a large jaw and large protuberant lips. The lower half of her face is as violent as the upper half is calm. In the eighteenth century, Goya depicted that section of the underworld inhabited by brigands and thieves, including scenes of the execution of criminals in the Spanish style. One of his brigands, about to be put to death, has a receding forehead and very pronounced orbital arches.

44

Political Criminals

Fanaticism

Economic or social fanaticism motivates most political criminals. In *Delitto politico* [*Political Crime*], I demonstrated that political criminals share the characteristics of criminals of passion and therefore are the opposite of the criminal type.[f] They have beautiful or what I would call anticriminal faces with broad foreheads, rich beards, and gentle, serene countenances.

Out of sixty political martyrs painted by D'Ayala, twenty-six have beautiful or at least harmonious physiognomies. Of the others, only four have abnormal expressions, one is pallid, another has a narrow forehead, several have protuberant cheeks, and two have rickets. Of the entire group, twenty-six are tall and only three are short.

Of the revolutionaries whose effigies are collected in the Museum of the Risorgimento in Milan, many were beautiful such as Dandolo, Poma, Porro, Schiaffino, Fabrizi, Pepe, Paoli, Fabretti, and Pisacane. Who does not admire the robust, harmonious beauty of Corday, Perowskaja, Kuliscioff, and Orsini?[g]

Sex and Age

Women are more numerous among political criminals than among criminals in general. Women make up 40 percent of the martyrs in the Christian catacombs and 14 percent of the nihilists,[g] with a preponderance of girls from eighteen to twenty-five years old.[10]

Many political criminals inherit their patriotic fanaticism or mysticism. The fathers of Corday and Orsini were fanatical revolutionaries; Booth's father was known as Junius Brutus and gave the name of a revo-

---

[f] Lombroso and Laschi, *Il delitto politico e le rivoluzioni*, Torino, Bocca, 1892
[g] Cesare Lombroso, *Delitto politico e rivoluz.*

lutionary—Welkes—to his son. Guiteau's and Nobiling's fathers were radical socialists.[11]

Honesty

Political criminals are the model of honesty. Charlotte Corday, for example, was a paragon of the honest woman, having at the age of twenty-five years the gentlest of souls and the sweetest demeanor. She passed her youth studying history and philosophy, including the works of Plutarch, Montesquieu, and Rousseau. Then inflamed by the words of some Girondin refugees, and perhaps by a secret love for one of them, she wed the cause. Present at the Convention when the Girondins were condemned to death, she decided to kill the person who was to blame. Although some deemed her a weak woman, she was able to kill Marat without help, driven by a passionate anger that she claimed "filled my heart and showed me how to reach his" (D'Abrantés, *Vita e ritratti di donne celebri*, 1838).

Another characteristic of political criminals is the lively desire to feel pain and suffer. As one of Dostoevsky's political heroes declares, "suffering is a good thing." This is the result of a true paradoxical tactile sensibility: passionate concentration on one single idea anaesthetizes the political criminal to pain, just as a powerful suggestion can make a hypnotized subject lose sensitivity. These passionate souls, whose ranks include history's most noble figures, are the pioneers in the struggles for political, religious, and social liberty.

Altruism

According to Hammon's study, anarchists are often inspired by an over-developed sense of altruism and an exaggerated sensitivity to the pain of others (see Lombroso, *Gli Anarchici*, 1894, 2d. ed.). The contradiction between their altruism and the cruelty of their deeds can only be understood in the light of the behavior of hysterics. Hysteria, the sister of epilepsy and a disease linked to the loss of sensitivity, usually combines extreme egotism with excessive altruism. This proves that altruism is often no more than a variant of moral insanity.[12]

Love of the Novelty

Another characteristic of political criminals is the absence of misoneism or the fear of new things.[13] Their unusual openness to novelty distinguishes them from most other men, especially those who have similarly weak educational backgrounds. In Hammon's inquiry into how and why they had become anarchists, his subjects frequently responded that they "felt a spirit of revolt and of revenge provoked by personal reasons or by particular books." "I suffered poverty," wrote Voght, a worker of twenty-four; "after two days with nothing to eat, a spirit of revolt *revealed itself in me*." Another confessed that "I read Victor Hugo, and my spirit rebelled against every modern oppression." This spirit of rebellion, which is often congenital or hereditary, appears without provocation.

Minimal Repentance

Because political criminals believe in the utility of their actions, they are fearless in the face of corporal punishment (Corday). Unlike other criminals of passion, they feel little sense of repentance. Nevertheless, they should not be confused with born criminals, whose indifference to life and absence of regret derives from lack of moral sense. Instead, political criminals combine impenitence with modesty and delicacy in all other aspects of their lives.

Madness

In many cases, fanaticism is kindled by madness and hereditary neuropathy. For example, Nobiling and Booth were both sons of suicides; both Haillaraud, who attempted to stab Bazaine, and La Sahla, who tried to assassinate Napoleon, had epileptoid fits.

45

Etiology of Crime
URBAN DENSITY, ALCOHOLISM, WEALTH, AND RELIGION

Density

It is easier to see the influence of civilization on crime if we examine the causes one at a time. First and foremost is population density because, as history shows us, little human behavior was considered criminal until human society reached a certain level of density. Among animals, the equivalent of crime is rare unless they live in groups, often domesticated. Savages have little outlet for their brutal instincts until they form tribes and clans; at this point crimes breaks out, as Ateneo, Herodotus, and Lucretius have shown. From primitive epochs to the present, the number and types of crimes have multiplied to the hundreds and even thousands.

In civilized countries, rising population density is correlated with increasing theft and decreasing homicide, except where temperature provides a countervailing influence (favoring theft in the north and homicide in the south). Table 25 shows the effect of density on various crimes in Italy, confirming that homicide is inversely correlated with population density. The large cities of Milan, Naples, Leghorn, and Genoa —although characterized by diverse races (Greeks, Celts, Ligurians) and climates (north, south)—also show a similar diminution in homicide figures over time. On the other hand, murder rates increase in regions of minimum density, which in Italy correspond to the hottest and most barbaric parts of the peninsula and, more often, its islands. Theft, rape, and violence against state officials diminish when villages begin to grow, but they rise again rapidly in the densely populated provincial capitals (Padua, Naples, Milan, Venice).

Immigration. Recent statistics for the United States, as shown in table 26, document high rates of crime in states with large numbers of immi-

Table 25: Population Density and Types of Crime

POPULATION PER SQ. KM.	RATE PER 100,000 INHABITANTS				
	HOMICIDE	THEFT	ASSAULT ON PUBLIC OFFICIALS	RAPE	SWINDLING
20–50	11	199	23.7	18.8	62.6
50–100	6.03	144.4	25.4	16.4	45.0
100–150	6	148	23.5	14.5	58.5
150–200	5.1	153	24.6	12.3	54.6
over 200	3.5	158	29.5	18.7	50.4

Source: Bodio, Annuario statistico italiano, Roma, 1894.

Table 26: Immigration and Rates of Crime

STATE	RATE PER 1,000 INHABITANTS	
	OF CRIME	OF IMMIGRATION
California	.30	3.3
Wyoming	.31	4.1
New York	.27	2.3
Montana	.19	2.9
Arizona	.16	3.9
Pennsylvania	.11	1.3
New Mexico	.03	.67

Source: Compendium of the Tenth Census (1880) of the United States, P. II, p. 1659.

grants, especially from Italy and Ireland. Out of 49,000 arrests in New York, 32,000 were immigrants (Brace, *The Dangerous Classes*). Immigrants belong to the human category with the greatest incentives and fewest barriers to committing crime. Compared to the resident population, newcomers have greater economic need, better developed jargon, and less shame; submitted to less surveillance, they more easily escape arrest. Thieves are almost always nomads.

Studies of emigration resolve a contradiction apparent in Italy and France: that certain crimes do not increase with rising birthrates. For example, thefts, which increase with greater population density, should increase with higher natality. Yet in France, where rapes and murders do increase in relation to density, thefts are inversely proportional to the birthrate. However, theft does not decrease with falling birthrates if immigration provides a countervailing force to swell the overall population.[14]

The opposite is true in Italy, which has an emigration rate of 193 per 100,000 inhabitants.[h] Regions known for crime and poverty almost always have the highest birthrates. Between 1876 and 1888, the birthrate for southern Italy was 40 per 1,000 compared to 36 per 1,000 for the rest of the peninsula. Yet as Del Vecchio has noted, higher mortality rates and emigration have prevented high population density in the south. For example, average family size is 4.10 persons in Sicily and 4.5 persons in the southern province of Basilicata, in contrast to 5.17 in the Veneto and 4.92 in Tuscany, both northern provinces.[15]

Alcoholism

Alcohol causes pauperism because alcoholic fathers may have blind, paralyzed, lame, or impotent progeny. If the family is rich, the members finish up impoverished and, if poor, they find every possibility of work closed to them. The worst fate awaits those whom alcohol renders paralytic or blind.

The nexus between alcohol and crime is not only social but pathological. Initial proof is offered by statistics that show the continual increase of crime rates in civilized countries. The crimes most associated with drinking are assault, sex crime, and political rebellion. In second place are murders and assassinations. Lastly come arson and crimes against property, although the latter are more common among habitual drinkers than the former. For good reason, few falsifiers and swindlers are drunkards; as they tell me, "you need your head in place to swindle."

Tobacco. Criminals use tobacco heavily compared not only to normal individuals but also the insane: 45.8 percent of criminals smoke tobacco, 25.88 percent of the insane, and 14.3 percent of the healthy.[i]

---

[h] Del Vecchio, *Sull'emigrazione*, 1892.

[i] Venturi, *Sull'uso del tabacco da naso nei sani, pazzi e delinquenti* (*Il Manicomio*, 1885, N. 2 e 3 and *Archivio di Psich.*, vii, 630).

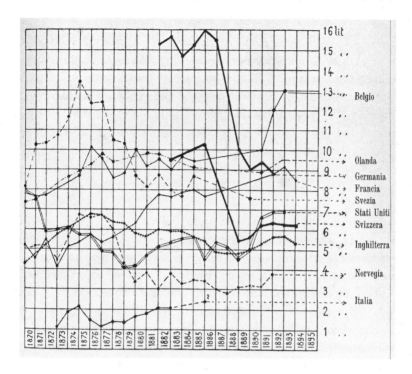

42 Consumption of Alcohol by Country
Editors' note: This table compares the consumption of alcohol (measured in liters/inhabitant) in ten countries, including the United States (no. 7). Lombroso proposed limits on the sale of liquor as a preventative measure against crime.
Source: Lombroso, *L'uomo delinquente*, Edition 5 (*Atlante*). Photo courtesy of the New York Library of Medicine.

Among criminals, the proportion of tobacco users is higher among violent criminals (48 percent) and murderers than among thieves and forgers (43 percent). Prostitutes in Verona and Capua chew tobacco almost constantly, and those who do not chew it, smoke it. Marambat established that passion for tobacco in children leads to laziness, drunkenness, and finally to crime.[j]

Morphine.   Other intoxicating substances also lead to crime. Malaysians commit homicides when they become inebriated by opium, which they call Hamook. The Chinese opium-eater seems apathetic yet at the same

[j] *Archivio di Psich.*, v, 378.

time is impulsive, homicidal, and suicidal. Rates of hysteria among female swindlers are heightened by morphine use. Morphine addicts in general show a diminished moral sense, which often leads them to swindling and sometimes to murder and sex crimes (Charcot, op. cit.). A perverse woman who had been addicted to morphine since childhood murdered her five-year-old daughter, blaming the drug for her violent, impulsive behavior (Guimbail, *Annale d'hygiène publique*, 1891).

Wealth

The influence of wealth on crime is a highly contentious issue, one that cannot be completely settled by studying statistics. However, we can start by calculating the wealth of each Italian province by the amount of total taxes paid by individuals and businesses. Table 27 shows that theft and crimes against the state rise with wealth, while murder rates fall. But statistics on offenses against morality reveal no clear pattern, being lowest where wealth is moderate and highest in areas of poverty. This contradicts the general opinion that morals offenses increase with prosperity. Even more contradictions appear if we consider specific years and regions. Thus we can draw few general conclusions, perhaps because taxes do not really reflect levels of wealth.[16]

Should we instead focus on economic crises to measure the connection between wealth and crime? Fornasari's (o.c.) admirable study shows no clear relationship between economic, commercial, and industrial depressions and rates of crime. Warning of the difficulty of measuring such complex relationships, Bodio found a correlation between economic downturns and rising crime only in the cases of bankruptcies, political crimes, and morals offenses.[k]

Does unemployment notably affect crime? In South Wales, unemployment has little effect on working-class criminality. In the United States, 82 percent of all homicides are committed by individuals with jobs, and only 18 percent by the jobless. Thus unemployment does not seem to constitute a major cause of violent crime.[l] Of course, most

[k] *Atti della Commissione per la statistica giudiziaria sul movimento della delinquenza nel 1893*, Sessione maggio 1895, Relazione di L. Bodio, p. 19.
[l] Fornasari di Verce, op. cit, 32–33, 44–48.

Table 27: Wealth and Types of Crime

| | RATES OF CRIME PER 100,000 INHABITANTS | | | | | |
| | wealth (1885–1886) | | | wealth (1890–1893) | | |
TYPE OF CRIME	max.	avg.	min.	max.	avg.	min.
against the state	70.6	66.0	43.0	55.13	39.45	37.39
against morality	15.6	13.4	19.6	16.5	15.28	21.49
theft	206.0	143.0	148.0	361.28	329.51	419.05
murder	11.3	17.0	23.0	8.34	13.39	15.40
swindling/fraud	–	–	–	81.39	53.27	46.53

Editor's note: Lombroso gives his sources as Bodio and Ferri for the crime statistics and the *Annuario del ministero delle finanze, Statistica finanziaria* (*Yearbook of the Ministry of Finance: Financial Statistics*) for the statistics on wealth. Maximum, average, and minimum levels of wealth refer to groupings of inhabitants based on the amount of taxes they pay into the national treasury. Crimes against morality include rape, incest, adultery, and the procurement of prostitutes. The table has no data on swindling and fraud for the years 1885–86.

criminals lack a steady job, but that is only because they do not want to work. Most unemployed individuals, on the other hand, had jobs but lost them for reasons beyond their control, unless they went on strike. In his book *The Relations of Economic Conditions to the Causes of Crime* (Philadelphia, 1891), Wright claims that all types of crime increase during industrial depressions, but he gives no proof. When he writes that 147 out of 220 convicted criminals in Massachusetts lacked regular work and that generally 68 percent of all criminals are unemployed, he forgets that criminals hate assiduous toil and avoid it.

Industrialization, rather than poverty, seems to cause crime. As industrialization spreads at the expense of agriculture, it attracts an increasing conglomeration of immigrants and workers to cities, who begin to abuse alcohol, which causes crime. Even in agricultural areas with a too-rapid increase in wealth we see a marked rise in crime.

Those who argue that crime is always a result of poverty have failed to research the other side of the question: when is crime the result of wealth? If not balanced by an elevation of character and broad religious and political ideals, acquisition of wealth leads to harm rather than good. Spencer has written that wealth can lead to either virtue or vice, depending on the character of a people. This is most true for excessive wealth that, like excessive power or advanced education, can fuel insolence, sexual abuse, alcohol consumption, and thus crime. In short,

wealth can both impede and engender crime, as is true with education, population density, civilization, and religion. In North America,
the states with the most severe crime rates show both the highest and
lowest levels of income, according to census reports.[m]

Thus not only wealth but also poverty causes crime. Lack of basic
necessities forces people to obtain the goods necessary for survival
through property crime.[n] Moreover, poverty renders man impulsive as
a result of cortical irritation that follows alcoholic intoxication and insufficient nutrition. When extreme need finds this type of fertile degenerative terrain on which to germinate, it naturally leads to certain forms
of homicide. These include, according to Colaianni, retaliation based
on the law that says, "take the life of he who takes your bread." This law
also encourages brutal elimination of individuals who threaten one's
family, reminding us of parricides and infanticides among savages.[17]

Indigence indirectly causes morals offenses, first, because poor men
cannot afford to hire prostitutes to meet their needs; second, because
work in factories and mines forces young people into precocious contact; and, third, because poverty leads to infantilism and femininity in
young boys.[18] Moreover, violent crime results from the terrible poison—wine and alcohol—that the working classes consume to brighten
their few hours of repose and assuage their pain and hunger. In addition, the poor, who are already subject to degeneration from inherited
scrofula, anemia, alcoholism, and tuberculosis, often develop epilepsy
and moral insanity.

The rich, on the other hand, can better resist criminal impulses because they are physically and morally fortified by sufficient nutrition and
good education. Yet wealth can also cause degeneration (from syphilis
and orgies) or encourage vanity and the desire to cut a figure in society,
a major cause of property crimes. Wealthy areas also attract gangs seeking fruitful outlets for crime.[o]

Though it may be true that need inspires the poor to do harm, they
generally commit only a few types of crime. The desires of the rich are
less urgent but more numerous, thus leading to infinitely more types
of crimes. Wealth also provides the means of executing them.

But it will be asked, why do nearly all convicted criminals come from

[m] Scribner's *Statistical Atlas of the United States*, 1880.

[n] Mayr, *Die Gezetzmässigkeit in Gesellschaftleben*, München, 1877; and Fornasari, o. c.

[o] See E. Ferri, *Dei sostitutivi penali*, in *Arch. di psich.*, i, p. 88; Idem., *Studi sulla criminalità in Fran-
cia* in *Ann. di Stat.*, S. 2a, v. xxi, pag. 183; and Fornasari, op. c.

the ranks of the poor? Statistics for 1889 in Italy (*Statistica penale per il 1889*) show the following rates of poverty per one hundred criminals:

	1887	1888	1889
Indigent	56.34	57.45	56.00
Poor[19]	29.99	30.77	32.15
Middle-class	11.54	9.98	10.13
Wealthy	2.13	1.80	1.72

These results confirm those of Dr. Guillaume, Stevens, and Marro, who have shown the enormous disproportion between rich and poor in the commission of crime.[p]

We must not, however, be misled by these statistics that seem to contradict the evil influence of wealth. As Marro has argued, not all those who break the law end up in prison. The rich are aided by their money, their families, their social relations, and their high levels of education in defending themselves in court and avoiding punishment. We have already seen that morally insane individuals with wealth can gain admission to private clinics and therefore are absent from statistics on public asylums and prisons. In the age-old class struggle, the justice system serves as an instrument of power and domination over the poor, who are considered guilty a priori for their poverty. A great poet has said "rags encourage the discovery of crimes, while gold covers and defends them" (Shakspeare, *Re Lear* [*King Lear*]).

Religion

The influence of religion is even more complex than that of wealth and civilization. There are extremely religious criminals (particularly in the countryside and uncivilized areas), as well as irreligious and atheist criminals. Criminals and honest men attend church at almost the same rate; in fact, the former often have higher attendance rates than the latter.[q]

---

[p] Guillaume, *État de la question des prisons en Suède*; Stevens, *Les prisons cellulaires en Belgique*; and Marro, *I caratteri dei delinquenti*, Turin, 1887.

[q] However, Maxime Du Camp observed thirty-three prisoners during mass and noted that three followed the mass; one had his head covered and stared at the altar; one knelt; one pretended to follow

Among 700 criminals, Ferri found only one atheist, one who was indifferent to religion, and seven who were extremely pious.[20] Several used religion to excuse their crimes. One claimed that "God instilled in me the instinct to rob"; a second that "Crimes are not sinful because even priests break the law"; and a third that "In confession the priest will pardon my bad deeds." Statistics show fewer criminals among atheists than among Catholics and Protestants, perhaps because atheists in Europe tend to be highly educated. For example, in Prussia (*Friedr. Arch. F. Strafsrech*, 1884), the rate of criminality among Catholics is 87 per 10,000; among Jews, 65 per 10,000; and among atheists, 37 per 10,000.

---

the mass but read the *Magasin Pitoresque*; one cried; and twenty-six read or worked. [These statistics on prisoners' behavior during mass add to thirty-two, not thirty-three as originally stated – Eds.]

46

Etiology of Crime
HEREDITY, SEX, AND POLITICS

Heredity

I examined 104 criminals and found that: 71 had hereditary abnormalities; 20 had alcoholic fathers; 11 had alcoholic mothers; 8 had criminal fathers; 2 had criminal mothers; 3 had fathers with insanity or meningitis; 5 had insane or epileptic mothers; 3 had prostitute mothers; 6 had insane siblings; 14 had criminal siblings; 4 had epileptic siblings; 2 had suicidal siblings; and 10 had prostitute sisters. These figures may not be exact because I had to rely on criminals' own statements. Under better research conditions, Virgilio found that 26.8 percent of inmates had criminal relatives, 21.77 percent had alcoholic fathers, and 6 percent alcoholic siblings.[r] Of those detained at the reformatory of Elmira, 13.7 percent had insane or epileptic parents and 38.7 percent had alcoholic relatives.[21]

Epilepsy. Knecht found 60 epileptics among the relatives of 400 criminals. Of 559 criminal soldiers, Brancaleone Ribaudo found epilepsy in 10.1 percent of their parents. Penta identified 9.2 percent of 184 born criminals with epileptic parents. According to a study by Clarke, 46 percent of epileptic criminals could trace epilepsy to their families, in contrast to only 21 percent of noncriminal epileptics.

Parental Age. Marro, who has studied parental age for various categories of criminals, writes that "a large number of perpetrators of crimes against property, except swindlers, have young parents."[s] The proportion of swindlers with aged parents is 37 percent, and it goes even higher for assassins and murderers, of whom 52.9 percent have aged parents — by far the largest proportion of any class of criminals. In addition, 38

---

[r] G. Virgilio, *Saggio di ricerche sulla natura morbosa del delitto*, Roma, 1875.

[s] Marro, *I caratteri dei delinquenti*, Torino, Bocca, 1887.

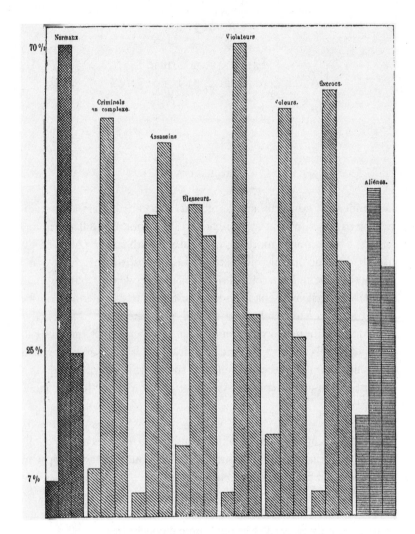

43 Age of Parents for Normal Individuals, Criminals, and the Insane
Editors' note: Juvenile delinquents, according to Lombroso, often have extremely young or extremely old parents. This graph compares parental age of normal individuals (far-left grouping), criminals (middle groupings), and the insane (far-right grouping). Within each grouping, the left column represents abnormally young parents and the right abnormally old parents.
Source: Lombroso, *Der Verbrecher* (*Atlas*). Photo courtesy of the Lloyd Sealy Library, John Jay College of Criminal Justice.

percent of murderers have aged mothers, compared to only 17 percent of normal individuals. Marro also noted that criminals (63 percent) were less likely than school students (70 percent) to have parents of similar ages.

We have seen that paternal heredity prevails over maternal heredity in both honest individuals and criminals. Children can more or less actively inherit hereditary characteristics, which are initially in a latent state and only gradually manifest themselves during childhood. The manifestation of hereditary characteristics follows the general growth of each organ, reaching the maximum when this organ is in its most energetic stage of development. The tension between the influence of the father, which favors variability and individuality, and that of the mother, which tends to conserve the average type, can already be seen in the nearly equal distribution of the sexes. Because mothers enshrine the principle of conservation, their constitutions energetically combat the transmission of diseases, especially from fathers. Children later play the same role in heredity as the parents of the same sex.

The most typical degenerative disease, after genius and cretinism, is criminality. We need only remember the story of the Juke family, whose great fecundity was followed by high infant mortality and finally by complete sterility, as also happens after the coupling of monsters or members of distant species.

Sex

Statistics show that female crime rates are much lower than those of men, especially if we exclude infanticide. In Italy between 1885 and 1889, men committed 286,825 crimes per year on the average and women 54,837. Experts have pointed out that women start to follow the path of crime at a later age than men. Oettingen argues that female crime rates peak between the twenty-fifth and twenty-seventh year, and Quetelet points to the age of thirty (compared to age twenty-four for men). Several factors explain women's limited involvement in crime, including their low rates of alcoholism and their lower levels of engagement in commerce.[t] For young women, prostitution constitutes a sub-

---

[t] Quetelet, *Physique Sociale*, 2a edizione, Bruxelles, 1869, pag. 313. Quetelet contradicts himself, however, on p. 354, where he locates the peak of female crime between the ages of twenty-four and

stitute for criminality; both behaviors are characterized by vagabond-age and sloth.[u]

Politics

Although they are crimes of passion, political crimes are nevertheless damaging and punishable because they offend the human sense of order and hatred of change, particularly in religious and political life. The young, inhabitants of hot countries, and educated and intelligent people play the greatest role in political crime.[v]

Density. Demographic density and industrial activity are correlated with rebelliousness and a progressive spirit. On the other hand, inhabitants of rural areas with low population are often quite conservative.[w]

Race Mixing. When grafted together, races become more progressive and revolutionary. This phenomenon relates to Darwin's discovery about plants, which require fertilization even when they are hermaphroditic. It also relates to Romanes's law, according to which the first cause of evolution is independent variation.[22] Ethnic mixing between European colonists and indigenous peoples in Spanish America has made the latter much more active commercially and intellectually, and finally more rebellious. Sicilians have a greater tendency to evolve and rebel than Neapolitans because Normans and Saracens interbred extensively in Sicily, especially in Palermo.

Bad Government. A government that neglects public well-being and persecutes its honest citizens incites revolts and revolutions. Persecution, as Machiavelli observed, transforms mere ideas into strong feelings.[23] On the eve of the American Revolution, Benjamin Franklin, in his pamphlet *Rules for Reducing a Great Empire to a Small One*, sum-

---

twenty-five (rather than thirty), and the peak of male crime between the ages of twenty-three and twenty-four. He believes that at other ages, male and female patterns of crime are similar.

[u] The full evidence for this appears in Lombroso and Ferrero, *La donna delinquente e la prostituta*; Roncoroni, o. c.

[v] Lombroso e Laschi, *Delitto politico*, 1890, Parte i.

[w] Lombroso e Laschi, *Delitto politico*, 1890.

marized the aspects of bad government that led people to rebel. In nations where political reform follows popular sentiment, uprisings seldom occur. Italy, in spite of its imperfections, provides such an example because the present form of government represents indisputable progress over its predecessors.

Class Inequality. In any form of government, the domination of one class or caste over others has always been dangerous, for it arrests the nation's organic development, predisposing it first to atrophy and later to the opposite but equally fatal phenomenon of violent revolution. For example, the dominant power of the Catholic clergy in Spain, Scotland, the Papal States, and Naples retarded progress and pushed those states to revolt. Where classes are in equilibrium, liberty prevails and revolutions become rare.

Epidemics of Idealism. Certain ideals can spread almost like epidemics. Once it was the monarchical ideal (the glory of having one's own king); then, with the French Revolution, came the ideal of popular sovereignty; and after that, the principle of nationality. The rage today is for the ideal of improving economic conditions, even though these are better now than in our fathers' times. In fact, the harvest failures that used to claim millions of victims now claim only a few hundred, and our workers have more shirts than the proudest aristocrats of old.

Inopportune Political Reforms. Only arrogant men, or those who are ignorant about human nature, can decree measures out of step with the temper of the times. They destroy ancient institutions and substitute new ones, not in response to popular demand but in imitation of other societies. Thus they provoke the resentment that every reform brings, and failing to blend the new with the old, create instability. The result is a weakening of state authority and continual revolution.

Economics. The influence of economic factors on the great revolutionary movements of recent centuries has been incontestably demonstrated by Loria.[x] Class struggle in England burst forth when the nobility started to vote for laws favoring landed property over industry. The

---

[x] *La teoria economica della costituzione politica*, 1885.

bourgeoisie, allied with Elizabeth, triumphed over the nobility grouped around Mary Stuart. The middle classes then allied with Cromwell and eventually elevated William of Orange to the throne.[24]

Industrial and commercial crises are more likely to influence local revolts than broad revolutionary movements. Yet it is nowadays impossible to contest the importance of economic factors in a nation's political life. The problem has changed little from the days of Aristotle, who demonstrated that aristocratic governments were threatened by revolution when some subjects were rich and others poor. Even in democratic or republican governments, the body politic will inevitably revolt when the poorer classes become substantial in size (*Politicon*, book V).

In our times, the enormous inequalities between capital and labor have become the main source of revolutionary ferment. Aggravated by today's financial speculations, these inequalities constitute a problem that classical political economists like A. Smith did not recognize. Like liberal economics, Darwin's theories, too, by documenting individual differences, seem to confirm the necessity of inequalities in wealth.[25] But against Darwin's theory comes that sentiment of humanity that was given its first breath by Christ and has not weakened with the passing of time—the reluctance to let a man who works die of hunger or a man who wishes to be useful go jobless.[26]

In Italy, thousands of peasants are forced to eat rotting maize without anyone, including members of parliament, trying to protect them. Goiter and cretinism deform entire populations in mountain regions, causing deafness, muteness, and albinism simply because not even a fraction of the money spent on wasteful monuments is devoted to supplying good water supplies. In many Italian plains, including those outside the two major cities of Rome and Milan, malaria decimates the population. If peasants protest with demonstrations and strikes, as they have done in the regions of Pavia, Mantua, and Polesine, the fault lies with the government, which has never solved these problems.[27]

47

Prevention of Crime

Ferri (*Sociologie criminelle*, Paris, 1890, p. 240) coined the phrase *penal substitutes* to refer to preventive measures for crime. For example, wide avenues and street lighting prevent thefts, holdups, and rapes better than police. Legislation to limit the hours of work for children and women prevents many offenses against decency. Reasonably priced housing for workers, workman's compensation, and civil responsibility on the part of business owners discourage vagabondage and strikes. As for the political order, a truly liberal government discourages insurrections and anarchist violence, just as freedom of the press impedes political corruption and civil rebellion.[28]

Scientific Policing

Hitherto policing was conducted much as wars used to be waged: randomly and on the basis of hunches. Successful investigations depended on the astuteness and dedication of a few individuals. What we need now is to apply the scientific method to the identification of criminals.

Of the many systems invented for this, Bertillon's is the most ingenious.[29] In the Paris police station where he worked, he collected thousands of photographs of criminals, which were easy to use as long as there were only a few of them, but less so once their numbers grew. Bertillon classified offenders according to the measurements of certain parts of the body that he considered invariable: height, length and width of the head, length of the left middle finger, length of the left foot, width across the extension of the arms, and length of the left forearm. This system rests on two assumptions: that the human body, once it has reached maturity, remains more or less the same; and that it is impossible to find two humans who are completely identical.

Sexual Crimes and Fraud

Sexual crimes and bank fraud are offenses that afflict advanced societies. How can we prevent them?

Sexual Crimes. Divorce effectively prevents adultery and other crimes of lust. In Italy, no fewer than forty-six murders a year take place in order to end a marriage that has become unbearable. Every day we see mothers pushed to the point of madness or crime by abuse from their spouses.

Some sex crimes are caused by congenital tendencies in born rapists with a cretinal diathesis that either stimulates the genitals or provokes insanity. Others are occasional crimes encouraged by the primitive level of rural society, lack of prostitutes as sexual outlets, or barriers to marriage.

Religious institutions like the Catholic Church have ruined some savage societies and even certain civilized nations. Where priests are condemned to celibacy, the confessional offers an occasion and instrument of crime.[30] Although the priesthood is one of the professions least stained by crime in general, statistics show relatively high rates of sex crimes, particularly pederasty. However, these rates are lower than they are for other celibate groups.

Civilization plays a role in the increase of sex crimes against minors by encouraging the proliferation of schools, particularly boarding schools. Schools provide opportunities for contact between teachers (who are often poor and therefore single) and pupils. Furthermore, one immoral youth can corrupt a hundred. In the growing cities, industry employs minors alongside adults. Certain types of factories and mines force children and adults to work seminaked in dark rooms.

Surveillance is necessary in schools and factories that employ youths. To prevent pederasty by male instructors, only women should be hired as teachers. Likewise, workshops should employ female guards to watch over youths working at night or in dark places. These would be easy and economical measures. Legislation should prohibit children beneath a certain age from work in mines. Another remedy for sex crimes by men would be for the government to encourage prostitution in rural areas, especially those where soldiers, sailors, and workers gather.

No law is able to prevent marriage from becoming unpleasant, but at least easy divorce would prevent antipathy from leading to nausea and crime.[31] Divorce would decrease the crime of adultery because spouses could legally find sexual satisfaction after separation. In the absence of divorce, separation leads to adulterous relationships and sometimes duels. When equilibrium between the call of nature and moral duty is established, we will see a rapid reduction in sex crimes, which flow as much from a lack of love as an excess of passion.

Not only must divorce be made simple, but weddings must become less commercial, love less difficult, and motherhood more respected. Above all, the law should legalize paternity suits and make reparation for seduction obligatory.[32] Then society would hold guilty not only the victim but also the seducer, who until now has been protected by smiles and silence. This has left the desperate victim to take justice into her own hands in order to eliminate the traces of her misadventure.[33]

These measures would prevent not only sexual crimes but also infanticide, suicide, murders, and, in short, all crimes committed for love. They are the crimes most worthy of human compassion, in which victim and perpetrator are most often honest beings.

Fraud.   Fraud and abuse of public trust, the most modern of crimes, can be committed only by people who are cultivated and pleasant. Through an evolutionary transformation, fraud replaces the harsh cruelty of primitive man with greed and lying, traits that are becoming widespread and are most dangerous in criminals.

As one goes from the countryside to the village and from the small city to the metropolis, the number of small-scale frauds and commercial deceptions grow in number and scope. Today, the gullible are engulfed by the elaborate schemes of joint-stock banks, which people with classy names and reputations protect. Furthermore, the parliamentary system encourages swindling and misuse of public money. For a politician, the steps are not great between giving public money to a newspaper here, to a friend there, and finally to himself. This is especially true of politicians who try to make up for a lack of cleverness with a lack of honesty, holding that *denaro del comun, denaro di nessun* (the government's money is nobody's money).

Excessive Wealth and Poverty

Crime is caused not only by poverty, as many maintain, but also by wealth acquired rapidly and in enormous amounts.[34] We need social legislation that mandates greater equity in wages, makes jobs more accessible, and reduces the hours of work for women and children.[35] We need to legalize strikes in more than theory, so as not to suppress the power of workers and their organizations.[36] Excesses of wealth are always harmful and should be limited by allowing workers to share profits and by progressive taxation, particularly on inheritances.

By taxing the rich, we could continue that progress toward economic equality that was initiated with the forced expropriation and subdivision of ecclesiastical lands and abolition of feudal entails by the state. Because the great latifundia of the Roman and Sicilian countryside guarantee great wealth to the few and misery to the many, I recommend forced expropriation in favor of the state.[37] We should remember the words of the great Cavour: "Either the upper classes concern themselves with the fate of the poor, or they accept civil war as inevitable."[38]

The first step toward equalization of wealth must be taken by the government and the ruling classes because we Italians are not used to organizing ourselves from below for political action. But after the government takes the first step, the neediest classes must advance their own cause through cooperatives and mutual aid societies.[39]

Extreme levels of poverty, however, cannot wait for cooperative societies, collectivism, and state aid. Charity, at one time the only guarantee against poverty, is still needed despite the progress of civilization. As time goes on, philanthropic initiatives must detach themselves from religion and transform themselves into measures of social welfare, cooperation, and, ultimately, collectivism.[40]

Education

We must abolish prison schooling, which favors recidivism and supplies new weapons to criminals. Conversely, we must make primary education available to the largest possible number of honest individuals. Born criminals should not be allowed to infiltrate elementary schools because education would harm both them and society. There should be special schools for born juvenile delinquents which render them less dangerous by channeling their energies into sport, sailing, hunting, or training for special occupations (such as butchery for the bloodthirsty). These occupations should include the military (which is a form of official butchery) and the circus (which satisfies the vanity of athletes).

Advances in criminal anthropology have now made possible the preventive isolation of criminals—the most important measure of social defense. Teachers are now able to identify in children the incurable signs of inborn criminality and to use these signs to distinguish between innate criminality and the temporary criminality of all youth. These signs include physiological and craniological anomalies in children, coupled with tendencies toward wrongdoing.

The family can be even more effective than the teacher in identifying signs of born criminality in children. Given the temporary criminality common to youth, parents need not be worried about or severely punish isolated criminal acts in children who do not display physical and psychological anomalies. In normal individuals, childhood wickedness evolves naturally into adult goodness, just as the fetus grows into the infant. Bad upbringing, however, can stimulate the vicious instincts of infancy until they become habitual.

Absurdities of the Legal System

Contradictions within the legal system lead to trials marked by wasted money, scandalous publicity, and uncertain outcomes.

Juries. The inappropriateness of juries for judging anything but political crimes is shown by the variation in the number of acquittals from year to year and place to place. For example, 50 percent of all trials end in acquittals in the southern city of Cagliari, while the acquittal rate is only 23 percent in northern Italy.[y] In Calabria, according to Taiani (*Rendic.*, p. 112), "the educated classes are never represented on the jury." Numerous cases demonstrate the complete ignorance of most jurors.

Jurors can be easily corrupted because they are answerable to no one and have nothing to lose through an acquittal. The frequent acquittals of criminals who have confessed to bribery show that juries often barter

[y] Lavini, *Del modo con cui è amministrata la giustizia,* Venezia, 1875.

away justice. The jury, indeed, is a cause of corruption: many honest people become corrupt as soon as they become jury members, according to the prefect Borghetti (*Relazione della giunta per l'inchiesta sulle condizioni della Sicilia*), because the Mafia loves to show off its power over the outcome of trials. According to another investigative report, the *Relazione Cantelli*, one parliamentary deputy actually complained when a certain trial did not provide a profit for the jury members.

Corruption of juries becomes a great incentive to immorality among the poor. Lower-class defendants, seeing that justice is anything but equal for all, feel free to revenge themselves against the society that condemns them. Although the jury system causes problems in England and America as well, justice does not fail as often among Anglo-Saxons as it does among Italians.

Pardons. Another problem in the Italian legal system is the right of one man—the king—to grant pardons, a practice that certainly negates those principles of eternal justice about which the opponents of criminal anthropology prattle continuously. How do our opponents contradict themselves? First, they affirm that justice is equal for all and derives from fixed norms, almost as if these norms were celestial emanations. But this theory falls apart like a pack of cards when convicted criminals are pardoned by a man who, although he may well be the most honest in the country, is only human. The practice of granting pardons is contrary to the spirit of equality that underlies modern society, for it favors the rich and encourages the poor to believe that for them there is no justice. As a result, the poor commit new crimes.

Misguided Theories. More than a few jurists and theorists, even the most enlightened, have called for the reduction of sentences in an effort to be up to date in applying the new science of criminal man. They misinterpret the anthropological discovery that many criminals are insane or feebleminded to imply that criminals should not be held responsible for their crimes. What they have not understood is that criminal anthropology, while not blaming the born criminal for his behavior, nevertheless prescribes for him a life sentence. We believe that those individuals least responsible for their behavior are most to be feared. Only sequestration can neutralize their innate, atavistic urge to crime, which resembles a wave that crashes within them when it finds high banks but overflows and floods when it does not. Many jurists, like Dutchmen in reverse, believe it possible to contain the wave by breaking the dykes—that is, by recommending abolition of the death penalty, stronger rights for defendants, and the granting of royal pardons—instead of measures to increase security and repress crime.

Does military history not teach us that a general would condemn his soldiers to perdition if he relied only on abstract philosophy, ignoring tactics and ballistics? Like military strategy, the proper functioning of the legal system requires knowledge of practical matters with little resort to philosophy. But our present professional class of jurists substitutes metaphysics for strategy by daydreaming of a free will that never was, of a liberty disconnected from material causes, and of a right to punish based on abstract legal notions rather than on social necessity. Not only do they fail to remove or reduce the sources of crime such as alcohol and juvenile gangs but they have introduced into our legal system an array of fashionable defendants' rights. At the same time, they have failed to enact legislation based on the new principles of social defense, such as taxing alcohol, instituting probation, and establishing criminal insane asylums and prisons for incorrigibles.

48

Synthesis and Penal Applications

The foregoing analysis vividly reveals the weakness of the old criminological edifice. Can we replace it with something more solid? If I am not blinded by my extensive study of the subject, I think it can be. To protect ourselves against crime, we need to focus on the criminal, not crime in the abstract. Up to 35 percent of all criminals are atavistic born criminals who differ physically from normal individuals. Many of their characteristics resemble those of primitive men and the colored races. The concept of atavism helps us to understand why punishment is ineffective against born criminality, and why crime remains at a constant, irreducible level.

Atavism and Epilepsy

The same anomalies typical of born criminals appear in the morally insane and, to an even greater extent, in epileptics. Table 28, prepared by Doctor Roncoroni, clearly proves that epileptics display all the atavistic characteristics of born criminals, as well as additional pathological anomalies. The born criminal's pathological traits may at first seem merely strange, but, as table 28 shows, they in fact resemble those of epileptics.

While we cannot ignore the social causes of crime, organic factors explain criminal behavior in 35 percent and possibly even 40 percent of all cases. Social causes are often nothing but the immediate determinant of the timing of a crime that, if it had not occurred at that moment, would have happened on another occasion because the congenital impulse was so powerful. We have proved this by identifying recidivists who continue to commit crimes even after their economic situation improves or after they are deported into an environment free of incentives to break the law. The organic roots of crime are again confirmed by the example of England, which has an ever-rising rate of recidivism despite its heroic efforts to eliminate the social causes of crime. In short, both

Table 28: Anomalies in Criminals and Epileptics

ANOMALY	CRIMINALS	EPILEPTICS	ATAVISM	ARRESTED DEVELOPMENT	DISEASE	ATYPICAL TRAITS
Skull:						
Too large	+	+		+		+
Microcephalic	+	+	+	+	+	+
Sclerosis	+	+	+	+	+	
Assymetry	+	+			+	
Med. occ. fossetta	+	+		+		
Abnormal indice	+	+			+	
Large orbital arches	+	+	+			
Low sloping forehead	+	+	+			
Wormian bones	+	+	+	+		
Simple cranial sutures	+	+	+			
Face:						
Overdeveloped jaw	+	+	+			
Jutting cheekbones	+	+	+			
Large jug ears	+	+	+		+	
Facial assymetry	+	+			+	
Strabismus	+	+			+	
Virility (in women)	+	+	+			
Anomalous teeth	+	+	+			
Brain:						
Anomalous convolutions	+	+	+	+		
Low weight	+	+	+	+		
Hypertrophied cerebellum	+	+	+			
Symptoms of meningitis	+	+				
Body:						
Assymetrical torso	+	+			+	
Prehensile feet	+	+	+			
Hernia	+	+	+	+	+	
Skin:						
Wrinkles	+	+	+			
Beardlessness	+	+	+		+	
Olive skin	+	+	+			
Tattoos	+		+			
Delayed gray hair/balding	+	+	+			
Dark and curly hair	+	+	+			
Motor anomalies:						
Left-handedness	+	+	+			
Abnormal reflexes	+	+			+	
Heightened agility	+	+	+			

Table 28: continued

ANOMALY	CRIMINALS	EPILEPTICS	ATAVISM	ARRESTED DEVELOPMENT	DISEASE	ATYPICAL TRAITS
Sensory anomalies:						
Tactile insensitivity	+	+	+		+	
Insensitivity to pain	+	+	+		+	
Overly acute eyesight	+	+	+			
Dullness of hearing,						
taste, and smell	+	+	+		+	
Psychological anomalies:						
Limited intelligence	+	+	+	+		
Superstitious	+	+	+			
Blunted emotions	+	+	+		+	
Love of animals	+	+			+	
Absence of remorse	+	+	+			
Impulsivity, cannibalism,						
and ferocity	+	+	+	+	+	
Pederasty/masturbation	+	+	+		+	
Vanity	+	+	+			
Sloth	+	+	+		+	
Passion for gaming	+	+	+			
Mania/paranoia/delirium	+	+			+	
Dizziness	+	+			+	
Causes:						
Heredity (alcoholism/						
insanity/epilepsy/						
old parents)	+	+				
Alcoholism	+	+				

Editors' note: This list has been shortened from a longer one of 81 anomalies. Lombroso is attempting to show how the first two categories of individuals, criminals and epileptics, share anomalies that might be caused by atavism, arrested development, disease, or atypical development.

statistics and the anthropological study of individual offenders indicate that crime is a natural phenomenon, or, as some philosophers would put it, a necessity, like conception, birth, and death.

Punishment

Once we stop thinking of punishment as retaliation or as a sort of civil excommunication, we can see that it must change direction completely.

44 Criminal Art
Editors' note: Lombroso's museum contains a large collection of water jugs,
sculptures, mechanical devices, and furniture made by prisoners. In this
example of criminal art, an inmate recreated the scene of his trial.
Source: Photo courtesy of the Museo Lombroso (Turin).

The purpose of punishment should be not the infliction of pain on the
criminal, but the well-being of society and restitution to the victim.
Punishment should be proportional less to the gravity of the crime than
to the dangerousness the criminal. There is a vast difference between the
future threat posed by an individual who kills a man for honor, politics,
or an ideal after leading a completely honest life and one who kills to
rape or rob, crowning a life already full of crime. In the first case, punishment is almost unnecessary because the crime itself tortures the perpetrator, who will never repeat it. In the second case, every delay and
mitigation of punishment endangers society. As Ferri aptly writes: "It
is impossible to separate the crime from the person who commits it."[1]

Crime is like an illness that requires a specific remedy for each patient. It is the job of criminal anthropology to establish the relationship
between criminals and their punishment. Punishment should vary according to the type of offender: the born criminal, the insane criminal,

[1] *Sociologie criminelle*, Paris, 1894.

the habitual criminal, the occasional criminal, and the criminal of passion.

Alternatives to Prison. Brief and repeated prison sentences should be avoided because prison is a school for crime. A few days in prison in the company of corrupt companions has little intimidating effect; instead, it cancels any fear of punishment and incites recidivism through contact with habitual criminals (Ferri, o. c.).

Thus we must find alternative methods of punishment for petty crimes. Some that have already been proposed include house arrest, judicial warnings, fines, forced labor without imprisonment, local exile, and corporal punishment.

The Probation System. Probation, widely used in the United States, constitutes an excellent penalty for minors and occasional criminals.[aa] Under probationary sentences, judges free nonrecidivist criminals but warn them that any lapse in behavior will bring imprisonment. The criminal is kept under surveillance by an agent of the state for a specified period; if the agent feels that the family does not provide a suitable environment, an underage criminal may be placed in a reformatory for morally abandoned youth. Should the juvenile commit another crime, he is returned to court and possibly prison.

In Massachusetts, the probation system produced such good results with minors that it was extended to adult criminals in 1878. Between 1879 and 1883, 2,803 individuals were placed on probation in Boston for crimes including drunkenness, receiving stolen goods, petty theft, and assault. Of these, 223 broke the conditions of their probation and were brought before the courts again, and 44 disappeared without trace.

Elmira Reformatory. In the United States, the Elmira Reformatory[bb] provides another alternative to prison; it was inspired, according to its founder, Brockway, by an earlier edition of *Criminal Man*.[41] The reformatory admits only young men between the ages of sixteen and thirty who have committed nonserious crimes. For each prisoner, Brockway studies the psychological condition, family background, and

[aa] Lombroso, *Les applications de l'anthropologie criminelle*, Paris, Alcan, 1891.

[bb] *The New York Reformatory in Elmira* by Alexander Winter F. S. S., with a preface by Havelock Ellis. London, Sonnenschein e C., 1891; *Fifteenth Annual Report of the Board of Managers of the N. Y. S. Reformatory at Elmira*, Transmitted to the Legislature, January, 1891, Reformatory Press.

causes of the crime; on the basis of this information, he designs an individualized program of reform that usually includes exercise, showers, massage, gymnastics, and a good diet. The aim is to reinvigorate the will, turn the inmate into his own boss, and give him a stake in his own liberation, which he will obtain as soon as he demonstrates that he is able to fend for himself. At the beginning of the month, Brockway himself assesses the physical condition of each inmate and establishes what amount of work will produce maximal results. Education consists of primary instruction and apprenticeship in a craft.

No one could be a greater supporter of this type of reformatory than I. It represents the first practical and serious application of the results of my research. The somatic study of each criminal, allied with practical and individualized training, cannot fail to lead to impressive results in criminals. Young adults will regain the habit of work and leave the reformatory with sufficient resources to prevent them from becoming recidivists in property crime. I do not believe, however, that the effects of such reformatories will be long-lasting for born criminals, many of whom have no moral sense (49 percent), left home before the age of fourteen (12 percent), have epileptic parents (12 percent) or alcoholic parents (37 percent), or manifest no sense of repentance (56 percent).

Criminal Insane Asylums. Criminal insane asylums can reconcile humane treatment with the need for social protection. While theories of punishment can be debated at great length, experts agree on one point: many criminals are insane. For them, prison is an injustice, liberty a peril, and most other provisions half measures that violate the demands of both morality and security. Only criminal insane asylums can provide an alternative to prison for those unhappy beings whose crimes have arisen out of morbid psychological impulses rather than inner perversity. For judges, criminal insane asylums provide an answer to the eternal conflict between justice for the insane and defense of society.

Types of Offenders

We now turn to the direct application of positivist penal theory to offenders according to sex, age, and crime. Punishment should vary according to whether the criminal is young or old; male or female; a country or a city dweller; and a criminal of passion, occasional criminal, born criminal, or insane criminal.

Sex. As I demonstrated in my book, *Criminal Woman, the Prostitute, and the Normal Woman*, female born criminality hardly exists except in the form of prostitution. For the female born criminal, the profession of prostitution itself acts as a penal substitute or crime preventative; it also acts as a dyke against that irresistible flood of male sexuality that would otherwise scandalize and threaten honest society.[42] Thus prostitution represents a case of symbiosis, discussed at greater length below, in which a crime or its equivalent must be tolerated because, although immoral, it provides social benefits.[43]

The majority of female criminals are occasional criminals, criminals of passion, or both in succession. Only between 11 and 20 percent of all female offenders have inborn criminal tendencies. Moreover, typically female crimes such as abortion, infanticide, and child abandonment are those that deserve the least punishment. Prison and other afflictive punishments are, therefore, much less necessary for women than for men. Because female crimes are almost always an effect of suggestion, their perpetrators are much less of a threat when they are distanced from the prompter, who is usually a lover or husband; it is sufficient to impose on women a judicial warning followed by probation. The small numbers of female poisoners, swindlers, and murderers should be interned for short periods in prison—or better still, a convent. Nuns can train them to replace sexual love—the most frequent cause of female crime—with religiosity. Honesty and religious fanaticism will eventually become substitutes for criminal tendencies. I have witnessed this process myself, even in a cellular prison where the nuns were not trained to reform inmates.[44]

Women who commit more than two or three offenses against public decency should be recognized by police as legal prostitutes and discouraged from practicing their profession in a secret and therefore harmful manner.[45] Given female vanity and the importance women place on clothes, knickknacks, and furniture, prison sentences for female offenders can often be replaced by penalties such as cutting their hair or confiscating their ornaments and furniture. Once imprisoned, female inmates must be made to work or go hungry.

Abortion. Abortion should be punished merely with a judicial warning, except in the case of professionals performing abortions for profit.

One of our leading jurists, Balestrini, has brilliantly proven that abortion does not constitute a crime. First, he argues that abortion does not undermine family order because most cases involve young, single women who are trying to avoid the creation of an illegal family.[cc] Second, abortion does not violate the legal protection of bodily integrity because the law punishes any abortion committed against a mother's will as a violent crime. Third, society derives no advantage from the birth of illegitimate children. Finally, it is contestable whether the fetus is a social being because the fetus is still at an animalian stage of evolution and not yet human. During the first few months after conception, only a trained embryologist can identify a future human. Thus the law should not prohibit abortions performed by women on themselves just as it does not prohibit individuals from potentially harming themselves in other ways, such as by exposing themselves to syphilis (Puglia, *L'evoluzione del delitto*, pag. 197).

The low conviction rate for abortion (28 percent of all cases) makes the law look ridiculous and the few sentences meted out appear unjust. "For every crime that by its nature goes unpunished, punishment becomes an incentive for additional crime" (Beccaria, *Dei delitti e delle pene*, XXXVI).

Infanticides. The same logic applies to infanticides, albeit to a different degree. The birth of an illegitimate baby brings no advantage to society and confers unjust infamy on its mother. Illegitimate children impose a burden on society, which must support them in foundling homes; and these institutions commit "legal killing" through high mortality rates. In Italy, for example, the mortality rate for foundlings is about 50 percent, with even higher rates in towns like Syracuse (73 percent) and Modica (99 percent).

Prison sentences for infanticide leave women completely depraved by removing them from their homes, denying them their habits of housework, and thereby ruining their prospects for rehabilitation at the end of their terms (Balestrini, op. cit.). Danger to society, which should form the basis of punishment, is completely absent in infanticide, which is a crime of occasion or passion and rarely repeated. Thus the penalty of judicial admonition is certainly sufficient.

[cc] Raffaello Balestrini, *Aborto, infanticidio ed esposizione d'infante. Studio giuridico-sociologico* ("Biblioteca antropologico-giuridica." Serie 2a, vol. iii). Torino, Bocca, 1888.

Youth. Prison is even less appropriate for youths than for women. Children require upbringing in families whose rectitude inspires morality and stimulates a sense of emulation, and which provide bland but benevolent treatment. For orphans and minors from corrupt families, moral education can be provided by charitable institutions, foster families, reformatories like Elmira, and agricultural colonies. Utilizing the new medical and psychological insights of criminal anthropology, these institutions promise to prevent the occasional crimes so common to childhood and in a few cases even improve, although not completely reform, the nature of young born criminals. Internment in reformatories will at least prevent juvenile delinquents from contaminating honest youths.

Old Age. There is nothing to be gained by sending the elderly to prison when they are already crippled and unable to commit harm. Detention in a workhouse, with special precautions to prevent corruption of others, is sufficient unless they have committed a series of vicious crimes.

Crimes of Passion. For criminals of passion, the remorse provoked by the crime is already a punishment in itself. Beyond this, fines, judicial admonition, or exile that takes the person far from those offended are sufficient to protect society since such criminals are not dangerous.

Political Criminals. The same applies to political criminals. If there is a type of crime that merits neither the death penalty nor even serious punishment, it is political crime. Many political criminals are simply insane, and mental hospitals are more appropriate for madmen than the prison or the scaffold. Even those who are sane deserve respect for their altruism. If their energies are channeled productively, they can be useful rather than dangerous to society. Furthermore, the majority of political criminals are young and at an age when audacity and fanaticism are at their highest; these passions nearly always fade with time.

Occasional Criminals. A prison sentence serves no purpose for occasional criminals who commit minor offenses and are not essentially dangerous. When violations by occasional offenders are more civil than penal, they should be punished by fines rather than incarceration. Financial restitution would not offend the public conscience and at the same time would provide compensation to the victim (Ferri, *Soc. Crim.*, pag. 620).

Adultery. Adultery, which used to be a serious crime under canon law, should constitute only a misdemeanor under modern penal codes. Because adultery is immoral, punishment would be appropriate if we could prevent the offense. But as Berenini says so well in his impressive monograph, *Offesa e difesa* [*Offense and Defense*]: "Can the law oblige a wife to love her husband and vice versa? If the law cannot command people to love their spouses, it cannot prohibit them from loving others. By dissolving natural marriage, adultery causes moral divorce, so why should civil marriage not be dissolved by legal divorce?[46] Why use force to maintain a disharmonious marriage that will become only more bitter after the scandal of a trial and a sentence?"[dd]

Criminaloids. The appropriate punishment for the first offense of an adult criminaloid who acted alone is a suspended sentence accompanied by bail, a judicial warning, and payment of damages or (if the offender has no money) forced labor. Only criminaloids who refuse to work should be sent to a prison.

Habitual Criminals. Recidivists and criminaloids who become habitual offenders should be treated like born criminals, with the following proviso: since their crimes are less serious (theft, forgery, fraud), their punishment should be less severe. While a born criminal's first offense, if it is serious, may justify a life sentence, the habitual criminal would need to recidivate several times before being declared incorrigible.

The ideal form of punishment for urban criminals is industrial work in the new large factories. Rural criminals should work on penal farms, with the most dangerous offenders assigned to the least healthy lands.[47] Minors should work in fields that have already been cultivated.

Insane Criminals. Criminal insane asylums are the only solution for insane criminals and for those numerous born criminals in whom epilepsy and moral insanity causes violent fits. Permanent internment in asylums will prevent insane criminals from transmitting their disease

---

[dd] The public prosecutor of Milan, Mazza, reached the same conclusion on the basis of common sense and the enormous number of suits for marital separation.

through heredity, from associating with ordinary criminals, and from forming criminal gangs. In addition, criminal insane asylums would reduce recidivism, the costs of additional trials, and the number of imitative crimes. I recommend special types of criminal insane asylums for alcoholics, epileptics, and those with pellagra.

Incorrigible Criminals and Born Criminals. Dangerous habitual criminals and born criminals must be interned in special institutions for the incorrigible. My proposal is not new, for in England—the international leader in finding practical solutions—the House of Lords as early as 1864 proposed that second-time recidivists be condemned to lifelong penal servitude. In Italy, respected statesmen and judges like Doria, Barini, and Manfredi have recommended establishment of a prison for incorrigibles (*Rivista di Discipl. Carc.*, 1875–1876). An agricultural colony for 4,500 incorrigibles already exists at Mexplas, Belgium, where inmates construct their own houses under the direction of only thirty to forty master builders (Joly, o.c.).

Death Sentence. When criminals repeat bloodthirsty crimes for the third or fourth time—despite being punished by incarceration, deportation, and forced labor—there is no choice but to resort to that extreme form of natural selection, death. Maintaining the death sentence does not mean using it often. It is sufficient that it should be suspended like a sword of Damocles over the most terrible criminals, those who have attempted to kill innocent people. This removes the last justifiable objection to capital punishment, that it is irreparable. The death penalty should also be applied to members of organized crime—*camorristi, mafiosi*, and brigands—who threaten the security and honor of our country. By creating violent, warlike conditions, they merit the same severe penalty as that meted out to traitors.

To claim that the death sentence contradicts the laws of nature is to feign ignorance of the fact that progress in the animal world, and therefore the human world, is based on a struggle for existence that involves hideous massacres. Born criminals, programmed to do harm, are atavistic reproductions of not only savage men but also the most ferocious carnivores and rodents. This discovery should not make us more compassionate toward born criminals (as some claim), but rather should shield us from pity, for these beings are members of not our species but the species of bloodthirsty beasts.

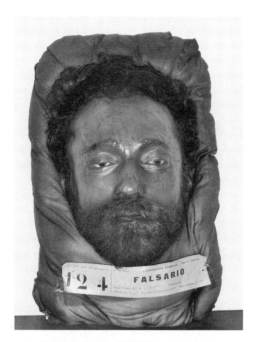

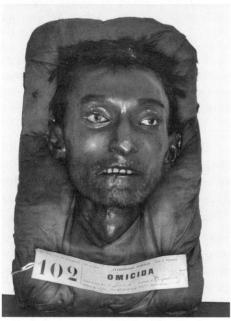

45 and 46 Two Death Masks
Editors' note: These death
masks, from Lombroso's
collection, represent a forger
(top) and a murderer (bottom)
who died in prison.
Created by a colleague,
Lorenzo Tenchini, they are
made of plaster covered with
colored wax and rest on
silk cushions.
Source: Photo courtesy of the
Museo Lombroso (Turin).

Practical Applications

The science of criminal anthropology has evolved to the point of offering both a theory of crime and practical applications of that theory. It can make useful suggestions in the struggle against crime, in contrast to traditional legal philosophy, which becomes ever more theoretical and has less and less to say about defending society. The new positivist criminology has also demonstrated its usefulness in the daily practice of psychiatry and forensic medicine.

Psychiatric Assessment. Forensic doctors and practical jurists who feel the impulse of modernity (as Majno put it so well) have made themselves the masters of the new science of criminal anthropology.[ee] It has become a precious tool for proving, for example, what part a suspect played in a particular crime or which individual among a group is the true ringleader. Until now, answers to these questions rested on fragile clues such as rumors circulating in prisons, the unreliable information of local officials, and the questionable documents in our barren judicial archives. As a result, almost half of all trials reach false verdicts, with innocents being incarcerated and many guilty people escaping punishment. The extent to which criminal anthropology can contribute to correct verdicts is demonstrated by several recent cases in which the new science played a role, albeit a small one.

For example, Gall . . . Maria of Lucera was found dead on June 19, 1886, at the age of sixty-six. Her corpse was in a state of advanced putrefaction, with her head covered by a sheet, her right arm bent under the torso, and the left arm outstretched. She was face down on the mattress, with a bloodied, broken nose. Suspicion immediately fell on her two stepsons, M. and F., who had bad reputations, had been seen in the area on that day, and had something to gain by her death because she was about to disinherit them.

I was summoned to the court to provide an expert assessment of the case.[48] According to the testimony of C., suffocated shouts were heard coming from the room of the victim on the night of the seventeenth. One of the suspects, the stepson M., had previously been sentenced for carrying arms, and he had swindled the victim of a large portion of

[ee] *Commenti di nuovo codice penale,* 1892–96.

her inheritance as soon as his father died. When a girl had rejected his advances, M. said he would like to strangle her as he had his mother; furthermore, he had threatened his brother over the division of their inheritance. Moreover, M. was named as the murderer by his brother F., who was less criminal and less inclined to evil.

Criminal anthropology served admirably on this occasion in deciding which of the two brothers was guilty. M. represented more completely the criminal type, exhibiting huge jaws, swollen sinuses, extremely pronounced cheekbones, a thin upper lip, large incisors (with the right larger than the left), a large head capacity (of 1,620 cc), tactile insensitivity (4.0 mm on the right and 2.0 mm on the left), and left-handedness. All of these physical anomalies, except the swollen sinuses and pronounced cheekbones, were absent in his brother, F. For these reasons, M. was deemed more criminal in his tendencies and convicted.

Criminal anthropology not only identifies criminals but also saves innocents from punishment. In one such case, a three-year-old girl was raped and contracted syphilis. Her mother offered the names of six suspects who were then arrested. All lived in the same building, had frequent contact with the child, and denied raping her. After studying them, I pointed out to the judge one in particular: he had obscene tattoos on his arms, Negroid physiognomy, and an altered field of vision that we traced to a recent case of syphilis. The confession followed shortly.

Pedagogy. Another immediate application of the new positivist criminology is to pedagogy. Anthropometric examination can explain the learning and discipline problems of certain children by revealing their criminal abnormalities, such as precocious physical development, cranial asymmetry, or small head size. Once identified as potential criminals, these children should be trained in suitable occupations, encouraged to emigrate, placed with moral families in foster care, or even given medical treatment.[ff]

Arts and Letters. Criminal anthropology can also be applied to literature, both in the interpretation of masterworks that foreshadowed its theories and in the creation of new forms of art. Our new science has

---

[ff] *Monist*, 1894, p. 398; Vitale, *Studi antropologici in servizio alla pedagogia*, Forlì, 1896; and Marina, *Ricerche antropologiche sui ragazzi*, Torino, 1896.

shaped many immortal works such as Dostoevsky's *The House of the Dead* and *Crime and Punishment*, Zola's *The Human Beast*, Rovetta's *Baraonda*, Garborg's *Kolbotubrew of Andre Skildringar*, Ibsen's *Hedda Gabler*, *Pillars of Society*, and *Ghosts*, D'Annunzio's *The Victim*, Capuana's *Profumo* and *Giacinto*, and Verga's *Lupa*.[99] We can also find applications of criminal anthropology in more distant branches of knowledge. Max Nordau,[49] for example, made use of my work to develop a critical theory of art, philosophy, and literature.[hh]

Symbiosis, or the Utility of Crime

Having arrived at the end of this work and looking back at the terrain tilled at such length, I realize that among the many lacunae of my theory is its underestimation of the rare but real advantages that crime offers to society. If we try to reconcile the Darwinian law, according to which only the organs useful for the species survive, with the fact that, as Spencer says, crime is on the increase (except in England and Switzerland), we must conclude that crime has a certain social utility, at least among less civilized peoples.

In my book, *Palimsesti del carcere (Prison Palimpsests)*, I documented a type of genius among prisoners, despite the general misery and malignity of their lives. Because degeneration causes cortical irritation in prisoners, they have a potential for genius unavailable to average men.[50] For example, I found these inspired words written on the wall of one prison: "Oh criminal code! Why do you inflict such severe punishment on fraud, while the Government of Italy, which sponsors immoral lottery games, is amongst the master swindlers of all time?"

Criminals share with geniuses a type of degeneration that produces not only evil but also new virtues. Just as brilliance of intellect in geniuses is counterbalanced by their energy and lack of moral sensibility, so, too, are the abnormal emotions of criminals accompanied by energy and openness to change. The organic anomalies of criminals counter the misoneism or fear of innovation that typifies normal individuals. Therefore criminals see more clearly than average men the defects of current governments. Their desire for change, coupled with

[99] Lombroso, *Le più recenti scoperte*, 1893, pag. 350.
[hh] *Degenerazione*, 2a edizione, 1896.

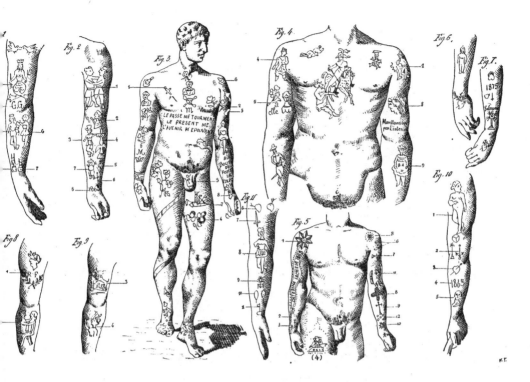

47 Tattoos of Criminals

Editors' note: Lombroso interprets several of the tattoos on the central figure, a French sailor (no. 3), as proof of his criminal personality: the inscription on his chest expressing torment and fright, the death mask above it, and the bunch of grapes on his penis. Flowers, according to Lombroso, commonly represent pederasty.

Source: Lombroso, *Der Verbrecher* (*Atlas*). Photo courtesy of the Lloyd Sealy Library, John Jay College of Criminal Justice.

their impulsiveness and inclination to do wrong, pushes criminals to the forefront of revolutions. Their crimes reveal the same innovative spirit as characterizes many revolutionaries and, while occasionally harming many to the advantage of a few, they introduce significant innovations. Consider, for example, the opening of the Suez Canal, which was crowned with universal approval despite being financed by fraud and swindle. In a similar vein, pirates—through their cleverness, energy, and absence of scruple—laid the basis for a useful institution, the English navy (Drake).

Among semibarbarous peoples, criminal organizations often take on the role of economic and political mediators for their own advantage and that of society in general. Practicing a sort of violent communism by defrauding and robbing the wealthy and powerful, they enrich themselves and at the same time provide a sort of summary justice in the absence of official justice. In Naples and in parts of Sicily, the Camorra and the Mafia traditionally exercised a type of popular justice among the common people that is still evident in brothels, taverns, and prisons. They offered shopkeepers and travelers a sort of insurance against brigands that the state failed to provide. This is why honest people have tolerated and sometimes have even assisted the Mafia and Camorra. Members of organized crime could not have continued to commit crimes for centuries if these misdeeds had not been socially useful.

Symbiosis. By admitting that crime sometimes serves a function, if only temporarily, am I undercutting the supreme purpose of this book? Is the fight against crime of no use and possibly even damaging? Oh no! If this were the case, my thirst for good and hatred of evil would make me destroy these pages. Fortunately, a less disconcerting conclusion can be drawn, however repugnant it may be to those who still advocate old methods of retribution against criminals. Rather than abolishing the fight against crime, we must employ less severe methods for preventing and punishing lawbreaking.

As social conditions improve, crime will lose its atavistic ferocity. Becoming more frequent but less violent, it will become less repugnant and savage in its forms, with fraud, swindling, and bankruptcy predominating. Education and public awareness will safeguard society more effectively against such economic crimes than will cruel repression. Social inequality is decreasing as basic human needs—education, lighting, and transportation—have been gradually satisfied by the state. Governments must now repair social injustices and remove one of the most pressing causes of occasional crime: insufficient work to survive in the struggle for existence. As social equality grows, another cause of crime, excesses of wealth, will disappear.

Sadly, born criminals are impervious to every social cure and must be eliminated for our own defense, sometimes by the death penalty. Yet the need for elimination may be diminishing, at least for those criminaloids whom we can assist in adapting to life. We can either develop medical treatments to modify criminaloids' most threatening behavior or put them to work in occupations that are repugnant to normal men but suited to their specific atavistic instincts: war for murderers, police spying for blackmailers and swindlers, prostitution for morals offenders, and colonization of unsettled lands for vagabonds. Society would derive great advantages from treating criminaloids in these ways.

The concept of symbiosis can best be applied to criminals of passion and political criminals, whose fervor for goodness and justice can be channeled into ambitious, altruistic works. Forward-looking nations can profit from this criminal energy and turn it to their benefit without risking entanglement with born criminals. Perhaps only the eruptions of moral enthusiasm that animate real criminals of passion and political criminals are capable of waking the apathetic masses of humanity to a new and useful future.

Appendix 1

This table provides a comparison of all chapters from the five original Italian editions of *Criminal Man* and offers insights into Lombroso's method of revising and enlarging his work. Lombroso never dropped chapters, usually incorporating them without change into subsequent editions. When he did modify a chapter, he retained his original argument but bolstered it by incorporating more data (for example, in "Criminal Craniums") or adding additional subtopics (for example, in "Etiology of Crime"). As this table demonstrates, Lombroso made the most substantial additions to his criminological theory in edition 3 (with new sections on the embryology of crime, children, and moral insanity) and edition 4 (with new sections on the epileptic criminal, insane criminal, and occasional criminal). The fifth edition constitutes for the most part a compendium of material from the previous editions except for the *Atlas*, a volume composed entirely of illustrations.

1876 Edition	1878 Edition	1884 Edition	1889 Edition	1896–97 Edition
			Volume 1	**Volume 1**
Preface	Preface	Preface	Preface	Preface
		PART I Embryology of Crime	PART I Embryology of Crime	PART I Embyology of Crime
		Chap. 1 Crime and inferior organisms	Chap. 1 Crime and inferior organisms	Chap. 1 Crime and inferior organisms
		Chap. 2 Crime and prostitution among savages	Chap. 2 Crime and prostitution among savages	Chap. 2 Crime and prostitution among savages
		Chap. 3 Origins of punishment		
		Chap. 4 Moral insanity and crime among children	Chap. 3 Moral insanity and crime among children	Chap. 3 Moral insanity and crime among children

1876 Edition	1878 Edition	1884 Edition	1889 Edition	1896–97 Edition
		PART II Pathological anatomy and anthropometry of crime	PART II Pathological anatomy and anthropometry of crime	PART II Pathological anatomy and anthropometry of crime
Chap. 1 Examination of 66 criminal craniums	Chap. 1 Examination of 101 criminal craniums	Chap. 1 Examination of 350 criminal craniums	Chap. 1 Examination of 383 criminal craniums	Chap. 1 Examination of 689 criminal craniums
				Chap. 2 Cranial anomalies
		Chap. 2 Anomalies of the brain and internal organs in criminals	Chap. 2 Anomalies of the brain and internal organs in 223 criminals	Chap. 3 Anomalies of the brain in criminals
				Chap. 4 Histology and pathological anatomy of criminal brains
				Chap. 5 Pathological anatomy of criminal bodies
Chap. 2 Anthropometry and physiognomy of 832 Italian criminals	Chap. 2 Anthropometry and physiognomy of 1,279 Italian criminals	Chap. 3 Anthropometry and physiognomy of 3,839 criminals; photographs[1]	Chap. 3 Anthropometry and physiognomy of 4,339 criminals; photographs	Chap. 6 Anthropometry and physiognomy of 6,608 criminals; photographs
		PART III Biology and psychology of the born criminal	PART III Biology and psychology of the born criminal	PART III Biology and psychology of the born criminal
Chap. 3 Tattoos in criminals	Chap. 3 Tattoos in criminals	Chap. 1 Tattoos in criminals	Chap. 1 Tattoos in criminals	Chap. 1 Tattoos in criminals
			Chap. 2 Metabolism	Chap. 2 Metabolism
Chap. 4 Sensitivity, emotions, and passions of criminals	Chap. 4 Sensitivity of criminals	Chap. 2 Sensitivity of criminals	Chap. 3 Sensitivity of criminals	Chap. 3 Sensitivity of criminals
		Chap. 3 Emotional sensitivity	Chapt. 4 Emotional sensitivity	Chap. 4 Emotional sensitivity
	Chap. 5 Suicide among criminals	Chap. 4 Suicide among criminals	Chap. 5 Suicide among criminals	Chap. 5 Suicide among criminals
	Chap. 6 Emotions and passions of criminals	Chap. 5 Emotions and passions of criminals	Chap. 6 Emotions and passions of criminals	Chap. 6 Emotions and passions of criminals
	Chap. 7 Criminals of passion			

[1] For this translation, we created a separate chapter for photographs, which constitutes new material introduced in edition 3; it does not include other repetitious material from the original chapter.

1876 Edition	1878 Edition	1884 Edition	1889 Edition	1896–97 Edition
Chap. 5 Morality of criminals; recidivism	Chap. 8 Recidivism; morality of criminals	Chap. 6 Recidivism; morality of criminals	Chap. 7 Recidivism; morality of criminals	Chap. 7 Recidivism; morality of criminals
Chap. 6 Religion of criminals	Chap. 9 Religion of criminals	Chap. 7 Religion of criminals	Chap. 8 Religion of criminals	Chap. 8 Religion of criminals
Chap. 7 Intelligence and education of criminals	Chap. 10 Intelligence and education of criminals	Chap. 8 Intelligence and education of criminals	Chap. 9 Intelligence and education of criminals	Chap. 9 Intelligence and education of criminals
Chap. 8 Jargon	Chap. 11 Jargon	Chap. 9 Jargon	Chap. 10 Jargon	Chap. 10 Jargon
	Chap. 12 Handwriting of criminals	Chap. 10 Handwriting of criminals	Chap. 11 Pictography, hieroglyphics, handwriting of criminals	Chap. 11 Pictography, hieroglyphics, handwriting of criminals
Chap. 9 Literature of criminals	Chap. 13 Literature of criminals	Chap. 11 Literature of criminals	Chap. 12 Literature of criminals	Chap. 12 Literature of criminals
			Chap. 13 Art and industry among criminals	Chap. 13 Art and industry among criminals
		Chap. 12 Organized crime	Chap. 14 Organized crime	Chap. 14 Organized crime
			Volume 2	
			PART IV The morally insane	
		Chap. 13 The morally insane and born criminals	Chap. 15 The morally insane	Chap. 1 Biology and psychology of the morally insane
		Chap. 14 Summary	Chap. 16 Summary	Chap. 2 Equivalence of the morally insane and born criminals
			Volume 2	
			PART I The epileptic criminal	PART V The epileptic criminal
			Chap. 1 Anthropometry, biology	Chap. 1 Anthropometry, biology
			Chap. 2 Characteristics; resemblance to the born criminal	Chap. 2 Characteristics; resemblance to the born criminal

1876 Edition	1878 Edition	1884 Edition	1889 Edition	1896–97 Edition
			Chap. 3 Statistics on criminal epilepsy; clinical cases.	Chap. 3 Statistics on criminal epilepsy; clinical cases
			Chap. 4 Hidden epilepsy; resemblance to moral insanity and criminality	Chap. 4 Hidden epilepsy; resemblance to moral insanity and criminality
			Chap. 5 Epilepsy without convulsions	Chap. 5 Epilepsy without convulsions in the morally insane
			Chap. 6 Physiology and etiology of epilepsy	Chap. 6 Physiology and etiology of epilepsy
			Chap. 7 Differences, analogies, and objections; atavism	Chap. 7 Differences, analogies, and objections; atavism
			Appendices to Part I	
			PART II The criminal of passion	PART VI The criminal of passion
			Chap. 1 Criminals of impulse	Chap. 1 Criminals of impulse
			Chap. 2 Suicide from passion or insanity	Chap. 2 Suicide from passion or insanity
				Chap. 3 Political criminals
			PART III The insane criminal	PART VII The insane criminal
			Chap. 1 Statistics	Chap. 1 Statistics
			Chap. 2 Biology	Chap. 2 Biology
			Chap. 3 Psychology; resemblance between the insane criminal and the born criminal	Chap. 3 Psychology; resemblance between the insane criminal and the born criminal
			Chap. 4 Psychology; types of mental illness	Chap. 4 Psychology; types of mental illness
			Chap. 5 The alcoholic criminal	Chap. 5 The alcoholic criminal

1876 Edition	1878 Edition	1884 Edition	1889 Edition	1896–97 Edition
			Chap. 6 The hysteric criminal	Chap. 6 The hysteric criminal
			Chap. 7 The mattoid	Chap. 7 The mattoid
			PART IV The occasional criminal	PART VIII The occasional criminal
			Chap. 1 Opinions, proverbs, statistics	Chap. 1 Opinions, proverbs, statistics
			Chap. 2 Pseudo-criminals, criminaloids, habitual criminals, latent criminals	Chap. 2 Pseudo-criminals, criminaloids, habitual criminals, latent criminals
			Chap. 3 Epileptoids	Chap. 3 Epileptoids
				Volume 3
				PART I Etiology of crime
Chap. 10 Etiology of crime	Chap. 14 Etiology of crime			Chap. 1 Climate
Chap. 11 Insanity and crime	Chap. 15 Etiology; insanity and crime			Chap. 2 Geography; disease
Chap. 12 Organized Crime	Chap. 16 Organized Crime			Chap. 3 Race
Chap. 13 Summary and conclusion; atavism	Chap. 17 Atavism in crime and punishment; summary			Chap. 4 Civilization
				Chap. 5 Population density
				Chap. 6 Nutrition
				Chap. 7 Alcoholism
				Chap. 8 Education
				Chap. 9 Wealth and poverty
				Chap. 10 Religion
				Chap. 11 Moral education; illegitimacy
				Chap. 12 Heredity
				Chap. 13 Age

1876 Edition	1878 Edition	1884 Edition	1889 Edition	1896–97 Edition
				Chap. 14 Sex; prostitution
				Chap. 15 Civil status, profession
				Chap. 16 Prison
				Chap. 17 Causes of organized crime
				Chap. 19[2] Causes of political crime
Chap. 14 Applications; prevention of crime	Chap. 18 Prevention of crime			PART II Prevention and penal policy
				Chap. 1 Penal substitutes; scientific police
				Chap. 2 Prevention of sex crimes and fraud
				Chap. 3 Control of alcohol
				Chap. 4 Measures against excessive wealth and poverty
				Chap. 5 Religion
				Chap. 6 Control of education; reformatories
				Chap. 7 Prevention of political crime
				Chap. 8 Prison
				Chap. 9 Rationalizing the law
				PART III Synthesis and penal applications

[2] Chapter 19 of Lombroso's original should be numbered Chapter 18. There is no Chapter 18 in his table of contents or text.

1876 Edition	1878 Edition	1884 Edition	1889 Edition	1896–97 Edition
				Chap. 1 Atavism and epilepsy in crime and punishment
				Chap. 2 Punishments according to criminal anthropology
				Chap. 3 Punishments according to sex, age, type of criminal
				Chap. 4 Successful reforms in England, Switzerland
				Chap. 5 Practical applications of criminal anthropology
				Chap. 6 The utility of crime; symbiosis
APPENDICES	APPENDICES		APPENDICES	APPENDICES **Volume 4** *Atlas*

Appendix 2

This is a complete list of the illustrations in the five original Italian editions of *Criminal Man*. We use Lombroso's own titles whenever possible, adding our own only to clarify or label untitled illustrations. Arabic numerals refer to page numbers. In the final column, we also use roman numerals; these refer to the tables in the *Atlas*, the fourth volume of the fifth edition of *Criminal Man*. We have not listed small illustrations inset into textual pages.

Note that Lombroso redid his illustrations for every volume; thus the content of some multi-image illustrations changed over time. In addition, his titles are not always consistent over time.

Illustration title	Present Edition	1876 Edition	1878 Edition	1884 Edition	1889 Edition	1896–97 Edition
Trococephalic Rapist from the Romagna	133	28	43	240	1:227	XXXV
Thief from Milan	223	31	47	245	1:232	XXXV; also 1:276
Tattoos of a Criminal Sailor	62	49	76	311	1, after 296	LXIV
Group of Assassins from Ravenna	67	65	after 112	after 396	1, after 388	LXXX
Homosexual Arsonist Nicknamed "The Woman"	53		48	247	1:233	XXXVIII; also 1:277
Physiognomy of Criminals I	52		after 48	after 246	1, after 232	XXXVI
P.C., Brigand from Basilicata			49	248	1:234	XXXVIII
Physiognomy of Criminals II			after 50	after 246	1, after 232	XXXVI
R., Sicilian Assassin; P., Assassin from Lucca			58	256, 257	1:246, 247	XLV; also 1:289
Handwriting of Criminals I			after 210	after 492	1, after 502	LXXV
Cavaglià's Water Jug			after 516	after 366	1, after 388	LXXXII

Illustration title	Present Edition	1876 Edition	1878 Edition	1884 Edition	1889 Edition	1896–97 Edition
Cranial Capacity of 121 Male Criminals	302			148	1:136	1:137
Weight of 137 Brains of German Male Criminals				194	1:183	1:191
Weight and Height of 400 Cadavers of Normal Men and Male Criminals from Bonn				221	1:207	XXV
Height and Arm Span of 800 Criminals	307			223	1:209	XXVI
Album of German Criminals I	203			after 258	1, after 250	XLVIII
Album of German and American Criminals				after 258		L
Album of German Criminals II				after 258	1, after 250	XLIX
Album of German and Italian Criminals				after 258	1, after 250	XLVII
German and Italian Female Criminals	129			after 278	1, after 264	LI
Sphygmography I				after 350	1, after 349	LXX
Sphygmography II				after 352	1, after 349	LXXI
Troppman's Drawing of the Scene of His Crime	240			after 366	1, after 388	LXXXI
Handwriting of Criminals II	112			after 495	1, after 498	LXXVI
Skulls of Gasparone and of a Thief					1, after 148	XXX
Types of Noses					1, after 162	
Skulls of Criminals I					1, after 164	XXVIII
Skulls of Italian Female Criminals					1, after 164	XXIX
Composite Photographs, Galtonian Method	232				1, after 180	XXVII
Thief from the Piedmont					1:231	XXXVIII
Nero					1:237	LX
Messalina					1:238	LX
Physical Anomalies Found in Criminal Photographs					1, after 252	
Tattoos of Criminal Soldiers	60				1, after 296	LXIV

Illustration title	Present Edition	1876 Edition	1878 Edition	1884 Edition	1889 Edition	1896–97 Edition
Tattoos of Criminals I					1, after 504	LXVII
Tattoos of Criminals II	353				1, after 504	LXVIII
Photograph Staged by the Killer C.					1:377	1:439
Ceramic Designs by Criminals I					1, after 504	LXXXIII
Ceramic Designs by Criminals II					1, after 504	LXXXIV
Handwriting under Hypnosis	242				1, after 502	LXXIX
Escape Tools Made by Prisoners					1:543	
Art of an Insane Criminal					1:545	
Album of Physiognomy of Criminals and Born Criminals					2, after 6	
Signatures of Epileptics					2, after 24	LXXVIII
Misdea					2:56	XXXVIII
Maps of Italy I: Homicide; Crimes against Custom and Family Order	116				2, after 82	I
Maps of Italy II: Reformatories for Epileptics; Crimes against the State					2, after 82	I
Gaits of Normal, Criminal, and Epileptic Men	254				2, after 110	
The Bandit Tolu					2:119	
Insane Criminals I					2, after 188	LIII
Insane Criminals II					2, after 188	LIV
Legal Proceedings and Alcohol Production and Consumption in France, 1849–1876					2, after 290	LXXXVIII
France, 1827–1869: Distribution of Crimes by Month of the Year; Relationship of Suicide to Alcohol Consumption					2, after 290	LXXXVIII
Belm . . . , a Chronic Alcoholic	279				2:314	2:429
Z, a Thief, Prostitute, Killer, and Liar					2:342	2:457
Guiteau	199				2:365	
Old Woman of the Vinegar (Palermo)					2:385	2:489

Illustration title	Present Edition	1876 Edition	1878 Edition	1884 Edition	1889 Edition	1896–97 Edition
Bar Graph of Anomalies in Various Types of Criminals I				2, after 386		
Bar Graphs of Anomalies in Various Types of Criminals II				2, after 414		
Portrait of Sgric . . . , a Born Killer and Morally Insane				2:437	2:554	
Baldness and Gray Hair among Various Groups					2, after 461	
Keenness of Taste among Various Groups					2:535	1:401
The Geography of Crime. Map-graphs of the Various States of Europe						II–XXIV
Anomalies in Three Criminal Skulls						XXVII
Skulls of Criminals II						XXX
Anomalies of the Brain, the Feet, and the Nasal Bones in Criminals	308					XXXI
Cortical Layers of the Frontal Lobes of a Normal Man and Epileptic Criminal						XXXII
Enlargements of Cortical Layers of the Frontal Lobes of a Normal Man and Epileptic Criminal						XXXIII
Anomalies of the Palm in Monkeys, a Normal Man, and Criminals	173					XXXIV
Types of Killers I						XXXIX
Types of Killers II						XL
Types of Killers III						XLI
Types of Killers and Thieves	117					XLII
Types of Killers and Robbers						XLIII
Types of Occasional Criminals						XLIV
Types of Italian Criminals						XLVI
Portraits of Epileptics	249					LII
Types of Russian Female Criminals						LV

Illustration title	Present Edition	1876 Edition	1878 Edition	1884 Edition	1889 Edition	1896–97 Edition
Portraits of Delinquent Women: Berland, Thomas, and Bompard						LVI
Types of Delinquent Children						LVII
Types of African Criminals	179					LVIII
Severed Heads of Criminals						LIX
Mattoids and Morally Insane Revolutionaries	286					LXI
Revolutionaries and Political Criminals of Passion						LXII
Anarchists						LXIII
Tattoos of *Camorristi*	87					LXV
Tattoos of Criminal Prostitutes						LXVI
Symbolic Tattoos	275					LXIX
Muscular Capacity						LXXII
Field of Vision of a Criminal Woman in Various States						LXXIII
Field of Vision of Born Criminals and Epileptics						LXXIV
Signatures of Mattoids						LXXVII
Prisoner Art						LXXXV
Drawing by Seghetti Showing His Execution	147					LXXXVI
Age of Parents for Normal Individuals, Criminals, and the Insane	326					LXXXVII
Types of Vicious and Criminal Boys	193					LXXXIX–XCIII
Types of Dinka						XCIV
Fields of Vision of the Dinka						XCV
New Fields of Vision of Criminals						XCVI
New Fields of Vision of Criminals and Prostitutes						XCVIII
Measuring Machines: Craniograph; Tachiantropometrical Device of Anfosso						XCVIIII, 3:325, 326

Illustration title	Present Edition	1876 Edition	1878 Edition	1884 Edition	1889 Edition	1896–97 Edition
Consumption of Alcohol by Country	319					XCIX
Brain Anomalies of Criminals						C
Types of Slavic and German Criminals						CI
Carnivorous Plants	169					CII
Prehensile Feet						1:233
Relationship of Crime and Suicide to Price of Bread, France 1843–1883						3:85
Relationship of Crime and Price of Bread, Italy 1875–1889						3:88
Relationship of Property Crime to Price of Bread, New South Wales, 1881–1891						3:91
Relationship of Homicide, Stabbings, and Cost of Wine, Italy 1879–1889						3:111
Children of London Vagabonds						3:435
Boys Abandoned by Vagabonds						3:436
Split of the Papycaceous Band of the Ethmoid in Criminals and Cretins						3:629
Fusion of the Optic Thalamuses in the Brain of a Prostitute						3:637
Underworld Characters with Scarred Faces						3:645
Hieroglyphics of the Camorra						3:653

Notes

Editors' Introduction

1 Lombroso and Ferrero 2004.

2 The dates of publication for the five editions of *Criminal Man* are 1876 (256 pages), 1878 (746 pages), 1884 (610 pages), 1889 (1,241 pages in two volumes), and 1896–97 (1,902 pages in three volumes plus a fourth volume containing 57 pages of text and 102 plates). For a detailed comparison of the five editions, see appendix 1.

3 There are only two English-language volumes that constitute partial translations of Lombroso's *Criminal Man*: Gina Lombroso-Ferrero's *Criminal Man* (1911) and Lombroso's *Crime: Its Causes and Remedies* (1911). They are discussed at greater length below.

4 For Lombroso's biography, see Gibson 2002; Wolfgang 1972; Frigessi 2003; Villa 1985; Baima Bollone 1992; and Bulferetti 1975. Delfina Dolza (1990) has written a book about Lombroso's two daughters and Luigi Guarnieri (2000) a fictional reconstruction of Lombroso's life. Gina Lombroso-Ferrero sketched the first outline of her father's life in *Cesare Lombroso: Storia della vita e delle opere narrata dalla figlia* (1915).

5 Beccaria 1986. This paragraph overemphasizes the contrast between Lombroso and Beccaria insofar as classical penology combined free will and determinism. Lombroso focused on the role of free will in Beccaria's thought in order to make his own determinist philosophy seem completely new. See Beirne 1993.

6 The First International Congress of Criminal Anthropology was held in Rome in 1885; it was followed by congresses in Paris in 1889 and in Brussels in 1892. On the debates at these congresses, see Nye 1976.

7 The estimated number of articles comes from Villa (1985, 283).

8 On the role of Lombroso's followers in the Italian criminal justice system, see Gibson 2002.

9 Lombroso-Ferrero 1972.

10 Lombroso 1968. The English translation of *Crime: Its Causes and Remedies* is twice removed from the original Italian text because it was based on earlier French and German translations of Lombroso's work.

11 An earlier book by Lombroso, *L'uomo di genio* (1888), was translated into English as *The Man of Genius* in 1891, but it is not a work of criminology.

12 The designation of Lombroso as "the father of modern criminology" has been repeated by many leading criminologists, including Marvin Wolfgang in his pioneering biographical article on Lombroso (1972, 232).

13 An invaluable collection of excerpts from a wide range of Lombroso's writings can be found in his *Delitto, genio, follia: Scritti scelti* (1995), edited by Delia Frigessi, Ferruccio Giacanelli, and Luisa Mangoni. Short selections from the various editions of *L'uomo delinquente*, however, form only a small part of this collection.

14 Villa 1985.

15 Gibson 2002.

16 Frigessi 2003.

17 Horn 2003.

18 See Mucchielli and Renneville 1994.

19 Wetzell 2000.

20 Davie 2004, 2005.

21 Rafter 1997. See also Rafter 1992.

22 Salvatore and Aguirre 1996.

23 Becker and Wetzell 2006. Other recent books on Lombroso include Chen 1992; Gadebusch Bondio 1995; Leschiutta 1996; Mazzarello 1998; Mella, Alvarez, and Arias 1999; and Rondini 2001.

24 On phrenology, see this volume, edition 1, footnote 30. See also Rafter 2005.

25 On moral insanity, see this volume, edition 1, footnote 33. See also Rafter 2004b.

26 On Guerry, see this volume, edition 1, footnote 38; on Quetelet, see edition 2, footnote 22. See also Beirne 1993.

27 According to Villa (1985, 188), Ferri first used the phrase *born criminal* in 1880.

28 Unless otherwise marked, quotations from *Criminal Man* refer to the present volume.

29 Lombroso is not consistent in his definition of the criminal type. In edition 4 of *Criminal Man*, Lombroso defines the full criminal type as an individual with five to seven anomalies at one place in the text, and five to six anomalies at another. In *Criminal Woman*, he includes a table that categorizes any woman with four to eight anomalies as constituting the "full type" (Lombroso and Ferrero 2004, 145).

30 In volume 3, Lombroso makes his claim that 40 percent of offenders are born criminals by averaging his estimate for born criminality among adults (23 percent) with that for children (59 percent).

31 Lombroso 1968, 365.

32 Lombroso-Ferrero 1972, 8.

33 Lombroso does not add new subcategories to his classification of criminals in edition 5; the first two volumes repeat lengthy sections from earlier

editions on the classification of criminals, and volume 3, which later became *Crime: Its Causes and Remedies*, summarizes these categories.

34 Lombroso 1876, 120.

35 Parent-Duchatelet 1836.

36 Lomboroso and Ferrero 2004, 80–81.

37 Ibid., 185.

38 Lombroso 1871, 222.

39 Rafter (2001, 2006b) develops the connection between the illustrations and the theory's success at greater length. For an analysis of narrative in Lombroso's work, see Gibson 2005.

40 See appendix 2 for a comparative chart of illustrations in successive editions of *Criminal Man*.

41 The artwork is the "Group of Assassins from Ravenna" (figure 9 in this edition), a photograph staged by the killers themselves to commemorate their crime.

42 Lombroso 1896–97, v. 4:iii; in addition, other illustrations are scattered through the three volumes that precede the *Atlas*.

43 Quoted in Colombo 2000, 36.

44 Our translation of *Criminal Woman* reproduces many of these pictures; see Lombroso and Ferrero 2004.

45 Lombroso 1891. This book was translated into French in 1894 and reprinted in Italian in 1996, but it has never been published in English. Most of *Palimsesti*'s images reproduce tattoos and other types of prisoner art; with few exceptions, these images reappear in one or more editions of *Criminal Man*. The book's title recognizes the multiauthored nature of this text, a palimpsest being a manuscript that retains traces of earlier writings.

46 Lombroso 1891, 40.

47 Lombroso 1896–97, v. 4:vii.

48 Lombroso 1876, 65.

49 The interpretation can be found in Lombroso 1896–97, 4:xvii; it refers to figure 47.

50 Lombroso's interest in codes and their decipherment was powerfully affected by Paolo Marzolo (1811–68), a linguist who hoped to derive a history of humankind from the study of language. Marzolo seems to have inspired Lombroso's choice of a medical career, to have sparked Lombroso's enthusiasm for scientific positivism, and to have suggested to Lombroso his theory of atavism. From the older man, moreover, Lombroso derived (at least in part) his faith in interdisciplinary approaches to the study of humankind, his interest in language and signs, and his conviction that the study of nature involved breaking codes. Lombroso named his first child (Paola) after Marzolo and dedicated to him ("the Darwin of Italian anthropology") his book *L'uomo bianco e l'uomo di colore*. On Marzolo,

see Colombo 2000; Frigessi 2003; Pancaldi 1991 (which traces Lombroso's theory of atavism to the Italian philosopher Giambattista Vico through Marzolo on page 148); and Villa 1985.

51 Colombo 2000, 116. Colombo presents preuglification versions of "P. C., Brigand from Basilicata" and of the "Thief from Milan, Sentenced Thirteen Times," on 117 and 118.

52 Portigliatti Barbos 1993, 1448.

53 Colombo (2000, 114) identifies Luigi Frigerio as an assistant to Lombroso at the insane asylum of Pesaro. Frigerio "sometimes sketched inmates," gathering the sketches in an album, "a bestiary" that Lombroso used for many years as source material. Also see Villa (1985, 132 n. 1), referring to Frigerio's help in creating the notebooks that constitute "the first iconographic nucleus" of *Criminal Man*. Portigliatti Barbos (1993, 1449) suggests that Lombrosian preconceptions may have influenced not only the poster drawings derived from Frigerio's originals but also the making of wax death masks of inmates for the museum (see figures 45 and 46).

54 Lombroso 1894, 5.

55 Ibid., 6.

56 Leps 1992, 11.

57 See this volume, chapters 22–23.

58 In 1892, the university, working with the Italian government, formally took responsibility for the institution, which remained open to the public until 1914.

59 We say "face," not "head," because Lombroso's brain was stored elsewhere. This list of the museum's exhibits is far from complete. Photographs and verbal descriptions of the museum can be found in Colombo 2000; Levra 1985; Portigliatti Barbos 1993; Regener 1999, 2003; and VI Congrès International d'Anthropologie Criminelle 1906.

60 Portigliatti Barbos 1993, 1441–42.

61 Regener 2003, 49.

62 Lombroso 1894, 2.

63 Regener 2003, 44.

64 Ibid., 47.

65 Colombo 2000, 10.

66 Lombroso's museum was widely imitated throughout Europe. Similar museums opened in Berlin, Dresden, Graz, Hamburg, London, Rome, and Vienna, and several remain open today (Regener 2003). Efforts are currently being made to reopen Lombroso's museum, which remains intact in Turin. No one expects it to serve its original goals; rather, the current aim is to put on display a riveting episode in the history of science and to encourage new readings of the institution's contents.

67 Lombroso 1894, 1.

68 Goring 1972.

69 Lombroso-Ferrero 1921, 435. On Goring, see also Beirne 1993.

70 Monachesi 1936, 404.

71 Glueck and Glueck 1934.

72 Hooton 1939a and Hooton 1939b. See also Rafter 2004a.

73 Monachesi 1936; Gibson 2002.

74 See our longer discussion of the influence of Lombroso on later theories of female crime in our introduction to Lombroso and Ferrero 2004.

75 The distinction between life-course persistent and adolescence-limited offenders can be found in the work of Terrie Moffitt and her colleagues; see, for example, Moffitt 1993; and Moffitt et al. 2001.

76 Ellis and Walsh 1997.

77 For an analysis of the distortions and misconceptions about Lombroso that have become standard textbook fare, see Rafter 2006b.

78 Lombroso's sentences often include pronouns without antecedents, numbers without units of measurements, and conclusions drawn from shifting numbers of cases. While long sentences containing many subordinate clauses are typical of nineteenth-century Italian, Lombroso's text is rife with sentences lacking parallelism and paragraphs lacking topic sentences, transitions, or both. We have smoothed out and cleaned up his prose to produce a grammatical and more flowing text.

Edition 1 (1876)

1 Lombroso begins his preface with an allusion to one of the major arguments of positivist criminology, namely, that criminals do not freely choose to break the law. Instead, he attributes their behavior in this passage to biological factors—their incurably "weak or diseased minds."

2 In this first edition of *Criminal Man*, Lombroso uses the term *healthy man* for what he would later call *normal man*. In both cases he implies the use of a control group of noncriminals, but he often fails to supply empirical data on "healthy" individuals.

3 Cranial circumference was one of several measurements used by criminal anthropologists to determine the size of the skull.

4 The numbers in table 1 do not always match those in this passage. Discrepancies between the tables and text occur frequently in *Criminal Man*, revealing Lombroso's inattention to detail.

5 Babies are born with open cranial sutures that normally close over time. Thus Lombroso is implying that many criminal skulls resemble those of undeveloped infants. On the other hand, Lombroso also regarded sutures that were too tightly closed as abnormal, enabling him to classify skulls with both loose and tight sutures as anomalies.

6 Lombroso labeled Giuseppe Villella a brigand, although historical sources

give conflicting data about his crimes, date of arrest, and place of in-carceration. Lombroso claimed that his examination of the anomalies in Villella's skull, especially the discovery of his median occipital fossetta, sparked his theory of atavism and the born criminal. The skull of Villella became, in Lombroso's words, the "totem" of his new school of criminal anthropology. According to Renzo Villa, however, Lombroso changed his description of Villella and the characteristics of his skull over time, a fact that renders the founding story of criminal anthropology more a myth than a scientific breakthrough. See Villa 1985, 148–49 and Baima Bollone 1992, 114–15.

7   These heights in meters are equivalent to 5 feet 6 inches; 5 feet 3.6 inches; 5 feet 2.8 inches; 5 feet 2.5 inches; and 5 feet 1.8 inches, respectively.

8   James Bruce Thomson (1810–73), chief physician at Scotland's Perth Prison, published influential articles based on degenerationist theory and arguing that many criminals are born criminals; these included "The Psychology of Criminals" in the 1870 issue of the *Journal of Mental Science*. Lombroso was fascinated by Thomson's work and cited it as evidence for his own theory. The Wilson to whom Lombroso refers was probably the British craniometrist George Wilson. The work of both men is discussed in Davie 2004, 2005.

9   These weights in kilograms are equivalent to 150 pounds and 138 pounds, respectively.

10 Johann Ludwig Casper (1787–1853) was a prominent professor of forensic pathology in Berlin.

11 Johann Kasper Lavater (1741–1801) attempted to turn physiognomy, or the reading of character from facial expressions, into a science. In the early nineteenth century, physiognomy flowed into phrenology, and later in the century, phrenology flowed into criminal anthropology. The Guido to whom Lombroso here refers was probably the Italian baroque painter Guido Reni (1575–1642).

12 The French criminal Martin Dumollard, famous for drinking his victims' blood, was executed in 1862.

13 The dynamometer, or strength-testing machine, used by Lombroso was oval in shape with a dial to record results. Subjects had to compress the oval to test "compressive strength" and pull at the oval to test "tractive strength."

14 Alexandre J. B. Parent-Duchatelet (1805–59) was the first European to conduct a large-scale study of prostitution, *De la prostitution dans la ville de Paris* (*Prostitution in the City of Paris*, 1836). Lombroso relied on Parent-Duchatelet's work for most of his early data on female crime. In this first edition of *Criminal Man*, Lombroso begins to establish his theory that prostitution—that is sexual deviancy—constitutes the typical and most widespread form of female crime.

15 Lock hospitals (or *sifilicomi* in Italian) were nineteenth-century institu-

tions for the internment of prostitutes with venereal disease. Although hospitals in name, they resembled prisons to which prostitutes were admitted forcibly by police. Lock hospitals provided criminologists like Lombroso with a captive female population for physical and psychological examinations.

16 In this summary of his conclusions on the anthropometry and physiognomy of criminals, Lombroso is referring (with only a few exceptions) to men. Some of his conclusions are based on material that we cut from this chapter.

17 The cephalic index was an important tool for nineteenth-century criminal anthropologists in their attempts to categorize races and identify born criminals. They obtained the cephalic index by multiplying the width of the skull by one hundred and dividing the result by the length of the skull. The resulting numbers enabled them to classify skulls into various categories including brachycephalic (or short-headed) and dolichocephalic (or long-headed). Born criminals fell into both categories; Lombroso considered their cephalic indices to be abnormal when the numbers deviated from the norm for their geographical region.

18 Imitation became an important criminological concept in the late nineteenth century, especially in explanations of crowd behavior. The French jurist Gabriel Tarde (1843–1904) is best known for applying the concept of imitation to the etiology of crime in his 1890 book *La philosophie pénale* (*Penal Philosophy*). In this first edition of *Criminal Man*, Lombroso anticipates Tarde as well as later criminological debates over imitation. See Barrows 1981.

19 Charles Darwin (1809–82), the British naturalist, elaborated the theory of evolution in his famous work, *The Origin of Species* (1859). For Lombroso, Darwin's theory confirmed his intuition that criminals were atavistic or throwbacks on the evolutionary scale. In the third edition of *Criminal Man*, Lombroso aspires to do for criminals what Darwin had done for plant and animal species.

20 The French thief and poet Pierre-François Lacenaire (1800–36) both shocked and fascinated public opinion with his murder of the widow Chardon and her son in 1835. The following year, he was executed by guillotine for his crime.

21 Lombroso was ambivalent about the death penalty, but in general he went from opposition to grudging acceptance of it as a means of social defense against recidivist born criminals and particularly violent members of organized crime like *mafiosi* and brigands. Yet he muffled his support of capital punishment in deference to the opposition of the majority of his positivist colleagues and the public in general. In 1889, Italy abolished the death penalty in its new criminal code.

22 The notorious French criminal Eugène François Vidocq (1775–1857) turned informer and finally became head of the French urban police force

in 1811. He is the model for both Jean Valjean and Inspector Javert in Victor Hugo's novel *Les misérables* (1862).

23   Lombroso often employs the word *precocity* to mean the premature development of physical or psychological characteristics or early indulgence in adult behaviors. In all cases, precocity signals abnormality for Lombroso.

24   This is Lombroso's first use of the term *positivist* to refer to his theory that true criminals are atavistic in nature and lack free will. He goes to pains in this passage to deny that positivism, which was materialist and therefore at odds with religion, encourages criminal behavior. As Lombroso explains later, positivism teaches that even if criminals lack free will to control their atavistic behavior, they should be disciplined and punished in the name of social defense.

25   Auguste Ambroise Tardieu (1818–79), a French pathologist and expert in forensic medicine, investigated many famous crimes.

26   Although Lombroso seems to echo Darwin in his use of *species*, he is not using the term in a rigorously scientific way. Throughout the various editions of *Criminal Man*, Lombroso periodically uses *species* loosely to mean social group or subgroup, rather than a biological classification.

27   Lombroso here refers to a number of European men of letters whose sexual activities or political views scandalized others, although it is not clear why he considers them all to have been criminals. Iacopo Bonfadio (1508[?]–50), a Genovese historian and poet, was executed for sodomy in 1550. Jean Jacques Rousseau (1712–78), the French philosopher, had to flee France to avoid arrest for his radical writings. Pietro Aretino (1492–1556), a prominent literary figure in Renaissance Rome and Venice, published bawdy poems. Brunetto Latini (1210–94), a Florentine statesman and poet, was a friend of Dante's, but in *The Divine Comedy* (c. 1308–1321) Dante consigns him to the section of hell reserved for sodomites. Ugo Foscolo (1778–1827), a poet and patriot, was imprisoned for debt. Lord George Gordon Byron (1788–1824) was famous for his numerous and varied sexual escapades, as well as for his romantic poetry.

28   By comparing this verse to the poems written by the famous Renaissance poet Petrarch about his love for Laura, Lombroso displays a fascination with and even admiration for prisoner art. This recognition of the creativity of some inmates tempers his general denunciation of born criminals as atavistic and animalistic.

29   These numbers total 120 rather than 105, perhaps because some prostitutes had more than one disease. Jean Etienne Esquirol (1772–1840) was the first psychiatrist to recognize the difference between insanity and mental deficiency; his data on prostitutes probably came from his work at the Parisian hospital of Salpêtrière.

30   Franz Joseph Gall (1758–1828), a Viennese physician, developed the basis for the science of phrenology about 1800. According to Gall and later phrenologists, the brain is the organ of the mind, and it consists of about

thirty separate organs or faculties such as combativeness, coveriveness, and destructiveness, which function independently. Phrenologists also believed that the more active an organ, the larger its size, and that the organs' relative size can be estimated by inspecting the contours of the skull. As a final element in the doctrine of phrenology, Gall's followers added the belief that the size of the faculties can be increased through mental discipline or decreased through illness or abuse. These fundamental ideas eventually became the basis of an international phrenological movement. While Lombroso did not endorse phrenology per se, he was closely familiar with Gall's work, and phrenological assumptions about the relationship of brain formation to behavior often lay behind his criminal anthropological claims.

31 Lombroso seems to contradict himself when he argues that the insane sometimes simulate madness. He probably means that some insane individuals are lucid enough to pretend not to know right from wrong in order to be released from legal responsibility for their crimes.

32 Pellagra is a disease characterized by skin eruptions, digestive and nervous disturbances, and, finally, insanity. It was widespread among Italian peasants of the Po valley whose diet consisted almost exclusively of corn polenta. Early in his medical career, Lombroso claimed to have identified the cause of pellagra as moldy corn; he clung to this explanation even after the origin of the disease was traced to niacin deficiency. Because pellagra infected only the poor and could cause mental illness, criminal anthropologists labeled it a social disease analogous to tuberculosis, syphilis, and alcoholism.

33 Lombroso barely mentions moral insanity in this first edition, but in the third edition, he elevates moral insanity to a cause of born criminality equal to atavism. The concept of moral insanity, one of the key psychiatric concepts of the nineteenth century, was first formulated by early psychiatrists to explain uncontrollable, undeterrable criminality. Lombroso occasionally cites the work of one of these authors, the English alienist James Cowles Prichard (1786–1848), who in fact invented the term *moral insanity* to label criminal behavior that seemed insane but was committed by people who suffered from neither delusions nor hallucinations. Prichard and other early psychiatrists defined moral insanity as a state of partial insanity in which only one faculty of the brain stops working—an iconoclastic idea at a time when insanity was almost by definition a state of total, unrelieved derangement. This definition attracted Lombroso, who needed a way to explain why some criminals who seemed perfectly normal were in fact insane. Toward the end of the nineteenth century, under the influence of Lombroso and other criminologists, moral insanity came to be viewed as an innate and heritable condition. Today it is called psychopathy.

34 Lombroso spent much of his life lobbying for the establishment of criminal insane asylums (*manicomi*). He considered them a humanitarian alter-

native to the practice of his day, that of incarcerating insane criminals in regular prisons. Criminal insane asylums would guarantee that insane criminals got treatment, while keeping them separate from ordinary insane individuals who posed no threat to society.

35 Angelo Messedaglia (1820–1901), an Italian statistician and economist, published a study of Austrian criminal statistics in 1866–67 entitled *Le statistiche criminali dell'Impero austriaco*.

36 Two forms of organized crime had become political issues in nineteenth-century Italy. The first, brigandage, was widespread throughout the peninsula before unification in 1861. After unification, a separatist movement developed in southern Italy; its members were branded brigands by the government and violently suppressed by the army and police. Second, the Camorra and Mafia—already active in Naples and Sicily, respectively, when Lombroso began his career as a criminologist—also caused social disorder for the new Italian state. Lombroso considered members of both groups to typify born criminality.

37 Lombroso is referring to the Jukes family. In 1877, Richard L. Dugdale, a New York City businessman, published *"The Jukes": A Study in Crime, Pauperism, Disease, and Heredity*, a work that influenced ideas about the causes of crime throughout the Western world, including Lombroso's ideas about the heritable nature of degeneration and criminality. Lombroso seems to have read an article about Dugdale's preliminary report on the Jukes, a 1874 report to the Prison Association of New York. He writes that he became familiar with it through an 1875 *Atlantic Monthly* article by Elisha Harris, a New York State public health official. However, the citation is incorrect, and Lombroso must also have been confused on other matters relating to the Jukes study, for he writes as though Harris himself had conducted and written it. In any case, Dugdale's horrific study of a rural clan that over seven generations had produced 1,200 bastards, beggars, murderers, prostitutes, thieves, and syphilitics helped persuade Lombroso and many others of the day of the validity of degeneration theory; it also seemed to demonstrate that criminality and other unfortunate tendencies are heritable.

38 The French lawyer André Michel Guerry (1802–66) was a pioneer in so-called moral statistics, the early movement to quantify and find patterns in social data, including patterns of crime. In the history of criminology, Guerry is best known for the development of shaded maps to indicate areas of lesser and greater crime, the precursor of today's crime mapping.

39 Here Lombroso is trying to deny that his theory will do irreparable harm to traditional legal theories propounded by the classical school, including that of criminal responsibility. He compares himself to a physician or scientist who refuses to use dangerous remedies.

40 In general, Lombroso did not in fact oppose measures, including indeter-

minate sentencing, to reform some categories of criminals. He is referring
here to his belief in the impossibility of rehabilitating born criminals.

Edition 2 (1878)

1 Lombroso also uses the term *habitual criminal* in edition 2 to refer to
   criminals in general. We have translated this term simply as *criminal* to
   avoid confusion with editions 4 and 5, where he identifies a new category
   of habitual criminals, defining it as a subclass of occasional criminals.

2 The high figure for Italian prisoners awaiting trial—38 percent of all inmates—is explained by the requirement of preventive detention for many
   arrestees by the nineteenth-century Italian Code of Criminal Procedure.
   Preventive detention was mandated for a variety of groups including those
   charged with felonies and those charged with misdemeanors who were va-
   grants, unemployed, or on police lists of suspect persons.

3 The French sociologist Emile Durkheim (1858–1917) also argued, in his
   famous book *Suicide* (1897), that social modernization increases rates of
   suicide. Unlike Lombroso, he explains this increase in purely sociological
   terms as an effect of the loosening of bonds of family, religion, and com-
   munity in nineteenth-century Europe.

4 In this early edition, Lombroso seems to believe that crimes of passion are
   extraneous to his topic and concentrates on "true"—or what he later calls
   "born"—criminality. In the later editions, as he develops a more elaborate categorization of crime, he begins to think that all types of crime fall
   within his purview—including crimes of passion.

5 The student Karl Ludwig Sand (1795–1820) murdered the playwright and
   conservative politician August von Kotzebue on March 23, 1819, for criti-
   cizing democratic student associations.

6 Felice Orsini (1819–58) was an Italian revolutionary who tried to assassinate Napoleon III on January 14, 1858, believing the French emperor to
   be leading the European opposition to Italian unification. Orsini was executed for his crime.

7 Lombroso's citation comes from a study of crime in France, where recidivist criminals were often sent to penal colonies in territories that formed
   part of the French Empire, like New Caledonia and French Guyana. These
   prisoners, who included men and women, were encouraged to marry and
   remain in the colonies after serving their sentences.

8 The English psychiatrist Henry Maudsley (1835–1918) became an influential born-criminal theorist in the late nineteenth century with his *Responsibility in Mental Disease* (1874; misspelled by Lombroso as *Responsability*
   at the end of this paragraph).

9 The French politician and writer Alexis de Tocqueville (1805–59) toured

American prisons with his colleague Gustave de Beaumont in 1831–32 and published a report entitled *On the Penitentiary System in the United States and Its Application in France* in 1833. Lombroso's reference to "Elam" should be to Captain Elam Lynds, the prison warden entrusted in 1825 with the construction of Sing Sing Prison in New York, one of the prisons later visited by Tocqueville and Beaumont.

10 Martino Beltrani-Scalia (1829–1909) was Italy's director of prisons for many decades and a leading prison reformer at the International Penitentiary Congresses. He founded the journal *Rivista delle discipline carcerarie* (*Journal of Prison Sciences*), which lauded positivist criminology and supported many of Lombroso's suggestions for legal and penal reform.

11 Hypospadias is a developmental abnormality in which the urethra opens on the undersurface of the penis in males and into the vagina in females. It is unclear why hypospadias would cause a man to be considered a woman.

12 Lombroso supports the assertion that crimes against persons increase in summer with a table, which we have not included, comparing rape rates by month in England, France, and Italy.

13 In was only in the nineteenth century that European Jews were emancipated, that is, granted the same civil and political rights as Christians. In many parts of Italy, definitive Jewish emancipation did not come until unification; Italian Jews took immediate advantage of their access to political office and provided Italy with mayors, members of parliament, and cabinet ministers. Lombroso, who was himself a Jew, preferred sociological to biological explanations for Jewish history and behavior.

14 Strabismus is a visual defect in which one eye cannot focus on an object because of weak muscles; therefore, that eye appears to wander or cross.

15 The French Agricultural Colony of Mettray, founded in 1839 by Frédéric Demetz, gained fame as a model reformatory for abandoned boys and juvenile delinquents. Architecturally different from traditional orphanages and prisons, Mettray was composed of cabins housing "families" of boys who learned agricultural and artisan skills in the presumably healthy air of the countryside.

16 Lombroso here contradicts his earlier assertion in the chapter on race that Jewish criminals, including members of the Cerfbeer family, were swindlers and thieves but not murderers.

17 Prosper Despine (1819–92), a French psychologist, strongly influenced late-nineteenth-century specialists in psychopathology.

18 On Dugdale's study of the Juke family, see edition 1, footnote 37.

19 Lombroso gives a figure of seventy-six (rather than seventy-seven) criminals in a more detailed table that has not been included here. The totals in this table include both the direct heirs of Max Juke and their spouses.

20 This quote comes from *The Betrothed* by Alessandro Manzoni (1785–1873),

the most influential Italian novel of the nineteenth century and therefore well-known to Lombroso's readers.

21 Italy, like most countries on the European continent, made prostitution legal in the nineteenth century as long as prostitutes registered with police and underwent regular health examinations for venereal disease. This regulation system differed from the legal prohibition of prostitution by most local statutes in the United States.

22 For Lombroso, England represented a nation where female crime was modernizing as women began to be convicted of "male" crimes like forgery and murder, as well as of traditional "female" crimes like infanticide and poisoning. Adolphe Quetelet (1796–1874) was a Belgian mathematician and astronomer who founded, with Guerry, the movement for moral statistics. He is best known for his statistical portrait of the physical and social traits of the so-called average man. Struck by the statistical regularities in crime rates over time, he presaged Lombroso in his attempt to identify the social and biological determinants of lawbreaking.

23 In Catholic countries of nineteenth-century Europe, foundling homes were widespread as a refuge for unwanted babies. Italy was the European nation with the highest number of abandoned children (37,000 in 1866), prompting speculation by Lombroso that rising rates of illegitimacy were fueling other social problems like crime. Italian foundling homes often had revolving compartments—called *ruote*, or wheels—on their doors in which mothers could deposit their unwanted babies anonymously. Because such babies lacked last names, foundling homes substituted suggestive monikers like Esposito (the exposed or abandoned one) or Colombo (the dove, symbol of innocence and the Holy Spirit).

24 For a definition of hypospadias, a malformation of the urethra, see note 11 above.

25 Lombroso here refers to an article by the English lawyer Edwin Hill, "Criminal Capitalists," published in 1871 (not 1872) in *Transactions of the National Congress on Penitentiary and Reformatory Discipline*, ed. E. C. Wines (Albany: Weed Parsons).

26 Lombroso was a strong proponent of so-called scientific policing, or the application of new technologies to the identification of lawbreakers. His disciple, Salvatore Ottolenghi, dedicated his life to encouraging the incorporation of anthropometry, fingerprinting, photography, and detailed record keeping into Italian police practice. Positivist research on crime rates was possible only after European nations began to collect statistics on crime, a practice pioneered by the French in 1825 with the publication of the first annual issue of the *Compte general de l'administration de la justice criminelle en France* (*General Account of the Administration of Criminal Justice in France*).

27 Italy's civil code (article 222) allowed parents to incarcerate children who

misbehaved, thus turning the population of reformatories into an amalgam of convicted juvenile delinquents and unruly children. Lombroso opposed this mixture of delinquents and "honest" children in the same institution, as well as the unwillingness of some parents to discipline and financially support their own children.

28   In this discussion of institutions for abandoned or criminal children, Lombroso shows his preference for state welfare over religious charity, a preference that would be strengthened by his conversion to socialism in the 1890s.

29   The cellular prison required inmates to remain in separate cells, both for work during the day and sleep at night. Intended to prevent communication and "moral infection" among inmates, the cellular prison was modeled on the Eastern (Cherry Hill) Penitentiary in Philadelphia. Debate raged in the nineteenth century about the merits of this Philadelphia model versus the Auburn, or collective, prison, where inmates worked together during the day and were separated only at night. By the late nineteenth century, Ireland had introduced a third model, where inmates began their sentences in isolation but could progress to work together through good behavior. Lombroso discusses the Irish, or graded, system in more detail below. Despite fierce disputes about the merits of each model, most European prisons in reality constituted an amalgam of types because of financial constraints and their location in buildings originally designed as monasteries, leper hospitals, or military fortifications.

30   In late-nineteenth-century Italy, the government routinely issued royal pardons that reduced the sentences of large classes of less dangerous criminals. Lombroso opposed this practice of granting pardons, believing that prisoners should gain freedom through good behavior and reform. He preferred indeterminate sentencing, where prison directors—trained in criminal anthropology—would determine when prisoners no longer posed a danger to society and could be released.

31   Despite the claim of early-nineteenth-century penal reformers that prisons would constitute a humanitarian replacement for corporal punishment, some early prisons retained instruments of physical discipline like the whip. Whips were unnecessary in the Philadelphia system, where inmates were perpetually separated. Some reformers accused the cellular system of promoting despair and, finally, suicide among inmates deprived of any human interaction except with prison directors and chaplains, but Lombroso disagreed.

32   Lombroso opposed the system of prison contracting, often used in Italian penitentiaries, which allowed private entrepreneurs or companies to organize prison industries and reap the profits. Instead, he preferred to have the state oversee prison workshops for the purpose of training and reforming inmates, as well as of gaining a financial return to cover the costs of the system. In Italy, as in the rest of Europe and the United States,

working-class political parties and unions opposed prison labor because wages for inmates were so much lower than those for free workers.

33 Individualization of punishment was a major demand of Lombroso and other positivist criminologists. They rejected Beccaria's plea for an abstract equation between crime and punishment, calling instead for punishment to fit the degree of dangerousness posed by each offender.

34 Despite his general support for cellular prisons, Lombroso sees them as unnecessary for incorrigible offenders, who—as born criminals—are already morally corrupted and incapable of reform. The idea of special prisons for incorrigible criminals, institutions where they would be held for life, was introduced by phrenologists in the early nineteenth century and became popular after 1870 as the great movement for prison reform began in the United States and Europe. To Lombroso, it seemed obvious that born criminals should be sent to such institutions since they were biologically doomed to recidivate. As eugenic ideas began to spread, some people added to the rationales for prisons for incorrigibles the idea that such institutions would help cut off criminals' bad germ plasm by preventing them from reproducing. Lombroso uses this rationale when he writes that prisons for incorrigibles "would gradually reduce that not inconsiderable proportion of criminality that stems from hereditary factors." He ends this passage on a Spencerian and social Darwinist note, observing that if we prevent born criminals from reproducing, we will be able to return to the process of natural selection, which encourages the fittest, and not the unfit, to produce more of their kind.

35 In his famous *Essays* (1588), Michel de Montaigne (1533–92) rejected the witch craze of his time, which condemned thousands of individuals (mostly women) to death for supposedly casting spells, consorting with the devil, and other acts without material proof. By citing this famous French renaissance thinker, Lombroso ennobles his defense of insane criminals, intimating that he—like Montaigne—will be proven right by history.

Edition 3 (1884)

1 Lombroso is contrasting the traditional philosophical deductive approach to legal thinking that dominated law schools of his day with his new positivist, inductive methodology. He is using *naturalistic* to denote his belief that crime is a natural part of social life, with its own statistical regularities over time, rather than an aberration that can be eliminated by the free choice of moral individuals.

2 This list of adherents of the positivist school of criminology is much longer in the original text, including the names of fourteen Germans, three Spaniards, four Russians, twenty French, six Belgians, two Hungarians, five English, and fifty-five Italians. To compile such a long list,

Lombroso included any researcher who used positivist—defined broadly as empirical—methods to study crime, rather than only those who more narrowly accepted his theory of the born criminal. By including criminologists who publicly criticized his concept of the born criminal—like Kraepelin, Lacassagne, and Benedikt—Lombroso gave the impression of having a much larger following than was in fact true. Yet the list does include a large number of foreign disciples of criminal anthropology, demonstrating the international reach of Lombroso's ideas.

The most prominent names on this list include two Germans who criticized Lombroso's theory but agreed with his focus on the criminal rather than the crime in assessing punishment: Franz von Liszt (1851–1919), a law professor who founded the modern school of criminal law in Germany, and Emil Kraepelin (1856–1926), a psychiatrist who wrote the first review of *Criminal Man* for a German scholarly publication. Two of the French representatives on the list, Alexandre Lacassagne (1843–1924) and Léonce Manouvrier (1850–1927), were leaders of the French revolt against the Italian concept of the born criminal at the International Congresses of Criminal Anthropology in the 1880s and 1890s, although both agreed that hereditary as well as social factors shape criminal behavior. Moriz Benedikt (1835–1920), a Viennese professor of neurology, was initially an admirer of Lombroso, but later joked that the existence of the median occipital fossetta in a skull could signal a predisposition to hemorrhoids just as well as criminality. Lombroso had a more loyal following in Italy, where the positivist school of criminology was led by the triumvirate of Lombroso and the lawyers Enrico Ferri (1856–1929) and Raffaele Garofalo (1851–1929).

3   Luigi Lucchini (1847–1929) and his journal, the *Rivista penale*, led the battle against positivist criminology in Italian legal circles. An heir of the classical school, he held prestigious positions as professor of law, parliamentary deputy, supreme court judge, and senator.

4   Lombroso discusses the assassins from Ravenna in edition 1 (figure 9 reproduces the illustration).

5   Lombroso seems to be drawing on Herbert Spencer's (1820–1903) theory that society has progressed from a simple to complex organization marked by increasing individuation. Spencer was more influential than Darwin among some Italian criminal anthropologists, who used the notion of *type* to indicate not only members of supposedly pure racial groups but also born criminals. In both cases, they taught, pure types tended to exist only in the past. It followed that born criminals in civilized society might exhibit only four or five atavistic anomalies because of the dilution of the criminal type by evolution.

6   Filippo Turati (1857–1932) is best known as a founder of the Italian Socialist Party in 1892 and one of its most prominent intellectuals. As a young man, Turati became enthusiastic about Lombroso's criminology, with its

materialist explanation of human behavior. But he soon became a critic of the positivist school's contention that even the advent of socialist society would not abolish born criminality.

7   In his successive editions of *Criminal Man*, Lombroso was increasingly influenced by his follower Enrico Ferri, who coined the phrase *penal substitutes* for measures that would either prevent crime or serve as alternatives to prison or corporal punishment. A lawyer and proponent of criminal sociology, Ferri put more emphasis than Lombroso on environmental factors in the etiology of crime. Lombroso shared Ferri's enthusiasm for penal substitutes like moral education, good housing, and even divorce to prevent crimes, and parole, suspended sentences, and other measures to keep minors and adult occasional criminals away from the contaminating atmosphere of prison.

8   Lombroso is probably referring to the Italian phrase used to wish people good luck (the equivalent to "break a leg" in English), which is *in bocca al lupo* (in the mouth of the wolf).

9   Alfred Edmund Brehm (1829–84) was a German zoologist best known for his encyclopedia *Illustriertes Tierleben* (*Illustrated Life of Animals*), from which Lombroso drew many of his examples of animal "criminality."

10   Lombroso seems to offer contradictory views in this passage about the criminality of animals. On the one hand, he admits that animal behavior is instinctual and not prohibited by any legal code; on the other hand, he wants to use examples of violence and supposed immorality in the animal world as evidence that crime as defined by legal codes is natural and rooted in all living organisms. Therefore, he is ambivalent about whether bad behavior in animals should be legally punished.

11   In the following section, "Crimes of Lust," Lombroso uses many examples that he will repeat in his later book of 1893, *La donna delinquente, la prostituta e la donna normale*.

12   Lombroso used the word *prostitution* in several ways: to indicate the exchanges of sex for money and, more broadly, to refer to all sexual intercourse outside of marriage. In both cases, he applies it only to women.

13   These terms refer to sex with animals (with horns, with beaks, with deer, etc.).

14   Lombroso here presents a confusing argument that law grew out of crime, or, more particularly, that legal punishment grew out of personal vendetta. With reference to his own day, Lombroso argued for the right of punishment on the basis of social defense rather than revenge; punishment should be tailored to the dangerousness of the offender, not the degree of anger or even harm sustained by the victim. He does, nevertheless, evaluate personal vendetta more positively for so-called primitive societies because it generated rules for the protection of the individual that would later be extended to the protection of society in general.

15   Lombroso's opposition to the jury system seems surprising in a nine-

teenth-century liberal soon to turn socialist. But because he believed that only criminal anthropologists had the expertise to understand criminals, Lombroso held that juries—and even most judges of his day—were unqualified to decide verdicts and set sentences. He also believed juries to be eminently corruptible.

16 In his analysis of childhood, Lombroso relies heavily on Ernst Haeckel's famous biogenetic law that ontogeny reproduces phylogeny or that each fetus goes through stages that repeat the evolution of the species. Therefore, physical or psychological characteristics that would be classified as anomalies in adults may be typical of children who—like savages—have not yet reached the higher stages of civilization. Normal children eventually outgrow these atavistic traits, usually during puberty.

17 See this volume, edition 1, footnote 33, on the place of moral insanity in nineteenth-century psychiatry. It is in the third edition of *Criminal Man* that moral insanity becomes central to Lombroso's theory, both here in relation to children and in chapter 28 as a supplement to atavism as an explanation for born criminality.

18 Lombroso is here mourning his son Leo, who died of diphtheria in 1882 at the age of six.

19 The Frenchman Jean de La Fontaine (1621–95) wrote a famous collection of fables.

20 By equating children with the morally insane—and even worse, born criminals—Lombroso radically reverses the early Victorian view of children as sweet innocents. He also medicalizes childhood as a diseased condition that requires constant moral monitoring and surveillance to identify youths with hereditary dispositions to crime. The implications of this view became apparent in Mussolini's Italy, which set up observation centers for any child labeled abnormal by parents, teachers, police officers, or fascist officials.

21 This list adds to seventy-seven, not seventy-nine, as Lombroso claims.

22 Italian nursery schools, which served children two and a half to six years of age, were both public and private.

23 Charles Julius Guiteau assassinated President James Garfield in 1881 and was executed for his crime the next year. The case raised international controversy among legal and medical experts, many of whom considered Guiteau—who claimed to have acted on the will of God—a case of moral insanity or hereditary criminality. Lombroso is here referring to the autopsy report of Guiteau's brain, which was reprinted in the American journal *Medical News*. In chapter 28 below, Lombroso refers frequently to Guiteau as a morally insane criminal.

24 Plethysmographs were devices that purported to record changes in blood circulation through the displacement of water in a tank or special rubber glove. Criminal anthropologists believed that they could measure the emotions of a criminal—and sometimes ascertain innocence or guilt—

through changes in heartbeat and blood circulation. In this respect, the plethysmograph was the forerunner of the modern lie detector.

25   In this paragraph, the number of cases shifts constantly and without explanation. The results of the genital tests imply that all the subjects were women.

26   Despite this acknowledgment of the need for a control group, Lombroso does not provide one, focusing exclusively on born criminals.

27   This list adds up to 220, rather than Lombroso's figure of 219.

28   This list adds up to sixty-three, rather than Lombroso's figure of sixty-six.

29   Lombroso tested three types of sensitivity: general sensitivity or the ability to feel a sensation; sensitivity to pain or the level at which a sensation becomes painful; and tactile sensitivity or the ability to feel two separate stimuli on the fingers.

30   An algometer is an instrument that measures sensitivity of touch and sensations of pain. Lombroso's algometer consisted of "an induction coil, put into action by a bichromate battery. The poles of the secondary coil are placed in contact with the back of the patient's hand and brought slowly up behind the index finger, when [sic] the strength of the induced current is increased until the patient feels a prickling sensation in the skin (general sensibility) and subsequently a sharp pain (sensibility to pain)" (Lombroso-Ferrero [1911] 1972, 246–47).

31   The esthesiometer, a device with two legs that were placed on the subject's fingers, measured tactile sensitivity. As the legs were gradually opened, the machine measured (in millimeters) when the subject could first feel the two separate points. Low readings on the esthesiometer (unlike on the algometer) indicated high sensitivity.

32   The French neurologist Paul Broca (1824–80) is best known for identifying the convolution of the brain that controls the ability for speech. He also invented several machines, like the dynamometer, for measuring the body and its functions.

33   Lombroso states that only thirty-six out of fifty-nine subjects blushed, but he then goes on to describe the extent of reddening in thirty-eight blushers.

34   In Italian, *sinistro* means both "sinister" and "left-handed."

35   Richard von Krafft-Ebing (1840–1902) pioneered research on human sexuality, including such behaviors as fetishism, incest, and homosexuality. His famous work *Psychopathia sexualis* reports the results of his physical and psychological examination of over two hundred cases of what he considered to be sexual abnormality.

36   This section is notable for the slippage in Lombroso's use of the terms *insanity* and *moral insanity*. The confusion arises partly from Lombroso's attempt to recast his earlier finding that criminals and the insane represented distinct categories into a new theory that incorporates moral insanity into the larger concept of born criminality.

37   Lombroso often uses prostitution to explain why women's rates of crimi-
     nality—and in this case moral insanity—were lower than might be ex-
     pected of beings whom he considered biologically, psychologically, and
     morally inferior to men. By defining prostitution as the female equivalent
     of male crime, Lombroso could argue that large numbers of women were
     in fact atavistic and degenerate, discovering an outlet for their deviance in
     prostitution, rather than in crime and moral insanity.

38   On the case of Callisto Grandi, see Guarnieri 1993.

39   Giuseppe Garibaldi (1807–82) conquered southern Italy for the cause of
     Italian unification. A Garibaldino government would have been a demo-
     cratic republic rather than the constitutional monarchy that ruled late-
     nineteenth-century Italy.

40   Prichard is identified in edition 1, n. 33, and Maudsley in edition 2, n. 8.
     Philippe Pinel (1745–1826), the founder of French psychiatry, wrote about
     a condition he called *mania sans délire*, the equivalent to Prichard's moral
     insanity. David Nicolson (1844–1932), a physician at England's Ports-
     mouth prison, published an influential series of articles on the morbid
     psychology of criminals in the *Journal of Mental Science* over the period
     1873–75. For more detail on the nineteenth-century debate over the defi-
     nition of moral insanity, see Rafter 2004b.

41   The revolutionist Masaniello (1620?–47), born Tommaso Aniello, led a
     short-lived rebellion of the poor in 1647 against the Spanish viceroy of
     Naples. Cola di Rienzo (1313–54) led a revolt against the Roman nobility
     and declared himself dictator in the name of restoring his city to the glories
     of ancient times.

42   The list in the original text is longer, emphasizing Lombroso's conviction
     that disease is a significant source of physical and psychological anoma-
     lies. In this confusing conclusion to edition 3, Lombroso suddenly adds
     disease, which can cause disorders in normal individuals from the fetal
     stage to adulthood, to atavism (an inborn condition of evolutionary re-
     gression), as a second constitutional cause of inborn criminality. What is
     unclear, however, is the role played in this new explanatory framework
     by moral insanity, a factor discussed at length in this edition, but then
     ignored in the conclusion. Nevertheless, Lombroso succeeds in this con-
     clusion in responding to critics who championed disease over atavism as
     the biological determinant of crime. He also broadens the definition of
     the born criminal to include individuals exhibiting abnormalities result-
     ing from disease as well as atavism.

43   This list of characteristics shared by criminals and primitive men is
     much longer in the original text; it demonstrates how ardently Lombroso
     worked at defending his concept of atavism in the face of severe criticism
     during the 1880s.

Edition 4 (1889)

1 Lombroso promised a second volume at the end of edition 3, but he never published it.

2 Earlier editions of *Criminal Man* were published in French in 1882 and 1887, in German in 1887, and Russian in 1889. This fourth edition of *Criminal Man* was the first to appear in more than one volume; Lombroso uses this preface to introduce the first two volumes of a projected longer work, but he never completed the additional volumes.

3 Lombroso has here added some new names to his list of collaborators, showing that he has continued to attract disciples to his new positivist school. These include Salvatore Ottolenghi (1861–1934), a forensic doctor and assistant of Lombroso's who went on to found the School of Scientific Policing in Rome in 1903. The school trained all Italian police administrators to identify criminals based on anthropometry, fingerprints, forensic photography, and Lombroso's list of biological and psychological anomalies. Luigi Frigerio, another of Lombroso's assistants, collected data and made a series of fine line drawings of criminal physiognomy for the early editions of *Criminal Man*.

4 Étienne Geoffroy Saint-Hilaire (1772–1844), a naturalist and zoologist, held that homologous organs show that all vertebrates are modifications of a single archetype; homologous organs (like human hands and horses' hooves) might have different functions, but their parts are connected in the same order. Darwin held that the survival of plant and animal species depended on adaptation to their environment. Adaptation occurs when random variations in organisms enable them to thrive in their particular environments. While citing Darwin positively, Lombroso distorts his theory by holding that evolutionary variations in humans are not random but instead have a teleological aim, that of transforming inferior savage peoples into civilized man.

5 In edition 3, Lombroso explained that the pure criminal type existed only in the past and that born criminals of his day represented only a diluted version of this pure type.

6 Paul Topinard (1830–1911), a French anthropologist, wrote a sharply critical review of the French translation of *Criminal Man* (1887) in which he claimed that criminals, although exhibiting a high rate of physical anomalies, do not constitute a type.

7 Composite photographs were pioneered by Francis Galton (1822–1911), the English psychologist, statistician, and founder of the eugenics movement. Galton overlaid photographs of the faces of a series of violent offenders in an attempt to identify the typical criminal face. Lombroso used the technique of composite photography to identify the typical criminal skull.

8 Lombroso here defensively asserts that his theory should not be applied to anyone but convicted criminals. This denial contradicts his earlier recommendation to keep children under surveillance for signs of born criminality; furthermore, his student Ottolenghi persuaded both police and prison administrators to examine suspected criminals for biological and psychological anomalies even before trial. See Gibson 2002.

9 Lombroso overstates his case here because he mentioned Darwin, albeit briefly, in his chapter on tattoos (beginning in the first edition). Although scholars such as Renzo Villa (1985) and Delia Frigessi (2003) do not consider Darwin to have been a major influence on Lombroso's initial theory of atavism, Lombroso had read *The Origin of Species* and *Descent of Man* before their translation into Italian and defended Darwin's theory of evolution in his early work, *The White Man and the Man of Color* (1871). Thus his acquaintance with Darwin is not as casual as this passage suggests.

10 The table contains no data on insane women.

11 Although Lombroso does not explain the significance of this data on menstruation, he argues in his book *Criminal Woman* that the early onset of puberty constitutes one proof of excessive sexuality in criminal women and prostitutes.

12 In nineteenth-century Italy, the birthrate was higher in southern regions like Sicily and Calabria than in the north.

13 Lombroso is implying that the low birthrates of female thieves demonstrates an absence of maternal feelings.

14 See figures 21–22.

15 Hypnosis became increasingly popular during the nineteenth century both as a medical tool and as popular entertainment. Lombroso seems to view hypnosis as a pathological state similar to hysteria, in which patients revert to earlier and more primitive stages of evolution.

16 Lombroso defines the mattoid, a person who is half-mad and often criminal, in more detail below (chapter 40).

17 In this confusing paragraph, Lombroso tries to answer objections to his earlier equation of born criminals with the morally insane by arguing, first, that it is almost impossible to collect enough cases to prove his point and, second, that it is difficult to compare (and thus equate) two groups that are nearly identical. He goes on to shift the focus of this edition from moral insanity to epilepsy. Epilepsy was a subject of growing interest among nineteenth-century psychiatrists, and Lombroso was not alone in classifying epileptics as insane and criminalistic. By adding epilepsy to moral insanity and to his even earlier explanation of atavism as a cause of born criminality, Lombroso here expands his born criminal theory to cover additional groups. He can now categorize almost anyone as a born criminal by using the diagnosis of hidden epilepsy, a condition with no visible symptoms.

18 It is unclear why Lombroso could believe that his figures for absence of

anomalies in male epileptics and criminals—63.4 percent and 75 percent—
were equal.

19 Lombroso does not give the outcomes of the sensitivity tests for the
    twelve remaining cases.

20 Fyodor Dostoevsky (1821–81), himself an epileptic, depicted prison life in
    his novel *The House of the Dead* and portrayed a murderer (Raskolnikov)
    in his celebrated work *Crime and Punishment*.

21 Lombroso recounts the story of Misdea later in this chapter.

22 Bénédict Auguste Morel (1809–73) worked as the chief physician in a
    French insane asylum where this woman evidently was a patient. In his
    famous book of 1857, *Traité des dégénérescences physiques, intellectuelles et
    morales de l'espèce humaine* (*Treatise on the Physical, Intellectual and Moral
    Degeneration of the Human Species*), Morel popularized the theory of de-
    generation, which predicted the progressive deterioration of not only in-
    dividuals but also European society from hereditary diseases leading to
    sterility. These diseases could result from immoral activities like drink-
    ing (alcoholism) and sexual activity (syphilis) or simply from the noxious
    atmosphere of polluted cities and factories.

23 Hidden epilepsy, which is still recognized as a diagnostic category, is today
    defined as a condition in which epileptic seizures present no external mani-
    festations but can be detected by an electroencephalogram.

24 The corresponding figures are 5′ 4″ in height and 124 lbs. in weight.

25 In this paragraph, Lombroso correctly explains that epilepsy can originate
    from different regions of the brain. Yet he also demonstrates the limits of
    the nineteenth-century understanding of epilepsy by identifying cortical
    irritation as a general causative agent.

26 Lombroso's conclusion here, that epileptics are less prone to criminalistic
    outbursts than born criminals, seems to contradict his general psychologi-
    cal profile of epileptic criminals.

27 An aura is a sensation, such as a strange taste or muscle twitch, which
    serves as a warning of an epileptic seizure.

28 Wilhelm Griesinger (1817–68) specialized in neurology and the treatment
    of the mentally retarded, a category that was sometimes defined to include
    epileptics.

29 Nineteenth-century thinkers commonly believed that the moral sense, the
    flower of civilization, must have been the last human attribute to have
    been formed during evolution. In *Criminal Woman*, Lombroso denies
    that women can have moral sense because women as a group have not
    reached the apogee of evolution already reached by white men.

30 Here Lombroso is trying to salvage atavism as a cause of crime, despite
    all he has now said about epilepsy, by arguing that epilepsy itself is a form
    of atavism.

31 Lombroso inexplicably ignores his largest category, *mania*, with its 286
    cases.

32 Lombroso is trying to argue here that most insane inmates enter prison with a congenital predisposition to madness that erupts under the inept discipline of prison directors. He downplays the possibility that incarceration itself transforms sane prisoners into madmen because he wishes to characterize criminality as rooted primarily in atavism, moral insanity, and epilepsy.

33 Satyriasis and nymphomania are conditions of inordinate sexual desire in men and women, respectively. In the nineteenth century, they were considered diseases.

34 In this chapter Lombroso elevates alcoholism from a cause of crime to a form of insanity. Although chronic alcoholism could lead to mental deterioration, as this chapter recounts in vivid detail, Lombroso fails to differentiate clearly between chronic alcoholism and ordinary drinking, which might lead to crime but not to insanity.

35 Lombroso suggests that his compatriots may have hallucinated about the Austrians in 1859 because Italy was fighting the Austrian Empire to gain independence and unify the nation. In 1889, when this edition was published, Italians were more likely to fear police agents and spies, who were employed by an Italian state that Lombroso considered repressive, and political criminals like anarchists, who were particularly active during the 1880s and 1890s.

36 Lombroso's analysis of hysterical criminals assumed an even more important role several years later in *Criminal Woman*.

37 The French neurologist Jean-Martin Charcot (1825–93) used hypnosis to investigate the causes of hysteria during his long career at the famous Salpêtrière hospital in Paris.

38 These figures do not add up to Lombroso's stated total of twenty-one.

39 In this chapter, Lombroso leans heavily on the theory of his positivist colleague Garofalo, who taught that that even the pettiest criminal is disfigured by moral anomalies. By quoting Garofalo, Lombroso casts doubt on the existence of an occasional criminal type who breaks the law solely for environmental reasons. Yet Lombroso never entirely renounces the category of the occasional criminal, perhaps out of deference to his other colleague, Ferri, who encouraged him to recognize the importance of social causes of crime. Lombroso's ambivalence about the occasional criminal shows his reluctance to let go of his beloved—and to him more fascinating—category of the born criminal.

40 Giacomo Girolamo Casanova (1725–98), who initiated his notorious life of love affairs and legal scrapes as a law student at the University of Pavia, recounted his escapades in a famous posthumously published memoir, *History of My Life*.

41 In this paragraph and those that follow, Lombroso recounts a famous English legal case of 1884, *Regina v. Dudley and Stevens*.

42 Although Lombroso states that criminaloids are "completely different"

from pseudocriminals, the two categories tend to run together. The main difference between them, in Lombroso's view, lies in the degree of predisposition to crime: pseudocriminals have none whatsoever, whereas criminaloids have a slight predisposition that opportunity can cause to ripen into criminal behavior.

Edition 5 (1896–97)

1   Lombroso studied 66 rather than 55 skulls in his first edition. However, he is correct in emphasizing the enormous increase in his sample, now comprised of 689 skulls. In this chapter on craniometry, Lombroso does not clearly indicate when he is drawing his conclusions from all 689 skulls; in several subsections of this chapter, he mentions a smaller number as a basis for his calculations.

2   For an explanation of the cephalic index, see edition 1, footnote 17.

3   The second column of this table adds to 98 percent rather than 100 percent.

4   We have shortened this list, which totals twenty-five anomalies in the original text. Lombroso uses a dauntingly long list of cranial anomalies to emphasize the validity of his original theory that the most dangerous criminals are biologically abnormal.

5   Lombroso is attempting to counter criticism of his statistical methods by recommending that rates of physical anomalies be calculated for subgroups of criminals rather than for criminals in general. In this manner, he can circumvent his adversaries' charge that no specific anomaly characterizes all born criminals by arguing that the various anomalies found in each subgroup should be added together to form a portrait of the criminal type.

6   Lombroso asserts in the preceding paragraph that Lacassagne studied 1,000, not 800, criminals.

7   A microhistory of the crimes and trial of the Old Woman of the Vinegar can be found in Fiume 1990; see also Lombroso and Ferrero 2004.

8   Lombroso does not specify the number of cases for this study of anomalous teeth.

9   Charlotte Corday (1768–93) stabbed the French revolutionary leader Jean-Paul Marat in his bath in 1893. As Lombroso explains below, she was seeking revenge for the guillotining of members of the moderate Girondin party by the more radical Jacobins, including Marat, during the Reign of Terror. There is some inconsistency between this passage and *Criminal Woman* (Lombroso and Ferrero 2004, 116–17), where Lombroso enumerates the "extraordinary number of anomalies" in Corday's skull. Anna Kuliscioff (1854–1925), a leading Italian socialist feminist, frequented Lombroso's household as a friend of his daughters, Gina and Paola. Al-

though she was arrested in 1898 during bread riots in Milan, she was an intellectual rather than a violent activist. It is odd to find the name of the writer Kuliscioff on the same list with Corday and other violent revolutionaries.

10 Anarchism and its Russian version, nihilism, called for the overthrow of the bourgeois state and its replacement with a society of economic equality. Anarchists were considered especially dangerous in the late nineteenth and early twentieth centuries because they made government authorities the target of their violent opposition to any form of centralized state control. Anarchist violence peaked in the 1890s with the assassinations of the French president Sadi Carnot and the Spanish prime minister Antonio Canovas; King Humbert of Italy was subsequently assassinated in 1900.

11 Lombroso has misspelled the middle name of the American John Wilkes Booth (1838–65), an actor whose rabid support for the Confederacy and its policy of slavery during the Civil War led him to assassinate President Abraham Lincoln in 1865 at the Ford Theater in Washington. Karl Edward Nobiling was an anarchist who tried to assassinate the German emperor in 1878; he later died of self-inflicted wounds.

12 See chapter 31 in Lombroso and Ferrero 2004, where Lombroso discusses hysteria at length and compares it to epilepsy.

13 *Misoneism* seems to have been a word coined by Lombroso to characterize a psychological trait that he believed inherent in normal individuals: their fear of innovation and new things. Blaming misoneism for retarding social and political change, Lombroso admired geniuses and even criminals who lacked this trait and therefore might serve as catalysts for progress. Lombroso returns to the problem of misoneism among normal individuals and the utility of criminals' openness to change in his final section on symbiosis in this edition.

14 Lombroso is arguing here that even in countries, like France, with falling birthrates, the total population may increase due to immigration. In this case, rates of crime correlate with changes in total population, not birthrates.

15 Lombroso's discussion of the effects of immigration on crime rates is convoluted and not entirely convincing. He seems to be trying to defend his general dictum—that theft rises and murder falls with increasing density —in the face of local statistics that often contradict this rule.

16 In this passage, Lombroso has to rely on crude measures for wealth—taxes paid by individuals and businesses—because the Italian state did not collect statistics on income.

17 The statistician and criminologist Napoleone Colaianni (1847–1921) was a leading critic of Lombroso in Italy, particularly of his theory linking high rates of violent crime in the south with racial inferiority and atavism. Lombroso's citation of Colaianni implies that the latter was a supporter of

criminal anthropology rather than an opponent who argued vigorously for a sociological explanation of the etiology of crime.

18   Lombroso's second point, that factory work promotes promiscuity because it forces girls and women to work outside the home and in close contact with the opposite sex, was a favorite lament of nineteenth-century social commentators. His third point, that poverty leads to infantilism and femininity in boys, is more obscure and possibly linked to his theory that bad environmental conditions, including poverty, may prevent boys from growing out of their stage of childhood criminality.

19   In this table, *indigent* means "beggar," and *poor* is our translation of the phrase, "has only the necessities of life."

20   Lombroso implies that the other 691 subjects of Ferri's study were moderately religious, but he does not discuss them directly.

21   Lombroso refers here to the reformatory for young men at Elmira, New York, superintended by Zebulon Brockway (1827–1920). He discusses it at more length later in this chapter.

22   The author of this "law," George Romanes (1848–94), was an English Darwinist.

23   The Italian author and statesman Niccolò Machiavelli (1469–1527) is sometimes considered the first modern political scientist because he analyzed effective government from the point of view of power politics rather than medieval religious ethics.

24   This passage refers to the long struggle in England during the sixteenth and seventeenth centuries between Protestantism and Catholicism, including the English civil war. Lombroso interprets this struggle in economic terms, labeling the Protestant cause bourgeois and the Catholic position aristocratic.

25   Lombroso here criticizes the classical theory of economic liberalism, formulated by Adam Smith in the eighteenth century, which advocates freedom of trade to bring wealth to nations. He then goes on to state that Darwin's evolutionary theory seems to confirm classical economic principles, a misinterpretation made by many social and economic thinkers of his day. Despite his advocacy of so-called social Darwinism, Lombroso offers one of his rare criticisms of Darwin when he argues against the necessity of economic inequality. In this passage, we can see a clash between Lombroso's reverence for Darwin's evolutionary theory and his socialist ideals.

26   Despite his Jewish heritage and materialist convictions, Lombroso curiously resorts to Christianity in this paragraph to bolster his argument that poverty is unjust and socially harmful. In the next paragraph, he returns to his more usual position that the government rather than the church should take measures to decrease economic inequalities.

27   This paragraph shows Lombroso's abiding concern for issues of public health and poverty that goes back to his studies of pellagra and cretinism as a medical student.

28 Lombroso's discussion of penal substitutes, from small measures like street lighting to major government reforms, demonstrates the breadth of his social critique.

29 Alphonse Bertillon (1853–1914), director of the identification bureau for the Paris police department, developed the first method for identifying recidivist criminals, a system based on anthropometry and standardized photography. While mug shots of criminals are still widely used, most police departments replaced anthropometry with fingerprinting after the turn of the twentieth century. Police preferred fingerprinting because it required less money and expertise than the multiple measurements required by Bertillon's anthropometric system; fingerprints were also easier to file and retrieve than identification cards based on anthropometry or photography.

30 As church attendance became feminized in nineteenth-century Europe, male commentators feared that priests were exercising undue influence over their female parishioners. They warned women of the danger of seduction by priests who might take advantage of the privacy of the confessional booth to violate their vows of celibacy.

31 In the nineteenth century, divorce was not legal in most Catholic countries, including Italy, and it was often difficult or costly to obtain even in Protestant nations like England. Thus Lombroso is taking a progressive stand in supporting the legalization of divorce, even though he bases his argument on the prevention of crime rather than the more popular rationales of his era, the secularization of marriage or women's rights.

32 By calling for the legalization of paternity suits and reparation for seductions, Lombroso is echoing a demand of the nineteenth-century Italian feminist movement that male seducers should be required to compensate women for loss of virginity and, more important, for support of illegitimate children born out of the relationship. Although he supports paternity suits on criminological rather than feminist grounds, he clearly sympathizes with unwed mothers and regrets the ignominy thrust on them by society.

33 Here Lombroso alludes to infanticide, a crime that he believed was caused not by inborn female perversity but by social condemnation of women who bore illegitimate children.

34 At about the same time as Lombroso wrote these lines, the French sociologist Émile Durkheim also warned of the perils of rapidly increasing wealth, which he believed might lead to anomie, or a sense of normlessness, in individuals who might subsequently commit suicide or crime.

35 In the nineteenth century, factories and mines employed large numbers of women and children who were subjected to twelve-hour days and unsanitary, dangerous working conditions like men, but who were paid even lower wages. Lombroso echoes the campaign of the Italian Socialist Party, and especially socialist feminists, in calling for so-called protective legisla-

tion to limit hours and provide improved working conditions for women and children.

36   In the nineteenth century, most nations banned unions, working-class parties, and particularly strikes. Lombroso is best able to reconcile his beliefs in positivist criminology and socialism in this chapter on the prevention of crime, where he expresses solidarity with the working classes and calls for an end to economic inequality.

37   At the time of unification, Italy had confiscated a large part of the vast lands of the Catholic Church; it had also tried to limit the possessions of the nobility by prohibiting fathers from disinheriting daughters and younger sons in order to pass down intact the family property to the eldest son. Lombroso is recommending further land reforms that would break up latifundia, the large estates in central and southern Italy that resembled the plantations of the American South.

38   The Piedmontese nobleman Camillo Cavour (1810–61) was the architect of Italian unification and the first prime minister of Italy.

39   Before the establishment of modern unions, workers in Europe and America organized cooperatives and mutual aid societies to provide themselves with accident, old age, and burial insurance, and sometimes with additional benefits like medicine and education.

40   Lombroso shows his preference for secular solutions to poverty by recommending that private charity, most of which was administered in Italy by the Catholic Church, evolve into public welfare, subjected to the control of the state and, ultimately, the collective will of the people.

41   The Elmira Reformatory was not in fact inspired by Lombroso's work, although it did conduct some criminal anthropological research. See Rafter 1997.

42   In *Criminal Woman*, Lombroso argues at more length that prostitution is both the typical form of female atavistic behavior and at the same time a behavior necessary to society. Women have low crime rates because they divert their abnormal tendencies into prostitution. Although immoral, prostitution is necessary to society because it provides a safety valve for the imperious male sex drive that might otherwise inflict itself on respectable women.

43   Lombroso defines his concept of symbiosis in more detail in the final section of this chapter.

44   The Italian state, like many Catholic countries, handed over the administration of women's prisons to orders of nuns in the nineteenth and early twentieth centuries. As a nonreligious Jew and a socialist, Lombroso generally opposed the interference of the Catholic Church in public affairs. It is a measure of his low regard for women that Lombroso recommends religiosity, as opposed to rational science, as best suited to mold their weak and immoral minds.

45   Rather than prohibiting prostitution, Lombroso wants prostitutes to

practice in public brothels under police surveillance. Punishment would fall only on so-called clandestine prostitutes, those who work alone and without state licenses.

46 Berenini is making a parallel between natural marriage, which is constituted by the moral and emotional bonds between wife and husband, and legal marriage, which must be approved by the state. For Berenini, and therefore Lombroso, it is illogical to insist on the indissolubility of the artificial bonds of legal marriage when the more fundamental ties of natural marriage have been destroyed by adultery.

47 Lombroso believed that the most dangerous adult male criminals should be sentenced to drain the marshes in Italy's malarial zones.

48 In his analysis of this case, Lombroso emphasizes the role he felt the criminal anthropologist should play in the courtroom—that of the expert witness. In his view, the biological and psychological training of criminal anthropologists made them better able to assess the guilt of defendants than judges, who still relied on old-fashioned legal philosophy based on the principles of free will and proportionality between punishment and crime.

49 The Romania-born Max Nordau (1849–1923), a philosopher, author, and physician, won Lombroso's admiration with his study *Degeneration* (1892). Lombroso dedicated volume 3 of the fifth edition of *Criminal Man* to Nordau, Hans Kurella, and Oskar Pfangst, whom he calls "the apostles of the new [positivist] school in Europe."

50 According to degeneration theorists, both genius and criminality are precipitated by the tendency to degenerate or devolve; it is the average man who is stable and unimaginative.

Glossary

This glossary is designed to guide readers to the meanings of Lombroso's key terms and concepts.

abnormality A term Lombroso uses in several different ways, to refer to (1) a deviation from a statistical average; (2) a deviation from law-abiding behavior; (3) a degenerative trait and therefore a sign of criminality.

alcoholism A chronic pathological condition caused by the habitual and excessive consumption of alcohol that can lead to nervous disorders and insanity. According to Lombroso, the consumption of alcohol constitutes a major cause of crime because (1) it loosens inhibitions against violence; (2) it occurs in taverns where criminals congregate and recruit accomplices; and (3) it becomes hereditary. In the fourth edition of *Criminal Man*, Lombroso revises his definition of the insane criminal to include a new subcategory, alcoholic criminals, a group that he predicts will grow because modern society encourages the production and consumption of alcohol.

algometry A procedure for measuring sensitivity to pain using an electrical apparatus called an algometer. By resting the coils of the algometer on the back of his subjects' hands, Lombroso measured both "general sensitivity," when they felt a prickling sensation, and "sensitivity to pain," when they felt an electrical shock. Lombroso held algometry in high regard because he believed that physical insensitivity correlated with emotional and moral insensitivity; thus low algometric readings were a sign of criminality. See also *sensitivity*.

anomaly A sign of deviance and hence of potential criminality. Originally, Lombroso used this term to refer to an atavism, but later he applied it to any degenerative trait. For Lombroso, an anomaly can be biological, intellectual, or psychological, and it can be detected through physical examination, an interview, visual inspection, or hearsay.

anthropometry The scientific measurement of the human body, body parts, and capacities for the purpose of establishing physical types (such as the criminal type) and identifying anomalies. As anthropology became established as a scientific field of study in the mid-nineteenth century, anthropologists relied increasingly on anthropometry to bring precision to their studies of human types.

arrested development A condition of a fetus or infant in which certain functions of the brain or neurological system fail to reach their full potential. In edition 3 of *Criminal Man*, Lombroso adds arrested development to atavism as a cause of physical and psychological abnormalities in offenders. He claims to prefer arrested development to degeneration as the explanation for how hereditary, prenatal, and childhood diseases can lead to criminal behavior, moral insanity, and epilepsy.

atavism A primitive form of humanity; a throwback to an earlier evolutionary stage in which humans were more savage, animalistic, and criminalistic than today.

born criminal Lombroso attributes born criminality to atavism in the first two editions of *Criminal Man*, but he later identifies moral insanity and epilepsy as additional causes. In his view, born criminals cannot avoid committing criminal acts; they are biologically destined to do so.

brachycephaly See *cephalic index*.

brigandage See *organized crime*.

cephalic index A measurement used by criminal anthropologists to categorize skulls based on their shape. The cephalic index is obtained by multiplying the width of the skull by one hundred and dividing the product by the skull's length. Skulls with numerically low indices were classified as dolichocephalic, or long-headed, and those with high indices as brachycephalic, or short-headed. Lombroso tried to use cephalic indices as a measure of criminality but found that they varied according to region and ethnic group. He therefore fell back on the argument that criminals could be identified by having cephalic indices at variance with the norm for their geographical area.

civilization A term used by Lombroso to indicate the advanced stage of social, economic, political, intellectual, and moral development reached by Europe in the late nineteenth century. In *Criminal Man*, civilization usually means the opposite of savage or primitive society and therefore the overcoming of violence, lawlessness, superstition, and sexual promiscuity. At times, however, Lombroso expresses ambivalence about some aspects of civilization—like industrialization and urbanization—that were producing new forms of property crime and encouraging vices like alcohol consumption and prostitution and that could lead to degenerative diseases.

classical school A philosophical approach to the analysis of crime and punishment based on Enlightenment beliefs about humans' capacity for rational behavior. The classical school is often traced back to Cesare Beccaria's 1764 *Essay on Crimes and Punishments*, a book that used deductive logic to argue for rationality and proportionality in criminal sentencing. While the classical school was in fact not a distinct group but rather an international philosophical orientation toward issues of crime and punishment, Lombroso and his followers identified it as a school in order to distinguish themselves from it. Their newer school of criminal anthropology called for science, not logic; induction, not deduction; and a focus on the criminal, not the crime or its punishment. See also *criminal anthropology*.

cranial capacity The volume inside the human braincase or skull. Lombroso assumes that cranial capacity is a sign of brain size and that brain size correlates positively with intelligence and other desirable traits. To estimate the cranial capacity of living subjects, Lombroso used head measurements such as cranial circumference. For the dead, he followed physical anthropologists' practice of pouring grapeshot or pepper seeds inside skulls and then comparing the relative amounts.

criminal In Lombroso's vocabulary, anyone who (1) has committed a crime or is capable of doing so; (2) has been convicted of a crime; (3) is in prison; or (4) bears a cluster of anomalies. When Lombroso applies *criminal* to plants and animals, he uses the term to denote lower organisms that have transgressed the moral codes of nineteenth-century Europeans. Thus confidently anthropomorphizing, Lombroso writes about polygamous llamas and the jurisprudence of ants. *Criminal* is synonymous with *delinquente* in Lombroso's vocabulary (but not equivalent to the softer English term *delinquent*, into which it is sometimes mistranslated).

criminal anthropology An approach to the study of crime that adopts the methods of physical anthropology and begins from the premise that science can discover the causes of crime by using the human body as fundamental data. Advocates of this approach—known as the positivist school, the Italian school, or the criminal anthropological school—defined themselves in opposition to the classical school. Whereas advocates of the classical approach focused on crime and (especially) punishment, criminal anthropologists called for a study of criminal types. Criminal anthropology was founded by Cesare Lombroso, who also emerged as its main exponent: from about 1870 to 1900, he and his followers were generally recognized as the world's authorities on criminal behavior. During this period, in which there existed no other scientific approach to the study of lawbreaking, *criminal anthropology* was also used as a synonym for what is now called criminology, or the study of the causes of crime.

criminal of passion Someone who breaks the law through a sudden outburst of emotion, usually one brought on by difficulties in love or politics. Unlike the born criminal, the criminal of passion has few or no anomalies.

criminal responsibility The degree to which an offender is guilty of a crime. According to the Enlightenment tenets of the classical school, offenders choose to break the law and thus are *legally responsible* for their crimes. Denying the existence of free will, Lombroso instead attributes lawbreaking to biological and social factors that determine all individual behavior. Society nevertheless has the right to punish criminals, who are dangerous and, in Lombroso's terminology, *socially responsible* for their crimes.

criminal type Someone with a cluster of physical anomalies; a synonym for *born criminal*. Lombroso usually defined the criminal type as an individual

with a minimum of five anomalies, but this number varies throughout the
editions of *Criminal Man* (and is not consistent with *Criminal Woman*,
where four anomalies define the criminal type).

criminaloid An offender who falls into the category of the occasional criminal but exhibits several anomalies typical of the born criminal. Although
slightly atavistic, such lawbreakers can be made useful to society if employed in occupations compatible with their abnormal tendencies.

death penalty A type of punishment carried out by hanging (or, in France,
by the guillotine) in Lombroso's time. In the eighteenth century, Beccaria had offered the first sustained critique of capital punishment, calling
it both inhumane and ineffective in preventing crime. In early editions of
Criminal Man, Lombroso hesitates to endorse the death penalty, which
was unpopular in Italy and abolished by the Italian Criminal Code of 1889.
But by the final edition of *Criminal Man*, Lombroso endorses a limited
use of capital punishment, arguing that it plays a natural role in the Darwinian struggle for existence and is necessary to defend society from the
most vicious born criminals.

degeneration A condition analogous to illness in which the human organism
is said to exist in a state of decay. While the early editions of *Criminal
Man* explain criminality in terms of atavism, a condition with which the
criminal is born, later editions also draw on the concept of degeneration,
a heritable or acquired condition in which the offender is said to gradually slip backward down the evolutionary scale. For Lombroso as for other
degenerationists, the deterioration can be physical, intellectual, psychological, or all three at once. Moreover, the signs of degeneration, such as
criminality, insanity, or epilepsy, are fluid and interchangeable, for they are
merely outward manifestations of the inner process of decay. At first associated with the work of Bénédict Auguste Morel, degeneration became
a leading explanation of crime and other social problems in the late nineteenth century in both the United States and Europe, laying the foundation for later, gene-based theories of criminality. See also *atavism*; *heredity*.

delinquent See *criminal*.

dolichocephaly See *cephalic index*.

epilepsy Technically, a chronic nervous disorder associated with changes in
consciousness and with convulsions. In the fourth edition of *Criminal
Man*, Lombroso introduces epilepsy as a cause of criminality comparable
to atavism and moral insanity. Thereafter, he periodically asserts that an
epileptoid personality characterizes all born offenders.

evolution In Lombroso's view, the most significant of all natural processes
because it is the one through which organisms become steadily more differentiated, complex, and civilized. Lombroso adopts Darwin's concept of
evolution but, like many of his contemporaries, he gives Darwin's ideas a
teleological twist, arguing that whatever is must be the result of evolution
and that it must therefore be socially useful and good. This sort of rea-

soning has given Lombroso a reputation for being a political conservative but, in fact, he reasons this way inconsistently and only when it suits his broader purposes to do so.

free will See *criminal responsibility*.

heredity The process by which traits are passed through the generations. Writing in a period before the discovery of the gene, Lombroso remains vague about how heredity might operate; he also does not show much curiosity about the process itself. Like other scientists of his generation, he assumes that degeneration is a heritable affliction. However, and again typically, Lombroso also adopts the Lamarckian position that acquired traits can become permanent and heritable. Thus he believes that an individual who is lazy, impoverished, or habitually drunken can acquire the degenerative tendency and pass it on through heredity to his or her children, in whom it might manifest itself in prostitution or criminality.

hysteria A psychological condition characterized by excitability and sudden mood changes. Perpetuating a long tradition, Lombroso associates hysteria with women in particular; in his view, as in that of many of his contemporaries, women generally lack rationality and self-control, which makes them more inherently emotional than men and thus more susceptible to hysteria. Lombroso regards hysteria as a form of insanity typified by lack of self-restraint, by suggestibility, and by a tendency to make false accusations.

individualization of punishment An approach that tailors punishment to the character of the offender rather than to the severity of the crime. In Lombroso's view, born criminals deserve incarceration for life in the name of social defense, while occasional criminals should be offered the opportunity for reform through flexible, indeterminate sentences or alternatives to prison. Criminal anthropologists claimed the expertise to make recommendations on appropriate punishments by examining and classifying offenders upon arrest; in the case of prisoners, they would decide when they were reformed and could be released. See also *penal substitutes*.

mattoid An offender who champions an idealistic and often altruistic political or religious cause but is in fact mentally unstable and dangerous.

median occipital fossetta (fossetta occipitale mediana) An anatomical peculiarity of the cranium that Lombroso interpreted as evidence for the atavistic nature of the criminal. Lombroso first detected this anomaly in 1872 while dissecting the corpse of the brigand Villella. At a midway point in the base of the skull, where a "normal" person would have a small bony crest, Villella's skull was indented, an abnormality that reminded Lombroso of the skulls of monkeys and lemurs. He instantly grasped (or so he said later) that the criminal must be a throwback to an earlier evolutionary type. For Lombroso, the median occipital fossetta became a key biological sign of the born criminal.

misoneism Hatred of change or innovation. In the final edition of *Criminal*

Man, Lombroso criticizes normal individuals for their misoneism, that is, their passivity and fear of new ideas. He admits to admiring criminals, and especially political criminals, for their energetic revolt against the social order, although change sometimes comes at the price of violence and destruction. See also *symbiosis*.

moral insanity A condition in which an individual remains normal intellectually but nonetheless lacks a conscience or moral sense; an early term for the state today termed psychopathy. Lombroso views moral insanity as an atavism or form of degeneration, associating it with born criminals and epileptics in particular. The subject of a book published in 1835 by the Englishman James Cowles Prichard, moral insanity was a widely recognized and much-discussed phenomenon throughout the nineteenth century. Integrating this popular concept with his notion of the born criminal, Lombroso helped prepare the ground for subsequent studies of psychopaths and sociopaths. His acceptance of moral insanity also contributed to the reconceptualization of criminality as a kind of disease or mental pathology.

normal individual A term Lombroso uses to denote individuals (1) with two or fewer anomalies; or (2) who have not been convicted of a crime or are not in jail or prison. In *Criminal Man*, Lombroso's control groups of normal individuals are usually made up of soldiers, a semicaptive population that offered a convenient source of bodies for examination and measurement. Even though he is aware that there are nondetected offenders in the general population, Lombroso constructs tables comparing honest or normal individuals with criminals, treating the two categories as dichotomous variables.

occasional criminal An offender with few or no anomalies who is pushed into criminal behavior by environmental circumstance (poverty, bad family, misfortune) or (in the case of women) by an evil man. Occasional criminals, because they are less degenerate than born criminals, can be reformed.

organized crime Lawbreaking carried out by a group rather than an individual. In *Criminal Man*, Lombroso focuses mostly on types of organized crime endemic in nineteenth-century Italy, such as offenses committed by brigands, the Camorra in Naples, and the Mafia in Sicily. Like other criminologists of his day, he believes that individuals tend to revert to primitive and violent behavior when acting in groups or caught up in crowds. He links the mafia-type organizations of southern Italians to their heredity, which, according to criminal anthropologists, preserved the racial traits of former Arab conquerors.

pederast A term used by Lombroso to refer to men who engaged in same-sex activities. In *Criminal Woman*, he uses terms that are similarly outdated today—*tribade* and *sapphist*—to refer to women in lesbian relationships.

penal substitutes Measures that either prevent crime or offer alternatives to incarceration as punishment for lawbreaking. Originally a phrase coined by Lombroso's follower, Enrico Ferri, penal substitutes came to occupy an increasingly significant place in Lombroso's plan to reduce occasional crime. Lombroso predicts that occasional criminals would have little incentive to commit crime if penal substitutes (such as land redistribution and better housing) improved the quality of their lives; if they continued to commit crime, alternatives to incarceration—including parole, suspended sentences, and fines—would keep them out of the corrupting atmosphere of prisons.

physiognomy The study of supposed correspondences between humans' exterior appearances, particularly their faces, and their internal states or character. The so-called science of physiognomy was founded by the Swiss theologian Johann Caspar Lavater (1741–1801), who elaborated his theory in his *Essays on Physiognomy*, a work first issued in German (1775–78). An early type of psychology, physiognomy was replaced in the early nineteenth century by phrenology, another early science of human character. Both efforts eventually flowed into Lombroso's criminal anthropology, with its strong emphasis on reading character from the head.

political criminals Individuals who break the law in the name of a political principle rather than for personal gain or revenge. As a liberal who had fought for the establishment of constitutional government in Italy, and later as a socialist, Lombroso tends to be sympathetic to political criminals. Believing them to be untainted by atavism and inspired by idealistic goals, he generally recommends mild punishments for their infractions of the law. Only for exceptionally violent political criminals—like the anarchists who assassinated heads of state—does he recommend harsh measures on the assumption that their ideology simply masks a deeper pathological condition such as moral insanity or epilepsy.

positivism an approach to science that stresses induction from carefully collected facts. Positivism is associated with the establishment of the social sciences early in the nineteenth century. Lombroso embraced the approach enthusiastically and, even from the perspective of his own day, uncritically, amassing facts and figures as though they had an existence independent of himself as their creator and drawing from them conclusions that he viewed as laws of criminal behavior, analogous to the laws of physics. This kind of naive or idealistic positivism is also reflected in his collections of photographs of criminals, from which he claimed to derive scientific conclusions about criminal anomalies, as well as in the collections of criminals' body parts and crime artifacts in his museum. His school is often described as the positivist school of criminology. See also *criminal anthropology*.

primitive peoples See *savages*.

prostitute A term that denotes (1) a woman who exchanges sex for money; or (2) any woman, but particularly one from the lower classes, who has sexual experience outside of marriage. Lombroso believes that in women, atavism is more likely to express itself through illegitimate sexual activity than through criminal behavior; thus he identifies the born prostitute, not the female born criminal, as the counterpart of the male born criminal.

psychiatry The branch of medicine that studies and treats mental illness. As a young medical student, Lombroso developed a lifelong interest in the new field of psychiatry and made it central to his theory of the born criminal. From the first edition of *Criminal Man* on, he emphasizes that born criminals are psychologically as well as physically abnormal; in the third edition, he elevates moral insanity to the level of atavism as a cause of crime. He champions special asylums for the insane criminal, a category that includes, by the fourth edition of *Criminal Man*, the alcoholic criminal, the hysterical criminal, and the mattoid.

race A group defined by skin color, nationality, or ethnicity. Using the term very loosely, Lombroso associates racial categories with ranks on the evolutionary scale and therefore (in his logic) with degrees of criminality as well. In one of his first books, *The White Man and the Man of Color*, Lombroso explains that in the earliest evolutionary stages, everyone was black, and that blacks today remain closer than other races to monkeys. As evolution progressed, it produced people with yellow skin and later white skin. The European races are the most highly evolved and therefore the most civilized. In phrases such as *the European races* and *the Italian races*, Lombroso also uses *race* as a synonym for *nationality* and *ethnicity*. He considers southern Italians inferior to northern Italians because the former have African and Arab blood. *Race* for him serves as both a descriptive and an explanatory term. Using the concept imprecisely, he can call on it to explain a wide range of phenomena.

recidivism The tendency to relapse into criminal behavior. Like many nineteenth-century criminologists, Lombroso blames recidivism for rising rates of crime and recommends harsh punishment for repeat offenders. The two types of criminals responsible for most recidivism, he believes, are born criminals, who cannot escape their hereditary impulse for lawbreaking, and habitual criminals, for whom occasional offending has become an instinct through repetition.

reformatory An institution for the correction and punishment of wayward youth. Although generally opposed to incarcerating juvenile delinquents, Lombroso approves of youth reformatories as a measure of last resort if they are small, separate inmates at night, and offer moral education. He lambastes the Italian legal system for permitting parents to intern disobedient but noncriminal children in reformatories where they are subject to moral contamination from criminal youth.

regression A process similar to that of degeneration in which a human organism slides backward and downward on the evolutionary scale.

savages Primitive people; individuals in an earlier state of evolution than white Europeans. Conceiving of savages as the ancestors of contemporary

Europeans, Lombroso pictures them as dark-skinned, uncivilized, and ani-malistic in their desires and habits. In the same category he places con-temporary peoples—Australian Aborigines, Africans, some Asians, and Native Americans—who in his view continue to exhibit these primitive traits.

scientific criminology See *positivism*.

sensitivity The ability to perceive through the senses. Believing that physical sensitivity increased with evolution, Lombroso tested offenders for sensi-tivity of touch, sight, taste, smell, and hearing. Although his results were mixed, he declares born criminals to resemble savage peoples in their insen-sitivity to pain. The physical insensitivity of offenders is correlated, accord-ing to criminal anthropologists, with equally atavistic moral and psycho-logical dullness.

symbiosis A term used by Lombroso to explain the social utility of crime. At the end of the fifth edition of *Criminal Man*, Lombroso takes a sharp turn from his general depiction of crime as dangerous to society to instead out-line the useful function of crime. Describing criminals as courageous rebels who fuel social and political progress, he envisions a future where less dan-gerous criminals—like criminaloids—can be employed in useful occupa-tions that harness their passions and energy. See also *misoneism*.

References

Baima Bollone, Pier Luigi. 1992. *Cesare Lombroso: Ovvero, il principio dell'irre-sponsabilità*. Turin: Società editrice internazionale.

Barrows, Susannah. 1981. *Distorting Mirrors: Visions of the Crowd in Late Nineteenth-Century France*. New Haven, CT: Yale University Press.

Beccaria, Cesare. [1764] 1986. *On Crimes and Punishments*. Trans. David Young. Indianapolis: Hackett.

Becker, Peter. 2002. *Verderbnis und Entartung: Eine Geschichte der Kriminologie des 19. Jahrhunderts als Diskurs und Praxis*. Göttingen, Germany: Vandenhoeck und Ruprecht.

Becker, Peter, and Richard F. Wetzell eds. 2006. *Criminals and Their Scientists: The History of Criminology in International Perspective*. Cambridge: Cambridge University Press.

Beirne, Piers. 1993. *Inventing Criminology: Essays on the Rise of Homo Criminalis*. Albany: State University of New York Press.

Bulferetti, Luigi. 1975. *Cesare Lombroso*. Turin: Unione tipografico-editrice torinese.

Chen, Xingliang. 1992. *Yi chuan yu fan zui*. Beijing: Jun zhong chu ban she.

Colombo, Giorgio. 1985. "Il 'delinquente' di Lombroso: Dall'album all'Atlante." In *La scienza e la colpa*, ed. Umberto Levra, 253–54. Milan: Electra.

———. [1975] 2000. *La scienza infelice: Il museo di antropologia criminale di Cesare Lombroso*. Turin: Bollati Boringhieri.

Davie, Neil. 2004. *Les visages de la criminalité: À la recherche d'une théorie scientifique du criminel type en Angleterre (1860–1914)*. Paris: Éditions Kimé.

———. 2005. *Tracing the Criminal: The Rise of Scientific Criminology in Britain, 1860–1918*. Oxford, UK: Bardwell.

Debuyst, Christian, et al. 1995. *Histoire des savoirs sur le crime et la peine*. Vol. 1. Brussels: De Boeck Université.

Dolza, Delfina. 1990. *Essere figlie di Lombroso: Due donne intellettuali tra '800 e '900*. Milan: Franco Angeli.

Drapkin, Israel. 1977. *Cesare Lombroso: El creador de la moderna criminologia científica*. Buenos Aires: Congreso Judio Latinoamericano.

Dugdale, Richard L. 1877. *"The Jukes": A Study in Crime, Pauperism, Disease, and Heredity*. New York: Putnam's Sons.

Dwyer, Ellen. 1991. "Stigma and Epilepsy." *Transactions and Studies of the College of Physicians of Philadelphia* 13, no. 4:387–410.

Ellis, Havelock. 1890. *The Criminal*. London: Walter Scott.

Ellis, Lee, and Anthony Walsh. 1997. "Gene-Based Evolutionary Theories in Criminology." *Criminology* 35, no. 2:229–76.

Erony, Susan, and Nicole Rafter, curators. 2000. *Searching the Criminal Body: Art/Science/Prejudice*. Albany: University Art Museum, State University of New York at Albany.

Ferri, Enrico. 1917. *Criminal Sociology*. Boston: Little, Brown.

Fiume, Giovanna. 1990. *La vecchia dell'aceto: Un processo per veneficio nella Palermo di fine Settecento*. Palermo: Gelka.

Frigessi, Delia. 2003. *Cesare Lombroso*. Turin: Einaudi Editore.

Gadebusch Bondio, Mariacarla. 1995. *Die Rezeption der kriminalanthropologischen Theorien von Cesare Lombrsoso in Deutschland von 1880–1914*. Husum, Germany: Mattiesen.

———. 1996. "La tipologizzazione della donna deviante nella seconda metà dell'ottocento: La prostituta, la criminale e la pazza." In *Per una storia critica della scienza*, ed. Marco Beretta, Felice Mondella, and Maria Teresa Monti, 283–314. Bologna: Cisalpino.

Garin, Eugenio, 1980. "Il positivismo italiano alla fine del secolo XIX fra metodo e concezione del mondo." *Giornale critica della filosofia italiana* 5, no. 1:1–27.

Garland, David. 1988. "British Criminology before 1935." *British Journal of Criminology* 28, no. 2:1–18.

Garofalo, Raffaele. [1914] 1968. *Criminology*. Montclair, NJ: Patterson Smith.

Gibson, Mary. 1982. "The *Female Offender* and the Italian School of Criminal Anthropology." *Journal of European Studies*, no. 12:155–65.

———. 1990. "On the Insensitivity of Women: Science and the Woman Question in Liberal Italy, 1890–1910." *Journal of Women's History* 2, no. 2:11–41.

———. 2000. *Prostitution and the State in Italy, 1860–1915*. 2d ed. Columbus: Ohio State University Press.

———. 2002. *Born to Crime: Cesare Lombroso and the Origins of Biological Criminology*. Westport, CT: Praeger.

———. 2004. "Labelling Women Deviant: Heterosexual Women, Prostitutes, and Lesbians in Early Criminological Discourse." In *Gender, Family, and Sexuality: The Private Sphere in Italy, 1860–1945*, ed. Perry Willson, 89–104. Houndmills, Basingstoke, UK: Palgrave Macmillan.

———. 2005. "Science and Narrative in Italian Criminology, 1880–1920." In *Crime and Culture*, ed. Amy Gilman Srebnick and René Lévy, 37–47. Aldershot, UK: Ashgate.

———. 2006. "Cesare Lombroso and Italian Criminology: Theory and Politics." In *Criminals and Their Scientists: The History of Criminology in International Perspective*, ed. Peter Becker and Richard F. Wetzell, 137–58. Cambridge: Cambridge University Press.

Glueck, Sheldon, and Eleanor T. Glueck. 1930. *Five Hundred Criminal Careers*. New York: Knopf.

———. 1934. *Five Hundred Delinquent Women*. New York: Knopf.

Goring, Charles. [1913] 1972. *The English Convict: A Statistical Study*. Montclair, NJ: Patterson Smith.

Gould, Stephen Jay. 1981. *The Mismeasure of Man*. New York: Norton.

Graziosi, Marina. 2000. "Women and Criminal Law: The Notion of Diminished Responsibility in Prospero Farinaccio (1544–1618) and Other Renaissance Jurors." In *Women in Italian Renaissance Culture and Society*, ed. Letizia Panizza, 166–81. Oxford, UK: Leganda.

Gross, Hans. [1911] 1968. *Criminal Psychology: A Manual for Judges, Practitioners, and Students*. Trans. Horace M. Kallen. Montclair, NJ: Patterson Smith.

Guarnieri, Luigi. 2000. *L'atlante criminale: vita scriteriata di Cesare Lombroso*. Milan: Mondadori.

Guarnieri, Patrizia. 1993. *A Case of Child Murder: Law and Science in Nineteenth-Century Tuscany*. Cambridge, UK: Polity.

Hamilton, Peter, and Roger Hargreaves. 2001. *The Beautiful and the Damned: The Creation of Identity in Nineteenth Century Photography*. Aldershot, UK: Lund Humphries.

Harrowitz, Nancy A. 1994. *Antisemitism, Misogyny, and the Logic of Cultural Difference: Cesare Lombroso and Matilde Serao*. Lincoln: University of Nebraska Press.

Hooton, Earnest A. 1939a. *The American Criminal: The Native White Criminal of Native Parentage*. Cambridge, MA: Harvard University Press.

———. 1939b. *Crime and the Man*. Cambridge, MA: Harvard University Press.

Horn, David G. 2003. *The Criminal Body: Lombroso and the Anatomy of Deviance*. New York: Routledge.

Leps, Marie-Christine. 1992. *Apprehending the Criminal: The Production of Deviance in Nineteenth-Century Discourse*. Durham, NC: Duke University Press.

Leschiutta, Pierpaolo. 1996. *Palimsesti del carcere: Cesare Lombroso e le scritture proibite*. Naples: Liguori.

Levra, Umberto, ed. 1985 *La scienza e la colpa: Crimini, criminali, criminologi: Un volto dell'Ottocento*. Milan: Electra.

Lombroso, Cesare. 1871. *L'uomo bianco e l'uomo di colore: Lettere sull'origine e le varietà delle razze umane*. Padua: Sacchetto.

———. 1876. *L'uomo delinquente studiato in rapporto alla antropologia, alla medicina legale ed alle discipline carcerarie*. Milan: Hoepli.

———. 1878. *L'uomo delinquente in rapporto all'antropologia, giurisprudenza e alle discipline carcerarie*. 2d ed. Turin: Bocca.

———. 1884. *L'uomo delinquente in rapporto all'antropologia, giurisprudenza ed alle discipline carcerarie*. 3d ed. Turin: Bocca.

———. 1889. *L'uomo delinquente in rapporto all'antropologia, alla giurisprudenza ed alle discipline carcerarie*. 2 vols. 4th ed. Turin: Bocca.

———. 1891. *The Man of Genius*. New York: Scribner's.

———. 1894a. *L'antisemitismo e le scienze moderne*. Turin: Roux.

———. 1894b. *Palimpsestes des prisons*. Lyon: A. Storck.

———. 1895–96. "Criminal Anthropology: Its Origin and Application." *Forum*, no. 20:33–49.

———. 1896–97. *L'uomo delinquente in rapporto alla antropologia, alla giurisprudenza ed alla psichiatria*. 3 vols. and *Atlante*. 5th ed. Turin: Bocca.

———. [1911] 1968. *Crime: Its Causes and Remedies*. Trans. Henry P. Horton. Montclair, NJ: Patterson Smith.

———. 1995. *Delitto, genio, follia: Scritti scelti*. Ed. Delia Frigessi, Ferruccio Giacanelli, and Luisa Mangoni. Turin: Bollati Boringhieri.

Lombroso, Caesar [*sic*], and William Ferrero. [1895] 1915. *The Female Offender*. New York: D. Appleton.

Lombroso, Cesare, and Guglielmo Ferrero. 1893. *La donna delinquente, la prostituta e la donna normale*. Turin: Roux.

———. 2004. *Criminal Woman, the Prostitute, and the Normal Woman*. Trans. Nicole Hahn Rafter and Mary Gibson. Durham, NC: Duke University Press.

Lombroso-Ferrero, Gina. 1915. *Cesare Lombroso: Storia della vita e delle opere narrata dalla figlia*. Turin: Bocca.

———. 1921. "Come mio padre venne all'antropologia criminale." *Archivio di antropologia criminale, psichiatria, e medicina legale* 41, no. 4:419–37.

———. [1911] 1972. *Criminal Man According to the Classification of Cesare Lombroso*. Montclair, NJ: Patterson Smith.

Mazzarello, Paolo. 1998. *Il genio e l'alienista: La vista di Lombroso a Tolstoj*. Naples: Bibliopolis.

McKay, Carol. 1996. "'Fearful Dunderheads': Kandinsky and the Cultural Referents of Criminal Anthropology," *Oxford Art Journal* 19, no. 1:29–41.

Mella, Ricardo, Anton Fernandez Alvarez, and Valentin Arias. 1999. *Lombroso e los anarquistas*. Vigo, Spain: Edicions Xerais de Galicia.

Moffitt, Terrie E. 1993. "Adolescence-Limited and Life-Course Persistent Antisocial Behavior: A Developmental Taxonomy." *Psychological Review*, no. 100:674–701.

Moffitt, Terrie E., et al. 2001. *Sex Differences in Antisocial Behaviour: Conduct Disorder, Delinquency, and Violence in the Dunedin Longitudinal Study*. Cambridge: Cambridge University Press.

Monachesi, Elio D. 1936. "Trends in Criminological Research in Italy." *American Sociological Review* 1, no. 3:393–406.

Morel, Bénédict Auguste. 1857. *Traité des dégénérences physiques, intellectuelles et morales*. Paris: J. B. Baillière, H. Baillière.

Mucchielli, Laurent, ed. 1994a. *Histoire de la criminologie française*. Paris: L'Harmattan.

———. 1994b. "Hérédité et 'milieu social': Le faux antagonisme franco-italien," in *Histoire de la criminologie française*, ed. Laurent Mucchielli, 189–214. Paris: L'Harmattan.

Nye, Robert A. 1976. "Heredity or Milieu: The Foundations of Modern European Criminological Theory." *Isis* 47, no. 238:335–55.

Pancaldi, Giuliano. 1991. *Darwin in Italy: Science across Cultural Frontiers*. Trans. Ruey Brodine Morelli. Rev. and exp. ed. Bloomington: Indiana University Press.

Parent-Duchatelet, Alexandre. 1836. *De la prostitution dans la ville de Paris*. Paris: Ballière.

Pick, Daniel. 1989. *Faces of Degeneration: A European Disorder, c. 1848–1918*. Cambridge: Cambridge University Press.

Pollak, Otto. [1950] 1961. *The Criminality of Women*. New York: A. S. Barnes.

Portigliatti Barbos, Mario. 1993. "Cesare Lombroso e il museo di antropologia criminale." In *Storia illustrata di Torino*, ed. Valerio Castronovo, 1441–60. Milan: Elio Sellino.

Quiros Cuarón, Alfonso. 1977. *Homenaje a César Lombroso*. Mexico City: Segretaria de Gobernacion.

Rafter, Nicole Hahn. 1992. "Criminal Anthropology in the United States." *Criminology* 30, no.4:525–45.

———. 1997. *Creating Born Criminals*. Urbana: University of Illinois Press.

———. 2001. "Looking at Lombroso: Space, Gender, and Representation in *La donna delinquente*." Paper presented at the workshop "Urban Space and Criminological Discourse," Vienna, 15 December.

———. 2004a. "Earnest A. Hooton and the Biological Tradition in American Criminology." *Criminology* 42, no. 3:735–71.

———. 2004b. "The Unrepentant Horse-Slasher: Moral Insanity and the Origins of Criminological Thought." *Criminology* 42, no. 4:977–1006.

———. 2005. "The Murderous Dutch Fiddler: Criminology, History, and the Problem of Phrenology." *Theoretical Criminology*. 9, no. 1:65–96.

———. 2006a. "Cesare Lombroso and the Origins of Criminology: Rethinking the Criminological Tradition." In *Essential Criminology Reader*, ed. Mark M. Lanier and Stuart Henry, 33–42. Boulder, CO: Westview.

———. 2006b. "Criminal Anthropology: Its Reception in the United States and the Nature of Its Appeal." In *Criminals and Their Scientists: The History of Criminology in International Perspective*, ed. Peter Becker and Richard F. Wetzell, 159–81. Cambridge: Cambridge University Press.

Regener, Susanne. 1999. *Fotografische Erfassung: Zur Geschichte medialer Konstruktionen des Kriminellen*. Munich: Fink.

———. 2003. "Criminological Museums and the Visualization of Evil." *Crime, History, and Societies* 7, no.1:43–56.

Renneville, Marc. 1994. "La réception de Lombroso en France (1880–1900)," in *Histoire de la criminologie française*, ed. Laurent Mucchielli, 107–35. Paris: L'Harmattan.

Rondini, Andrea. 2001. *Cose da pazzi: Cesare Lombroso e la letteratura*. Pisa: Istituti Editoriali e Poligrafici Internationali.

Salvatore, Ricardo D., and Carlos Aguirre, eds. 1996. *The Birth of the Peni-*

tentiary in Latin America: Essays on Criminology, Prison Reform, and Social Control, 1830–1940. Austin: University of Texas Press.

Tarnowsky, Pauline. 1889. *Étude anthropométrique sur les prostituées et les voleuses*. Paris: Bureaux du Progrès Médical.

Velo Dalbrenta, Daniele. 2004. La scienza inquieta: Saggio sull'antropologia criminale di Cesare Lombroso. Padua: CEDAM.

VI Congrès International d'Anthropologie Criminelle. 1906. *Le Musée de Psychiatrie et d'Anthropologie Criminelle dans l'université de Turin*. Milan: Bocca.

Villa, Renzo. 1985. *Il deviante e i suoi segni: Lombroso e la nascita dell'antropologia criminale*. Milan: Franco Angeli.

Wetzell, Richard F. 2000. *Inventing the Criminal: A History of German Criminology, 1880–1945*. Chapel Hill: University of North Carolina Press.

Wines, Frederick Howard. 1895. *Punishment and Reformation: A Historical Sketch of the Rise of the Penitentiary System*, 229–65. New York: Thomas Y. Crowell.

Wolfgang, Mavin E. [1960] 1972. "Cesare Lombroso, 1835–1909." In *Pioneers in Criminology*, ed. Hermann Mannheim, 232–91. 2d enl. ed. Montclair, NJ: Patterson Smith.

Index

CESARE LOMBROSO (1835–1909) is widely considered the founder of criminology. His book *L'uomo delinquente* was first published in 1876.

MARY GIBSON is a professor of history at John Jay College of Criminal Justice at the City University of New York. She is the author of *Born to Crime: Cesare Lombroso and the Origins of Biological Criminology* (2002) and *Prostitution and the State in Italy, 1860–1915* (1986).

NICOLE HAHN RAFTER teaches at Northeastern University in the College of Criminal Justice and in the Law, Policy, and Society Program. She is the author and editor of many books on crime, law, and gender, including *Creating Born Criminals* (1997) and *Shots in the Mirror: Crime Films and Society* (2nd ed. 2000).

Library of Congress Cataloguing-in-Publication Data
Lombroso, Cesare, 1835–1909.
[Uomo delinquente. English]
Criminal man / by Cesare Lombroso ; translated and with a new introduction by Mary Gibson and Nicole Hahn Rafter, with translation assistance from Mark Seymour.
p. cm.
Includes bibliographical references and index.
ISBN 0-8223-3711-8 (cloth : alk. paper) — ISBN 0-8223-3723-1 (pbk. : alk. paper)
1. Criminals. 2. Criminal anthropology. I. Gibson, Mary. II. Rafter, Nicole Hahn. III. Title.
HV6038.L5813 2006
364.3—dc22   2005034058